V&R

Handbook of Theme-Centered Interaction (TCI)

Mina Schneider-Landolf, Jochen Spielmann, and Walter Zitterbarth (Editors)

Translated by Joseph Smith

With 16 figures and 3 tables

Vandenhoeck & Ruprecht

Thanks to Frida Müller-Blas who so gracefully enabled this translation and publication by bequeathing the RCI International.

German original edition: *Handbuch Themenzentrierte Interaktion (TZI)*, 3rd ed. Göttingen: Vandenhoeck & Ruprecht, 2014.

Bibliographical information published by the Deutsche Nationalbibliothek

The Deutsche Nationalbibliothek lists this publication in the Deutsche Nationalbibliografie; detailed bibliographic data available online: http://dnb.d-nb.de.

ISBN 978-3-525-45190-8
You can find alternative editions of this book and additional material on our website: www.v-r.de

Typesetting: Satzspiegel, Nörten-Hardenberg
Cover: SchwabScantechnik, Göttingen
Printed and bound in Germany by ⊕ Hubert & Co., Göttingen

Printed on non-aging paper.

Table of Contents

Part IV: The Differentiation of TCI

Part V: Facets of TCI

Part VI: Interactions: TCI and ...

Preface

TCI is alive and well! And this book is proof thereof. Under the direction of three editors, no fewer than 39 bright men and women came together to explore 53 different aspects of TCI corresponding to the state of the art of research into this theme in the year 2008. That is an impressive amount of "we-ness"! What makes TCI so special – so particular and essential and different from all other approaches – is how it is taught and put into practice as well as how it is theoretically substantiated. The discussion surrounding these points is still in full swing, though many insights are clearly in place. For instance, that the "inventor" of TCI, Ruth Cohn, is an amazingly inspirational human being who developed TCI from very pragmatic considerations, that she is a gifted psychologist and teacher – and a woman devoted to caring for this planet. Some 2000 years after Christ walked this earth things don't look so rosy for the human race; our will and our skill to coexist in harmony, be cooperative and just with each other are being tried daily. Still, according to Ruth Cohn, that should not hinder us from embarking on new paths that are not the product of technical progress. To seek out inventions that increase the quality of human life and human relations. TCI is just such an "invention" by connecting psychological and pedagogical findings with ethical considerations and a learnable armamentarium. The basic question is this: Is it possible to combine the success of a common endeavor with the success of interpersonal relations such that each and every individual is able to give and receive exactly what he or she has to offer and needs?

These things don't just happen when everything is left to run its course. Rather, there is a distinct need for someone to lead the group or the team according to prevalent rules. That the most important principles of leadership are doubly valid – at once externally and within each individual (self-management) – is a surprisingly ingenious fact (just mentioned as an aside). Being able to lead a group has to be learned, and this learning process includes both practicing the art of leadership as well as learning the tenets on which this subject was founded. This book serves to show readers the intellectual horizon of TCI with all its questions and answers. Whatever a good leader (in the TCI sense of the term) needs to have grasped is systematically treated in this volume. It is also meant to help practitioners keep up with the research going on at the university level, which is concerned largely with theoretical explication and empirical evaluation. Having these insights scientifically anchored extends their shelf life and livelihood considerably.

Indeed, TCI lives! Whenever I lead a seminar, situations always come up in which my own TCI soul rises to the occasion and takes flight. For example, during a discussion of a case history I notice that the group has become silent, and that the energy level of the participants has fallen to near zero. What to do? Should I position myself at the flipchart? Should I initiate a "lightning session," saying something like: "So where did you all go to? I'm clearly feeling your reticence, which can mean any number of things: contemplation, embarrassment, unease, alienation, emotional involvement. Maybe everyone is feeling something different. I'll pass this little egg around, and whoever holds it in the hand can say what is moving him or her at this moment!"

This method of repositioning one's "I" (the protagonist) to become a "we" is what I experienced again and again from Ruth Cohn – that's where the little marble egg idea comes from. It is both simple and ingenious: Lost souls bounce back to life again; the group becomes a group again, reconstituted. Much of what had remained unspoken is now voiced, worked through, discussed. And sometimes a depth to the theme at hand occurs that is wholly unexpected (always be aware). An ingenious method?! Indeed, although it is not just a method, something to be "used." Rather, it also demands great insight, poise, and courage: the insight that this "we" is important; the poise to allow discordance and obstacles to enter, indeed to invite them in; the courage to wake sleeping dogs that may be rabid toward my style of leadership or reject the protagonist altogether.

That is what is at once so special, so valuable, and so difficult about TCI: Every intervention is embedded in an *umwelt*, and only by combining it with a proper diagnosis of the situation at hand, controlled by human feelings and qualities, can it display its true nature. The bachelor student who wants to know how best to prepare for a multiple-choice test – what is right and what is wrong? – doesn't have a chance. Nor does the professor preparing to give just such a test.

Yet things get even more complicated. Would it have been so definitively and completely wrong to have held a lecture at the flip-chart? Would that have represented a TCI blunder? As long as the lecture corresponded to the lecturer's intention to explain something, and if that intention was his or her way of fulfilling an impulse to revitalize the group, then maybe it could have increased both the audience's knowledge and vitality. A group leader is also important, and what the leader thinks is relevant also has its place – among all the other equally important matters. So the lecture wouldn't then have been totally wrong? Once I remarked to Ruth Cohn that I had held a seminar that was "not quite pure TCI" and she nearly bit my head off. She said: "Pure TCI – a nice formulation to be sure, but simply not true – is called by others 'classical TCI' or 'proper TCI.' And that is really wrong. Why? Because TCI does not prescribe dogmatic rules, but rather is open to the peculiarities of the respective theme, the personality of the group leader, etc."

So: The principles and main ideas of TCI are not *normative* but present a horizon of options for coherent behavior, whereby "coherent," as most have likely deduced, corresponds to the thinking of Ruth Cohn. Coherency is defined by the double agreement with, first, the "truth of the situation" ("Globe") and, second, the one's inner truth. Put another way: Leading a TCI group must reflect both one's own character and the situation at hand. Dealing with a human condition by looking for coherency against the background of the systematic doctrines and the philosophy of TCI is always driven by experience and creativity. Encouraging others to behave creatively would be a disaster for the multiple-choice test of our undergraduate student – though that does not contradict TCI.

TCI is alive and well, and this book serves to further that endeavor! I hope that Ruth Cohn, now approaching her 100th birthday, may once again experience that her life's work is flourishing – and, as mentioned here, continues to grow. Being one of the first to get to read what follows I want to most heartfully thank the three editors and the 39 authors involved for their contributions!

Friedemann Schulz von Thun

Foreword

More than 40 years have now passed since Ruth Cohn first developed and published *Theme-Centered Interaction (TCI)*. Since then many have taken part in TCI workshops, heard lectures at congresses, visited courses, and taken extensive training. This helped them to deal with their own personal development, to increase their involvement in a humanization of society in general, and furthered their professional standing. Their application of TCI in various fields, for example, in education, the workplace, social work, adult education, church and theology, management training, counseling, and supervision led to TCI becoming a very differentiated and integrative approach.

How TCI is understood today is also a product of the many experiences and reflections gathered over time. The discussions surrounding TCI resulted in changes to the basic concept because of many teachers and researchers who were adapting and adopting it; some terms had to be defined more precisely, others were added to the existing list.

This process lasted many decades, and today we find it opportune to offer a new handbook to treat the concept of TCI in an exhaustive, systematic, and scientific manner. This volume is organized like TCI itself.

TCI offers a concept for holistic learning and working which is based on theoretical premises as well as methodologically practical guidelines. The individual elements work only in conjunction with each other. In order to present them in the necessary detail and thus to analyze them more precisely, however, we have decided to treat them separately in this handbook, though in practice that will not be the case.

Depending on the discipline in question, TCI must be differentiated and discussed individually. For that reason, it was important to us to present as broad a picture of the theoretical background as possible in addition to the many different forms found in practice. This includes a number of controversial positions, which are mentioned and discussed as such, without resolving any conflicts.

This handbook has a number of goals: As a *theoretical treatise*, it offers a systematic presentation of the entire concept of TCI; as a *reference work* it enables the reader to get a quick overview as well as clear definitions of the individual terms and keywords involved; as a *handbook and textbook* if provides access to the methods concerned.

The basic idea behind this volume stems from Jochen Spielmann. It was then taken up by the editorial team of Mina Schneider-Landolf and Walter Zitterbarth as well as many other committed and experienced TCI colleagues who wrote the individual contributions. We thank each and every one of those who have gone down this common pathway.

Special thanks go to Günter Presting of the publishing house Vandenhoeck & Ruprecht, who enabled the publication of this volume, and to the many people on the publisher's staff who worked so diligently.

It is our hope that those who read or browse in this handbook will experience new learning processes, that persons already interested in TCI will obtain the comprehensive information they need, and that experts in TCI will be just a little inspired, irritated, or validated – and that a new understanding of the concept of TCI emerges for all of these groups of readers.

For those who have no knowledge of TCI at all, the first contribution "What Is TCI?" serves as an excellent introduction. For those who desire an overview of how the individual parts of TCI fit together, we recommend the contribution of Mina Schneider-Landolf "The Systematics of TCI." Those searching for a more biographical or historical and political approach should definitely read the article about "Ruth C. Cohn" and the article on the "Historical and Political Background." Persons more interested in how TCI relates to their own personal professional activities are directed toward Section VI, which deals with the interactions between TCI and the respective discipline. A reader searching for a more systematic approach to TCI will, in addition to the general sections, enjoy the two sections "Systematics of TCI: Theory" and "Systematics of TCI: Practice."

Note: Most of the contributions in the sections "Systematics of TCI" are arranged in three subsections: Definition, Origin, Explanations. This serves to help the reader to compare the various chapters. Many of the contributions in the other sections also employ this scheme.

Cross-references are marked with → and the respective title of the contribution. Since the various authors often refer to the same secondary literature, we decided to print a common reference section for the entire book.

Mina Schneider-Landolf
Jochen Spielmann
Walter Zitterbarth

What is TCI?

Jochen Spielmann

The abbreviation TCI stands for "theme-centered interaction" and was developed by → Ruth Cohn in the 1950s and 1960s, her goal being to promote "living learning." With that, Ruth Cohn meant a working and learning that equally involved the intellect and emotions, body and soul, thoughts and feelings, action and reflection.

Presently, TCI has been introduced into many different fields – in schools, therapy, business, social work, adult education, church and theology, management training, counseling, supervision, etc.

In the 1970s it was often employed in individual personality development as well as for promoting social-therapeutic concerns.

Since the 1980s, however, TCI has been understood primarily as a concept for leading groups and teams and as such has since become broadly adopted, especially in adult education, schools, business contexts, church work, social work, and at the university level.

Since the mid-1990s, based on the various experiences and demands gathered in the different fields, TCI has been transformed into a concept specially suited for shaping social situations. Today, TCI can be seen in the following trends and forms:

- For leading groups and teams,
- For leading and accompanying learning processes,
- For controlling communicative and cooperative processes,
- For supporting individual development processes and for self-guidance (→ TCI as Lifestyle),
- For social therapeutic purposes,
- For management purposes (management concept, leadership concept),
- For shaping social situations (→ TCI as a Professional Educational Concept),
- For shaping counseling situations (counseling, supervision, coaching).

Thus, the following definition is relevant today:

TCI is a comprehensive, holistic action concept that has the goal of shaping situations in which humans interact, work, live, and learn together such that they consciously experience each other as humane and humanizing. The focus lies on taking action in groups, teams, and organizations. TCI represents a differentiated method of observing situations as well as controlling and accompanying social processes. This includes the tasks such as planning, leading, intervention, reflection, analysis, and diagnosis. The overall goal is to create professional and learning processes producing optimal results that reflect the common goals, the interactions between the various parties involved, and the individual interests and their circumstances.

TCI relies on a vision of humanity and a value system that reflect the ability of humans to change and learn; its premise (→ Axioms, → Chairperson Postulate, → Disturbance Postulate) is that work and learning processes can indeed be done in a humane and humanizing spirit. Ruth Cohn combined her own experiences with very divergent theories and approaches to form TCI (among others, → Psychoanalytical Fundamentals, → Influence of Humanistic Psychology, → Educational Fundamentals, → Jewish-Christian Influence).

The theoretical basis lies in the → four-factor model of TCI, which says that the processes and interactions active in social situations and living learning situations can be described by four different factors: (1) the → I – every individual, (2) the → We – the interaction among those involved, (3) the → It – the cause at hand, the contents, the tasks, the goals that brought everyone together, and (4) the → Globe – the circumstances and conditions under which group actions take place. One special characteristic of TCI lies in its distilling the breadth of social situations down to these four factors, making them manageable. The four-factor model is well suited for interpreting and understanding situations. In addition, it helps when developing concrete action strategies. The symbol Ruth Cohn used to depict this ability was a triangle embedded within a circle.

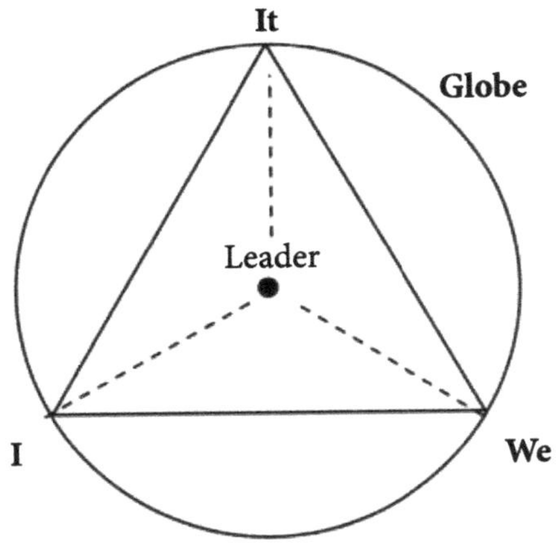

Figure 1. The four-factor model of TCI.

It was Ruth Cohn's assumption that these four factors are equally important, and that there exists a sort of dynamic balancing (→ Dynamic Balance) between them which enables living learning and cooperative learning, transparent interactions, and growth-enhancing communication. This process is the product of finding a → theme and choosing the proper → structures and the fitting → work and social forms. All of which is controlled by the principle of → participative leadership.

Institutionally, TCI is represented by the Ruth Cohn Institute for TCI International, which serves as the overarching organization for the many regional and national TCI institutes in Germany, The Netherlands, Belgium, Austria, Switzerland, and Hungary. TCI International offers authorized TCI seminars and a broad range of educational and training courses (see under www.ruth-cohn-institute.org).

Ruth C. Cohn

Heidi Greving

Ruth Charlotte Cohn (née Hirschfeld) was a German Jew born in Berlin in 1912 who lived a carefree life there until the year 1933. Her early goal in life was to become a poet, but in the end, she chose to study economics and psychology at the Universities of Heidelberg and Berlin. Following some very troubling experiences with National Socialism she decided to leave Germany in 1933 and headed toward Switzerland. She returned to Berlin only once to settle some personal matters. The trip back to Switzerland was to be her last border crossing for a long time.

She was one of the lucky ones, she said later:

> I experienced the horrible things of those days very intensely. That I was even able to live in Zurich seemed to be to a strange and fateful gift. My whole life long I saw that as a defining challenge to do something with the fate I had been dealt, to pay thanks. (Farau & Cohn, 1984, p. 213)

In Switzerland, she married her long-time friend Hans Helmut Cohn and thus enabled his parents to get out Nazi Germany in time. Only many years later did she speak about the fears she suffered on behalf of her friends and relatives still in Germany until she left Europe for the United States.

Up to 1941, Ruth Cohn studied psychology as well as education, theology, literature, and philosophy in Zurich and did her psychoanalytic training at the Swiss Society for Psychoanalysis.

> Although I learned much about myself and other people [through psychoanalysis] [...] the pain I felt inside, the longing, became ever more intense – a longing for something unknown, something I had to find. [...] Sometimes my analyst would try to console me [...] by saying "We'll find 'it,' don't worry. 'It' just takes time." (ibid., p. 215)

It was to take a long while before Ruth Cohn actually found "it." In the meantime, she had to meet many challenges as a Jewish emigrant. But during that time she never lost sight of her vision of social therapy; she never doubted

> that psychoanalysis would trigger a new, more humane era. The deep self-knowledge that psychoanalysis provides enables paths to better self-management and new ways to educate others. (ibid., p. 216)

In 1941 Ruth Cohn left Switzerland with her husband and child.

> We were put in a sealed train car and traveled through the unoccupied part of France. After a veritable odyssey [...] we reached Lisbon and got on one of the last ships to cross the ocean after the outbreak of World War II. (ibid., p. 217)

Ruth Cohn had to overcome many obstacles to establish herself as a psychoanalyst in the United States. Being without a medical degree, she failed to get a work permit for the New York Psychoanalytic Institute – despite her many excellent references and credentials – though she was permitted to work with children. This made her angry – as if the problems of children were any less important than those of adults!

First, she worked as an assistant teacher in the Bankstreet Schools which provided progressive teacher training. This position proved to be a rich and positive experience for Ruth Cohn.

> Living learning: I had yet to discover this term and had not heard it used by others. Looking back, I now know that Bankstreet was the source of my love for → living learning: following the tracks laid by a child's interest. (ibid., p. 327)

At the same time, this sort of educational activity made clear to her that therapists need a much broader and much more comprehensive training that includes studies from the social sciences.

Thereafter, under very difficult conditions – personal illness and her role as a working single mother – Ruth Cohn commenced her therapeutic work in improvised surroundings.

> I had been told that "appearances" [...] were absolutely necessary for the success of any psychoanalytic practice. Well, that was not true, but then again maybe only because I didn't believe in it from the very beginning. (ibid., p. 229)

Instead, her attention was directed toward helping many people to grow developmentally through therapy. She pondered the connection between poverty and sickness:

> We need a therapeutic form of education and more just economic conditions (ibid., p. 230).

In 1948 Ruth Cohn met the Viennese psychoanalyst Theodor Reik, who – against the monopolizing tendencies of the medically oriented New York Psychoanalytic Institute – founded a psychologically based psychoanalytic training institute, called the National Psychological Association for Psychoanalysis (NPAP). Ruth Cohn assisted him in this endeavor and early on became the Head of the Training Committee responsible for the curriculum.

This position offered her many new avenues to implementing an open form of psychotherapy based on interpersonal relationships. Harry Stack Sullivan's thoughts in this direction had impressed her, so that she sought out contact with the psychoanalyst Ruth Forster in order to delve deeper into Sullivan's form of therapy. What she experienced confirmed what she had been envisioning all along: a sound, reality-based method oriented toward concrete problems as well as a warm-hearted but sufficiently distanced personal relationship. This turn of events encouraged her to continue working on her own therapeutic ideas.

A further step "on the road to holistic therapy" (ibid., p. 242) was her attention toward bodily signals. During the therapy of a young woman a decisive developmental juncture was initiated through physical contact. Yet because of the taboo in classical psychoanalysis against physical contact of any type, it took many more years before Ruth Cohn could completely integrate bodily signals into her therapeutic thoughts.

At the time, therapists leading group therapies were achieving ever greater success, not just by working through neurotic symptoms, but especially by improving the communicative skills of lonely people suffering from the aftermath of World War II. Despite her initial skepticism concerning group therapy, Ruth Cohn was impressed by this turn of events, and especially her meeting with Jacob L. Moreno and his psychodrama was to excite her.

> One day by chance I noticed a sign in an alleyway on Upper Broadway inviting people in to take part in "Psychodrama Theater." Well, that's just what I did. There was a stage there, seats for an audience, and two "directors" who each were able to draw a person from the audience up and onto the stage to perform their own respective conflicts. The roles of those involved in these conflicts [...] were distributed to volunteers. I was fascinated by this ingenious method. (ibid., p. 257)

This sort of creative therapeutic group work served to rejuvenate psychotherapy, though only Ruth Cohn's friendship with Asya Kadis could completely remove her reticence toward group therapy.

All of the experiences mentioned above proved useful for the training of young psychoanalysts. For Ruth Cohn, however, the problem of countertransference remained. In 1955, as Head of the Training Committee of the NPAP, she initiated the first private workshop with nine advanced analysis trainees to deal with countertransference.

> On the evening before the first workshop, I was very restless. I had failed to think through completely exactly how I was going to teach the theme of "dealing with countertransference." [...] I thought it might strengthen their courage if I just recounted the first case in point. (ibid., p. 266)

Thus, Ruth Cohn took part in her own experiment and was successful. The workshop attendees went along with it, and this sort of seminar became a permanent institution at the NPAP.

> In the countertransference workshop we learned [...] to better recognize and work through [...] our own weaknesses and strengths. To our own surprise, we discovered what was unknown at the time and eventually came to called "mirroring." The group mirrored both the characters and the problems of the patients as well as those of the respective therapist. In this

> manner problems of transference and countertransference became completely situated in the here and now and thus became treatable as part of the process of the group's interaction with the therapists. (ibid., p. 269)

In 1962 Ruth Cohn became an active member of the Academy of Psychotherapists (AAP). It was a time of greater liberalism in the United States because of the civil-rights movement. The AAP was a place where representatives of both classical psychoanalysis and newer, more modern approaches could meet and exchange ideas. Ruth Cohn now experienced and help to frame Humanistic Psychology, always in close contact with George Bach, Henry and Vivian Guze, Fritz Perls, Ervin Polster, Carl Rogers, Virginia Satir, John Warkentin, and Carl Whitaker. Her relationship was particularly intensive with two of the most important representatives of the humanistic-therapeutic movement (or as she called it "experiential therapy"), namely, Fritz Perls (gestalt therapy) and Carl Rogers (client-centered psychotherapy). From this emerged her own brand: theme-centered interaction – TCI.

> The patient is not an empty vessel and the therapist does not have a hose as his disposal. Giving and taking are existential necessities. [...] For experiential therapists, the way the therapist concentrates on the patient and the way the therapist sincerely tries to engage the patient as a partner (and not as a guru) are indispensable prerequisites to gathering emotionally correctable experiences. Healing is a product of the depth of new experiences – especially when the strength of early traumatic experiences can be corrected by the emotional power of the therapeutic relationship. Such power arises from the authenticity of feelings and their communication. (ibid., p. 279)

With these thoughts in mind, Ruth Cohn approached more and more nontherapeutic groups, her goal being to further a tolerant and accepting atmosphere amenable to constructively working on the problem at hand. It was during this time that she had the following dream:

> One night [...] I dreamed of an equilateral pyramid. Upon awakening, it was immediately clear to me that I had indeed "dreamed up" the basis for my work. The equilateral pyramid of my dream meant the following: Four points determine my group work, and they are all interconnected and equally important. They are:
>
> - The person interacting with others and with the theme at hand (= I);
> - The group members who become a group by attending to the theme at hand and through their interaction (= We);
> - The theme at hand, that is, the task being before the group (= It);
> - The environment, which influences the group and is influenced by the group – the *umwelt* in the narrowest and broadest sense of the word (= Globe). (ibid., p. 343)

Out of the pyramid arose the image of a triangle within a circle. The core part of Ruth Cohn's teachings had been born, and the theory of experiential therapy had received a powerful new component.

"I've got it – now we can finally begin teaching it," Ruth Cohn told her colleagues following this dream, as Norman Lieberman reports (ibid., p. 345). Together with Lieberman and others, Ruth Cohn founded the Workshop for Living Learning (WILL) in 1966 in New York. Many group therapists and supervisors from that institute came together there with Ruth Cohn to implement TCI in nontherapeutic groups, teams, teaching facilities, and institutions.

One of the first workshops to be held at WILL was entitled "Segregation – Collision – Co-Existence – Integration," which had the expressed goal of integrating Blacks and Whites in social institutions.

The first members of WILL tended to be group psychotherapists of various schools, whereas eventually people from all sorts of different disciplines (especially counseling and education) were trained as TCI group leaders (→ Training over the Course of Time).

In 1968 Ruth Cohn was invited to attend the Fourth International Congress on Group Psychotherapy in Vienna. After 27 years' absence, she once again touched down on European soil.

> I felt uneasy at first, being in this German-Austrian environment, surrounded by the unaccustomed German language. But that soon passed in light of the heartfelt welcome I received from my colleagues. (ibid., p. 376)

> At the end of the congress, an elderly gentleman came up to me and excitedly said: "I now realize why they let us contemplate things in silence and allowed us to speak as 'I': That was their way of avoiding mass suggestion and mass hysteria." I had never thought about silence in this way. [...] That this was one of the first comments a participant from Germany offered on TCI made me feel happy for a long time. (ibid., p. 380).

The bridge to Germany had now been opened, and in 1970 Ruth Cohn became one of the speakers at the Psychotherapy Meeting in Lindau. Further engagements in Europe were to follow. Up to the year 1973, Ruth Cohn spent her vacation going to TCI workshops and congresses in Europe. She discovered a great pent-up demand among her colleagues in Europe from all types of experiential therapy. Initially, mostly registered psychoanalysts came to her workshops, later people who worked as counselors, teachers, and pastors. Besides the important elements of experiential therapy, her search for a holistic concept of humankind (ibid., pp. 357 ff.) was what led teachers and theologians to the teachings of Ruth Cohn. The first book in German about TCI by Matthias Kroeger entitled *Themenzentrierte Seelsorge* (Theme-Centered Pastoral Work) was witness to the enormous influence Ruth Cohn had obtained in Germany

> What stood out most to me [...] in Germany was the need to fill the gaps in both knowledge and experience which had been left behind by the Nazi times and the war. (ibid., p. 384)

Ruth Cohn's activities on both sides of the ocean had become so diverse that, in 1971, she had to admit "you can't burn the candle at both ends" (ibid., p. 384). She decided to leave

New York. For the next 3 years, she traveled back and forth between the United States and Europe.

In 1974, she found a new domicile for her activities at the Ecole d'Humanité in Goldern am Hasliberg near Bern, Switzerland. Exchanging work for an apartment was a success, and thus began a new era in her life, "a great panorama before me from a small flat."

> I didn't really think about the apartment much. It didn't matter that it consisted only of one large room and two further small ones with bevels. I always went directly to the balcony door and there it was: glaciers surrounded by the soft lines of the mountains, covered nearly to the top ridge by a dark forest. There was a waterfall and below an immense snow-dabbed winter valley between the mountains. I stood on my balcony and was speechless. Two thoughts crossed my mind: "That's a sight reserved for farmers" and "Maybe I can find God while I'm here." (ibid., p. 391)

> The solitude of the mountain became the new home to my thoughts. (ibid., p. 427)

Here she wrote her important autobiographical work *Gelebte Geschichte der Psychotherapie* (The Living History of Psychotherapy, 1984) in which she discussed philosophical, sociocultural, and psychological matters, in a dialog with the works of her late colleague and friend Alfred Farau.

In 1979, Ruth Cohn received an honorary doctorate from the Psychology Faculty of the University of Hamburg, and again in 1994 she was given an honorary doctorate from the Institute for Psychology of the Philosophical-Historical Faculty of the University of Bern. Since the 1980s Ruth Cohn had looked increasingly at the role of social problems; ecological and political threats directed her attention to the → Globe.

Upon turning 80 she said the following in an interview:

> I believe that there is something good in human beings. [...] It has to do with respect for life, respect for nature, respect for other humans. [...] I think it might be possible that, say, in 50 years the appropriate methods [of TCI] will no longer be appropriate, and something new will appear. As long as humankind exists [...] even 1% hope is justified. (Heidbrink, 1992, pp. 315 ff.)

During the next years, Ruth Cohn remained publicly active as an honorary member of WILL International organization, inasmuch as she was able to do so.

> Growing old means two things: Keep saying "I can still do it" and accept the fact that, in light of decline, "I can't do it anymore." (quoted by Löhmer & Standhardt, 2006, p. 29).

Since 2003 the TCI International organization bears her name: the Ruth Cohn Institute for TCI International (→ The Institutionalization of TCI).

Ruth Cohn passed away in Düsseldorf on 30 January 2010.

Part I

Foundations of TCI

The Historical and Political Background of TCI

Helmut Johach

1 Existential Borderline Experiences and the Struggle with Fascism

Ruth Cohn repeatedly pointed out that her flight from Nazi Germany, only a few weeks after the Nazis had usurped power in 1933, and their continued threats through fascism, decidedly influenced the development of TCI (Cohn, 1975a, pp. 220 ff.; Cohn, 1979, pp. 873ff.; Farau & Cohn, 1984, pp. 462 ff.). Her years of university studies, the founding of a family, and her work at a psychiatric clinic near St. Gallen in Switzerland were overshadowed by the events going on in her now fascist neighboring home country – not the least the disenfranchisement experienced by the Jews after the Nuremberg laws, the state-supported pogroms against the Jews (played down by the belittling title of "Night of Broken Glass"), the takeover of Czechoslovakia, and the attack on Poland in 1939, which started World War II. When, in 1940, the news broke in Swiss radio that the German Army had crossed the border into Switzerland, she seriously considered suicide to avoid falling into the hands of the Nazis. She could pass her daughter on as the illegitimate child of the daughter of the head of the clinic – but what would happen if the Germans discovered that they were shielding a Jewish baby? "Was is not our duty to kill her as painlessly as possible beforehand?" she asked herself (Farau & Cohn, 1984, p. 466).

In the end, Ruth Cohn and her husband did not have to make the choice between suicide and torture, between the painless death of her child and the chance of her meeting a gruesome end: The news of the border crossing turned out to have been a hoax. Nevertheless, Ruth Cohn said that the situation was for her "the main borderline experience" of her life, that it influenced her later life and played a decisive role in the "further development of her values system" (ibid., p. 467).

Yet, it was not only this existential experience, but also her political consciousness of the "horrors of the times" (ibid., p. 213) that led her to make the dangerous journey with her daughter and her husband from Switzerland to the United States. At the time she had no specific theory of fascism, though she was a convinced follower of democracy who had been shaped by the events of the Weimar Republic. And like so many others from the Jewish intelligentsia, she had been drawn to Marxist ideas[1], though she reacted very negatively to the *social-psychological mechanisms* the fascists used to secure their rule in people's heads and hearts. Especially effective was the demagogic use of the "brown propaganda," the demonstration of military might, the "national-ethnic" unity shown at the Nazis' yearly Nuremberg Party Rallies, and the initially broad support offered by the population during the first years of the war for the fascist politics of conquest. They were successful in suppressing objections to all the spying and informing that went on and displacing the will to annihilate anything considered non-Aryan from the consciousness of most Germans. Even while living in Switzerland during her university studies and in her volunteer work for refugees, which she did parallel to her training analysis, Ruth Cohn was always devoted to the question: "How can the insights we garner from our couch work be made available to more than just the one patient being treated? Can we reduce or even prevent prejudices, mass hysteria, and their spread through our psychoanalytic knowledge?" (Cohn, 1979, p. 874). With this, she meant that psychology and therapy should not be limited to dealing solely with the mental problems of individuals.

2 The Social-Therapeutic Claim of TCI

In an article written together with Anita Ockel entitled "The Concept of Resistance in Theme-Centered Interaction" (Cohn & Ockel, 1981) as well as in her own work "Living History of Psychotherapy" (Farau & Cohn, 1984), Ruth Cohn commented on the political intention of TCI to go beyond just dealing with fascism. There she speaks of a sort of "social therapy" (Cohn & Ockel, 1981, p. 178) as well as of an "approach to a humanistic social therapy" (Farau & Cohn, 1984, p. 334). This thought too stems from her own therapeutic training under the National Socialist regime. She said she thought it "surely must be possible, in the midst of all the horror going on in the world" (Cohn & Ockel, 1981, p. 178) to expand the experiences gathered on the psychoanalytic couch[2] to beyond the purely personal and reach all of society, by taking "little steps, tiny little changes of direction" (ibid., p. 178). The most important prerequisite would be not to suppress the *fear of threatening developments*, but rather to allow them to surface and to draw the proper consequences from them. She

1 "At the time [i.e., in Berlin of the 1920s] you were either a Communist or a National Socialist. You were a liberal only if you were already old. I, of course, chose Communism and read Marx with great enthusiasm. However, what I didn't like was the teaching that children were to be separated from their parents. That's why I didn't join the Communist Party" (Ruth Cohn from a conversation she had with Edith Zundel, in Zundel & Zundel, 1991, p. 73). Matthias Kroeger also notes from his conversations with Ruth Cohn that she had "since her school and university days been well aware of and drawn to Marxist themes" (Kroeger, 1992, p. 112).

2 The original title of her first book, which appeared in the Klett publishing house, was "The Couch Was Too Small" (cf. the Preface to Cohn, 1975, p. 7).

later expanded her thoughts on such possible threats in her writings against the background of the atomic arms race that was going on between the two superpowers of the time, to include the dire chance of nuclear war as well as the ecological dimension involved – the "catastrophic destruction of the Earth" (ibid., p. 188). The task, she thought, was not to close a blind eye to such life-threatening developments. The normative fundamentals of TCI, like any other approach to humanistic ethics, include promoting life and living growth – not destroying it. This naturally leads to the second philosophical-ethical axiom: "Revere all living things and their growth" (Farau & Cohn, 1984, p. 358).

It is important to see the *political* dimension contained within this axiom, which by the way also plays a major role in other ethical proclamations (e.g., by Albert Schweitzer[3]). The "reverence" mentioned does not refer to a feeling any one person has; rather, it designates a basic life-affirming tenet we should show toward our fellow human beings and toward nature as such. It is present in and emanates from all the interlaced connections of the "Globe." Ruth Cohn emphasizes that the relationship we have to the Globe is not a one-way street, but has "reciprocal effects" (ibid., p. 357). With this, she means that it not just a matter of the influences the "Globe" has on the individual and the group, but the opposite as well: that changes are necessary for our relationship toward the "Globe."

Especially two possible distortions can occur which should be avoided: First, there is the danger of hubris, of an inflated self-esteem by thinking that one, as an individual or together with others in a group, can "unhinge" the world; second, that one resigns too quickly when faced with the overwhelming power of global developments – "What can I really do about it?" Ruth Cohn's answer as the founder of TCI was to formulate an important insight and a guiding principle: "I am not all-powerful; I am not powerless: I am partially powerful" (Farau & Cohn, 1984, p. 360).

One should note, however, that Ruth Cohn always spoke of the social-*therapeutic* and not any social-*political* claims TCI made[4]. Her statements foresee a reflective moment of "becoming aware" (Cohn & Ockel, 1981, p. 178) – which is not the same as uttering a behavioral guideline or a making a call to take up any specific social model. Yet, it is also not an invitation to political arbitrariness. Against the background of Ruth Cohn's life and that of the other Jewish founders of TCI (among others, Norman Liberman, John Brinley, Yitzchak Zieman) we may assume that they rejected all forms of totalitarianism, and that they further condemned xenophobia, racism, and anti-Semitism. To quote Ruth Cohn again: "Humanistic Psychology and the related discipline of Humanistic Education is concerned with *how* people live and how love can counter murder and cruelty. Everything else is rather secondary" (Farau & Cohn, 1984, p. 467).

---

3 "The reverence toward all life that arises from the mindful will to live comprises the affirmation of life and the world and is intertwined with an ethical stance." This reverence toward life in no way allows an individual to forsake his interest in the world. "That is what demands that we deal with all living things that surround us, that we feel responsible toward the world" (Schweitzer, 1984, p. 46).

4 The subtitle of an anthology edited by R. Standhardt and C. Löhmer *Free to Act: Social-Political Perspectives of TCI Group Work* (1994) prefers, it seems, to blur this distinction.

3 Political Objectives During the Founding Phase of TCI

In the United States Ruth Cohn met, among others, Fritz Perls, the co-founder of gestalt therapy, who like her had fled Nazi Germany as a Jewish therapist (see Johach, 1999, pp. 11 ff.). She was, to be sure, impressed by his therapeutic skills, but rejected the so-called "gestalt prayer" ("I am I and you are you and if by chance we find each other, it's beautiful; if not, it can't be helped") because of what she felt was the call for "blinded egoism" (Cohn, 1975, p. 102). Early on she also distanced herself from the typical American call to "do your own thing" and emphasized the necessity of being thoughtful of the opinions and needs of others. Thus, in the TCI system, the requirement contained in the → chairperson postulate to be aware of one's own feelings and needs is coupled with the conscious perception and the "identical human respect" (Farau & Cohn, 1984, p. 359) for the feelings and needs of others. This is one of the major differences from the self-fulfillment approach, which takes little notice of fellow human beings.

That these principles were valid not just for small groups, but for whole societal conflicts as well, is manifested in the activities of the WILL Institute, which was founded in New York in 1966. Following the McCarthyism of the 1950s, precipitated by the Cold War, which caused a veritable hunt for Communists among the intellectuals of the country, the United States of the 1960s were characterized by comparably liberal politics. The civil rights movement under the leadership of Martin Luther King fought for the equality of the Blacks and had some success in helping to enact the respective legislation (e.g., equal voting rights in the Voting Rights Act of 1965). This did not, however, mean that racial discrimination came to an end from one day to the next. One of the first workshops carried out by the founders of the WILL Institute was concerned with the "Separation – Connection – Coexistence – Integration" of Blacks and Whites. (By the way, this was also the first WILL workshop to address the theme of the emancipation of women; cf. Farau & Cohn, 1984, pp. 346 ff.) Another workshop reported on by Yitzchak Zieman took place in 1968 in a poor neighborhood in a part of New York populated mainly by Blacks. The theme of the workshop was how parents could fight for more participative rights in their children's schools, which the largely white teachers and school authorities were adamant to prevent (Zieman, 2002, pp. 162 ff.). The goal of the workshop was to break down prejudices and reservations and achieve more direct participation.

The examples given above show that, from the beginning, TCI was attuned to political effectiveness, in the sense of *understanding and cooperation* – and that it rejected all forms of suppression and violent confrontations between the various social groups.

4 TCI and Politics in the Present Discussion

Today, the matter of the political effectiveness of TCI is being discussed on various levels. For example, Helmut Reiser differentiates between the description of TCI as a "system of political education" and the alternative depiction of TCI as a system for "power-political actionism." The latter description is, in his opinion, clearly *not* the case (Reiser, 1996a, p. 33). Based, on the one hand, on the sociological theory of increasing differences in social systems (economy, politics, jurisprudence, etc.) and the increasing individualism present in the lifestyles of our "risk society" (Beck, 1986), on the other hand, the political question is as follows: Not just our behavior in large collective groups is of major importance, but also the effects of the incalculable consequences of industrialization and technical progress (e.g., fractured work histories or ecological problems). What we don't need is more action, but more reflection, which in light of the many different influences we are faced with demands a "moratorium for decisions, a hold on the implementation of life experiences" (Reiser, 1996b, p. 32). This "reflection moratorium" is not situated on the political level, but rather, according to Reiser, where TCI contains the element of "reflexive identity formation" (ibid., p. 32). Political action is related to the collective creation of opinion, to assuming power, and to asserting interests; TCI, on the other hand, has the goal of creating "consciousness and decision-making skills in the individual" (ibid., p. 33).

The question "Is TCI political in nature?" also surfaced in the discussion between Manfred Krämer and Walter Zitterbarth (Krämer & Zitterbarth, 2006). From the outset, Zitterbarth limits what is political to "democratic decision-making processes, legislative procedures, and things that are institutionally determined" (ibid., p. 9) – what in English is generally termed "polity." Krämer, on the other hand, envisions a much broader definition of the term "political," which he thinks concerns the "democratization of social areas" (ibid., p. 9) – or what in English is generally termed "politics." According to Krämer, political action is not limited to institutional procedures of representational democracy (e.g., elections), but has more to do with the individual self-determination and codetermination of those concerned; it is a matter of "overcoming rigid, traditional communication structures" (Krämer, 2001, p. 34). In the end, it also has to do with "the development and humanity of society" (Krämer & Zitterbarth, 2006, p. 11). Krämer's latter interpretation of TCI reads like one of the visions of the student movements from 1968, whereas Zitterbarth's more modern interpretation reminds us of Luhmann's model of system theory. The latter presumes sophisticated sections of society that are subject to their respective principles. Politics is one thing, and the correct execution of educational events is another. For this reason, Zitterbarth rejects the social-therapeutic claim TCI makes as a "promise of salvation" (ibid., p. 13) that it can never realize.

If you keep up with the ongoing discussion, you might get the impression that the further development of the theory of TCI ended up limiting the group-educational concept to the idea of *personality development*. In an interview with Manfred Krämer, however, Ruth Cohn protested against just such a constriction.[5] On the other hand, the continued

5 "TCI does not mean just individual self-realization. I read in a book that TCI is concerned with the development of the individual. That angered me, even then, since TCI does not attend to a person's psychological development but to the person's socialization" (Ruth Cohn in Cohn & Krämer, 2002, p. 22).

specialization and professionalization of TCI in the various disciplines poses the question: Should we really relinquish the vision of TCI influencing or changing social circumstances? Put another way: Should we give up on the idea of creating a more just and humane society so that the implementation of TCI in practice can function more smoothly?

From the history of TCI and the painful experiences that prompted the humanistic impulse and the value system of TCI, we know that this question cannot receive an outright "Yes" as an answer. How political TCI is must be occasionally reexamined in accordance with the changing social circumstances – the quest is never simply over.

The Psychoanalytic Foundation of TCI

Angelika Rubner

The theory behind theme-centered interaction (TCI) as developed by the psychoanalyst Ruth Cohn has its roots in both psychoanalysis and Humanistic Psychology. The following contribution is concerned with the psychoanalytical roots of TCI and the common features shared by psychoanalysis and TCI. First, the two approaches need to be defined.

The practice of psychoanalysis as taught by Sigmund Freud is, on the one hand, a *diagnostic method* directed toward uncovering and becoming aware of the unconscious meaning of language, actions, imaginary events (dreams, fantasies, hallucinations), and symptoms. On the other hand, it is a *psychotherapeutic method* based on just such examinations which, by interpreting a patient's resistance, transference, wishes, and fears, serves to strengthen their ego to withstand the inundation from the Id or the constrictions of the Super-ego. Third, psychoanalysis is a *psychological theory* that systematizes the results of the psychoanalytic examination and treatment methods (Laplanche & Pontalis, 1973, p. 410).

TCI, like psychoanalysis, is a *diagnostic method* directed toward capturing the themes and processes occurring at that moment in a group situation. Second, it is an *educational method* that serves to improve the collective learning and work in groups. Third, it is a *psychological theory* that describes and systematizes the events that go on in a group, its psychodynamics, and its targeted work.

This attempt to define TCI similarly to psychoanalysis points up many similarities and differences in the two methods. The commonalities are related to the roots of TCI in psychoanalysis; the differences (which are not the main concern of this article) result first from the synthesis with → Humanistic Psychology and, second, from the fact that TCI is not primarily a psychotherapeutic but an educational method.

1 Which Discoveries and Developments from Psychoanalysis Found Their Way into TCI

Freud was the first to make *inner (subjective) experiences* the object and tool of scientific research. But a person's experiences can be verified only from within and tapped only from the outside, which increases the subjective responsibility for presenting the truth and the expression thereof. In TCI, we find the practice of introspection as demanded and promoted by psychoanalysis in the demand that all expressions of feelings be authentic and all thoughts be unclouded. This thought is included in the → chairperson postulate, which arises from the axioms and value system of TCI: "Be aware of your inner life and your inner environment [...]. Give and take, as you see yourself responsible for yourself and for others" (Farau & Cohn, 1984, p. 359).

The second postulate of TCI is "disruptions and passionate involvements take priority" (→ Disturbance Postulate), which is derived from the concept of dealing with resistance in psychoanalysis. On this Sigmund Freud said: "Whatever disturbs the progress of analysis is resistance" (Freud, 1900, p. 521). The definition of disturbance in TCI is thus nearly identical to the use of the term resistance in psychoanalysis: "Anything that obstructs the plan, the goal, the task, a person's theme or an interactional group is a disruption" (Ockel & Cohn, quoted acc. To Löhmer & Standhardt, 1992, p. 185). Even if TCI doesn't go as far and as deep in working through disturbances as psychoanalysis does with resistance, the Disruption Postulate of TCI still corresponds to the postulate found in psychoanalysis that one must first work through resistance before addressing content: "Disruptions take priority."

Freud's discovery that the individual should not be seen as an isolated unit, but as a part and an expression of his or her relationships to the environment led Harry Stuck Sullivan (1947) to establish his theory of interpersonal relationships, and to further develop his concept of the nonneutral, empathetic therapist. For Sullivan, the therapist is a "participative observer" (Sullivan, 1947, p. 347). Ruth Cohn's own concept of a "participating group leader" may be traced directly back to Sullivan's influence as well as to the experiences she gathered with group psychoanalysts who had changed their approach from the originally neutral and abstinent position to one of existential partnership with their patients.

Ruth Cohn was always quick to insist on dealing with *values*, which for her meant committing oneself to relieving the world of fear and misery, of loneliness and indignity. These thoughts may also be found in the demands of her predecessor Alfred Adler, who was the first so-called depth psychologist to introduce ethics and education into the therapeutic setting. He even went further and interjected analysis into the social fabric, developing the term "community feeling" (Adler, 1911). His influence is often overseen, not the least by Ruth Cohn, who first read Adler, as she admitted herself, while writing the book *Living History of Psychotherapy* together with Alfred Farau, a disciple of Adler (Farau & Cohn, 1984, p. 442).

The experiences gathered in psychoanalytic groups, namely, that it is possible to create an atmosphere of trust by demanding authenticity and an open and responsible exchange of feelings, led Ruth Cohn to conclude that these phenomena should be introduced and pursued as well in nontherapeutic groups. TCI, with its principles of group education, is the attempt to create just these conditions that enable trustful cooperation (cf. as well → We).

2 Similarities Between Psychoanalytic Group Therapy and TCI

The vehicle used to communicate in these two approaches is the same: language. Both methods foresee that all thoughts, feelings, ideas, fantasies, and body signals be expressed through the use of language.

Working with time: Despite all the differences in their conceptions of time, psychoanalysis and TCI are both methods that refer to the *here and now* and that have built-in time limits.

Interaction and *relationship* are important factors, too. Both TCI and psychoanalysis assume that an "interactive approach to the entire situation" (Streeck & Bell, 1994) is created when words and understandable visual means of communication and gestures are employed. Both also define behavior as something situated not just on the performance level, but also on the relationship level.

For psychoanalysis and TCI, the *environment* is something that is framed – and subjectively interpreted – by our own respective mental state.

The role of the group leader/group psychoanalyst: Psychoanalytic group therapy and TCI both see the group analyst/group leader as part of the *system referred to as a group*. The analyst/leader participate in this system and are affected by any changes to it that may come about. Both are responsible for the group atmosphere, and both must, if they are intent on instigating a developmental and change process in the group, continually reflect and try to understand themselves. They both use their self-conceptions to understand what is going on in the group process, and they both must be able to identify with all members of the group. They should not be prone to partiality, that is, regardless of the empathy they may have, they must maintain the distance necessary to allow them to understand and interpret what occurs. Both the TCI group leader and the psychoanalyst must too conform to their own demand for selective authenticity. They always act from the position of interactive involvement – structuring, focusing, regulating, and emphasizing what happens in the group setting. They actively influence the situation, alone through their presence and the role they have been given.

Exploiting transference phenomena: Freud's discovery that transference occurs in all human interactions (Freud, 1910) is a topic that is observed and used in TCI as well. Much as psychoanalysis uses transference to influence the therapeutic situation, TCI discretely employs transference to achieve desired educational effects. For example, the demand made of the TCI group leader to be both role model and model participant is based on the effectiveness of transference: Without transference – the linking of earlier role models, such as mother, father, siblings, and others, to the group leader – the role model function of the group leader would remain futile. There would be no reason for identification. However, transferences, whether positive or negative in nature, develop not only between group members and the group leader, they can also occur among the group participants. The TCI group leader must be aware of the fact that some of the reciprocal reactions of participants and some of the distortions in their perception can be dealt with and tested against reality if they are interpreted as re-appearances of feelings and fantasies directed toward earlier important persons in life (→ We).

Dealing with countertransference phenomena: Psychoanalysts use their own reactions to the analysand – that is, countertransference – to understand and interpret that person's unconscious expressions and emotions. As part of their interpretations, they pick from the mass of material presented what they deem useful for explaining the ongoing situation. Thus, Freud called for "authentic psychoanalytic communication," whereas Ruth Cohn demands "selective authenticity." Ruth Cohn repeatedly emphasized that the TCI leader, despite all the leadership functions that go along with the role, should always remain part of the group and be subject to its feelings, fears, desires, and positions, just like the other participants. Consciously dealing with this fact enables the leader to make the proper diagnostic decisions with respect to the group atmosphere and the prevailing attitudes. These, in turn, form the basis for further thematic and structural actions. If group leaders are to be "selectively authentic" in their interventions, then they must purposely choose from the many reactions at their disposal those that promise to foster further development in the individuals involved, the group processes, and the subjects being treated.

Finally, a word about a feature historically common to the founders of psychoanalysis and TCI: Both Sigmund Freund and Ruth Cohn were Jews. According to René König, the sociological background, the double identity, and the more or less intensive discrimination and marginalization the Jews experienced should not be seen as completely negative factors; rather, they were also (perhaps for that very reason) triggers for their sharp analyses and demands for change in social mores. "The whole lived social circumstance pushed the Jews nearly automatically to take a theoretical stance toward social existence" (König, 1975, p. 133). In the Jewish tradition, as opposed to the Christian tradition, "the social element [. . .] is basically the only dimension amenable to human life. For this reason, the ethics of life in this world – a positive morality – go all the way back to ancient Judaism" (ibid., p. 127). That these are two descendants of Jewish tradition may, I think, be found in the thoughts of Sigmund Freund and Ruth Cohn. First, the role of morality and human values, to which Freud said: "Morals are self-evident" (quoted acc. to Hartmann, 1973, p. 11). Ruth Cohn postulated the following in her philosophical-ethical axiom: "Respect is due all living things [. . .]. The humane is valuable, the inhumane is threatening" (Cohn, 1975, p. 12). Second, an ambivalence emerges from the Jewish cultural-historical background which can be found in their demand for resistance toward oppressive social mechanisms, on the one hand, and the simultaneous interdiction of any form of aggression, on the other hand, the result of the fundamental law in Judaism to suppress all expressions of aggression. It would go far beyond the scope of this article to study the overall role of Jewish thought in psychoanalysis and TCI – but it would indeed be an interesting topic to pursue.

The Influence of Humanistic Psychology on TCI

Wendy Hecker

The previous article (→ Psychoanalytic Foundations of TCI) clearly showed the psychoanalytic background behind TCI. The same may be said for the Humanistic Psychology movement, which too is based on psychoanalysis. This contribution is concerned with the influence of North American Humanistic Psychology and Experiential Psychology on the rise of TCI.

1 Humanistic Psychology

Humanistic Psychology considers itself to be the "third force" beside Behavioral Psychology and psychoanalysis – and yet it distances itself from both of them, which it accuses of presuming a mechanistic and (cultural) pessimistic image of humankind, respectively. Whereas Behavioral Psychology reduces the individual to a collection of measurable stimuli and reactions, psychoanalysis stems from 19th-century thought and claims that humans are ruled by their instincts and can – at best – learn to ward off or control said instincts. The primary focus of Humanistic Psychology, on the other hand, lies neither in a scientific approach nor in controlling things, but in empathy, understanding, and liberation.

The basic tenets of Humanistic Psychology were laid down in 1962 as part of the "four-theses program" of its founders (Maslow, Bühler, Rogers, Köstler et al.; see Revenstorf, 1983, p. 70):

- Human *experiences* stand at the center of attention.
- An individual cannot be reduced to certain qualities and characteristics (*nonreductionism*).
- Objectivity is not the main criterion of relevant psychology research, but rather the *meaningfulness* of the results of research for human existence.
- Humanistic Psychology aims at helping people to develop their *positive powers* and to maintain *human dignity*.

The program of Humanistic Psychology thus contradicts psychoanalysis and behavioral therapy and pits itself again the "increasing alienation of humans toward themselves, others, society, and history" (Quitmann, 1996, p. 27). Because of a loss of orientation toward traditional value systems such as religion, family, and society, the search is on for new guideposts.

1.2 The Conception of Human Life in Humanistic Psychology

Widely varying intellectual currents contributed to the conception of human life found in Humanistic Psychology, among others, phenomenology, European existential philosophy, Marxism, Far Eastern philosophy as well as the Old Testament. These very divergent influences show that Humanistic Psychology does not represent a very consistent theoretical structure, but rather concentrates on the development of what constitutes human life. The Humanistic Psychology movement was caught up in and eventually assimilated many of the intellectual trends present in the 1960s. Each of the master Humanistic Psychologists, in turn, contributed their own special aspects, some of whom ended up founding their own schools of thought and spreading their own teachings (examples are Virginia Satir, Wilhelm Reich, Carl Rogers, Fritz Perls, and Eric Berne).

One of the basic conditions of human life, for example, was formulated by Erich Fromm and Ruth Cohn as *fear and freedom*: The more we humans can register our fears and our lack of freedom, the more liberated we become. Goldstein, Bühler, Maslow, and Rogers also speak of the importance of freedom, albeit emphasizing *human potential* as well as *growth* and *self-realization*. The concept of *contact* was the focus of attention in Fritz Perls' Gestalt Therapy.

The terms *choice, decision*, and *responsibility*, well known from Existential Philosophy, are also characteristic of Humanistic Psychology. As an individual you are basically responsible for your own life – whether you want to or not. We must continually make decisions, choose paths, and suffer the consequences. We can no longer expect help from some all-knowing God, fate, or some other deterministic value system. The aspect of *presence in the world* is understood such that mental development does not occur solely by coming to terms with our past or by orienting ourselves to the future, but rather arises by experiencing the Here and Now. Meaning, values, a holistic life, and self-fulfillment are the cornerstones of Humanistic Psychology.

The vision of human life propagated by Humanistic Psychology is strongly dependent on European, in particular German, intellectual traditions, not surprisingly so, since German émigrés such as Goldstein, Fromm, Perls, Bühler, and Cohn contributed considerably to both its theory and practice.

1.3 Resistance

The term *resistance* is understood differently in Humanistic Psychology than in psychoanalysis. In Humanistic Psychology, resistance is a form of contact. But what does "contact" mean here? Broadly speaking, it means how our self organizes itself in daily life (Wheeler, 1993) – and resistance is just one part of that organization. Resistance is not seen as opposing contact, but rather as a part thereof. This is an important extension of Freud's original concept of resistance.

Working with a countertransference group led Ruth Cohn to an insight concerning resistance: Parallel to the subject of countertransference the group can develop its own transference phenomena that grow and gain influence in the group if not checked. This insight led to her postulate: "disruptions take priority," one of the cornerstones of TCI. Unlike in psychoanalysis, in TCI resistance is not thought of as a defensive mechanism, but rather as an important contribution to the group situation.

1.4 Holistic Approach

Humanistic Psychology repeatedly emphasizes, sometimes in a rather naïve and extremely optimistic manner, that the individual must be seen as a totality. Gestalt Psychology, which arose at the beginning of the 20th century as a child of the perception research going on at the time (by, among others, Wertheimer and Köhler), referred to a holistic form of information processing that conformed to its own natural laws of physics. For example, it says that the human gestalt has the natural tendency toward completeness and for this reason must always be viewed as a whole – not as the sum of the individual parts. But holistic principles are also valid for "thought gestalts": "The thought becomes whole when suddenly a meaning is revealed (the 'aha experience')"; or valid for "need gestalts that also want to be whole" (Revensdorf, 1985, p. 12). The most important thing is to see the entire phenomenon and not just the individual parts thereof – and to recognize that there is a natural tendency to go forward with development toward a complete gestalt.

In 1961, at the yearly Congress of the American Academy of Psychotherapists (AAP), Ruth Cohn discovered this long-desired holistic approach, which heeds to feelings, reasoning, body, and environment. Thereupon, she began exchanging regular correspondence with a number of colleagues. In her later book *Living History of Psychotherapy* (Farau & Cohn, 1984) she calls out John Warkentin and Carl Whitaker as being the most important contacts at the AAP and writes the following: "I was fascinated. I felt this corresponded to a piece of my own journey: to allow myself to enter into an emotional-metaphorical search for my own reactions to my patients" (ibid., p. 275).

2 Experiential Therapy

Some of the AAP members from the East Coast had joined together as early as the mid-1950s and called themselves "experiential therapists." Well-known representatives of this school were John Whitaker, John Warkentin, Vin Rosenthal, Virginia Satir, and (sometimes) Carl Rogers (Farau & Cohn, 1984). The basics of "Experientialism" were similar to those of Humanistic Psychology. Ruth Cohn considered herself one of the founders of this movement (Quitmann, 1996), which however did not get a foothold as an independent method in the United States or Europe. Today the term "Experiential Therapy" is virtually unknown.

As to the typical characteristics of Experiential Therapy, Ruth Cohn had the following to say:

Encounters in *partnership*: an existential equality of the analyst and the analysand despite their very different functions; maximum *authenticity* toward oneself and clear communication toward others (both within and outside of the therapeutic situation); emphasis on the *Here and Now*; *holism*: humans are holistic beings and should be treated as a psychosomatic entity; situations within and outside of therapy should be discussed for their *relevance to reality*; *exercises on perception and judgment* can be introduced; experientialism emphasizes the *inner experience*, the *subjective life* of a human being. Experientialism does not believe that human life can be reduced to measurable units or observable behavior; the demand for *nonhierarchical standards* and a corresponding lifestyle; what a patient (or student) is, can, and does is important – not what a patient is not, cannot be, or cannot do; that is, the therapist is attuned primarily to the *potential of a human being* and only secondarily to that person's illness; the nondetermined component of a human being. All of this is favorable to making *autonomous decisions* in the sense of self-actualization. (Farau & Cohn, 1984, pp. 278 f.)

With this Ruth Cohn formulated her own personal humanistic value system that later found its way into the axioms and postulates of TCI.

2.1 The Relationship Between Therapist and Patient

The groundbreaking work on this subject was done by Carl Rogers. Rogers demanded from the therapist authenticity, acceptance, and empathy; the therapeutic atmosphere should be one of mutual respect and esteem (Rogers, 1961, 1942). The "philosophy of dialogue" propagated by Martin Buber (1983) was one of the basic philosophical and theoretical guideposts for this relationship. Although psychoanalysis also leans in this direction, the emphasis in this therapeutic school put on partnership goes far beyond that found in psychoanalytic thought. Here, the therapist is explicitly present as an individual and, as opposed to psychoanalysis, not primarily just a projection surface.

The following quote by Ruth Cohn shows how important the idea of partnership in the relationship between therapist and patient was to her. Healing, she said, happens in the presence of a strong, authentic interpersonal relationship:

The patient is not an empty vessel and the therapist does not have a hose as his disposal. Giving and taking are existential necessities. If the one or the other in a partnership fails to provide these functions, it is pathogenic [...]: Healing is a product of the depth of new experiences – especially when the strength of early traumatic experiences can be corrected by the emotional power of the therapeutic relationship. Such power arises from the authenticity of feelings and their communication. (Farau & Cohn, 1984, p. 279)

I think it's important at this juncture to mention that some humanistic therapists and group leaders misused the demand for fair cooperation in the relationship between the therapist and patients or group members as a license to deal irresponsibly with ongoing processes. In such cases, Ruth Cohn's call for authentic feelings and their direct communication was not accompanied by the necessary *selective authenticity*. The incidents of countertransference that subsequently occurred were then only insufficiently worked through (or not even understood).

3 Group Therapy

Following World War II, interest in the United States in group therapy and group processes in general exploded. It became clear that many more people could be reached via group therapy than by individual therapy or the even more time-consuming individual analysis. A group provides the participants with the feeling of togetherness; it can be a social corrective factor in a way individual therapy cannot. Ruth Cohn received many further impulses for her own work in groups from Moreno's teachings on psychodrama. And her friend Asya Kadis, a pioneer in group work, was able to convince Ruth Cohn to further develop her thoughts on working with groups.

Besides being an experiential therapist and reaching out to her colleagues at the AAP, from 1962 to 1970 Ruth Cohn profited greatly from her contact with Fritz Perls and gestalt therapy. Under his leadership, she discovered what it meant to live in the Here and Now, to squeeze through the "bottleneck," to look at "unfinished business" (earlier experiences that still inhibit one today), the effectivity of role-playing, and other gestalt techniques. These were later integrated into TCI.

4 Further Developments – from Therapy to Education

In light of the diversity that Humanistic Psychology and its offshoots represent, it seems only logical that Ruth Cohn eventually developed the wish to reach even more people by working with groups. One goal of Humanistic Psychology is to become involved in the political and social fabric of society. Ruth Cohn's approach of "living learning" was suitable for groups of all types that were learning to constructively communicate and to generally develop the human potential propagated by Humanistic Psychology.

The Educational-Pedagogical Fundamentals of TCI

Helmut Reiser

Ruth Cohn developed the educational-pedagogical concepts of TCI experimentally and intuitively from the experiences she had gathered in group therapy and from her interaction with the many therapeutic, social, cultural, and political trends of the day – not primarily from any scientific debates about educational theories. In her biographical texts she describes this development as a process that led her from one task to another: training psychoanalysts, leading the supervision of social workers and managers, solving problems in organizational development, looking at tasks from community work, working together with teachers and in the school environment (cf. Cohn, 1975, p. 119). Both she and her colleagues addressed the scientific background based on their expanding interests in TCI. The development of the educational background of TCI was the result of a years-long learning process.

In the first part of this contribution, I would like to look at what Ruth Cohn herself wrote about the history of the educational-pedagogical foundations of TCI, how they interacted with educational-pedagogical tasks, and resulted in the basic tenets of TCI. In the second part, I point out some of the basic principles and their connections to other educational-pedagogical approaches (→ Living Learning).

1 The Biographical Background of Ruth Cohn

Without any claim to completeness, I would like to limit this inquiry to the early 1970s when teachers and educational scientists began directing their attention toward TCI. This was the time when Myron Gordon's book on TCI originally appeared (1972), when WILL Europe was founded, and when Ruth Cohn moved to Switzerland and started working at the International Landschulheim "École d'Humanité" (1974).

In her memoirs, *The Living History of Psychotherapy* (Farau & Cohn, 1984), Ruth Cohn dedicates a whole chapter to the "Living History of Pedagogics" (pp. 324ff.). There she describes a number of situations in which she was confronted with educational tasks. Her first contacts were driven by her primary desire to become a psychoanalyst. In order to better understand how her adult patients were as children, during her studies she spent time in a kindergarten. What remained stuck in her memory was the contradiction between external order and internal organizational skills (ibid., p. 325). The subject of the inner development of children also proved to be important during her next phase at the Bankstreet School in New York where she practiced "progressive education" (1941/1942). There, too, she was not primarily concerned with becoming a teacher, but a psychoanalyst. However, at the time Ruth Cohn, who was not a medical doctor, was not allowed to work as a psychotherapist; it was suggested to her that she concern herself with treating children, so she ended up working as a "student teacher" in the famous Bankstreet School. She considered this time a "fantastically positive experience" (ibid., pp. 326f.). In 1984, she wrote about it: "Bankstreet provided me with the fundamentals for my later educational-therapeutic work" (ibid., p. 325). The was impressed with the fact that the children there were treated as "real and important people" and not as objects of an educational process (ibid., p. 326). "When I look back I see that Bankstreet was the source of much living learning" (ibid., 327). The "unnatural" demand of adults that children should be nice and kind and need no guidance whatsoever leads to the adults not being respected for what they are, and that children fail to develop an inner stability. In 1969, in a contribution to an anthology entitled *Group Therapy Today*, she wrote: "The pendulum of the frustration-gratification scale swung far too high to the side of permissiveness" (Cohn, 1969, p. 105). The children were being excessively bound to group experiences, they had to do without a place to retreat to in order to concentrate on their own "inner being" – one of the most important ideas in Ruth Cohn's educational theory, as may also be seen in TCI methodology. The reason behind this lies in her perception of "within and without" and in the perception of the beauty of nature (Farau & Cohn, 1984, p. 328). Sometimes, she thought, one just needs to pause and be quiet in order that "our internal and our external parts – self-realization and world-realization – [...] autonomy and interdependence may meet" (ibid., p. 378). Her realistic view of child development, however, is based not solely on intuitive presumptions, but also on hard scientific research. A few years later, while writing a review article for an anthology, she was once again concerned with the psychoanalytic research on childhood and discovered that her views were being supported: "I read about 150 different pieces, summarized about 100 of them, and learned just about everything known about child development before and after birth" (ibid., p. 333).[1]

In her memoirs Ruth Cohn notes another stage in her "Living History of Pedagogics": "being a mother: living learning" (ibid., pp. 329ff.), i.e., learning from her own children. The next step in her work with educational tasks were the years she devoted to the training of psychoanalysts: Since 1949 she taught the "psychoanalytic theory of child development" (Löhmer & Standhardt, 1995, p. 448).

According to Ruth Cohn, the birth of TCI took place in 1955 during her psychoanalytic training at the first countertransference workshop (Cohn, 1969, pp. 106f.). In what corresponds to the German practice of supervision, the rules and procedures

1 The timeframe of 1953 supplied for this bibliographic article would seem to refer to the publication year of the volume *Infancy* in the series *Progress in Clinical Psychology*.

of the TCI method were devised (or, as Ruth Cohn would say, "discovered"). Together with other colleagues, she developed a series of nontherapeutic workshops concerned with themes stemming from psychotherapy (ibid., p. 111). Queries from outside of psychotherapy led to experiences gathered through, among other things, team supervision, team groups in social agencies, and teamwork in hospitals. "As I gained in skill with these theme-centered interactional workshops, I began to test out and refine further the method for various other themes, groups and purposes" (ibid., p. 111). These were from supervision, teamwork, organizational development, political education, and self-awareness.

In 1969, in an article for the *Journal of Group Psychoanalysis and Process*, Ruth Cohn asked: "Can the passionate interest filling the group-therapeutic room be transferred to the school classroom?" (Cohn, 1969/70, quoted acc. to 1975, p. 112). She emphasized the importance of feelings during the learning process without actually focusing on the school situation.

A look at the existing texts shows that subjects from the realm of school and teaching were added to TCI only later. The great resonance TCI experienced in the educational setting turns up when TCI became more well known in the German-speaking countries of Europe. According to a footnote in the text (Cohn, 1975, p. 152), the first article to deal in any detail with the subject of schools was "On the Humanization of the School"[2] resulted from a workshop held for teachers attended by a physician, Gerd Iversen, the editor of a regional medical journal, who published the text in 1973. Via this winding road, TCI eventually fell on the fertile soil of German pedagogics.

When Ruth Cohn returned to Europe, her initial interest still belonged to the subjects of group therapy, especially at the congresses held in Vienna (1968), Bonn (1969), and Lindau (1970–1972). Later (1973/1974) she worked for a few months at the "Westfälischen Kooperationsmodell (WKM)" (Cooperative Model of Westfalia) in Vlotho, an organization devoted to the education of adolescents, teachers, and families – and, thus, in explicitly innovative pedagogical surroundings. In 1974, she lived and worked at the Ecole d'Humanité in Goldern am Hasliberg in Switzerland. From the descriptions we have of her activities there, provided by Armin Lüthi and Natalie Lüthi-Peterson (Lüthi et al., 1995, pp. 281–288) and by Ruth Cohn herself (Farau & Cohn, 1984, pp. 386–401), we see that she considered it her job to support and supervise the development of the school. The result was, among other things, poignant insights into inequalities and imbalances, the effect of a pleasant atmosphere, the conscious autonomy of adults, how to reduce hierarchy, and how to ensure the proper development of a partnership.

2 This article goes back to the idea of the "revolutionary evolution in the classroom" (cf. Kuebel, 2001, p. 433).

2 TCI Pedagogics

From the biographical stops in Ruth Cohn's life and the many contributions she penned up to that time we can deduce some of the basic principles of the pedagogics oriented to TCI.

During the 1970s some of the emancipatory and progressive educational goals in German pedagogics were combined, preparing the way for the subsequent impulses that emerged from TCI. In addition, the social and political ideas of equality, social justice, and partnership championed by Ruth Cohn emanated humane and reconciliatory tones – despite her sharp social criticisms. Her return to Germany from exile as a German Jew as well as her personal charisma also garnered much positive resonance.[3]

The approach TCI took toward pedagogics was based on its developmental view of the child and of humans in general, which were based on the humanistic side of psychoanalysis. The idea of the parallel existence of autonomy and interdependence as the driving forces behind development appeared to many to be a more logical and balanced approach to human psychology than the restrictive misunderstandings the so-called progressive educators of the day posited toward psychoanalysis. Ruth Cohn was very much aware of the necessity of implementing restrictions in education.

TCI propagates a combination of visionary ethics with realistic educational actions – a nod to Ruth Cohn's inclination to propose paradoxical combinations (above all autonomy and interdependence). In 1994, she wrote: "I am very impressed by the way paradoxes (or seeming paradoxes) are accepted" (Cohn, 1994, p. 367). She then provides an example for one of her paradoxical statements: "We only have very little time, so we've got to proceed slowly" (ibid., p. 328). This way of thinking corresponds to the daily business of teaching, which is infused with all sorts of paradoxes and antinomies. On the relationship level, we find the paradoxes closeness and distance, which are to be seen not as poles at the opposite ends of a spectrum, but as a dialectical pair: I must keep my distance from you in order to come closer to you. This makes it clear that in TCI Ruth Cohn was primarily concerned with sharpening our perception. Perceiving what is going on inside and outside of us leads to a consciousness and the ability to make free decisions. Affects play an important role in the decisions made by an individual and in we-processes. Intuition can be schooled by consciously becoming aware of bodily signals – both of one's own body and those of others. Body and soul are considered an entity.

The physical/affective/cognitive experiences of educators allow TCI to be directly effective in pedagogical practice, regardless of its theoretical background in educational science. Nevertheless, it is possible to pin down which theories and concepts are compatible with TCI and which are not.

TCI can generally be conceived of as a "progressive educational" concept (→ Living Learning). There are also many remarkable parallels to the teachings of Martin Buber

3 Characteristic for Ruth Cohn was her support for the protesting students at the 1969 DAAG Congress in Bonn.

("philosophy of dialogue"; see his "Speeches on Education," 1925), which Ruth Cohn had not previously been confronted with but are later referenced repeatedly (e.g., Reiser, 1987). Connections to TCI may be made to the similar principles of gestalt pedagogics (see Reiser, 1983); the "theme" principle of TCI also runs parallel to many educational theories (Klafki, 1991, pp. 118–135). TCI formed the basis of the Hamburg Model of Learning-Theoretical Didactics (Schulz, 1980). Others refer to its "pupil orientation" and its "relationship didactics" (Miller, 1997, pp. 71 f.). Reiser (2006) describes TCI as a "psychoanalytical, systemic concept." On the other hand, educational theories and approaches that do not foresee the joint development of autonomy and attachment nor put mental and interactional self-regulation at the center of their concepts are incompatible with TCI.

TCI and Philosophy

Walter Zitterbarth

1 The Philosophical Influences on Ruth Cohn

It is difficult to precisely determine the influences philosophy had on TCI. Ruth Cohn was interested in philosophical matters only in a rather broad sense – in particular in those philosophers who had played a role in the development of Humanistic Psychology and other psychotherapeutic movements she felt close to.[1] Paramount to her interest in philosophical thought were certainly phenomenology and existentialism, though other schools were of interest inasmuch as they were concerned with anthropological questions. For example, during her time in Switzerland in the 1930s she once spent a whole semester shuttling back and forth between Zurich and Basel in order listen to lectures by Paul Häberlein on the subject of conscience.

Ruth Cohn once said her favorite intellectual direction and form of therapy was experientialism (Cohn, 1979, p. 875), a term that was not widespread in Germany and has a number of meanings. On the one hand, this designation serves to help delineate between the rather dark and despairing European flavor and the more cheerful North American version – to which Ruth Cohn felt more attached. The latter type had an optimistic outlook and found its clearest proponent in Rollo May.[2]

On the other hand, the term experientialism acts as a defensive position toward all attempts to objectify and denature the human soul, as is often found in the scientific treatises on materialistic or mechanistic approaches to psychology, for example, in behaviorism. Humanism and the experiential life of human beings are set in opposition to such thrusts; here again, we encounter the thoughts of Martin Buber, who said we should always differentiate between the I-You relationships between human beings and I-It relationships between human beings and things (Buber, 1962).

1 See Quitmann, 1985, pp. 197 f.
2 Ruth Cohn describes May's work (1958) as the philosophically most defining influence on her own concept of therapy.

2 Attempts at a Philosophical Underpinning of TCI

A number of attempts were made to provide philosophical support for TCI beyond the remarks made by Ruth Cohn herself. The most extensive one was done by Hanneke Ehlich and Ingo Majewski (1995), who made the attempt to deduce TCI axioms and postulates from basic philosophical tenets. Kant's categorical imperative, for example, was used to modify the first axiom by repealing the equality of autonomy and interdependence in favor of interdependence: Autonomy is then of importance only within the network of interdependence. A similar conclusion results for the first postulate if one were to, as these authors do, read: "Be your own chairperson" as a categorical imperative, the result being that one's own needs are valid only in the context of others.

The fact that in the end not a single axiom and not a single postulate of TCI is left untouched suggests that these authors were concerned less with supporting the theory of TCI with philosophical arguments than they were with providing a legitimization for a revamping of TCI. The two main philosophers chosen for support – Plato and Kant – were treated not as partners in dialog, but as infallible authorities. Both Kant's ethics and Plato's cosmology are considered declarative systems with unlimited value and a clear meaning: No interpretation necessary. Such secret dogmatism is clearly difficult to reconcile with the basic principles of living learning.

A somewhat older attempt to philosophically underpin TCI stems from the year 1987, when Eleonore Olszowi, unlike her later colleagues, did not attempt to deduce the entire system of TCI from philosophical premises, but rather pursued a much less radical goal: to show the "parallels" between TCI and Existentialism, especially that of Sartre. This she does, for example, by looking at the → chairperson postulate (she still calls it Chairman Postulate), which in her opinion contains the following statements:

1) The subject cannot be reduced to something more elementary – despite all the tendencies to the opposite, namely, to make the subject a mechanistic thing. Thus, for Sartre Existentialism is the "only theory" that "does not make him [the human being] an object" (Sartre, 1961, p. 25).
2) All human beings are responsible for their own actions. Sartre: "If indeed existence precedes essence, then humans are responsible for what they do" (Sartre, 1961, p. 12).
3) All human beings are responsible for other human beings. Olszowi thinks that Ruth Cohn's theory of the interdependence of humans is contained in this statement, but lacking elsewhere in the TCI literature. In Sartre, she detects a greater level of responsibility: "And if we say that human beings are responsible for themselves, then we are not intimating that humans are responsible only for their own individuality, but rather that they are responsible for all other human beings" (Sartre, 1961, p. 12).
4) Some further attempts by Olszowi to show parallels between TCI and the Existentialism of Sartre would seem to have been less successful. Sartre's idea of freedom, for example, is much more absolute and does not contain "conditional inner and outer borders." It is also difficult to imagine that Sartre's statement that "every truth and

every action involves an environment and a human ego" (1981, p. 8) reflects the TCI axiom concerning independent and interdependent human behavior.

3 The Adaptation of TCI to Pragmatism

The least reimagined part of TCI would seem to its adaptation to certain basic positions of North American pragmatism. Also, Ruth Cohn never mentioned this direction as having inspired her. And yet we may assume that she was exposed to such influences – by the very fact of living in the United States and teaching at Bankstreet School. Pragmatism was one of the predominant philosophical trends in North American even in the second half of the 20th century.[3] Here I would like to provide three examples of how TCI and pragmatism were related:

1) Ruth Cohn's description of the first axiom of TCI that humans are equally autonomous and interdependent has an interesting parallel in the social psychological teachings of George Herbert Mead (1968). In order to uphold the identity of every organism, Mead calls it a "self" and confers two behavior-based identity poles: the "I" and the "Me." He designates the "I" to be the more spontaneous, creative, and active dimension of the "self"; the "I" causes the self's reactions to the expectations of others to be unpredictable. Whereas the "I" in this scenario comprises the subjective and autonomous part of the "self," the "Me" is the controlling, limiting, socially conditioned part of a person. "Me," which in TCI stands for the dimension of interdependence, is – unlike the "I" – controlled by conventions and habits, something available to all other people as well. The call by TCI to pay equal attention to autonomy and interdependence is thus present in Mead's demand to find a long-term balance between behavior in which I am like no one else and behavior in which I am just like everyone else. The social psychologist Erving Goffman (1975), who was closely aligned to pragmatism, took up Mead's thoughts and developed them further by saying that humans have a double identity: Their biographical data are vertically aligned, along a timeline, to comprise their "personal identity," which reflects the distinctiveness of each and every individual. On the other hand, the many roles that we play at any one point in time may be seen horizontally as our "social identity," which defines our sometimes rather conflicted relationships to numerous social groups.
2) In the context of a conversation, Ruth Cohn said the following: "We are dealing here with values and with the meaning of human life" (1985, p. 15). And then she goes on to say, "I am more and more convinced that the basis for every rational argument for ethics lies in beliefs that cannot be rationally supported" (1985, p. 14). No one before Ruth Cohn had emphasized the connection between beliefs and values so cogently as the philosopher and psychologist William James, one of the founders of pragmatism.

3 A good introduction to these matters may be found in Nagl (1998).

Science, according to James (1897), tells us to strive for truth and avoid error, meaning it deduces two formulations of the same rule and gives priority to the latter. Thus, science amasses considerable knowledge but, according to James, limits our access to the truth. On the other hand, if we prioritize the search for truth without steadfast knowledge when we have in fact reached our goal, then we support our willingness to search for answers in places where no certainty may be found. This, in turn, provides sufficient opportunity for beliefs to arise, especially when we are concerned less with the critical assessment of insights and more with the creative process of discovery as such. According to James, especially with respect to moral matters, we simply cannot wait for an exhaustive argumentation, but have to act even in the absence of certainty. Belief becomes especially important in situations where trust is involved or necessary. James notes the example of falling in love: Without some measure of insecure belief in the existence of love, there can, in fact, be no love. In this sense, James thought there are situations where our beliefs in something can contribute to its very creation. Ruth Cohn's belief in life and the meaning of life would seem to be a good example confirming James' position.

3) In her book *Living History of Psychotherapy*, Ruth Cohn develops a theory that was unusual at the time of its emergence: the "hypothesis of an innate organismic value system" (Farau & Cohn, 1984, pp. 467 ff.). The idea behind this theory is that our social value systems are not simply subjective and arbitrary constructions, nor do they consist of abstract entities in some separate sphere beyond human actions. This idea may be found in a precursor from the classical philosophy of pragmatism: In his work *Theory of Valuation* (1939), Dewey concerned himself with the development of values and covered some of the same ground as Ruth Cohn did, namely, by seeking an alternative to the dilemma posed by having to choose between value-theoretical subjectivism and objectivism. In order to understand what values are, Dewey considered it necessary to begin with organismic behavior, which for him contained a number of preferences, that is, unreflected priorities of certain behavioral tendencies toward others, relative to the demands of the environment. The most important thing, Dewey thought, was that these preferences do not arise solely from conscious decisions, but, as it were, precede them. Dewey thought it impossible that complex and rational value hierarchies could arise without such organismic impulses. This theory of Dewey's was not, to be honest, completely original, even at the time. The Irish philosopher Francis Hutcheson (1694–1746) had attributed to humans an innate morality that gives birth to emotions such as cooperation and brotherly love. The Scottish moral philosopher David Hume (1711–1776) took up this thought and spoke of a sixth sense, responsible for human decency, which we humans are born with in addition to the well-known other five senses.

4 TCI and Philosophy Today

Such naturalistic approaches have once again, at the beginning of the 21st century, become popular. The instinct for good and evil – a sort of moral compass – seems to be implanted deeply in our biological makeup. This sentiment is widespread not only among researchers from the natural sciences, but also among philosophers, such as the legal philosopher Matthias Mahlmann (1999). On the one hand, this stance agrees with the hypothesis of Ruth Cohn concerning the existence of an innate organismic value system; on the other hand, it contradicts the reigning opinion from the past 50 years held by many philosophers, legal experts, and psychologists who generally agree that moral opinions represent completely conscious decisions – and thus reject any presumption of a moral instinct. They consider all forms of manners and civility to be the product of education, religion, and social pressures.

The best-known consequence of such an approach is the moral development model of Lawrence Kohlberg (1974), according to which human moral development progresses in individual steps that must proceed in a very particular and immutable order. The ever-growing differentiation in the individual moral judgment postulated in this model results from the experiences every human being has in the course of his or her lifetime. Here, too, there is no room for a moral foundation in the sense of innate moral judgment. The new philosophical approach, on the other hand, viz. that successful employment of reason is dependent on a functioning emotionality (Engelen, 2007), has been an integral part of TCI for over 30 years now.

If, for some reason, we had to come up with a clear opposite position to the basic position held by TCI, then likely the Kantian approach would be the first choice. Kant derived his Categorical Imperative completely from reason; for him, feelings and affects played no role – they are no more and no less than the confusions of the mind, a mental illness so to speak. From the vantage point of TCI, however, this one-sided preference for reason as the true nature of mankind exaggerates human autonomy and neglects human dependency (interdependence) and all the associated facts of infirmity and suffering. What led Kant to so completely repress the physical nature of mankind is unknown; some (see Böhme & Böhme, 1983) have presumed this may reflect his own unacknowledged personal fears.

Jewish-Christian Influences

Dietrich Stollberg

1 The Intellectual Background

It occurred to me quite early on – and this is surely no coincidence – that *all* of the early proponents of TCI were Jews: Ruth C. Cohn, Ruth Ronall, Frances Buchanan, Norman Liberman, Yithchak Zieman, and many others. It is also not a coincidence that the psychological component of TCI ("Globe") contains the psychoanalysis of Freud, Adler, and other Jewish psychoanalysts, in particular Reich and the social research done by Lewin under the name of group dynamics, the psychodrama of Moreno as well as Humanistic Psychology[1]. Finally, there was Fromm, who presented a synthesis of philosophy, psychoanalysis, and Zen. It was Fromm's work that bridged the gap to the Institute for Social Research headed by Max Horkheimer, to which Theodor W. Adorno and Herbert Marcuse belonged and which was closely connected with both the Frankfurt School and psychoanalysis. To illustrate the philosophical background of TCI, Kroeger (1973) points toward both the Holism propagated by Kurt Goldstein and the teachings of the Frankfurt School. Ernst Bloch also belongs in this group. From the early days onward, Martin Buber, the religion and social philosopher, belonged to the University of Frankfurt and its milieu. Buber's philosophy of encounter and dialogue as much as the principles emerging from the Frankfurt School and their critical theory may be found in the very basic theoretical and practical foundations of TCI (see Reiser, 1987). Since its founding in 1912, the University of Frankfurt (as well as the Institute mentioned) was closely connected to Judaism through its many benefactors and staff members.[2]

---

1 The only major non-Jewish representative of Humanistic Psychology was Rogers, whose encounter groups were affected by TCI. An important role was played by Ruth Cohn's organismic thinking.

2 On this subject, see the relevant article by H. Johach. (1999). Das Erbe der jüdischen Emigranten in der Humanistischen Psychologie [The legacy of the Jewish emigrants in Humanistic Psychology]. *Themenzentrierte Interaktion, 13*(1), 7–28.

2 Religious Aspects

Whether Ruth Cohn or her followers were Jewish or not would, in fact, be of no import if there were not certain characteristics of their approaches that are integrally linked to Judaism, the history of Judaism, and Jewish beliefs.

A comparison of Judaism and Christianity immediately reveals that, of course, Christianity began as a Jewish movement. The ancient Christians believed that the eschatological predictions Judaism had so long awaited had indeed been fulfilled: Jesus, the desired Messiah, had come to them. That is to this very day the major difference between the two religions: Judaism is still waiting for the Messiah, whereas Christianity sees the prophecies as having been completed (even if they are still waiting on the end of times). However, these two religious movements can hardly be differentiated in many of their basic tenets. Especially those philosophies that highlight the themes of *relationship* and *hope* (examples being Buber, Bloch, Levinas) are closely related.

The *anticipation (and possibility) of fulfillment* – that is the central category of the Jewish-Christian perception of the world. When Bloch speaks of these categories with respect to the creation of the world, he speaks of *Realutopien* (feasible and viable utopias here on Earth). *Hope* has been one of the central motifs in Jewish thought since the very beginning: Hope is what at work when the Jews were freed from Egyptian slavery (the Exodus motif); what led them to the Promised Land; what protected them from their enemies and the series of new occupiers of Palestine; it was what enabled their escape from Babylonian captivity. Hope and desire are also directed toward the (re)erection of the Kingdom of David and his return. Hope continued beyond the destruction of the Temple on Zion in 70 AD and the end of the state of Israel until its new foundation in the year 1948. The hope of obtaining a new/old home always played a major role in Judaism, both literally and figuratively – ever since its nomadic beginnings some 3000 years ago.

The motif of the diaspora (Exodus 11) is relevant here, too. The tale told in Exodus refers to the whole of humanity, but throughout much of antiquity Jews were scattered and tried to return, if possible, at least once a year to Jerusalem. In the New Testament, the story of the Pentecost (Acts 2) takes up this theme: The desire for *unity and understanding* is connected to *overcoming the diaspora* of the Jewish people. Despite its long-term scattering, the Jewish people never ceased to exist or become completely absorbed in other peoples, but rather retained its identity as the "chosen people" – regardless of whether one was a strict observer or not. The vision of the last days, with a universal and globalized world religion with its center on Zion, always lay before them. The idea of heeding a global calling, for example, in the promise made to Abraham that all peoples of the world shall be blessed, is one of the oldest and most basic ideas of Judaism.

Christianity retained nearly all of the terms and categories it inherited from Judaism, albeit in a rather spiritualized form, for example, *hope for liberation*, the *Promised*

Land, the *call to minister*, the idea of the *Kingdom of God*, the *universality of life* (which became especially strong in Christianity), *apocalyptic* and *eschatological phantasies* of the end of time as well as *socialistic ideals* (Acts 4).

Both religions are concerned with relationships: the relationship between God, His people, and the individual members of His chosen people. Again and again, covenants are made, broken, and renewed between God and His people. The basic commandment is: "Love the Lord your God with all your heart and with all your soul and with all your mind – and love your neighbor as yourself" (Matthew 22, 37–39). This triangle contains the "I-You" relationship as well as the "I-We" relationship and "I-We-Theme" relationship.[3] The Old Testament prophets speak repeatedly about the damaged, but remediable relationship between God and His people.

Further, both religions are social religions: The goal is not the salvation of the individual[4], but the salvation of the entire people of God, which originally comprised only the 12 tribes of Israel but eventually came to be more universally and liberally understood (especially in Christianity) to go beyond that one people to include all of humanity.[5] Zionism, Israeli nationalism, and Jewish cosmopolitanism are often at odds with each other. The (pacifist) concept of cosmopolitanism may be found explicitly in TCI in the idea of the "Globe" and in the axioms.

The two religions also belie their social basis in the Old and New Testament calls to exhibit merciful behavior toward the needy. The goal of creating a dynamic balance between "I," "We," "Theme," and "Globe" is to avoid any one-sided emphasis of egocentrism, altruism, neutrality, or environmentalism.

The original nomadic tradition of the Jews, the charismatic leadership of the judges during the first years of settled life in Israel, the negative experiences with monarchic rule after David and Salomon, the repeated occupations, and finally the loss of the Promised Land, the experience of being "tolerated" in the diaspora and repeatedly being subjected to pogroms – all that contributed to the pathos which the idea of freedom assumed over time – and which today is still one of the main characteristics of liberal Judaism. In addition, there is the long tradition in orthodox Judaism with its strict adherence to the written word, which in turn resulted in a strong longing for freedom as counterreaction. Even the ancient Christians were concerned with this theme: Jesus is depicted as the defender of a more humane attitude toward the rule of law when he says "The Sabbath was made for man, not man for the Sabbath" (Mark 2,27). That is clearly a humanistic concept, found as far back as in the prophets of the Old Testament and take up many times since, particularly by the Reformers, when pious legality threatened to stifle human free-

3 This triangle is an old archetype in the Jewish-Christian tradition. At its middle lies the eye of God, often containing the name of the Jewish God. Two overlaid triangles result in the Star of David. In Christianity it serves as the symbol for the Trinity.

4 Individualization is a relatively recent development that was articulated in Christianity only during the Reformation, even though its proponents quoted Paul and St. Augustine in its defense.

5 The rejection of a religious claim to absoluteness is a relatively new phenomenon within the churches.

dom and individual responsibility. Wilhelm Reich thought the cause lay in the sedentarization of the Jews; Erich Fromm postulated a vulnerability of the (Jewish) bourgeoisie to adopt authoritarian structures, heteronomy, and a lack of willingness to assume responsibility.

That TCI propagates freedom should not be surprising in light of the comments on religious history given above. The → chairperson postulate, for example, is a basic democratic principle that is difficult for people to accept who are accustomed since their childhood and school days to being submissive and conforming to leadership. The political dimension of TCI is present in this principle and in the way in which conflicts are resolved. The vision of "peace and righteousness" (Psalm 85,11) is one of the very basic motifs of the Bible. Even though the God of Israel was originally conceived as a successful warlord, He is also the God of peace. "God's peace" in "shalom" is this central concept; participation in this peace may be found through Aaron's blessing (Numbers 6, 26) as well as in the promises of the prophets and others: "Peace be on Israel" (Psalm 125, 5; 128, 6). The motif of peace is even characteristic of those who survived the Holocaust – more so than the motif of revenge, which the God of Israel reserved for Himself (Deuteronomy 32, 35).

Not to forget the Jewish love of life. Different from Christianity and despite (or maybe because of) its long history of suffering, Judaism is known for its extraordinarily positive attitude toward life, creativity, and the Here-and-Now mentality. Prudery and a puritanical lifestyle have no place in Judaism. "Pleasure plays a major role in the life of the rabbis. For they are the ones who teach that, in some distant (eschatological) future, humans will have to answer for everything they liked and yet failed to enjoy" (Petuchowski, 1980, p. 20).

3 TCI Is an Approach, Not a Religion

"It is certainly difficult to understand Judaism without looking at the Jewish faith, even if representatives of → Humanistic Psychology [...] do not belong to orthodox Judaism. The influence of the Jewish religion is clearly recognizable in all three" (Johach, 1999, p. 26). Johach is referring to the "Messianic nature [of Judaism], which means not being happy with what is, but hoping for something better [...] even if only in very small things, in changes in the Here and Now" (ibid., p. 26). Petuchowski describes rabbinical thought as follows: "They approach things 'concretely,' not abstractly. Strongly differing opinions can exist side by side, and they do not try to harmonize them, to force them into some coherent system. Rabbinical theology remains directed toward life itself. [...] Experience comes first, leading to tradition. And the stronger the religious experience is, the less purely reason-driven reflection comes into the picture. [...] According to rabbinical thought, the chasm that exists between God and humans can never be bridged. [...] They are thus always conscious of the purely human nature of life" (Petuchowski, 1980, pp. 11 f.).

All of which is true of Ruth Cohn's work. This makes Johach's comment all the more apt: "I see [...] the reception in Germany with somewhat mixed feelings, since it introduces such features as the desire for systemization, literalism, and pedantry into the picture, losing along the way the creativity and joy of experimenting that played such a major role in the beginnings. I see this trend on the rise at least in TCI training. [...] We can confront the danger of slipping into literalism and empty formalism, which deeply contradict the very foundation of Humanistic Psychology, [...] only by reminding ourselves that creativity, levity, and exuberance, all of which are characteristic of the Jewish soul, are the best means to prevent the stiffness of persevering in staid forms [...]" (Johach, 1999, p. 27; see also → Interculturality and Diversity). TCI comprises a certain level of chaotic creativity, joy of life, sensuality, and eroticism in addition to all sorts of socially critical impulses.

A few years ago I took part in a service in Israel on the eve of Sabbath, in the old Kabbalist[6] city of Sfat (Safet). We arrived on time, took a prayer book, and sat down. Two men were running around, making the well-known rocking motions practiced in Judaism while praying. They took no notice of us. Now and then someone else would enter the room, take a prayer book, and begin to pray out loud – not, however, by first taking a seat in a pew, but still roaming around, stopping here and there, praying, sitting, roaming. This continued for some time. It suddenly reminded me of my TCI experiences: We were experiencing a congregation in which everyone was moving to their own rhythm ("I") as well as communally praying ("We") a common prayer ("Theme"), all of which was set in the context of a devout tradition in a highly developed modern society ("Globe"). At some point in time, the apparent chaos we were experiencing cleared, and I was reminded of an old saying I had once heard: "It's like being in a Jewish school."[7] And that's the way it should be: creative, vibrant, and free.

6 Kabbala refers to a Jewish mystical movement (kabbalah) that mixes traditional theology with pantheological philosophy and interprets Biblical texts allegorically.

7 A Jewish school (or "Jew school") refers both to synagogues as well as Talmud schools where it is generally very loud and seemingly chaotic: Some repeat or discuss their texts out loud, whereas others walk around, and still others learn silently on their own. Today I live in what is known as "Franconian Jerusalem" – the 1000-year-old city of Fürth in Germany – near the former so-called "schoolyard," where earlier three synagogues and a number of other teaching annexes and living quarters once stood before being burned down in the awful "Crystal Night" of November 1938. The Jewish cemetery is on the other side. We walk by it daily, meaning the Jewish tradition is always present in my life. From the "schoolyard" you can see the neighboring Christian church in the old part of Fürth. Up until the Nazi reign of terror the Jews and Christians lived peacefully next to each other.

Humanism

Peter Vogel

1 Humanism in TCI

TCI arose on the basis of Humanistic Psychology, a term coined by Abraham Maslow (1908–1970) to describe the new and exciting movement within North American psychotherapy following World War II. Yet the designation is fuzzy and became the repository for many very different psychotherapeutic methods and approaches that, generally speaking, emphasized individuals and their opportunities for development and growth.

For Ruth Cohn, the term *humanistic* had a very distinctive meaning to it, not the least because of her experiences as an immigrant German Jew. In 1973 she wrote: "To know that I matter; to know that you matter. To know that every human being matter, whether black, white, red, yellow, or brown. That the Earth matters. That the Universe matters. That my suffering matters. That your suffering matters. (If you don't care about my suffering and I take no interest in your misery, then both of us will be annihilated by hunger, sickness, and mass murder.) Respect for life is important. Skills and knowledge are important. Knowledge without respect for human life results in gas chambers and napalm factories. Humanity without knowledge cannot produce bread, houses, hospitals, or schools. It cannot heal broken bones or comfort souls" (Cohn, 1975, p. 109).

"Humanistic" is an adjective Ruth Cohn used whenever she wanted to describe the goal of all therapeutic and educational strivings: "A humanistic approach to values is based on the unalienable presumption that human life is a reality that must be maintained and advanced. Being a human being does not mean just being thrown senselessly into the world; it means finding a meaning to life in the realization of the individual self that is part of the community of all human beings" (Farau & Cohn, 1984, p. 443).

Against this background, Ruth Cohn's TCI proposes to "lead to a humanizing, consciousness-raising approach to education" (Cohn, 1975, p. 7). That goal is valid to this very day. Humanism, humanistic – these are terms that describe both the background and the goals of TCI.

2 Background and Variations of these Terms

Humanism is a designation for various intertwined historical movements that arose in 14th-century Italy. Different from Medieval Christian traditions, humanism put the individual human being at the center of its considerations. From Italy, the movement spread during the next centuries throughout Europe to exert a strong influence on art and philosophy, the natural sciences, politics, and pedagogics. By returning to Roman, as well as later to Greek, influences, it searched for guidelines and norms to living the proper life. Increased emphasis was put on educating people to become true humans, on *humanitas*. The goal was a well-rounded, uplifted personality that is capable of living life according to reason and structuring the common life with others. Humans should become what they, being images of God, were meant to become, and this venue should be available to all members of the species.

In the centuries to follow, the idea of humanism became associated with a number of other movements. Especially during the Enlightenment of the 18th century, with its motto sapere aude ("dare to know"), it called on the grandness and the dignity of the rational human being. In 1798, in his Oratorium "The Creation," Joseph Haydn sang the praises of humans: "In native worth and honor clad,/ with beauty, courage, strength adorn'd,/ to heav'n erect and tall,/ he stands a man,/ the Lord and King of nature all./ The large and arched front sublime/ of wisdom deep declares the seat./ And in his eyes with brightness shines/ the soul, the breath and image of his God" (Feder, 1999, pp. 219 ff.; English text from Naxos Records, translator unknown). Typical of the time and typical of humanism in its many variations is the overall positive picture it paints of human life. The abysmal, faithless sides of humans, the depths of their entanglement with guilt and fate, are blinded out.

The holy words of humanism throughout time are this: reason, progress, love, freedom, community, harmony. However, this educational ideal came to be dismantled in the trenches of World War I and in the gas chambers of Auschwitz; it had proved to be incapable of preventing such catastrophes. Belief in a God in whose image mankind had been formed and who provides mankind with values and meaning had largely vanished. This did not signal the end of all efforts to establish humanism and to humanize the world; but humanism had to be re-invented and humane behavior underpinned in reality.

In light of these events, Jean-Paul Sartre (1905–1980) wrote a polemic in 1945 defending existentialism as humanism. Following the many shocks to mankind over the past years, he saw humans as alone in the world, left to no one but themselves to find their way. There were no signs that could help in this endeavor: "Man is damned to be free. Damned because he did not create himself and yet free because, being in the world, he is responsible for everything he does" (Sartre, 2005, p. 155). To the objection that this view of things is pure subjectivism, Sartre responded: "In order to obtain any piece of truth about myself I must go through another human being. The other is indispensable to my existence, as is the knowledge I possess about myself" (ibid., p. 166).

3 The Adoption and Modification of the Term in TCI

When TCI uses the term "humanism" or "humanistic," it is adopting a number of different insights and perspectives on humanity and the good and true life which flowed together into this tradition for many centuries. Of particular importance, I think, are the ideas of the freedom to decide (autonomy), the ability to grow (optimism), and the necessity to assume responsibility (ethics).

3.1 The Freedom to Decide (Autonomy) (→ Axiom 1)

Freedom was always one of the highest values to be found in humanism. But how can freedom, following all the seductions that took place during the National Socialist reign in Germany and in light of an apparently predetermined, godless world, be renewed and thrive? Here, Ruth Cohn highlights European existentialism and writes: "In European Existentialism [...] I see the ascent of a mind that is free of positivistic materialism and determinism; a mind that desires humane values. Decision, courage, autonomy – those are humane values. Even if the room for autonomous decisions is small, there is always a way to exert an influence" (Farau & Cohn, 1984, p. 430). The idea of human autonomy may be found in TCI in Axiom 1.

3.2 The Ability to Grow (Optimism) (→ Axiom 2)

In light of all the awful experiences of World War II, it is legitimate to ask how TCI can truly believe that every human being possesses the ability to grow and prosper; how it can assume that the chairperson (→ Chairperson Postulate) really does lie within us and both strives and succeeds in doing the right thing to others. I see this optimism as founded in the practical experiences gathered in therapy: Humans are capable of discovering on their own – in the accompaniment of others – creative solutions to their problems; they can change their lives and they can develop in ways previously not envisioned. Apparently, this capacity is deeply ingrained in each and every one of us. This positive view of mankind was supported by the generally positive mood found in the United States following the war. Ruth Cohn describes this feeling as being very different from the tragic-serious existentialism of Europe at that time: "The *American form of existentialism* of the 1950s and 1960s [...] was an ode to life, the golden motto of a life well lived and fully enjoyed. It meant living completely in the Here-and-Now, applying oneself to what is valuable to the individual – be it with regard to esthetics, material things, sexuality, friendship, or personal efforts" (Farau & Cohn, 1984, pp. 430 f.). In TCI the ability to grow is found in Axiom 2.

3.3 The Necessity of Assuming Responsibility (Ethics) (→ Axiom 3)

Ruth Cohn, of course, sees very clearly that humans – despite all the hope we have for development – can also become perverted into monsters endangering the planet. For this reason, she desperately pleads for decisions based on an explicit value system. For her, empathy and solidarity were the major pillars of her ethics: "I want to have eyes that look out of my room, beyond the flowers and the waterfalls, and the birds, beyond the meadows and mountains and beyond national borders, to see the boats afloat on the cold waves, full of women and children, raped by pirates, bereft of their last grain of rice and the last shirt on their back. I want to have ears that hear the cries of those drowning, the cries of men in torture chambers [...] and the cries of women and children who must witness the pain of martyrdom of their loved ones. I want to encourage all those people who have suffered a misery they did not invite, not to resign, not to feel helpless, but to use their imagination and their capacity to act to express their solidarity and to remain active for as long as we can still feel the autonomous forces alive in our souls" (Farau & Cohn, 1984, p. 374).

4 Extensions, Contradictions, Impulses

4.1 Role of Autonomy in TCI and as Lifestyle (→ TCI as Lifestyle)

Despite all its humanistic insights and foundations, TCI is still not interested in delivering a complex theory of human existence. Rather, it prefers to reflect on the experiences people have in therapy and workgroups; it prefers to provide people with assistance in self-development and in assuming responsibility for themselves, others, and the environment. Leading from that concept are many lines connecting TCI with a philosophy of lifestyle: Not some ideal image of mankind against this background, but rather a "sober, realistic humanism [...] that purposely does not draft an ideal image of mankind, but puts the concrete existence of individual human beings at its core and looks deeply into the face of the other" (Schmid, 1998, pp. 177f.). The amazing similarity between philosophy as lifestyle and TCI may also be seen in the question of how free we actually are to make autonomous decisions in light of the many tempting things to choose from and the many voices denying freedom of choice, declaring it to be nothing but an illusion: "What is important is to make choosing the central matter of all lifestyles; to raise our sensitivity toward choice; and to make the act of deciding a conscious one" (ibid., p. 193). Jens G. Röhling, in his article entitled "TCI and the Philosophy of Lifestyle" (2005), presents in detail the many interactions between TCI and a philosophy of lifestyle.

4.2 Growth and Fragment

Among other things, TCI is directed toward helping people to grow mentally, to become identical with themselves. This humanistic concept of identity serves to protect the individual from being overwhelmed by the group or by society in general. Yet every stage of ego development is replete with disruptions and losses – life is not just about growth and gains. And what does "becoming identical" even mean in light of our fractured biographies, the wounds we suffer, and the guilt we bear? Henning Luther introduced as a counterpoint to the new "dictation of identity" the image of life as a fragment: "On the one hand, we have fragments as reminders of a now wrecked but former whole, a torso, ruins, scraps from the past. On the other hand, we have unfinished works that have not – yet – reached their final form, fragments of the future" (Luther, 1992, p. 167). Viewing life as a fragment and living life in rebellion against the compulsion to continually develop seems to me to be an appropriate and hopeful way of viewing human life: "In each stage of ego development we always also represent the ruins of the future – building sites that are as yet unknown, whether and how progress will even be made. The only thing we know is that the foreseen building is not yet finished" (ibid., p. 170).

4.3 Tradition and Ethics

In Axiom 2 Ruth Cohn says very generally: "Respect for growth affects all ethical decisions. What is humane is valuable, and what is inhumane threatens our values" (Cohn, 1975, p. 120). She leaves no room for doubt as to what her values are and where she derives her maxims: "The ethical human being is not guided solely by thoughts and logic, not by feelings alone, but by a holistic conscience. That includes conscious and unconscious transpersonal and spiritual endeavors" (Farau & Cohn, 1984, p. 478). With this, she clearly shows that we are responsible not only *to* our conscience, but also *for* our conscience, which may have to be (re)adjusted and (re)built over time. It is my understanding that she is referring to discussions surrounding the formative cultural traditions (e.g., antiquity, Christianity, humanism). However much one may value the inner forces and the potentials present in human beings, when we are concerned with ethics and values, we must remember what Fulbert Steffensky (2002, p. 125) called his "reluctant plea for authority": "You cannot win by relinquishing yourself to authorities. On the other hand, you cannot experience who you are and how you should behave solely by listening to your own monologs and rejecting everything besides your own insights, your own wisdom, your own conscience. [...] I need to interact with a text that knows more than I do; I need to interact with a tradition that is older than I am. [...] I need the images, the life plans, the wisdom that others before me have constructed and that others besides me still construct."

Part II

The Theory of the TCI System

The Systematics of TCI

Mina Schneider-Landolf

Part of the practical and theoretical development of TCI included the longstanding attempt to prepare and present a meaningful and systematic collection of *all* important elements. The task was to identify the basic determinants of TCI and to ask how the various individual components fit together and are interconnected. Such a systematic approach should be more than just a mere recounting of the individual elements and also do justice to the concerns raised by Ruth Cohn regarding social therapy and personality development (→ Historical and Political Background), the theoretical considerations (→ Part II: The Theory of the TCI System), and the practical guidelines for leading a group (→ Part III: Practical Applications of the TCI System). A systematization is also necessary in order to transmit and teach TCI as well as for determining its place in the scheme of other scientific concepts.

1 The Development of a Systematization of TCI – Ruth Cohn 1975

The first attempt at systematization was done by Ruth Cohn herself in 1975 in various articles included in her book *From Psychoanalysis to Theme-Centered Interaction.*[1] In the chapter "The Foundation of the Theme-Centered Interactional System" consists of three → *axioms* (ibid., p. 120), Ruth Cohn described the anthropological premises of TCI. From there, she deduced two *postulates*: the → Disturbance Postulate and the → Chairperson Postulate (ibid., p. 121). The fundamental features of this method are as follows:[2]

- The *Structure Model* (later called the → *Four-Factor Model*) with the four factors found in group interactions *I – We – It – Globe*. The first three are depicted as the corner points of a triangle contained within a circle, the Globe.
- These three dimensions must be held in a → *dynamic balance* in the workings of a group. The *Hypothesis of Equal Importance* of the three factors (and the Globe) (ibid.,

1 Published in German as *Von der Psychoanalyse zur Themenzentrierten Interaktion*, this book contains a collection of various articles that in part had been previously published by Ruth Cohn in English. On the one hand, it contains case reports of her work with groups as well as, on the other hand, theoretical and methodological thoughts and the philosophical-ethical premises of TCI.

2 The basics of this method are described in the later chapter in this volume entitled "The Theme as Focus of Interactional Groups" (p. 111 ff.).

p. 160) defines the premises for → *living learning* in a group. Living learning, in turn, is the higher-level goal of all leadership behavior, the utopia of the best-possible group process (ibid., pp. 111, 119).
- The group leader controls the process by setting a → *theme* and by stipulating a particular → *structure* (ibid., p. 113).
- → *Auxiliary rules* as means of intervention serve to support the group work.

How this dynamic balance is achieved among the "I," the "We," and the "It" in a group or school class, how leadership is exerted in such a group (ibid., 1975, p. 161), and what role *participative leadership* and *selective authenticity* may have (ibid., p. 189) is explained in further chapters of this volume using case examples. These methodological aspects, however, are not part of the classification system.

These methodological-theoretical basics of TCI were imparted and taught in the initial years in courses that took place in the "Workshop Institute for Living Learning" (WILL).

On this point Raguse (1984, p. 55) said the following: "The concept of TCI seems to be so varied and so clear that only the formations of Ruth Cohn [. . .] are repeated: Axioms and postulates [. . .] as the bearers of a humanistic value system and concept of mankind; auxiliary rules as group norms; the concept of participative leadership; balance; and the theme." Raguse sees the problem in the practical implementation of these theoretical formulations. Transferring insights gained in a TCI course to the outside reality of one's own field of work is not easy. The question is: "How can we describe TCI and how can we answer the question of what is not yet TCI and what is no longer TCI?" (ibid., p. 56).

From the very beginning Ruth Cohn and others instructing TCI (the so-called "Graduates") attached great importance to their position that TCI is both an *approach* (value orientation as formulated in the axioms) as well as a *method* (the practice of group leadership and self-leadership). Simply following the methods taught and the auxiliary rules without the value orientation part would not correspond to the objectives set down by Ruth Cohn concerning social therapy and personality development.

Based on the early publications and the experiences gathered in the respective TCI courses and workshops, various different visual aids depicting the overall concept of TCI were developed to be used in the teaching context. The goal was to extensively develop the individual building blocks according to the two aspects of approach and method, and to demonstrate how these two aspects are connected. Various terms such as "model" (a model of living learning), "method" (method for group leadership), or a "concept" (a group-therapeutic concept, a group-educational concept, a pedagogical-therapeutic concept) were employed.

A method often used in Switzerland in the 1970s (see Figure 1) was prepared by M. Zollmann[3]. This illustration depicts the relative importance of the different elements, go-

3 Extracted from the course materials used in TCI methods courses.

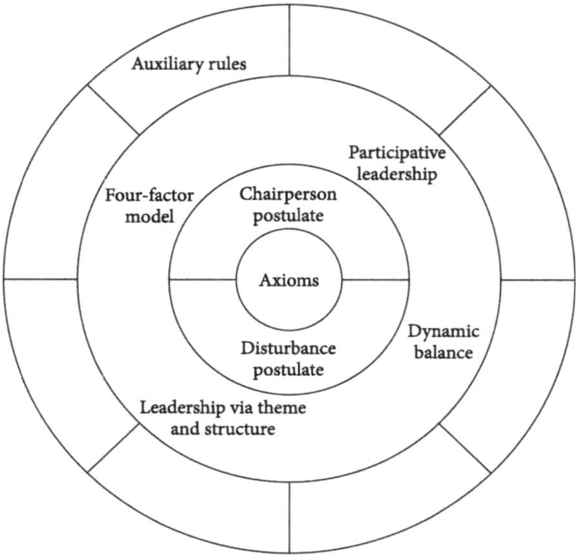

Figure 1. The approach and method of TCI according to M. Zollmann.

ing from the center to the periphery; "approach" lies in the middle and the postulates are near the axioms. The central methodological elements lie near the center; the auxiliary rules at the periphery. The model clearly demonstrates what at that time was considered part of TCI and what was being taught to the TCI group leaders.

2 Matzdorf and Cohn 1983/1993

The joint publication of Paul Matzdorf and Ruth Cohn in 1983 was their contribution to the German-language *Handbuch der Psychotherapie* (Handbook of Psychotherapy, Volume 2, ed. by R. Corsini, pp. 1272 ff.). It represents the first comprehensive depiction of the entire "TCI system" in a single text. There, TCI was introduced as an "educational-therapeutic concept" (p. 1274) and as a "compass for a more humane life." The authors differentiated between theoretical foundations and methods. This early publication, however, did not gain much recognition beyond psychotherapeutic circles. However, the revision prepared in 1992, with revised chapter headings but with the same basic systematics, published in the anthology edited by C. Löhmer and R. Standhardt entitled *TZI – Pädagogisch-therapeutische Gruppenarbeit nach Ruth C. Cohn* (TCI – Educational-Therapeutic Group Work According to Ruth C. Cohn) was much more accessible.

In 1993, Matzdorf published his graphical interpretation of the TCI system in the form of a house.[4] The value system, represented by the axioms as the compass for methodolog-

4 This depiction had already been published in the 1980s in the teaching materials for TCI courses.

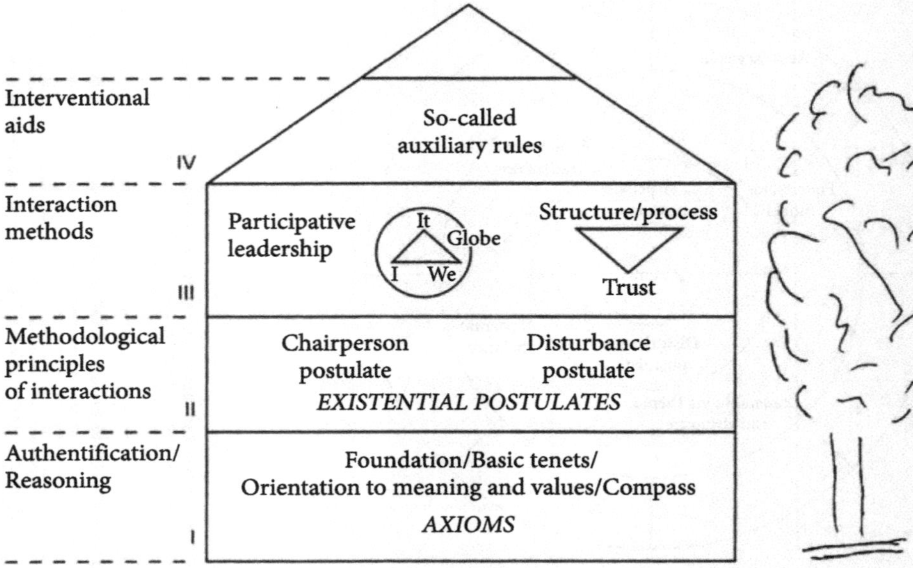

Figure 2. The TCI house according to P. Matzdorf (1993, p. 339).

ical actions, formed the foundation of the house – on which the postulates were situated as the superordinate basic methodological principles. Further methodological-practical guidelines formed the next story, and at the very top lay the so-called auxiliary rules and further techniques such as games and exercises (which are not necessarily specific to TCI).

This model provides an overview of the elements contained in TCI and demonstrates the necessity of anchoring the methodological approach to the level of the value system (without a foundation there can be no upper floors).

Matzdorf himself says that this image does not attempt to depict all of the important systemic connections between the various levels. “Exactly how the elements affect each other is not shown in this model, though it can be explained using this model” (Matzdorf, 1993, p. 342). To this end, Matzdorf looks at the interconnections among the elements in detail in the text by presenting TCI as a comprehensive educational action concept that encompasses the different levels shown (see Figure 2). This clearly expresses that TCI is more than just a “method for leading groups.”

The depiction shown in Figure 3, known as the “Tree” by Annedore Schultze (1995)[5], is also widely used.

Schultze integrates the historical background and the personal history of Ruth Cohn into the figure. She says (1995, p. 17) she wants to emphasize the “roots and branches” of TCI. Besides the axioms, these important influences form the roots of the tree from which

5 I am in possession only of Schultze’s publication from 1995, although it well known that her tree illustration was developed by her much earlier and used in her many training courses.

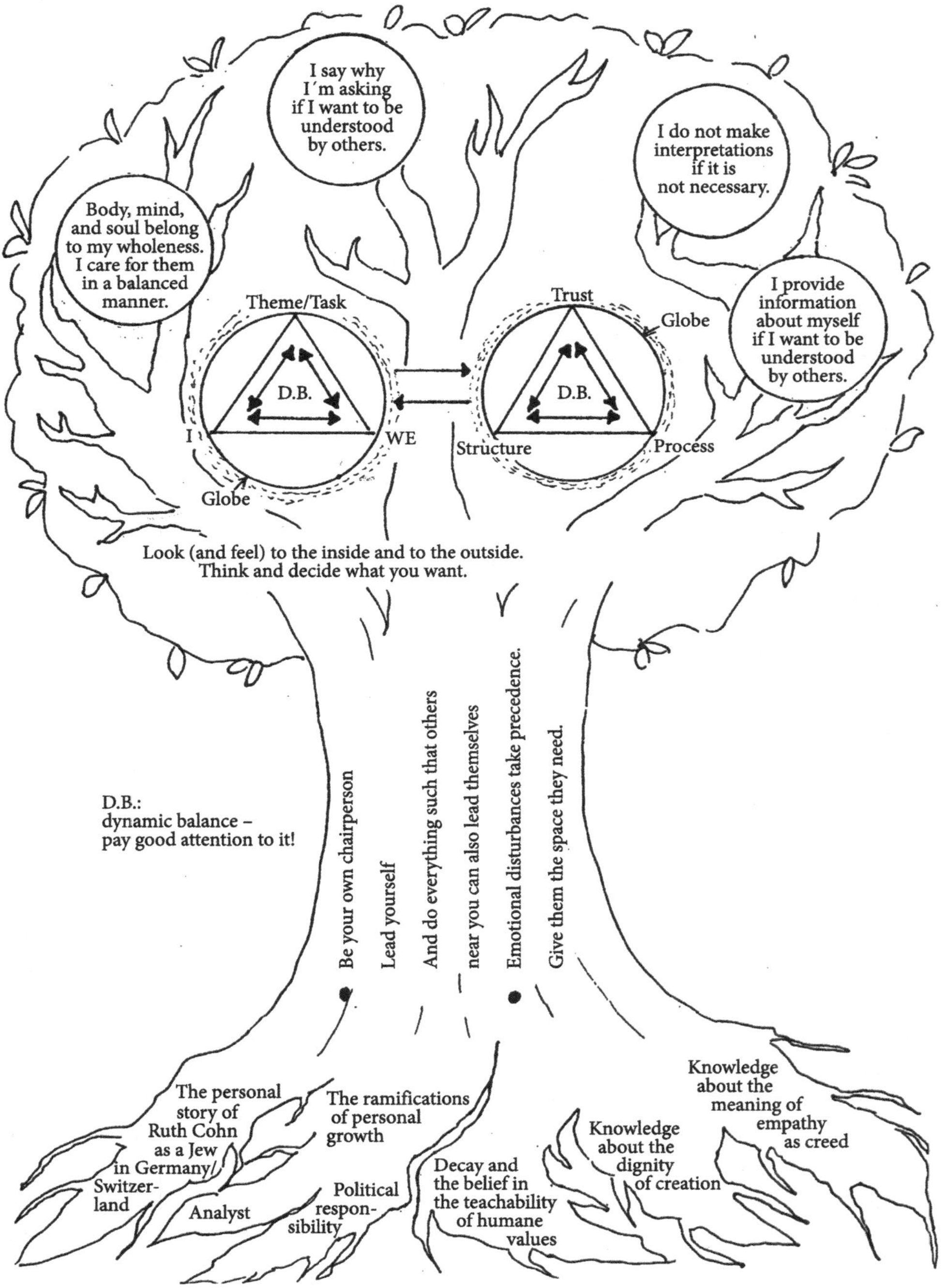

Figure 3. The "Tree" by Annedore Schultze.

the methods developed: The postulates as the basic methodological principles form the trunk of the tree from which the further methodological elements stem. This structural model containing → dynamic balance as well as the triangle "Structure – Process – Trust" lie at the base of tree's crown; the auxiliary rules are the fruits.

3 Discussion

These two depictions – the TCI house and the TCI tree – were subsequently used in many TCI training courses to illustrate the "whole" of TCI. Especially the TCI tree provides a good overview of the various levels and individual elements.

The TCI tree also proved to be an appropriate means of stimulating learning processes when introducing TCI methods. Annedore Schultze said that the picture of the tree "helped me to realize that TCI is a living organism that serves to stimulate the process of growth both in the individual and in the group" (1995, p. 14).

Teaching practice revealed that there are a number of different ways to assign the individual method components to the various levels. In some depictions, for instance, the → four-factor model and the → structure – process – trust triangle as well as leadership via → theme and structure are seen as the basic methodological principles in the trunk. In some TCI houses, on the other hand, → dynamic balance, leadership via → theme and structure, leadership as → participative leadership are missing completely. Still other TCI houses put the postulates on the outside.

There have also been a number of critical remarks concerning these images: "Basically, there's no reason why there can't be different, parallel attempts at systematizing TCI. After all, didactic instruments do not presume to depict true content. On the other hand, the tree model can be misleading by supporting the notion that TCI is a natural occurrence, whereas a house is clearly an object, something created by human hands. The picture of a house correctly emphasizes the constructed basis and the model character of the TCI system" (Zitterbarth, 2001). Philipp Rubner (2008) also criticized the different versions of the house model, saying he could not understand the logic involved in the different levels. He then offered his own version of a new depiction of the "whole system" of TCI, purporting to better show the factual relationship between the individual elements.

To date, no consensus has been found among those who teach TCI concerning a systemization of its structure. What is not disputed is, first, the differentiation between the basic philosophical stances and the statements about value orientation (the → axioms and the derivative → postulates) and, second, the fundamental methodological principles or positions, to which the → four-factor model and → dynamic balance belong.[6]

Opinions also differ with respect to the meaning and implications of leading a group via a theme (is that a basic methodological principle or rather a technique?), how to un-

---

6 On this, see the working paper of the International Graduate Conference IGK 1996.

derstand and allocate → participative leadership and → selective authenticity (which are missing in some models), how to deal with transference, the meaning of → leadership interventions (about which there are few publications besides those of Ruth Cohn).

Thus, it is not surprising that Schreyögg (1993), in an article in the journal *Globe*, which is dedicated to TCI, remarked that TCI does have a clear metatheory (the axioms) as well as well-formulated theoretical hypotheses (the four-factor model and the equilibrium hypothesis), but that it is missing a clear idea of its methodology (→ Critical Matters in TCI). At this level, Schreyöff is aware of only the leadership intervention in the form of gestalt-therapeutic techniques. For her, the four-factor model, with its hypothesis of the equal importance of "I," "We," and "It," forms the core theoretical principle.[7] However, she fails to discuss the question of how dynamic balance can best be implemented both methodologically and practically (using process control through theme and structure? through forms of leadership intervention? through participative leadership?). It would appear that important aspects of TCI-specific methods are not properly treated in the existing publications.

To many who were trained in TCI in the 1970s and 1980s (the time of the "therapeutic society," see Kursbuch 1985), their own experiences and personal development were more important than understanding the methodological ins and outs of TCI leadership.

In addition to her criticism of TCI methods, Schreyöff sees TCI as one of the first "integrative action models" to adhere to the idea of the theory of an integrative psychotherapy that bridges other methods and schools. Besides her demand to differentiate the → "Globe" idea, she suggests improving TCI theory by introducing a four-part systemization that includes the levels of metatheory, theory, action theory, and praxeology (1993, pp. 18–22). Her critical article prompted a heated discussion and a more in-depth look at the knowledge structure of the TCI system.[8]

These methodological uncertainties can at times be rather irritating for those training in TCI. And they do not help to promote TCI and its place in the educational market very well either. The call for a more reliable and common understanding of TCI is understandable. On the other hand, the discussion surrounding the methodological problems causes some TCI disciples to worry whether future progress based on direct experience with TCI and the collective "living learning" process might come to a halt. During the pioneer phase of the WILL (Workshop Institute for Living Learning) in the 1970s, it was the multiplicity of courses offered on TCI that impressed and convinced the followers. Each course reflected the respective personality of the graduates, their multifaceted biographies[9], as well

---

7 Schreyöff assigns the structural model with the egalitarian hypothesis to the theory level (as one of the theoretical assumptions of group processes). In my opinion, this reasonable differentiation between metatheory and theory did not receive the proper recognition with the Ruth Cohn Institute.

8 On this controversy, see also the rejoinder by Helmut Reiser in 1993 in the journal *Themenzentrierte Interaktion*, *7*(2), p. 52.

9 The first teachers were North Americans, Germans, Dutch, Swiss, Austrians, both with and without traumatic wartime experiences; the children of perpetrators and the children of victims. Most of them

as their various methodological competencies, whether in psychoanalysis, body therapy, art therapy, or other approaches of all types. It was the diversity of the different leadership styles and the methods chosen that led some to be irritated at, others to reflect on and implement TCI in their lives.

4 Recent Systematization Attempts of TCI: Reiser and Lotz (1995/2005/2006)

In 1993, Helmut Reiser's answer to Schreyögg's criticism and suggestions for systematizing TCI resulted in his own depiction of "TZI als ein pädagogisches System" (TCI as an Educational System). This work was then published in 1995 together with a contribution by Walter Lotz (Lotz & Reiser, 1995). Reiser is an educational researcher who has certain basic ideas about the relationship between positions (approaches, convictions, opinions), thought processes (theory), and behavior in pedagogical situations – all of which are cardinal matters in the training of teachers, remedial teachers, and educators. He uses the term "system" to represent the idea that connections exist between the different levels and elements – as well as the ruptures that clearly delineate the various levels from each other. The most important thing is how a thought is carried out: The practice of educational behavior (in TCI this means the method of leading a group) cannot be deduced from a theory. Rather, the practical experiences gathered flow into the formulation of a theory. Theoretical concepts (from education, psychology, and sociology)[10] serve to reflect on practice (understanding the present group situation or a past group process as the basis for planning the next methodological step or as the reasoning behind an intervention). This confers a special role to the two postulates, which connect all levels and operate as bridges between the axioms, the method, and the techniques. For this reason, in his scheme, they are situated outside of the three levels. He understands the chairperson postulate and the disruption postulate as "higher goals" in the group developmental process and learning process[11]: They represent the action call to implement the axioms.

Similar, but with a different thrust, was Matzdorf's understanding of the postulates. With his concept, Reiser (1993) wanted to describe and present "the common core of convictions, representations, and behavior patterns" – the "generative core system" of TCI, as he put it – in its totality. The previous arrangement, going from bottom to top (cf. the TCI house shown in Figure 2 and the TCI tree shown in Figure 3), is thus turned on its head.

---

were born just before or during the war and were quite willing to confront and work through their own life story.

10 One may ask as this juncture why the hypothesis of dynamic balance, which is necessary to understand living learning, cannot be construed as a theoretical construct and assigned to the level of theory, as Schreyögg suggested.

11 A more detailed exposition is not possible here. For further information, see the article "TCI as a Professional Educational Concept" in this volume.

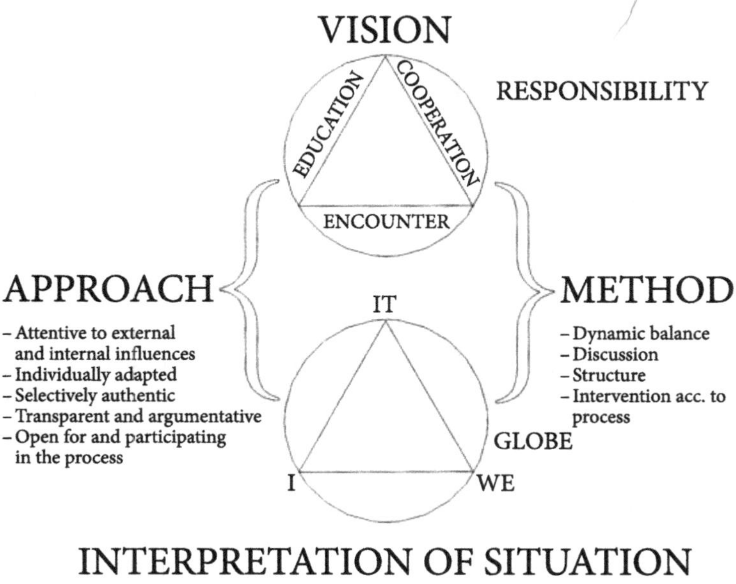

Figure 4. Walter Lotz: A TCI model for socioeducational behavior (Lotz, 2003, p. 110).

Table 1. Orientation levels of TCI as depicted by Helmut Reiser (1995, p. 17), put in **bold** for a better comparison with the previous illustrations).

Theoretical level	**Axiom 1** (a) Autonomy ------ (b) Interdependence (c) Consciousness **Axiom 2** (a) Humanity ------ (b) Life (c) Necessity of evaluative decision **Axiom 3** (a) Free decision ------ (b) Reality (c) Expansion of boundaries	
Methodological level Model of group work	(a) Unity ------ (b) Difference (c) **Dynamic balance** (a) Internal perspective ------ (b) External perspective (c) **Participative leader**	**Postulates: Disruption postulate, Chairperson postulate** (a) with respect to subject (b) with respect to reality, (c) with respect to awareness and decision
Techniques level **Specialization acc. to task and field**	– Perspective of change – Respect for other position – Starting point from subjective basis – **Process control** by theme and structure – **Auxiliary rules** – Situation-specific, field-specific, and task-specific variations and techniques	

Reiser (2006) also saw the necessity of expanding the techniques derived from the various areas of application and action fields (such as school classes, training group, personality courses, workgroup or team, supervision, counseling) (see also → TCI as a Professional Educational Concept).

Reiser's coauthor and discussion partner, Walter Lotz (1995), agrees with many of his basic tenets. However, Lotz does see the importance of theme and structure differently. For him, these "essential tools" belong to the very core methods of TCI; in this, he agrees with Kroeger (1992), Schreyögg (1993), and Schneider-Landolf (→ Theme), who consider the theme principle to lie at the core of the TCI method. Lotz regards TCI as a "professional action concept" that goes beyond educational applications. It is available to be employed more broadly, also for socioeducational situations, in counseling, and in dyadic therapy. This approach fits the fact that, today, TCI is used by experienced TCI leaders in many very different fields. The hotly discussed problem of transferring knowledge gained in a TCI course to one's own field is seen here differently. The question is wrong: Every action concept must deal with the particularities of the respective situation (the respective "Globe" conditions), to which TCI is then applied. To this end, Lotz introduced two new terms into the system: the *situation* and the *vision*, the two poles between which the methodological action of a TCI leader or some other professional action is situated. With this image, Lotz took leave of the picture of a house with its various levels and created a new, successful image that clearly marks the intended connection of methodological action with value orientation and with theory orientation (or the methodological basic principles).

5 The Situation Today (2008)

Many of the various evaluations and classifications of the individual methodological elements in the TCI system, an example being the meaning of theme as a leadership tool or as a methodological principle, result from the variety of situations and fields in which TCI is applied. It makes a difference whether someone is using it to teach, lead, parent, counsel, discuss, treat, or do research. Depending on the situation, which has to be defined exactly, the vision of "living learning" or "cooperation" may have to be replaced by other visions from a more humane world – which in turn will influence the respective method chosen.

All of the various systematizations and graphic representations given above are employed today in TCI training courses and publications. The complex interrelationships between knowledge ("to know that") and skills ("to know how"), between thinking and action, between basic methods and situation-oriented techniques and tools, are often not properly portrayed – and perhaps insufficiently clarified. The discussion continues.[12]

12 This discussion is especially being held among the teaching staffs that offer the basic courses, in the yearly theory workshops, in part in the journal *Themenzentrierte Interaktion* as well as at the international conference of lecturers/teachers (ILK).

An Introduction to the Axioms and Postulates

Anja von Kanitz

In the humanistic-liberal arts, it is highly unusual to speak of "axioms" and "postulates." Ever since Kant, the use of these expression has nearly completely been limited to logico-mathematical contexts. The origin of the two terms lies in antiquity, whereby it remains unclear whether they were part of mathematics or philosophy. There is also no consensus as to their exact differentiation. In fact, in logics and mathematics, sometimes no difference is made between axioms and postulates at all, both of which are used to designate a principle that can be accepted without further proof. In TCI this is true for the use of "axiom." The closest attempt to more exactly differentiate between the two terms (in the TCI sense) may be found in the writings of Geminos (2nd century BC), who says that axioms concern perceptibility, whereas the postulates deal with implementation. What prompted Ruth Cohn to adopt these two terms is unknown.

TCI is a value-based system for working in groups. Ruth Cohn herself considered the basic ideas behind TCI to be axioms, that is, something that has been recognized as true and nonnegotiable prerequisites for working with TCI. At the core of her humanistic concept lie human beings, their relationship to the world, and their ability to develop and influence their surroundings. The three axioms of TCI bear a great resemblance to the Preamble of the European Constitution (Charter of Fundamental Rights), which speaks of the "the inviolable and inalienable rights of the human person, freedom, democracy, equality and the rule of law as universal values." In both cases, we are dealing with principles that are valid for all subsequent initiatives. How these principles are dealt with in concrete situations depends on the matter at hand. Thus, they form both the basis and direction for the daily challenges involved in responsible actions, though they do not prescribe any one particular path. On the other hand, they do categorically exclude certain decisions and actions – in the case of the European Constitution, for example, taking someone into custody for no lawful reason, in the case of TCI working in institutions that serve to harm humans and their development. Support for National-Socialist (Nazi) organizations, for example, with their explicit goal of discriminating against and annihilating certain groups in the populace, would not be compatible with the axioms of TCI. Thus, if the axioms are fixed orientation points within the TCI concept, then the postulates (like those of Geminos) may be seen as concrete aids in the practice and implementation of TCI.

The clear commitment of TCI to human values – to the ability of humans to develop and to make own decisions – without a doubt goes back to the traumatic experiences under the Nazi regime and the devastating results it had for millions of individuals. The experience of being persecuted, of having to flee one's home country, of suffering from fear for life and limb, of having to live in exile – that was the background to Ruth Cohn's concerns about the future: How can we help to prevent other people from being existentially threatened or exterminated? TCI, with its axioms oriented toward the value of individual life and its postulates and methods that deal with emancipation and (self-)responsibility, may be viewed as her attempt to answer her own question.

With TCI and its role in educational endeavors Ruth Cohn wanted to ensure appreciation for the insights contained in the axioms. Working with TCI should empower people to actively participate in humanizing human relationships under their respective circumstances. She saw this as a process that must be continually renewed and never reaches a final point. Working with TCI and its axioms in the sense of Ruth Cohn means forever struggling for a humane form of society in the respective framework of the individuals involved. TCI is not bound to any one philosophy, political party, or religion; it rejects only those groups whose direction does not correspond to the axioms.

The explicit formulation of the axioms occurred long after the initial experiences with TCI workshops and seminars. Ruth Cohn noticed that the characteristic structure and process techniques of TCI were sometimes being (improperly) employed in very different ways in practical group work, especially if they were not expressly linked to humanistic values. If one adopts the → chairperson postulate without respect for the ideas of interdependence and the shared responsibility for one's surroundings, then it can be interpreted (and implemented) as a sort of carte blanche for self-realization at the expense of others: a here-and-now philosophy with a penchant for hedonism. In order to counteract the discretionary repurposing of TCI, Ruth Cohn combined the educational concept of TCI with the value-based foundation laid down in the axioms.[1]

The three axioms complement each other, beginning with an existential-anthropological stipulation, an ethical-socially oriented approach, and a political-pragmatically oriented realization.

1 These were first published in German in 1975.

Axiom 1: The Existential-Anthropological Axiom

Uwe Faßhauer

> "Human beings are psychobiological entities and a part of the universe. They are equally autonomous and interdependent. The autonomy of individuals is all the much larger, the greater they are aware of their interdependence with all and everything" (Farau & Cohn, 1984, p. 357)

1 Definition

The first axiom in TCI is referred to as the existential-anthropological axiom. The central formulation, repeated by Ruth Cohn many times, is that of a "psychobiological entity," which means that physical, intellectual, mental, as well as emotional and (indirectly) spiritual-religious needs, perceptions as well as both conscious and unconscious human experiences are considered to be inseparable basic units. They form the basis of the holistic principle of theme-centered interaction and its conception of humankind.

Second, this axiom formulates a dialectic contradiction pertaining to culture and society. Between independence and individual responsibility, on the one hand, and mutual dependence among humans, on the other hand, lies individual development marked by increasing consciousness (synthesis). What lies between these two poles is considered by TCI to the anthropological constant. Personal and individual development always takes place in connection with other human beings when "themes" (tasks) are being processed. The poles of this field consist of primordial human needs: nearness and belongingness as well as individuality and diversity.

2 Origin

The origin of Axiom 1 clearly lies in the mutual influences exerted during the 1930s to 1960s from parallel developments present within Humanistic Psychology. The holistic view of human nature found in TCI arose through the influences of Wolfgang Köhler, whose lectures Ruth Cohn visited while still living in Berlin; and of Kurt Goldstein, whom she was personally acquainted with. It is based on the hypothesis of the psychosomatic integrity of personality (Cohn, 1992, p. 11), that is, TCI does not foresee a separation between rationality (cognition) and feelings (emotions). The corporeality of all human activities lies at the core of TCI theory. The resulting needs and impetus play a major role in both learning groups and workgroups. TCI is based on the insight that meaningful and sustainable learning goes far beyond reason and concerns "the whole human being as a psychosomatic – and thus emotional and sensual – being" (Cohn, 1975/1992, pp. 116ff.).

This holistic understanding of human nature results in a number of connections to psychology, therapy, philosophy, and politics, all of which initially influenced Ruth Cohn and later the entire TCI concept. A glance back reveals that Ruth Cohn's approach was clearly connected to existential philosophy and phenomenology as well as being influenced by humanistic-oriented pragmatism (John Dewey) and the philosophy of dialogue propagated by Martin Buber, though she never made any direct, conscious remarks or published any scientific treatises in this regard. She was aware of the philosophical positions of Kierkegaard from her own readings, and she visited lectures by both Heidegger and Jaspers in Berlin and Zurich during her studies. She became acquainted with Buber, Sartre, and Camus only much later. Seeing humans as part of the universe is an expression of her holistic view of mankind. Her recognition of religious feelings and spiritual needs as basic anthropological conditions occurred during her teenage and college years when she read Spinoza and Goethe (Quitmann, 1996, p. 207).

3 Explanations

Axiom 1 says that humans are more than the sum of their partial functions; that humans can grasp their interdependence and are thus capable of choosing and deciding; that humans live toward fulfilling their goals and values, which is also an expression of their autonomy (Kroeger, 1993).

Neuroscientific Proof

The holistic view of human beings as psychobiological entities leads to the view that there is a physical basis for all mental processes (cognition, emotion, motivation, volition) as well as all actions and interactions. Perceiving and respecting the various signals emitted by one's body as well as the nonverbal signals used to communicate are thus deducible operationalizations.

The results of modern research have strengthened the argument that humans are psychobiological entities. Especially findings emerging from the neurosciences have added to a rapidly growing body of evidence of scientifically well-founded insights concerning the complex interactions that occur between cognitive, emotional, mental, and physical processes (e.g., Roth, 2004). One central concern of such research lies in the neuronal correlates of consciousness, memory, and emotion. A neuronal and hormonal substrate can be associated with certain emotional and mental states. Put another way, feelings and thoughts have a material (biological) correspondence or even basis. This has led to increased knowledge about the functional structure of the brain: Certain areas of the brain are responsible for concrete tasks, while at the same time being connected to other areas in very complex ways, for example, to the limbic system, which influences and activates emotionality. Emotions have a situational signal function, making a broad and consciously social orientation possible. In this way, emotions take on a central practical role by controlling various forms of social interactions. These are always based on innate impulses (pulse, breathing, muscle tension, etc.) that are not always consciously sensed. They occur in the reciprocal dependence of intimate, personal, and social relationships. For many years now we have been able to deduce how to establish holistic learning processes like those that have been discussed and implemented in school pedagogics (e.g., Hermann, 2006) as well as for group work according to TCI.

Social Scientific Proof

The way we experience the diverse relationships of life is embedded in the dialectical contradiction between autonomy and interdependence. In TCI, autonomy is understood as independence, individuality, and personal responsibility. A high level of self-efficacy and a stable self-image are further characteristics of this idea, which is part of the humanistic goal of obtaining emancipation and reaching maturity. Further, raising one's own consciousness about both internal and external as well as social matters involved with one's personal development is closely related to the neohumanistic concept of education. In TCI, the individual is regarded as being capable of developing as well as being willing to develop; individuals can bear the responsibility for realizing their own potential without restricting the needs of others in the process. In what transacts *between* autonomous individuals and their interdependent counterparts – whether individuals, groups, society at large, or in some central matters in our globalized world even all other human beings – lie actions, that is, *interactions*.

Specific to TCI is the understanding that humans are embedded in social networks, contexts, circumstances, etc. According to TCI, this form of integration should not be seen as a post de facto delimitation of unlimited/expressed freedom or autonomy, which tends to be egocentric and egoistic. Rather, characteristic of TCI are equitemporality, equivalence, simultaneity, and the reciprocal conditionality of the dialectic of autonomy and interdependence. This dialectical basis of Axiom 1 is substantiated in the postulate of the Chairperson.

The development of an "I" – personal development in life – occurs in our relationships to other human beings ("You," "We") and to subject matters ("themes"). This is not necessarily limited to our reactions to personal experiences or self-development. TCI generally differs from all other approaches of Humanistic Psychology because of structural inclusion of the "theme." According to TCI, only by having to deal with tasks, themes, and other factual matters does a human being become a complete human being. This is where we notice the similarity with the neohumanistic educational ideals and other progressive educational concepts from the 19th and early 20th century.

Different from the "being-in-a-relationship" idea of Martin Buber, a "theme" has no less value than a personal relationship, but is in fact equal to it. Themes, things, and tasks are thus not foreign to humans, something that a burden to humans and must be overcome in order to live a free and happy life. Quite the opposite, they form an unavoidable part of our humanity – they are the prerequisite to our humanity and shield us from too much relationship, too much emotion, too much intimacy. "We become humans only by concerning ourselves directly with themes, in particular those themes that go beyond our own selves" (Kroeger, 1993, p. 112). Echoes of the subject of alienation found here go back to Marx, whom Ruth Cohn studied at school.

The laws of group dynamics and psychoanalysis are generally recognized and heeded by TCI. But the political experiences Ruth Cohn had with fascism reveal that it is the function of the autonomous, responsible, and yet independent and conscious "I" to counteract the momentum of group-dynamic processes and their unheeded implementation.

Spiritual Proof

That religious feelings and spiritual needs play a role in TCI is based on the basic tenet that human beings as psychobiological entities are part of the universe. Ruth Cohn herself came from a family that, from our modern perspective, would be called assimilated Jews. They did not actively practice their religion, and religion did not lie at the center of family life. Yet, again and again, a feeling of transcendence showed up in various forms of her search for meaning life. That God lived in all things was something she was so convinced of from her childhood on that she considered it useless to even ponder (Cohn, 1988, p. 226). She speaks of an "inner hereafter" corresponding to the Divine within humans, something she says she became aware of during contemplation. She (and thus TCI as well) agreed with Humanistic Psychology that humans have an innate sense of value that must be exercised or withers away. The goal is to free that sense of value from the limitations of purely rational consciousness and to root it emotionally. This thought is also found in Jewish pedagogics, in particular in Hebraic Humanism. The concept of TCI, however, is not a religion and certainly not a replacement for any religion. It makes no claims to providing statements about the true nature of human life or the relationship of individuals to a transcendent, God-like being. TCI leaves these matters to humans themselves and to their various confessional/ideological positions. They are confronted with a concept that clearly lies within the Judeo-Christian tradition, albeit with a strong tendency toward Jewish pedagogics and the educational ideal of enlightened Neohumanism.

3.1 Critical Reception

The critical reception of TCI as a constructivist-systemic concept of holistic competence development and effective teamwork gradually replaced the original social-therapeutic and political approach advocated by Ruth Cohn, her expressed goal having been to contribute to establishing a humane society. The reception of TCI today is guided particularly by those aspects of the method laid down in Axiom 1. In vocational education, for example, we find concepts that have become the standard in the development of holistic professional competences since the 1990s (Ott, 2007). Today, TCI is considered only one of many different concepts and enjoys relatively little recognition (Faßhauer & Schapfel, 2008). This is also valid for the way TCI, a clearly holistic, resource-oriented approach defined by ethical standpoints, is implemented in educational, school, and religious settings.

3.2 Controversies

The acceptance of the axiomatic basis is a necessary, albeit insufficient reason for working with and discussing TCI. There are a number of controversies among practitioners of TCI regarding the concrete way it is conceived of and adapted to shifting social and global circumstances. For example, the role of spiritual and religious themes has been intensively discussed. The implicit criticism of rationality contained therein was one of the earliest pillars of TCI, which also corresponded to the social mainstream at the time of its founding in the 1950s and 1960s. Another pillar was psychoanalysis, which – at least in the purely Freudian flavor – represents the attempt to introduce rationality to highly complex inner life and to illuminate the irrational influences that affect our presumed rational thought processes. TCI as a methodological pillar of Humanistic Psychology is committed to the traditions and principles of humanistic educational ideals and the Enlightenment. This implies a critical and distanced approach to religious-theological-spiritual impulses.

3.3 Further Development

Presently, Axiom 1 is not a primary object of systematic discussion within TCI; no efforts are being made to formulate or revise the content in another way. Sometimes suggestions are made to expand or make its contents more concrete (Zitterbarth, 2001). Being a practical method, however, TCI need not offer a comprehensive conceptual system; it must only be compatible to valid insights made by other methods as well as to important insights of the relevant academic research. There is thus presently no need to reform this axiom.

Axiom 2: The Ethical Axiom

Peter Vogel

"Respect is due all living things and their development. Respect for development is what stands behind value-based decisions. What is humane is valuable, what is inhumane is threatening." (Cohn, 1975, p. 120)

1 Definition

Ruth Cohn called the second axiom the "ethical axiom" (Farau & Cohn, 1984, p. 357) and goes on to be more specific: "Being a human being means, for example, not torturing any living being and killing no more of them than is necessary to sustain and further life (in particular that of humans). The notion of 'killing' expressly includes the killing of mental and intellectual capabilities."

On the one hand, these words seem clear – who would not support a position against torturing and promoting life and humanity! On the other hand, they are not completely clear when it comes to making concrete decisions about what is, in fact, humane. For example, is it necessary for the survival of humans that thousands of geese be euthanized at a geese farm because somewhere in the vicinity one animal was found with bird flu? Is it the proper thing to insert a feeding tube into the stomach of an 85-year-old patient who has been in a coma for days and can no longer eat in order to keep him/her alive in that state for another few months? Or should artificial feeding be abandoned and the patient allowed to die?

The second axiom is not particularly precisely defined and in fact, raises more questions than it answers. First of all, it says that we should have a basic reverence and respect for the life of others (be it humans, animals, plants), but also for other opinions and lifestyles we encounter – even those opinions and lifestyles that we find strange or repelling. It also says that development, growth, and maturity are important goals for all human beings, so that any threat to these goals must be thwarted. Respect for life and growth thus necessarily demands evaluations and decisions on our part. But then again, cancer cells are also living beings, and cities can suffer from too much development. Vigor and growth alone do not guarantee a good life. Furthermore, death and decay are also a part of life. What is humane in any one situation is thus not always so easy to say. For Ruth Cohn, however, there was never any question about what was humane and what was not.

2 Origin

Ruth Cohn got her inspiration for the second axiom from the Judeo-Christian tradition (→ Judeo-Christian Influences) behind Humanistic Psychology. Upon turning 80 in 1991, Ruth Cohn looked back and said the following: "I tried to put the Judeo-Christian message of reconciliation and love into a humanistic value system for my time. I would hope that TCI and other approaches could continue this tradition into the 21st century" (quoted acc. to Löhmer & Standhardt, 1992, p. 33). As to the origin of our ability to make value-based decisions, she postulated an "organismic [= innate] value system" (Farau & Cohn, 1984, pp. 466, 471), as it were, an inherent talent to make ethical judgments: "What I mean is that there exists a moral sense implanted in us from birth, much as we have eyes to see. Yet it depends on the circumstances how, when, and what we actually see" (Cohn, 2002, p. 82 (→ TCI and Philosophy).

It depends on the circumstances – and circumstances were what shaped Ruth Cohn's passion for a more humane world! The most profound impressions resulted from her experiences as a German-Jewish immigrant in Switzerland and later in the United States. What she had to live through should never again happen to anyone; there should never be another "Hitlerization" of the world (Farau & Cohn, 1984, p. 42). That was the powerful motor behind her engagement as a therapist and behind the development of TCI.

A further impulse occurred during the 1950s in the scope of her psychotherapeutic practice in the United States. It became clear to her that the "popular form of value relativism" found in the psychotherapy of the day "leads to loneliness and alienation. Most people lament less their sexual problems [...] than they do an 'inner emptiness': 'Who cares at all, I just feel so empty.' [...] Technology has made an abundance of material goods possible while also creating broken families, broken work relations, and broken souls. This distress has slowly led to the insight that psychotherapy too must deal with values" (Farau & Cohn, 1984, p. 439).

Ruth Cohn found further inspiration concerning the matter of values in the new, holistic view of life that spread among the intellectual elites of the United States during the 1960s and 1970s. The scientist and physicist Fridjof Capra spoke of a new era and of a necessary paradigm shift in our attitude toward the Earth if humanity is to survive. Everything has to do with everything! Ruth Cohn integrated these thoughts into her own approach: "From Humanistic Psychology to Holistic Act" was not by chance the title of the important final chapter in her book "The Living History of Psychotherapy." She quotes Fridjof Capra from an interview he gave: "The insight that everything is embedded in other systems means that we must consider the influence of our own actions on these systems. And that is not being done today, neither in the national economy nor in politics – and least of all in science" (Farau & Cohn, 1984, p. 614).

For Ruth Cohn all of these ideas, impulses, and experiences led to the ethical axiom. In a summary of the concept of TCI published together with Paul Matzdorf in 1992, she says about the second axiom: "When people are not concerned about their ability to love and to make ethical decisions (which is part of their autonomous and interdependent self), there are no limits to the rule of might, the oppression by few of many, the exploitation of humans and nature [. . .] The importance of the second axiom emerges from the historical situation we are experiencing today: the imperative nature of values" (Matzdorf & Cohn, 1992, p. 61). This is the background against which she sees things such as the "evaluative decision" or "inhumaneness" that led to her formulation of the second axiom. Today, we can see in this axiom the task of ensuring a more humane world. The basic direction is clear, though it still remains a matter of debate which paths and which decisions can best lead us there in a specific situation.

3 Explanations

Part of the discussion surrounding the second axiom is concerned with various ethical questions. For example, Jens G. Röhling looks at how we treat violence and aggression in TCI groups, "since in certain humanistic-based educational concepts we find the ideal of aggression-free behavior, which of course cannot be realistically realized" (Röhling, 2000, p. 58). "Respect is due all living things" – this is also valid for the fascination humans have for violence and aggression, if we are not to suppress it. Karl-Ernst Lohmann wrote a long essay entitled "Interkulturelle Gruppen leiten" (Leading Intercultural Groups), which was not expressly concerned with the second axiom. However, he did deal with the question of how people from very different cultural contexts can work together professionally on sometimes rather opposing "truths"; he ponders where the limits of one's own values are with respect toward those of others: "In an American-Arabic workgroup some of the participants admitted to being anti-Semitic when they discovered that there were Jews among the American participants" (Lohmann, 2003, p. 88). Without referring directly to the second axiom, but squarely within the humanistic approach of TCI, Jörg Ewen (2003) asks about the ethical stance of managers. This is part of a trend: the clear necessity for managers in large corporations to take an ethical stance since their actions affect many people and many jobs (→ TCI for Managers).

Nevertheless, in all of these cases the second axiom fails to provide true orientation and does not answer the question of what is to be done in any particular situation. The contribution by Walter Zitterbarth (2001) entitled "TCI und Ethik" (TCI and Ethics) is more radical. For example, he ponders what TCI would be missing were there no axioms at all, and whether there aren't other more precise and thus more helpful approaches to ethics. In addition, he suggests modifying the second axiom as follows: "Respect is due all living things in their growth and decay. It includes respect for the whole human being. For that is what conditions value-based decisions" (ibid., p. 104). This approach avoids limiting the existing limitation of the second axiom to growth as a human value. Yet the question about concrete actions remains unanswered.

4 Further Development

Most people can agree on what they generally consider to be "humane" or "life promoting." Ruth Cohn used such terms as autonomy, interdependence, individuality, cooperation, and responsibility. Modern brain research has discovered that humans are by nature attracted to cooperation, empathy, and communication (Bauer, 2002, p. 34). This provides neurobiological support for the innate sense of value postulated by Ruth Cohn as well as underpinning the humanization of the world foreseen by TCI. But these big goals are of little value when we are confronted with solving concrete ethical problems.

In order to make ethical decisions in conflict situations, we need to discuss them and to talk about the ethical insights and designs of both those who went before us and our contemporaries. This is the reason behind many hospitals today adopting ethical counseling for their staff, where ethical problems encountered in the care and treatment of patients are looked at in an interdisciplinary fashion by professionals from the fields of medicine, theology, and psychology as well as by relatives and the nursing staff. In the Western hemisphere, frictions may arise in modern ethical approaches because of the Old Testament commandments as well as because of newer insights propagated by bioethics, as Zitterbarth (2001, p. 103) noted in his article: When dealing with humans, the following principles should be heeded: "1) Respect for the autonomy of the other person; 2) the principle of loss prevention; 3) the principle of duty to care; 4) the principle of justice."

Experience clearly shows (especially the Holocaust) that the human conscience does not simply jump into action on its own, but rather must be constantly regenerated and developed. We are not responsible only *to* our own conscience, we are responsible *for* our conscience (→ Humanism)! The innate ability of humans to make humane decisions, the organismic value system, as Ruth Cohn phrased it, "like all other skills we have, has to be regularly trained and fostered if it is to properly develop and flourish" (Matzdorf & Cohn, 1992, p. 62). Of course, we do not begin the implementation of our ethical efforts from point zero, but rather stand on the shoulders of those who have lived before us, who pondered and acted, who drew up commandments and prohibitions, rules, and guidelines. Their insights are not binding for us, and indeed many of them we will choose to leave behind. We are free to take our own steps. But these traditions remain the starting point for our contemplations and the breeding ground for our actions.

Axiom 3: The Pragmatic-Political Axiom

Anja von Kanitz

> "Free will occurs within certain internal and external limitations, though these limitations may be extended. We judge freedom as given when we are healthy, intelligent, materially secure, and mentally mature; better than being sick, hampered, or poor and suffering from violence or a lack of maturity. Being aware of our universal interdependence is the basis of all humane responsibility."
> (Cohn, 1983, p. 120)

1 Definition

The third axiom concerns above all the freedom to decide and determine things so innate to all human beings. This freedom is limited by the internal and external boundaries that are particular to every individual, and that may be extended to varying extents. Inner limits are set by the mental mechanisms described by psychoanalysis as well as by limitations concerning one's own body, certain skills, or the lack thereof as well as by the availability and type of learning and experiential opportunities in life. External limits concern one's social and global environment, which we do not completely have at our command, but rather exist in a certain form and can be influenced only marginally or with the help of others. The extent of freedom we enjoy is also based on the material resources available, an insight that goes back to the theories of Marx, for which Ruth Cohn found support in her own biography. The most important thing, especially when working in educational settings with TCI, is to train the perception of one's inherent freedom within the given limitations and to acknowledge that a certain latitude does exist for extending this freedom. Testing the limitations and strengthening one's capacity to act plays a special role in the practice of TCI. The goal is to increase the level of freedom and the abilities of the individual based on humanistic values; individuals should perceive themselves as active subjects who can decide consciously, take a formative influence on their environment and structures, and take responsibility for their own actions. The educational theory of groups has the goal of strengthening the individual in connection with an understanding for the inherent interdependence with one's surroundings both near and far as well as with all other human beings. This was Ruth Cohn's political and pragmatic answer to the Holocaust. Both the call "Never again" and the prevention of such human-made catastrophes of all types are best effected by ensuring the power of value consciousness the ability of each and every individual to act and to assume responsibility. This is why as a psychotherapist she considered TCI to be a group method. She wanted to reach as many people as possible with her freedom-oriented, emancipatory, subject-strengthening teachings. For her, the target audience was everyone who worked in education and therapy, especially those who were disseminators among their peers.

2 Origin

This axiom was likely a reaction to the fatalistic ideas spread by European existentialism during the 20th century. World War I with its many victims and the subsequent difficult years full of economic and political crises had caused many to doubt the previously held certainties in life – belief in God, human reason, the blessings of technology. Toward the end of the 1920s, the first existential-philosophical discussions emerged, especially in Germany and later in France, where the main themes were the meaning of life and the many disillusioning answers to such questions (→ TCI and Philosophy). One of the basic motifs of all existentialistic trends was the idea of the individual as a subject who has been thrown into an absurd and meaningless world – alone, frightened, mortal – in search of the meaning of existence and the proper way to live life without resorting to higher beings of any type. Ruth Cohn's colleague and friend, Alfred Farau, was convinced that the creed of the meaninglessness of human existence paved the way for evil and allowed "Hitlerization" to take over the world. The feeling of meaninglessness produced egoism, indifference, brutalization. Ruth Cohn, on the other hand, saw the consequences of the insights of the various existential philosophers more positively. She saw existentialism as a necessary disengagement from materialism and determinism, as the acknowledgment of the individual as a subject equipped with the freedom to decide for himself whether to say "yes" or "no" in the respective situation. The courageous commitment to an uncertain existence could free up reserves and enable one to live life squarely grounded in one's environment and together with other human beings. The most important thing was to be oriented toward humane values and to possess a deep understanding of human society. The trend toward relativizing values and embracing nihilism found in the 20th century led, in her opinion, to loneliness and alienation from others. She also observed these phenomena in her therapeutic work, when patients spoke more of the "meaninglessness" of life and of an "inner emptiness" than they did of sexual problems, work problems, phobias, or compulsions. Left alone with the problems of humanity (she noted as examples violence, genocide, economic colonialization, overexploitation of natural resources, benefits for the few, among others), individuals were overwhelmed and developed feelings of despair and futility. To that she countered with the following idea: "Being a human being does not mean just being thrown senselessly into the world; it means finding a meaning to life in the realization of the individual self that is part of the community of all human beings [...]. Humans are able to discover things, to decide for themselves, to consciously change the way the world is. This means both passion and burden and leads to the important question: 'How can I/we change things? What are my/our standards for deciding?' And that is what we call values" (Farau & Cohn, 1984, p. 444).

3 Explanations

The question is now being discussed intensely whether the third, the so-called political-pragmatic axiom directly or indirectly commits us to political action. And if it does, in what form? Cornelia Löhmer, Helmut Johach, Günther Hoppe, and other authors derive from the values conveyed by the axioms a clear social-political responsibility and thus the call to action. "Theme-centered interaction wants to help change society. It is not value-free, but, quite the opposite, is based explicitly on maintaining a more humane life in a more humane world" (Löhmer, 1994, p. 26). Johach is of the opinion that the working life of many people is shaped by market and contractual relations, performance pressure, and competition. Such structures demand orientation toward humanistic principles: "If not a complete 'dropping out,' then at least, at some select junctures, a conscious bucking of the inhumane tendencies in a modern-day consumer society with its emphasis on performance and competition" (→ Humanism) (Hoppe, 1994, p. 85). Günter Hoppe assumes that TCI, being a method of living learning, necessarily means being critical toward society from the outset (→ Influences of Humanistic Psychology) (ibid., p. 66). Like psychoanalysis, TCI is directed toward the inner life and brings suppressed and limited self-experiences to light. "In this way, they [psychoanalysis and TCI] create a counterweight to superficiality and self-alienation – both of which are major social problems today" (ibid., p. 66). Hoppe thinks that the invitation contained in the third axiom to position oneself clearly against inhumane structures and power displays of the "Globe" is underdeveloped in both the organization and practice of TCI. The political force of TCI is too weak. He calls for a third postulate in the TCI concept: strengthening political desire for change. His short formula (derived after a number of revisions) is as follows: "Get involved! Step in! Become engaged!" The longer version is this: "Deal with the external world, deal with the Globe that surrounds you, deal with its image in you. Get involved and change what you can change in the sense of humanization" (ibid., p. 76).

Hoppe's suggestion for expanding TCI theory never caught on. The fact was that most authors who addressed the political background in the literature were unhappy with the social-political commitment of the TCI organization and that of many TCI teachers and wanted to see a greater orientation toward the "Globe" (→ Globe) – and overall more political activism. Manfred Krämer, in fact, spoke of an "obligation": "Every human being has the obligation to do his part. People who are humanistically oriented have the obligation to become involved. Success in life should not be reserved for the elite" (Krämer & Zitterbarth, 2006, p. 14). Walter Zitterbarth, on the other hand, see TCI as an anthropological-educational concept that is active only in the preliminary stages of social areas or partial systems. For him, TCI is not particularly political in nature: The TCI teacher should be content with using the TCI concept to create quality education – and that is not a political event (ibid., pp. 8 ff.). TCI can be emancipatory and reinforce personal development, he thinks, but only in the sense of Kant's enlightenment, which is an important prerequisite to becoming politically active – if desired. But TCI is not inherently political (ibid., p. 15). Johach in turn thinks that TCI does have a political mandate, but that the political repercussions of TCI are factually limited since TCI did not become successful in many countries – and even in Germany and Switzerland it is mainly used in the counseling, therapy, education, and pastoral care of persons who work professionally in communication (1994, p. 90).

These differences of opinion whether the TCI concept in general, and the third axiom in particular, contains the implicit call to political activism – and how exactly such activism should be expressed – are rooted in the various available definitions of what constitutes "politics" and "political." Some already view a strengthening of the chairperson (→ Chairperson Postulate) as being "political," whereas others think acting "politically" means an active involvement in social and political discussions and the proactive reform of inhumane structures. Ruth Cohn's idea of politics is a broad one: "Everything I do, whether I feed myself or teach, is political because it is connected to everything else. That is my political doctrine" (Cohn & Schulz von Thun, 1994, p. 42). Ruth Cohn assumes that every human being (even though only one of many billion on the planet) is inseparably connected with what happens in the world and is thus, to that billionth part, responsible. Both directions are wrong, she thinks: Hedonism, the suppression of responsibility and the limitation of one's consideration to one's own well-being, is just as bad as self-sacrificing oneself for the misery of the world. "Once I am happy with doing what I can do, suddenly I can do more" (ibid., pp. 60 f.). Ruth Cohn herself thought TCI was a way of actively resisting inhumane tendencies: "From the very beginning, TCI was an expression of an idea that there must be a way for us to be active in the midst of all the horror in the world – to counter the horror by taking small steps, tiny changes in direction [...]. It was my wish to help as many people as possible to become conscious of these things – much as psychoanalysis does for individuals. I especially wanted to reach children and their parents [...]. At the time I did not believe, and still don't today, that human cruelty is an insurmountable law of nature. Rather, it is a chain that has yet to be broken, a chain of frustration and beatings. I do not believe that it is a law of nature that refugees must be thrown into the ocean, that millions of children must die of malnutrition" (Cohn & Ockel, 1981, quoted by Löhmer & Standhardt, 1994).

For Ruth Cohn the strategy of taking small steps is in itself political in nature – as is the growing consciousness TCI offers as a means of personality development. This generalization of other people, in the sense of "It is your responsibility to get involved," cannot be directly deduced from these thoughts and would also contradict the chairperson concept she developed. Nevertheless, a deep understanding of one's own autonomy and simultaneous connectedness with the world support the ability of an individual to take up a position that may even go against the mainstream. Ruth Cohn cherished the hope that such skills would also lead to a greater desire and greater courage to exert one's social influence in a direction that maintained high esteem for human life.

The Chairperson Postulate

Jens G. Röhling

1 Definition

> "Be your own Chairman, the Chairman of your self. That means: (1) Be aware of your inner reality and of your environment. (2) Consider every situation to be a proposition for your decisions. Take and give as befits being responsible for yourself and for others" (Cohn, 1975, pp. 120 f.).

The Chairperson Postulate is a humanistic call to be autonomous, self-responsible, self-assertive, and not controlled by ideals or authorities. This postulate is at once a motive and a goal in the overall concept of TCI, and it is used in exercises in self-direction and group management. It has both intrapersonal and interpersonal dimensions to it – and thus also social and political ramifications.

This postulate was first mentioned in writing in 1968. Later, in a nod to the changing understanding of gender consciousness, was renamed as the "Chairperson Postulate" (Matzdorf & Cohn, 1992). Originally it was referred to in publications (and in practice) as a "rule" (Kroeger, 1985; Heigl & Heigl-Evers, 1984). Today, the term "postulate" is used, much as Ruth Cohn envisioned it from the beginning (→ Axioms and Postulates). The term is appropriate inasmuch as we are not dealing here with a norm for which compliance is sanctioned. Rather, it is a call to enact a certain way of living. The designation as "postulate" also better fits the dilemma Kroeger noted about formulating the content. How this postulate is lived, however, remains part of individual responsibility.

Ruth Cohn adopted the term from the vocabulary used in the American Congress. "Chairman" represent a very specific form of group leadership and is more widespread in the United States than in Europe; some of the inherent double meaning gets lost in translation: being Chairman of one's self and Chairman of a group. Ruth Cohn explained the term as follows: "[...] that everyone is his own chairman, who is responsible for internal perception and who is externally responsible for his choices as an entity and as part of the universal community" (1968, p. 151). Ruth Cohn herself sometimes also used the term "own leader" (e.g., Farau & Cohn, 1984, p. 359). Stollberg (1982, p. 19) made the suggestion to just continue using "Chairperson" in German and to adapt it to the respective situation: "Everyone is their own teacher, chairperson, seminar host, mayor [...]." Schulz von Thun (1998, p. 67) used the term "Oberhaupt" (= head, leader, ruler).

The true meaning may be realized by imagining the term "chairman" literally. Kroeger (1992, pp. 100f.) offers the following explanation: "The chairperson of a workgroup initially does not make any decisions, but rather ensures that everyone present gets the chance to speak, and that they are able to truly speak their mind. Yet a chairperson is also aware of his or her own opinion and expresses it as such. This means that the adult chairperson, in the TCI sense of the word, has to take great care to first become aware of his or her own differentiated and multifaceted internal and external reality."

Ruth Cohn again: "Lead yourself with all confidence: Look inside at what it looks like there, what you want, and what you should do. And look around you at what surrounds you. Decide between all realities what and how you want to act" (Cohn, 1975, p. 214).

1.1 The Intrapersonal Dimension

Ruth Cohn's experiences under the Nazi regime created the most important motif behind the Chairperson Postulate. She was particularly careful about the differences between considering what "should" be done (i.e., morals and ethics), what one would "like" to do (i.e., one's own desires), and what "must" be done (i.e., reality) (Cohn, 1968, p. 150). The danger is that confusion may arise if the ideas of "should," "like," and "must" are mixed together without due consideration and mistaken for volition. "Will" (or "volition") occurs as a result of the contemplation process that includes "should," "like," and "must" (Farau & Cohn, 1984, p. 345). It was Ruth Cohn's hope that careful discrimination, along with the proper contact with one's "organismic value system," would lead to strong personalities that could not be manipulated or succumb to the pull of the masses. Therein lies the origin of the political-social effectivity of the Chairperson Postulate (→ Historical and Political Background).

The "I" listens to many more voices than those of "should," "like," and "must." The role of the "I" as chairperson is to allow all these different voices to be heard – and then to make a well thought-out and self-responsible decision. Such a decision is all the more mature, the more inner voices that come into play. In this sense, the Chairperson Postulate is primarily a postulate about how to live life, about living a successful life. It is thus often referred to as the "existential postulate" (Matzdorf & Cohn, 1992, p. 66).

When practicing the Chairperson Postulate, it can be helpful to use the four-factor model of TCI: What would I like and need ("I"), what do others want and need ("We"), what does the task demand ("It"), and what does the "Globe" demand, enable, or prevent?

1.2 The Interpersonal Dimension

In interactional groups, the Chairperson Postulate means the following: "Practice perceiving both yourself and others; give yourself and others the same attention; respect all facts such that you extend your freedom of decisions; take yourself, your environment, and the task at hand seriously" (Farau & Cohn, 1984, pp. 359f.). Through his or her selective authenticity, a well-trained chairperson can motivate others to become better chairpersons themselves, who in turn motivate others through interaction. The chairperson is attuned to all voices present in accordance with the four factors.

For those who are leading groups (learning groups, teaching groups, workgroups, etc.), the Chairperson Postulate becomes the guideline for managing such a position: Leading in such a way that the members of the respective group are put in the position to assume responsibility for themselves. This can be all the more successful, the more authentic the group leader is. Thus, the leader is in effect a model participant.

2 Origin

The Chairperson Postulate combines a number of motifs stemming from the Enlightenment and → Humanism: the concept of an "inner diversity," the idea of self-responsibility, the idea of reaching a balance between self-responsibility and responsibility for others, or between self-care and other-care.

The concept of the inner group includes everyday experiences like those so well described by Goethe in his famous sigh "Two souls, alas, dwell in my breast" (Faust). But there are many other examples from literature. The ancient Greek maxim: "Know thyself!" (Temple of Apollo at Delphi) includes the multiplicity of the self by making it self-reflective – as I and me (Schmid, 1998, 239). Kierkegaard, the founder of existentialism, also said: "The self is a relation that relates itself to itself."

Freud's tripartite teachings of psychoanalysis also include this thought. The Chairperson Postulate is only a slight variation on Freud's maxim: "Where Id is, there Ego shall be." In Humanistic Psychology we find the concept of inner diversity: Fritz Perls applied it in therapy, and parallel to Ruth Cohn, Eric Berne developed his own ideas about "ego-states": The "should" in life is related to one's "parent-ego," the "like" reflects one's "child-ego," and the "will" relates to one's "adult-ego," although the analogy doesn't always work.

Even Augustin's motto: "Ama et fac, quod vis" (Love and then do what you want) is related to this concept.

The Chairperson Postulate should be understood above all in the sense of the holistic-existential motto from the Enlightenment "Sapere aude" ("dare to be wise," Horace) or Kant's saying "Have the courage to use your own reason." Clearly, the idea involved in the Chairperson Postulate is not new, though the thought of presenting it in a graphic form with an "emotional" basis (Matzdorf & Cohn, 1992, p. 66) is new (→ TCI and Philosophy).

3 Explanations

3.1 Further Development

It was especially Friedemann Schulz von Thun (1998) expressly took up Ruth Cohn's idea and developed it further in his Communication Psychology (→ We). He speaks of an *inner team*. Further, he describes the tasks and functions of the chairperson or leader: control, moderation, integration, conflict management, team development, personnel selection, and operations management with respect to the inner team (ibid., p. 70). At the same time, the leader is responsible for perceiving the external situation. The goal is to become an "authentic acting and communicating subject." Schulz von Thun developed methods for the inner team to take up positions.

In addition to → Humanistic Psychology, one should note the approach of Wilhelm Schmid (1998), who coined the term *subject of reflected life skills*, which means more or less the same as Ruth Cohn's concept of chairperson. Schmid's idea of *life skills* adds to the *self-direction* aspects of esthetics and values: It is not just a matter of being self-determined instead of being other-determined; self-direction should enable one to live a "good" life, that is, a worthy life.

Also, Peter Bieri's "The Craft of Freedom" (2001) reads like a description of the Chairperson Postulate.

The above-mentioned "hypothesis of an organismic value system" formulated by Ruth Cohn (Farau & Cohn, 1984, pp. 467 ff.) is a central component of Humanistic Anthropology and is supported by the results of modern neurobiological research (Bauer, 2002, pp. 64 ff.).

The Chairperson Postulate and the concept of the "inner group," however, challenge the usual *concept of identity*. Initially, the concept did not foresee any differentiation between "I" and "not-I" except at the somatic level. The "I" (or ego) is a complex of very different, in part contradictory, factors. New discussions are continually taking place within the "inner team" about who the chairperson is and who the ego is. Röhling (2005) thus, in an extension of Schmid's (1998) thoughts, suggests abandoning the identity concept in favor of a coherence concept. Whereas strictly speaking identity always means staying the same, the coherence concept allows development and change.

3.2 Controversies

It is a wrong and abbreviated approach to the Chairperson Postulate to suggest that, with the Chairperson Postulate, TCI is promoting egoism, arbitrariness, and laxness (see Kroeger, 1992b). Whenever the Chairperson Postulate is quoted in this manner, it has clearly not been completely understood. In particular, it must be seen in connection with the first axiom, the existential axiom, and thus includes the aspect of interdependence. The abbreviated misunderstanding of this concept neglects those parts of our personality that aspire to obtain – and indeed desperately need – contact, communication, and help from others. In short, it negates all social skills and needs of the chairperson.

There is a linguistic uncertainty that should be discussed: Some people who practice TCI say: "I discovered my inner chairperson" (an example is Arndt, 1992) or they say "I perceive my inner chairperson" – as though the chairperson were "not-I," some special part of one's ego, something that lies completely outside of one's ego. However, being the chairperson *is* the ego-function per se. In both cases the following is meant: "I am aware of my self-responsibility as chairperson." As an alternative suggests the following: "I perceive myself as chairperson." Even simpler: "I am the chairperson of myself."

Kroeger (1985, p. 29) sees a "meaningful linguistic dilemma" in this postulate. The postulate "Be your own chairperson" includes the possibility that sometimes we are in fact *not* our own chairperson. It also has a descriptive function: Everyone makes decisions that are sometimes based on incomplete information or without due respect for more low-level impulses. With this, the postulate takes on several meanings: Be aware of the fact that you have made a decision, then you can no longer make others responsible for your actions. The most important thing to remember when dealing with this dilemma is the perspective (as Bieri says): From an internal vantage point, we have the feeling of deciding autonomously; from an external viewpoint we may conclude that we are being controlled externally. The opposite case is also often found.

Becoming a chairperson is a process: The more you become aware of your internal and external workings, the more mature and autonomous your decisions become.

In light of the challenges posed by (post-)modern life, the aspects surrounding freedom of decision contained within the Chairperson Postulate may not always be viewed positively; sometimes, the burdensome necessity to decide raises its ugly head. Thus, the question is: Do I have to be a chairperson *all the time* – or can't I sometimes just get along without deciding? It's easy to imagine situations in which you suspend self-responsibility, for example, while experiencing (sexual) desire, while listening to music, or enjoying some other form of art, when you just let others decide for you. Whether it is the wise thing to do and in your own interest may be doubted, however. The dilemma involved in formulating this postulate is also an existential dilemma: If we as human beings are *always* on call – always responsible – then at some point in time that burden will become overbearing. On the other hand, if we surrender responsibility, then we fail to experience many important aspects of human life. Since we cannot completely solve this dilemma, we adopt a paradoxical formulation: Even when you are not deciding something, you bear the responsibility for your nondecisions.

The case is different for people who are clearly limited in their ability to made decisions, that is, in their ability to be a chairperson. Examples are unconsciousness, mental incapacity, or immaturity (children). "The freedom to decide is greater when we are healthy, intelligent, financially well off, and mentally mature than when we are sick, limited, poor, or suffer from violence and immaturity" (Cohn, 1975, p. 120). Ruth Cohn would surely agree that sickness, poverty, or immaturity do not count as excuses for a lack of self-responsibility. No one is responsible for the social, economic, political, and historical situation into which they were born. Yet everyone is responsible for leading their life under the circumstances encountered. However, we must differentiate between those circumstances we can influence and those we cannot. Regardless, the Chairperson Postulate may serve as an impulse to escape the role of victim and take action. Ruth Cohn used dramatic words to warn against intervening too early in the self-direction of others: "Too little help is theft, too much help is murder" (Farau & Cohn, 1984, pp. 284f., 359f.).

The Disturbance Postulate

Sarah G. Hoffmann

1 Definition

Disturbances play a central role in TCI. Ruth Cohn referred to the development of the term disturbance as "one of the most important steps leading from psychoanalysis to TCI" (Ockel & Cohn, 1992, p. 185).

The second postulate of TCI reads as follows: "Note the hindrances along your way, both your own and those of others. Disturbances take precedence; failing to solve them prevents or delays growth" (Cohn, 1975, p. 121). The original definition of this postulate was: "Disturbances and passionate involvements take precedence." Ruth Cohn paraphrased the term "disturbance" as follows: "Disturbances do not ask for permission; they are simply there: pain, joy, fear, distraction" (ibid., p. 122). Elsewhere, she speaks of "antipathies," "perturbation," "passionate feelings," "involvements" (Farau & Cohn, 1984, p. 360).

According to Ruth Cohn, disturbances are real conditions that counteract the conscious intentions and tasks of a group. They use up energy and hinder living learning. Sometimes, however, they also redirect attention to important aspects that, under more stringent conditions, would be lost or even consciously repressed. According to the Disturbance Postulate, disturbances occur in group situations and contribute to maintaining a dynamic balance.

If there are a multitude of disturbances, Ruth Cohn suggests attacking first the personal ones and then the factual ones. She warns against putting practical matters front and center while ignoring personal matters. Yet in life-threatening situations, or when absolutely pressed for time, then one should first take action instead of reflecting or treating. "Never analyze in a burning house [. . .]. On the other hand, don't set the house on fire in order to be able to use practical matters as an excuse for neglecting personal disturbances" (Farau & Cohn, 1984, p. 361).

2 Origin

Ruth Cohn describes how she came to understand the effectivity of the Disturbance Postulate during a workshop she conducted on the day after the assassination of President John F. Kennedy (cf. Cohn, 1975; Farau & Cohn, 1984). Instead of getting to the matter at hand right away or discussing the shock this tragedy had caused, she suggested that the participants take a while to ponder their own feelings and thoughts the assassination had created in them. Then, in a second step, she formulated a theme they could discuss that connected the "external" disturbance to the actual theme of the workshop. In doing this, she understood that not only in extreme situations was it both meaningful and productive to look at a disturbing situation. "Very often personal or collective attention to an apparently remote matter can connect it closely to the matter at hand" (Farau & Cohn, 1984, p. 342).

The postulate that disturbances take precedence is grounded in the concept of resistance in psychoanalysis and its axiom that "resistance comes before content." Whereas classical psychoanalysis understands resistance as a form of defense and an unconscious opposition to repressed needs or guilt feelings, in TCI resistance is more broadly defined: "Whatever gets in the way of the plan, intention, task, or theme of an individual or interactional group is what I call a 'disturbance'" (Ockel & Cohn, 1992, p. 185). Besides resistance, external distractions and events in the immediate surroundings can cause disturbances. Ruth Cohn considered disturbances in the social, political, and ecological "Globe" to be of particular importance. It is not surprising that she even illustrated the history of the Disturbance Postulate by using a disturbance stemming from a political event. For her, the social-therapeutic relevance of TCI was methodologically valuable.

Within TCI the demand that "disturbances take precedence" may be seen as the other side of the coin of the Chairperson Postulate. These two postulates are dialectically related to each other and take a positive stance (Chairperson Postulate) and a negative stance (Disturbance Postulate) toward human learning and developmental processes. They are both derived from the axioms and represent "clarifications of existential phenomena and noninterchangeable rules" (Cohn, 1975, p. 123).

3 Explanations

The Disturbance Postulate is today well known, albeit often completely misunderstood. "Disturbances take precedence" is often repeated in management training situations as a hard and fast rule of communication, and it is often one of those tenets from the "TCI curriculum" that sticks from pedagogical training during teacher education. It is also part of the moderation method (Klebert et al., 1987) and as such has gained a good foothold in various educational settings.

However, in addition to the positive echoes and the apparent easy integration into the stock principles furthered by Humanistic Psychology and education, especially in the 1970s and 1980s there were also a number of controversies surrounding its theoretical value and practical application. The standpoints expressed in this (largely internal) discussion touched on five main aspects: First, the normative or normalizing character of this postulate. Second, the rather fuzzy nature of the concept of disturbance. Third, the degree of reality contained within disturbances. Fourth and fifth, TCI is said to give precedence to emotions and avoids dealing with conflicts.

Seen from the present-day perspective, some of these objections would appear to reflect above all the sensitivities of the *zeitgeist* during the seminal days of the 1970s. They deflect attention to the most important differences between TCI and other methods and educational concepts – and they reveal the provocative power contained in the simple sentence "disturbances take precedence."

3.1 Normative Aspects of this Postulate

At the beginning of the 1970s, even the simple formulation of postulates seemed to be provocative. In the German journal *Gruppendynamik*, for example, the objection was raised that TCI contradicts even the slightest consensus of all emancipatory movements by laying down goals and norms. Postulates, it was claimed, lead only to new dependencies (Vogt & Cohn, 1975). An empirical-quantitative, psychoanalytically oriented study by Mahr (1979) on the priority of disturbances even expressed the concern that the inherent paradox contained in this postulate could cripple progress and create more or less insoluble psychological conflicts. The author also bemoaned conceptual and methodological fuzziness, saying that the "law of disturbance precedence" (his formulation) failed to differentiate itself from the auxiliary rules.

In fact, Ruth Cohn's concept is not well suited to strict categorization; it becomes understandable only after considerable paraphrasing and is easily misunderstood when used to normalize reality.

Ruth Cohn said the following about instrumentalizing individual elements of TCI and arbitrarily mixing and matching auxiliary rules and postulates: "My original excitement about auxiliary communication rules faded in the face of the avalanche of mechanical interpretations of 'Cohn's rule system' written on the walls of many institutions and burned into the brains of their members – without an understanding of the heart and soul of the axioms and postulates" (Farau & Cohn, 1984, p. 362).

3.2 The Basis for the Disturbance Postulate

The breadth of the Disturbance Postulate (ranging from antipathies to passionate feelings, from a toothache[1] to street noises) often leads to a banalization and a loss of meaning for the second postulate. For this reason, Raguse (1992, p. 273) referred to the Disturbance Postulate as a "dead metaphor" and called for its complete removal from TCI. He thought

1 On this, see the article by Ruth Cohn, in which she used a toothache as an inspiration for her thoughts: "The Experiential Therapies – Autism or Autonomy?" (Cohn, 1975, pp. 97 ff.).

the Disturbance Postulate denoted "everything bothersome that occurs between Heaven and Earth, between individuals, groups, societies, and sovereign states." Instead of putting so much emphasis on disturbances, he suggested keeping it simple: "If someone is not feeling well, then it's okay to shelve the matter at hand for a while" (Raguse, 1987b, p. 135).

However, this objection ignores two things: First, the Disturbance Postulate is not a strict behavioral mandate; it does not relieve individuals or groups from grappling with and deciding about how to deal with the respective situation stemming from the disturbance. "Dealing with disturbances is part of the art of living and the nature of groups" (Farau & Cohn, 1984, p. 361). Second, the fact that disturbances occur at all is a meaningful part of TCI. According to learning theory, disturbances belong to the elementary conditions for learning processes (Hoffmann, 2005): They represent moments of indecision that occur when new, unaccustomed, or strange things are encountered. Such moments necessarily demand our attention and cause interruptions. We are then forced to decide whether to reject or relativize what is happening – or whether to use the event to learn something in the sense of changing cognitive structures.

3.3 The Reality of Disturbances

Sometimes it is maintained that Ruth Cohn's formulation that "disturbances exist" contains a problematic idea of reality. Raguse (1987b), for example, thought her view involved a positivistic understanding of science, which postulates reality independent of any subject. Horst Siebert (2000), the founder of so-called constructivistic adult education, said that TCI suggested that disturbances were discernable entities. Siebert's objection, however, ignores the fact that the North American flavor of TCI is clearly grounded in existentialism and experiential therapy. According to its radically subjective look at things, the reality of disturbances depends on the ability and willingness of the participants to become involved with the disturbances. Disturbances become real when the participants acknowledge them as such.[2] In addition, the event character of disturbances plays an important role in TCI: When a disturbance occurs, it may be a "moment of high awareness and expression [...]. It is a moment of creative chaos that includes the chance for all to experience the new and realize the greatest gains" (Rubner, 1992, p. 69).

3.4 Dealing with Emotions

A further point of criticism of TCI and its Disturbance Postulate concerns its approach to emotions. In 1980, Günther Bittner (1980, p. 53) wrote in the journal *psychosozial* that

2 This formulation may be traced back to the "Thomas theory" of the American sociologist couple W. I. and D. S. Thomas, who said that "if men define situations as real, they are real in their consequences."

Ruth Cohn could apparently "deal with everything except with negative feelings." Judging by the practice of TCI, he thought the second postulate should read: "Emotions take precedence over factual matters and comments" (ibid., 1980, p. 61).

The difference between TCI's aspirations and its sometimes failed practice caused critics to concentrate on how TCI group leaders deal with their own disturbances. Being participants themselves, they are responsible for maintaining a dynamic balance and not just for leading the group, but also themselves – if necessary by prioritizing their own disturbances. This means they need not only the proper methodological tools, but also "educated feelings" (Cohn, 1975, p. 114). And, as Raguse (1992a) demands, they should have at their command a sort of intrepidity when difficult matters come up during the group process.

3.5 Dealing with Conflicts

Klaus Vopel (2000), in his article "Ein Update für die TZI" (An Update for TCI) took a detailed look at the Disturbance Postulate and noted that, in his opinion, it represented a relatively superficial substitute for the absence of a well-rounded theory of conflict and power in TCI. His suggestion for updating the Disturbance Postulate would be to reformulate as "disturbances and conflicts take precedence" (ibid., p. 81).

Whenever rivalities, jealousies, and aggressions fail to appear to the usual degree during TCI seminars, some feel that the seminar is divorced from reality. Belz (1992), on the other hand, thinks that one of the strengths of TCI lies in its ability to create a constructive and emotionally accepted work and group atmosphere. According to Belz, the reason lies not so much in the touted esteem of TCI or its elimination of destructive elements, but in its acknowledgment of the antinomy of destructive and constructive forces. "'An unrealistic atmosphere and an unrealistic lust for harmony' [...] do not correspond to the methodological and philosophical concept [of TCI], even if they are – clearly – part of the wishful thinking all humans entertain" (Belz, 2001, p. 61).

4 Further Development

With its volume "Störungen als Beitrag zum Gruppengeschehen" (Disturbances as a Contribution to Group Dynamics; Rubner et al., 1992), a working group of TCI teachers from Munich helped considerably to clear up and further develop the concept of disturbances and the way TCI deals with disturbances. The authors studied various sources of disturbance and their effect on the group process from a systemic perspective. They concluded that there is a complex potential for disturbance in every group that is manifested in its own specific way in the Here and Now, and that it acts to mitigate, compensate, or neutralize such disturbances. For this reason, a disturbance should not be seen "as distracting from the 'real theme' of the group, but rather as a contribution to the 'real theme' and treated as such" (Rubner et al., 1992, p. 17).

According to this working group, the Disturbance Postulate means only giving priority to recognizing and understanding disturbances – not to prioritizing the working through of disturbances.[3] If necessary, TCI group leaders must accept the fact that not every disturbance can be eliminated. This position, however, does mean abandoning certain therapeutic aspirations and the image of TCI as an independent educational concept.

3 Compare the original reading of the Disturbance Postulate of Norman Liberman, who worked with Ruth Cohn on developing TCI: "Distractions from the theme by any individual at any time take precedence and are to be dealt with" (1971/2001, p. 89).

The Four-Factor Model of TCI

Hermann Kügler

1 Definition

According to TCI, the processes and interactions that are active in situations – and thus also in all groups – are affected by four factors: the "I," the "We," the "It," and the "Globe."

- "I" stands for the individual, the group participant (→ I).
- "We" stands for the interconnectedness that is strengthened (or weakened) by the interactions of group work (→ We).
- "It" means the matter that lies behind the group coming together in the first place, the task at hand that is to be dealt with (→ It).
- "Globe" is understood in TCI terms as the circumstances and conditions under which the group works (→ Globe).

In TCI the following is true: The interplay between these four factors enables or hinders → living learning and cooperative work, transparent interactions, and growth-stimulating communication. These four factors are equally important. "The equality hypothesis is the most important principle of TCI. It says that the interactional group is attuned not only to the matter at hand, but equally to persons, groups, themes, and the Globe. I am as important as you and as we are; we are just as important as our task, even though we are all dependent on the equally important surroundings both near and far" (Matzdorf & Cohn, 1992, p. 74).

The four-factor model is optimal for interpreting and understanding situations as well as assisting in developing action strategies and visions. The four-factor model of TCI may be employed in both a factual and a lively manner; it is appropriate for planning and leading processes as well for diagnosing and analyzing situations. In this way it is not limited solely to group-management tasks. That all four factors are equally important does not mean, however, that they occur in all phases with the same intensity and demands. The task of the TCI leader is rather to ensure a dynamic balance between "I," "We," and "It" (→ Dynamic Balance).

The symbol for the four-factor model is generally depicted as a triangle within a circle or sphere. Ruth Cohn first adapted her original intuition by changing the image of a pyramid within a sphere to that of a triangle. She thought it would be easier to convey its

Figure 1. The triangle in a circle, used as a logo for TCI.

meaning on paper and blackboard by using a two-dimensional depiction of the circle. However, this form does make it less clear that the "Globe" refers to both the spatial and the temporal conditions in the broadest sense. Perhaps the best image would be "a multilayered, transparent sphere that extends to eternity. The often used circle can only suggest what is actually being portrayed" (Cohn, quoted in Amman, 1992, pp. 146 f.).

Over the history of TCI there have been a number of attempts to depict the four-factor model using a single symbol or image to illustrate the entire reality of its purpose (e.g., Amman, 1992, pp. 146 f.; Langmaack, 2001, title page; Kuebel, 2002, pp. 399–404).

2 Origin

Ruth Cohn developed the four-factor model based on her own experiences with groups. She attempted to discover what factors were responsible for maintaining the vigorous learning processes that occur in encounter, experiential, and therapy groups. It was her experience that living learning arises as a result of paying attention to the world of emotions and the personal situation of the individual group participants. The group atmosphere is furthered or hindered when everyone can express themselves. A clearly formulated theme demands that everyone take part in the conversation. And the group structure is able to reveal and test the interpersonal complications (Farau & Cohn, 1984/2000, pp. 111–119).

After many years of practical work in psychotherapy and education, Ruth Cohn developed the basics of TCI. For her the following dream was crucial: "One night [...] I dreamed of an equilateral pyramid. Upon awakening, it was immediately clear to me that I had indeed 'dreamed up' the basis for my work. The equilateral pyramid of my dream meant the following: Four points determine my group work, and they are all interconnected and equally important. They are:

- The person interacting with others and with the theme at hand (= I);
- The group members who become a group by attending to the theme at hand and through their interaction (= We);
- The theme at hand, that is, the task being discussed by the group (= It);
- The environment, which influences the group and is influenced by the group – the *umwelt* in the narrowest and broadest sense of the word (= Globe).

It seemed to me that these four points were able to symbolize *every* group, that is, there is no group that is not defined through these four points. And yet nowhere, regardless of where I looked, whether in our own groups or in the secondary literature, did I find such a definition of the group. The most important thing to me was the *equilaterality of the pyramid* as my dream had suggested. This meant that all four points are equally important. The *equilaterality of I, We, It, and Globe provided a basic definition of group management within TCI.* All other models of groups tended to emphasize one or more points: Encounter groups emphasized the I or the I/We; school classes emphasized the It or the It/I; universities emphasized the It. Then I changed the symbol of the pyramid into a triangle within the sphere in order to create a better image" (Farau & Cohn, 1984, pp. 343 f.).

In her publications, we do not learn whether and to what extent she grappled with the other theories of group models from North American sociology and social psychology of the 1950s. In the early 1970s, however, she did admit that, "for example, I taught five models of group interaction for many years, even though I had not studied their historical connections and scientific or philosophical meaning" (Farau & Cohn, 1984, p. 383).

"Today it is hardly imaginable," she later wrote (Matzdorf & Cohn, 1992, p. 49), "how revolutionary these ideas of interactional groups and psychological themes in the groups of that time really were. Much of what is known today on the group market was discovered by us then in many hours of exciting creativity."

With the four-factor model, Ruth Cohn discovered an instrument that transports living learning to all places where people gather for educational, organizational, scientific, and social-political purposes (Cohn, 1989, pp. 25–29).

3 Explanations

3.1 Reception

In 1987 Klaus-Volker Schütz wrote about the role of TCI in the canon of other types of group work. He differentiated between group psychotherapy, group dynamics, and group pedagogics. The various models of group psychotherapy are primarily directed toward the individual "I"; their therapeutic work is thus concerned mostly with changing the ego-structure of the individual client. Group dynamics, on the other hand, concerns itself with the "We"; group-dynamic laboratories are mainly interested in obtaining insight into the group-specific operating dynamics in order to understand the processes and structures present. Group pedagogics, in turn, refer to the dimension of content, something Ruth Cohn called the "It." Yet none of these approaches tapped the social and historical background like TCI does.

Schütz concludes that the four-factor model of TCI enables a multifactorial approach to understanding the group. "Whereas TCI speaks of a dynamic balance of all relevant factors found in the group situation, the three main social-psychologically based paradigms of group work tend to concentrate on only one of these aspects, with respect to their basic orientation" (1987, p. 18). It is this recognition and demand for balancing the "I," the "We," and the "It" in the "Globe" which form the basis for TCI group leadership.

Barbara Langmaack notes that many people are better acquainted with the subject level – the "It" within the triangle – and feel more secure there than on the psychosocial level of the "I" and the "We." As an example, she uses the image of an iceberg where only a seventh of the overall size is visible, whereas the major part lies hidden beneath the water level. When working with human beings it proves to be true again and again that the danger of "collision and sinking" lies in the hidden part and not in the size of the visible portion (2001, pp. 51–71).

The four-factor model as the central instrument of TCI is undisputed (see Section 3.2 below). The term "factor," which is derived from the Latin word meaning to "produce, create, make" and thus means literally "the maker," is quite clearly employed to denote each of the four variables that determine the processes and interactions in groups. To date it has not been a subject of controversy how these factors are actually constructed.

In addition to the term "four-factor model," the secondary literature contains other designations such as "structure model" (Matzdorf & Cohn, 1992, pp. 70–75; Ewert, 2008, pp. 23–25 & p. 228). The term "four-factor model" expresses that, from the vantage point of the TCI, the "I," the "We," and the "It" in the "Globe" are the determining variables in group processes and interactions. Authors who prefer the term "structure model" lean more toward emphasizing the action aspect: Someone who uses TCI to lead a group accepts and accentuates the dynamic balance between "I," "We," and "It" in the "Globe."

Thus, for the sake of clarity, I would suggest using the term "four-factor model" since the term → "structure" in TCI terminology means something different than the term "structure model" expresses.

The triangle in the sphere (or, more simply put, in the circle) is employed in the work materials and as a standard depiction of the four-factor model. It is today generally a well-known trademark of TCI. Even those who themselves do not actively work with TCI still use it.

3.2 Controversies

Even Ruth Cohn herself noted that the influences of the → Globe on the individual and the group are in principle "infinite" (Cohn, 1988). For this reason, the "Globe" is the one factor that is most difficult to grasp. Statzer (1995) forwarded the theory that the triangle and the sphere (or circle) thus represent different factors and should not necessarily be considered to be equally important. Further discussion on this matter concerning the importance of the Globe is presently taking place (Hoffmann, 2008).

Further, it has to date not been thoroughly discussed whether time should be considered as an aspect of the "Globe" or not – or whether time should be seen as an independent entity. As far as I can ascertain, only Achim Battke (1995) has discussed this matter, and further considerations remain outstanding (Kügler, 2008). Thus, the following questions remain unanswered at the moment:

- *On the theory of TCI:* Does time belong to the "Globe" or to the structure, to "I" and "We"? Where is time a constant and where can it be shaped? Or is time a factor of its own that has to date been neglected in TCI theory?
- *On TCI training:* How much time should be expended in the training of TCI leaders? Do the usual 5-day courses still represent the optimal way to ensure personal development? If so, why is that the case?
- *On TCI application:* Which is the best time structure for supervision, dream work, personality courses, methodological courses? What is possible on a single evening course, in a 90-minute course, in a 5-minute exchange? "Slow is good, fast is bad" – is that still true?

Craemer's proposals (1988) to add a "two-pole" or a "triad" to the four-factor model of TCI or to turn the triangle into a pentagon consisting of the elements "I – We – Theme – Globe – Leadership" never caught on and to this day have remained individual approaches that failed to generate discussion. Yet they may serve as starting points for new considerations: The "I" of the leader in the four-factor model is not precisely differentiated from the "I" of the group participants. For this reason, Langmaack (2001, pp. 203–206) rightly points out that the leader must be attentive to both his or her own "I" as well as to the "I" of the individual group participants.

A look at the pertinent secondary literature shows that the correct designation of the third corner of the TCI triangle was long contested (Kügler, 1997). The fuzziness or equation of "It" and "Theme" led to a number of ambiguities. Reiser and Lotz (1995, pp. 126–131; Lotz, 2003, pp. 156–173) kept "It" and "Theme" separate and justified their position (→ Theme). I have also suggested adopting more precise terms (Kügler, 1997, p. 25) since we are dealing here with the methodological benefits emerging from a differentiated approach to a neutral and unrelated matter ("It") and a thematic issue ("Theme").

3.3 Further Development

There have been repeated attempts to depict or extend the relationships that go on between the four factors. In the following, I would like to point out and discuss some of them. None of these attempts, however, has been able to catch on.

As early as 1982 Dietrich Stollberg (1982, pp. 136–145) pointed out the transfer problems that arise when people trained in TCI attempt to apply what they have learned to their everyday (professional) situations. Large groups, member or plenary meetings consisting of several hundred persons, or a hierarchically organized group demand very different strategies than a smaller group in which direct communication between all participants with each other is practiced and desired.

Irene Amann (1992) made the attempt to show the spiritual aspects of TCI. Her thoughts considered the triangle within the circle as corresponding to the ancient symbol of humanity. Through its concern for our environment and the large community of human beings living on the Earth, TCI could provide important impulses by drawing attention to the interconnectedness of humans with "all that is."

Like Stollberg, André Dörfler (1998) notes that organizations and institutions are not groups as such. Companies, schools, churches, hospitals, clubs, and political parties are more complex social systems than simple groups and accordingly function differently. Especially the functions of the individual employees are more starkly differentiated; work processes are formalized; the participation of the lower levels of the hierarchy is often possible (and meaningful) only through surrogates. Using the four-factor model so well known from group work in large organizations and institutions may not properly fit their complexity. The four-factor model was originally developed for working with limited-size interactional groups in which the participants can directly and immediately communicate with each other. Anyone who wants to use the structure model of TCI for working with large organizations and institutions should have extensive knowledge of their peculiarities (→ Globe; → TCI as a Professional Educational Concept; → Generative Leadership; → TCI and Organizational Development). In such cases, the challenge lies in adapting the four-factor model of TCI as needed.

For seminar and training groups, Barbara Langmaack (2001, pp. 203–206) differentiates between the "I" of the group leader and that of the participant. Marion Bönsch and Kathrin Zach (2006) go even further: In teaching and training groups the "I" in the triangle within the circle denotes both the "I" of the leader as well as that of the individual participant. If a co-leader is present, the situation becomes even more complex. The term "We" also refers to relationships of the participants of a group among themselves as well as the relationships between the participants and the leader (→ We). "In order to determine where the problems lie in such situations, it is imperative that we differentiate between the trainer and the participant" (Bönsch & Zach, 2006, p. 20) (→ Participative Leadership). Bönsch and Zach extend their depiction of the triangle within the circle to become a model of a pyramid within a sphere (p. 21) with the following parameters:

- Individual participants, group of participants, trainer, co-trainer,
- Theme (in their depiction the "It" is unfortunately equated to the "Theme"),
- The "Globe" as a sphere around a pyramid.

Figure 2. Depiction of the four-factor model by P. Rubner (2008, p. 88).

Walter Lotz made the extensive attempt to spell out the four-factor model even further. He portrays this differentiation in a separate contribution in this volume (→ Differentiation of the Four-Factor Model).

Philipp Rubner (2008) attempted to summarize the various elements of TCI in a single schematic illustration (see Figure 2). The "3 × 4-factor model" that resulted proposes to present an overview of both the individual elements as well as the structural interactions and reciprocal conditions of the elements in the entire TCI system.

Rubner takes up the four-factor model and extends it by adding the levels of "Method" and "Approach," thereby constructing a sort of navigational map of the TCI system. His depiction has the advantage of connecting the levels "Approach" and "Method" dynamically with the level of "Model" and showing their mutual influences.

Only future practical applications and considerations of the experiences with these new models will show whether such differentiations of the four-factor model prove to be acceptable.

The "I"

Walter Lotz

1 Definition

The "I": A nominalized personal pronoun that is one of the four categories in the TCI structure model of "I – We – It – Globe." These four categories, in turn, represent the four equally important factors in all learning and work processes and thus also in the way theme-centered interactions take place. In the TCI literature, the explanations of the "I" factor are generally kept short (e.g., Farau & Cohn, 1984, pp. 352 f.; Klein, 2002, p. 94; Kroeger, 1992, pp. 97 f.; Langmaack, 2001, p. 48; Löhmer & Standhardt, 2006, p. 27; Matzdorf & Cohn, 1992, p. 71). The "I" simply stands for the individual and that person's relationships. The idea of "I," which in TCI reappears more specifically in the form of the Chairperson, is in the writings of Ruth Cohn not depicted in any compact and theoretical way, but rather very vividly in its many various pragmatic facets. In her general comments on TCI she repeatedly refers to herself, to her own experiences, and to the great meaning of personal development – also with respect to functional roles such as leading a group. She thereby emphasizes the role of the individual personality in such actions, something that is also true for therapeutic work: "Introducing yourself as an individual into therapy means learning to voice things about yourself. For example, as a therapist, I am not just a therapist but *also* a woman, an immigrant, a mother, a friend. I have a certain mood, and I have my own development behind me. This means that at that moment I try to accept myself as I am and become aware at that moment of my own inner reality" (Cohn, 1975, p. 100).

The importance of being a self-descriptive person is a common theme found in many examples in the writings of Ruth Cohn. It is impossible to reproduce the clarity and directness of her texts in a compact manner, so we will concentrate on presenting the essence of her idea of "I" in three anthropological-philosophical treatments.

2 Reception: Prerequisites and Characteristics

2.1 The Self-Conscious "I" Between Autonomy and Interdependence

According to Ernst Tugendhat (2003), we humans are all "I-sayers" who can uniquely express ourselves in a self-reflexive way. By using the word "I" the speaker does not refer to something within him- or herself, but rather refers to his or her complete self.

Such use of language, however, does not mean that we can refer only to our own present state of affairs: "I'm freezing!" could easily be shown by revealing the goose bumps on our skin or other nonverbal means. We can go beyond such expressions and point out something that exists in time and space, for example, an experience we had: "Yesterday I experienced something really strange." In this sentence (1) an "I-sayer" claims (2) to have experienced something (at some point in time) that (3) may be described as being strange. The "I-sayer" thus introduced his or her own inner life into a depiction of three-dimensional reality (of the speaker, the situation, and the concept). The "I-sayer" can also compare these ideas with other ideas (and thus with other experiences), evaluate them, and determine his or her own actions from a self-reflexive position in light of the various circumstances and possibilities, desires, and fears.

Through "I-saying" we expressly refer to ourselves as individuals who are different from all other individuals and all other things. All "I-statements" reveal the most innate feelings and wishes, goals, and rationales of that one person: "As an individual, I can feel, sense, and acknowledge my own feelings like no one else, namely, subjectively. [...] I alone and no one else can experience my perceptions, ideas, feelings, and thoughts; no one besides me has my memories and my desires and makes decisions for me" (Farau & Cohn, 1984, p. 354). Because, in the end, only I can refer to my own inner states, I gain self-confidence: as an "I-saying" person among all other "I-saying" persons who is separate from all others – who can also refer to their own inner feelings. This innate ability to self-express enables the "I-sayer" to make his or her own direct experiences the object of a verbalization and thereby to emerge from his or her own world. At the same time, the speaker experiences him- or herself from the speaker's perspective as the center of his or her universe. Thus, every "I-sayer" takes him- or herself seriously. By attributing our own self-awareness to all other humans as well and thus recognizing that they too live at the center of their universes, we develop "an awareness that others also takes themselves seriously and that he lives in a world in which he can take others seriously" (Tugendhat, 2003, p. 30). This perspective of simultaneous differentiation and integration marks the origin of the first axiom concerning autonomy and interdependence.

2.2 The "I" as Person: Experiencing Oneself and Acting in a Relationship ("We") and in Reference to Others ("It"/"Globe")

An individual is an indivisible, living entity who exists through their own being and act in their own regard. Humans are individuals by virtue of the unity of their self-consciousness. Despite the various different states in which we exist in the world, and despite the very different feelings in which we experience these states, our self-consciousness provides us with a unified idea that we are the ones who are having (have had, will have) these feelings. This makes clear that – despite all the various states and feelings – the unified nature of an individual emerges from our knowledge about our state, which demands a certain level of objectivity toward what is experienced. An individual is thus not a substance, but rather develops consciousness in the self-assurance of being "above and beyond situations" and of acting independently as an entity. That is the subjective perspective.

Another equally basic, intersubjective perspective shows that the ability to become a person does not emerge from the individual and does not emerge of its own accord. Rather, humans are social beings that gain their autonomy in social settings; becoming a person is an event that takes place *between* human beings: "I become through my relationship to You; and as I become, I say You. All real living is meeting" (Buber, 1984, p. 15). Being addressed and answering – being acknowledged as a person by others – comprise the basis for the development of personhood. In this sense there are only persons "in the plural, since the social character of personhood is bound to the reciprocal acknowledgment" (Hühn, 2004, p. 812).

We are persons not solely through our individual uniqueness, but also through the relationships that correspond to the particular existential situations we encounter in life. "Humans become persons through threefold relationships: in the relationship to other persons, in the relationship to the world, and in the relationship to oneself" (Schleißheimer, 2003, p. 154). TCI illustrates these threefold relationships by applying the three procedural factors "I," "We," and "Globe" (and the "It" as the "small part or aspect of the world of things and events") (Matzdorf & Cohn, 1992, p. 72).

2.3 The "I" in Light of Humanistic Principles: Equality, Freedom, Responsibility

A conception of human life based on human dignity and the free development of personality is tied to the recognition of the three basic tenets, which are simultaneously the cornerstones of humanistic ethics (cf. Schleißheimer, 2003, pp. 174–200):

1) *Equality:* Despite all the differences we humans display in daily life, we still assume that others think, feel, and behave as we do. In doing this we forget that the thoughts, feelings, and actions of every "I" emerge from the unity of that person's own self-consciousness. We thus ignore the authenticity of selfness that substantiates the very uniqueness of an "I." If we look at the formal relationship others have to themselves, to other human beings, and to the objects that surround us, we see that this relationship includes the same perspectives as our own. If I observe myself as a person who disposes over my own self, then I necessarily have to attribute this same self-disposition to others, and with it recognize an equality of being in the world. Any differences that may occur result from the authenticity of selfness, the equality that arises through the ability to self-dispose – the position that lies behind one's own self-assertion, which is in principle also that of others as well. The self-conscious "I" thus has two reference points:

its own authenticity as a function of its independence and its personal authority as a function of the equality of all.

2) *Freedom:* The idea of searching in life for a meaning to one's life and shaping one's life according to own criteria is called "conditional freedom" (Cohn, 1975, p. 120), which is something very different from "willful freedom" and "chosen freedom." Thus, individuals have the task of determining their own life within the limits of what is possible and the scope of what is not predetermined (e.g., through instincts). In this sense, we do not decide for or against freedom, but rather are "damned" to exist through our very being (cf. Sartre, 1943). In addition, we do not simply choose a lifestyle from a stockpile of past sample life plans; rather, we must create our path by actively confronting our traditions and our existing possibilities. Making decisions and taking responsibility are thus the central components of freedom.
3) *Responsibility:* Those who (within the limits of the given conditions) see themselves as free to decide and in a relationship to others necessarily become aware of their responsibility. Vice versa, they become aware of their freedom by recognizing their responsibility. A completely free individual bears just as little responsibility as one who is completely determined in his or her behavior. Only the fact that our freedom is conditional and limited leads us to assume responsibility for what we do or fail to do. The idea of responsibility includes the idea of "answering" in a dialogical situation: I answer (to/for) someone – even if it is only my inner voice questioning my behavior. In addition, this form of "providing an answer" assumes a general claim to justify responsibility. Those are the objective and contextual perspectives of personhood.

These principles of the Humanistic Action Concept address the following constellation: Being the subject of his or her own decision-making ("I"), a person justifies his or her behavior by taking reference to other persons ("We") and with respect to those things and conditions ("It"/"Globe") for which he/she is responsible. Thus, the autonomous-interdependent "I" is involved in relationships that form the basis for "living learning." The "I" as a factor in this process represents the irreducible significance of the person in learning and working.

3 Critique

The TCI approach reflects an image of mankind that, on the one hand, is well reasoned and, on the other hand, vulnerable to criticism from a number of vantage points. The philosophical criticism considers the "I" to be a constructed fiction; the psychological criticism notes that the "I" is hardly the master of its own house; the sociological criticism sees the "I" as lost in the whirlwind of changing social stagings; the neuroscientific criticism is leveled at the only apparent free decision of humans, preferring biochemical determination. So, in the end, it is a matter of perspective: The "I" is the product of internal conditions and external influences; it must continually be renewed and is easily damaged; it has to deal with its own sense of reality and illusion; it suffers from its own individual self-reflexive nature; and it must answer the question: "Who am I?" When we peruse all possible considerations and relativizations, TCI represents the "vision of a human being who can rise above himself and his own consciousness, growing both internally (in his unconscious realm) and externally [. . .]; who is both related to and independent of others; whose 'I' is capable of entering into relationships with both humans and things and is not concerned solely with its own well-being. Only then can the desired autonomy in interdependence ensue – in light of all internal and external hazards" (Kroeger, 1992, p. 106).

The "We"

Mina Schneider-Landolf

1 Definition

The "We" stands beside the "It," the "I," and the "Globe" as one of the four elements in the TCI structure model describing the factors active in groups based on these four categories. Ruth Cohn herself defined "We" as follows: "The We is not a psychobiological organism like the I, but rather a *gestalt* that arises through the respective I and its interaction. Like all other *gestalts*, it is more than the sum of its parts. Strictly speaking, the We represents a number of people in the same room at the same time who have reference to each other and have gathered around common theme" (Farau & Cohn, 1984, p. 354). Elsewhere she used the terms "community" or "group" to describe the "We" (Cohn, 1975, p. 113).

The *gestalt* of "We" is thus formed through the common occupation of individuals with a single matter, a learning material, a task, a problem – what the TCI four-factor model calls the "It." The emphasis lies on the ensuing personal encounters between individuals and the resulting conscious and unconscious effects. The "We" comprises the mental processes that occur between the individuals in a group, the entire network of "I-You" relationships[1] as well as the dynamics that drive the group as a whole. In the terms of social psychology, it means the interaction, the communication, and the interpersonal relations in a group with all respective qualities – to which the relationships between the participants and the leader also belong.

This approach necessarily means a delimitation from an identification widespread in TCI circles: equating the "We" with a positive "We-feeling." This reflects the fact that this term is sometimes used in groups to refer to the pleasant feeling of close attachment that arises.[2] And if this feeling of attachment is missing, then the cry is: "This group is not a

1 Martin Buber also used the term "We": For him, the "I-You" relationships were of utmost important because that is where an independent "I" comes to fruition. There are other parallels in the use of the term "We" – as well as a number of differences. Schiffer (1996) provides a detailed comparison of the various instances.

2 Generally, a positive, trustful atmosphere quickly arises in a TCI group and is interpreted by the participants to mean "'We' are an especially good group." This exhilarating feeling of community is colloquially (and even in some group models) referred to as a "We-feeling" – a term that does not occur in TCI. The danger is that the necessity of disturbances and controversies on the path to optimal

We." Ruth Cohn herself conceived of "We" in a much broader sense: that it can develop and change quantitatively as a result of the increase in interactions, and qualitatively through the type of relationships between the individual participants.

Ruth Cohn's choice of the term "We" represents a phenomenological-existential approach – different from a systemic-constructivist approach[3] or social-psychological approach. She saw the term "We" as better suitable to what the participating persons (and that includes the leader) experience and perceive. This comprises how they experience the atmosphere in the whole group, whether as distanced and cold or as warm and cordial. But it also underscores the quality of the relationships among the individuals present in terms of nearness–distance, affection–repulsion, strangeness–intimacy, dominance–dependence.

2 Origin

Ruth Cohn's understanding of "We" only partially agrees with the term "group" as found in the social psychology and in group therapy of her time. Below I discuss both the agreements and deviations between the TCI approaches to "We" and these other concepts.

2.1 The Idea of the Group as an Object of Social Psychological Research

The rise of TCI occurred parallel to the intensive phase of social psychological research into group processes in North America in the 1960s, particularly its discovery of group-dynamic rules in the so-called *t-group laboratories*. The scientific interest of the day was directed toward the social influence on perception, social attractiveness, interpersonal relationships, the sources and effects of social power, and the roles and structures that occur in groups.

Ruth Cohn's concept of "We" certainly includes these phenomena but does not correspond in all aspects to the research concept of "group" in the social-psychological or sociological sense of the word.[4] One could presume that these theories did play a role in her development of "We," especially in the practical applications within the encounter groups flourishing at that time in the United States. Ruth Cohn deliberately took a phenomenological approach to interaction and interpersonal dynamics; she emphasized the subjective perspective of those experiencing and participating in a group – which in turn influences the gestalt of the "We" and is influenced by the "We."

The respective complex network of mutual influences and relationships of the "We" is experienced differently by those involved in the group than by a researcher studying the group: less consciously, less comprehensively, in smaller snippets.

---

cooperation becomes factored out of the equation.

3 Here, see the detailed comparison of Reiser (2004).

4 See the comparison of the systemic approach with that of TCI in Reiser (2004).

The overall group has its own dynamics and its own rules. Social psychology describes this as a power structure (= "Who's in charge here?"), as a popularity hierarchy (sociogram), as an interaction pattern (Bales, 1950), as task and role distribution, as group norms, or as interaction styles (Argyle, 1969; Hofstätter, 1973; Lindzey & Aronton, 1969; Müller & Thomas, 1974).

2.2 Encounter Groups and Group Therapy

The development of TCI is closely connected to the overall large interest that occurred in the 1970s concerning psychotherapy in groups and in encounter groups, including the newer approaches stemming from → Humanistic Psychology (e.g., gestalt groups, encounter groups, transactional analysis, psychodrama, bioenergetics), which proposed to further personality development. Ruth Cohn's own experiences in and with groups, however, were not limited to these areas; she was also concerned with task-oriented learning groups, work-groups (such as teams in hospitals), with complete teaching staff, and with training seminars for prospective psychotherapists (→ Educational Fundamentals). It is not surprising that the "We" in TCI always consists of the trinity *person, group*, and *task* (or *theme*) – which stands in contrast to the purer models of encounter and therapy groups of the day.

Ruth Cohn's writings contain only a few explicit passages in which she gives her opinion of the other group models.[5] Thus, in the following, I mention only some aspects where there are agreements or similarities.

2.3 The Psychoanalytic View of Groups

Despite the above-mentioned clear positioning of TCI within the group movement of Humanistic Psychology, Ruth Cohn always remained a psychoanalyst. Besides the "Here-and-Now" of ongoing interaction in a group, she also implicitly saw a "Then-and-There" of the early, formative years with important persons and important groups from the past (Kroeger, 1993; Reiser, 1995). Early experiences of security or deprivation, safety or fear influence how one views and shapes present relationships in the "We": Past feelings and behavioral patterns are (unconsciously) transferred to persons present in the group (Rubner, 1992). The first experiences of relationship with one's parents affect how one later interacts with group leaders, and relationships with siblings influence how other group members are experienced: Sometimes they are loved or hated, feared or admired with an intensity that is not rooted in the ongoing events. Thus, in my opinion, the impact the

5 A comparison of psychoanalytic, gestalt-therapeutic, and experiential-therapeutic therapy groups may be found in Cohn (1975, p. 76). An exception to the rule is her dispute with Fritz Perls and his gestalt groups, where she clearly distanced herself from his "gestalt prayer." This matter is discussed in detail in Kroeger (1992, p. 100).

unconscious has and the phenomenon of transference both clearly belong to the "We" of TCI. However, in contrast to the therapeutic dyadic relationship of psychoanalysis, in TCI the term transference does not refer to the transference neurosis found in psychoanalysis, but has a broader and more encompassing meaning – the transferences that occur among the group members. "[In group therapies] the transferences are spread out over many persons instead of being limited to one [the analyst], though they forfeit none of their illusionary power in doing so" (Farau & Cohn, 1984, p. 260).

Ruth Cohn's approach to transferences drew on concepts found in Humanistic Psychology, in accordance with the ideas of Carl Rogers (1969, 1974), which diverge starkly from how psychoanalysis understands the role of the group leader (of a psychoanalytic therapy group): TCI groups strive for a strong direct relationship to the leader from the outset, with as little irrational distortion as possible.

We share the opinion that transference must be seen, and treated, as a disturbance of the actual encounter. The justification for transference stemming from the individual's biography remains valid and becomes more significant in the course of treatment. The therapeutic method of choice, however, is not to reinforce the symptom to trigger regression, but the direct reaction of the therapist (or teacher) to the patient's (or pupil's) illusion. Transference should be considered a disturbance of the encounter in the Here and Now and treated through a realistic reaction by the therapist (Farau & Cohn, 1984, pp. 576f.).

Such a reaction becomes possible when the therapist (or group leader) presents a relationship offer in the sense of Humanistic Psychology, i.e., not one of psychoanalytic abstinence, but as someone who encounters others as an authentic person (see Rogers, 1961/1969).[6] Ruth Cohn, however, narrows Rogers' idea of maximum authenticity by using the term *selective authenticity* to describe a selective openness that respects the situation and is acceptable to others (Cohn, 1974, pp. 188–190). The group leader participates in the group process as an active and involved person, with all of his or her individual strengths and weaknesses (participative leadership).

2.4 Communications Psychology

Inasmuch as TCI judges the quality of relationships and encounters to be important to the ability of the group to work effectively, this insight agrees with the findings of communications psychology as propagated by Paul Watzlawick (1969).[7] In his analysis of the communication that takes place between individuals, he differentiates between the aspects of content and relationship. Besides the verbally communicated facts of the situation (the

6 See the detailed depiction of the parallels between Carl Rogers and Ruth Cohn in Kroeger (1973). The further development of psychoanalysis to group therapy according to Sullivan also changed the strict abstinence of the analyst.

7 But also note the further development in Europe in the writings of Schulz von Thun (1981), whose communications psychology combines the two aspects and explicitly refers to the influence of TCI.

"It" of TCI), the aspect of the relationship is present, which tends to remain nonverbal and analog, expressed through facial expressions, gestures, body position, and voice intonation. This nonverbal part of communication is interpreted by one's counterpart and may, of course, be misinterpreted. In TCI, the "We" aspect gets much attention, since in theory the "I," the "We," and the "It" all have the same importance; the guidelines in the auxiliary rules say that one should pay great attention to bodily signals and always speak as "I" and not broadly (→ Auxiliary Rules). This relationship aspect can, and indeed should, be brought up in TCI and made an object of discussion.

2.5 The Anthropological Foundations of "We"

The importance attributed by TCI to "We" is based on the anthropological assumption that, in their mental development, humans are dependent on other humans (sensu Portmann, Winnicott, and Mead): There can be no "I" without "We." A child needs the emotional attention of an "acceptably good mother" (Winnicott) to ensure proper mental and intellectual development. In addition, a child requires the experience of interacting with other human beings, both as mirrors and as models (Mead, 1968). Or, as Martin Buber (1923) expressed it, the interactions with a "You." Here, again, we find the opposing poles of being a human being who is a free and independent "I" as well as deeply conscious of our dependence on others.

This tension between autonomy and interdependence is what Ruth Cohn meant by the anthropological assumption in → Axiom 1, to which she added: "Every you as well as every 'We' and every experience we make leave traces behind in an individual's 'I-Self' [...]. Thus, interdependence means both our external (social) and universal integration as well as a constitutive moment of consciousness of our self, of subjectivity" (Matzdorf & Cohn, 1992, p. 56).

We humans insert into every group situation our own social needs for esteem, for respect, for belonging, for social appreciation. Depending on the respective early experiences we have gathered, the group situation may also arouse our social fears: Will I be loved? Will I be seen and accepted as I am? Do I belong here? Ruth Cohn's anthropological assumptions on the development of personality (as well as her assumption of an organismic value system) show great conformity with those of other representatives of → Humanistic Psychology, in particular with Carl Rogers (1961, 1969). "The common thread in these various approaches is that the relationship to other humans is not secondary to the one's autonomy, but imperative to the development of the personality and the human self. [...] Only by interacting with others do I create a conception of me and myself" (Kroeger, 1992, p. 104).

On this matter Lotz (2003) points to the social philosopher Honneth (1994), who broke down the necessary "psychosocial recognition relationships" among humans: He differentiates between recognition through emotional attention, recognition through attention to one's personal status, and recognition through social esteem.

3 Explanations

3.1 The Shaped "We" of the TCI Group

Different from psychoanalytic therapy groups or in group dynamics, in TCI the development of "We" (the group process) is not left to chance events.[8] Rather, the leader of a TCI group has a goal and a vision of how to create an optimal "We": by creating an atmosphere of mutual esteem ("every I is important"), of respect for differences, of open communication as well as close contact among all participants. According to TCI, the goal of workgroups and learning groups is cooperation (Cohn, 1975). In this sense[9], the group process and the development of the group's dynamics are not left to chance, but are actively shaped and influenced by the leader. The TCI-specific methodological steps involved to ensure the optimal development in a cooperative learning group or workgroup are provided in detail in a cooperation model created by Belz (1988) as well as by Klein (1992), and Langmaack (1989) (→ Phase Models).

Thus, each group shapes its very own "designer We," which does not completely conform to the typical course of the psychoanalytically oriented group phase models.[10] The TCI leader controls the process, and to this end very consciously uses methodological instruments such as → work forms and social forms as well as theme formulations (→ Theme) that concentrate on relationship experiences and social needs, which in turn can then be addressed in the group. The many available means of feedback –metacommunication and collective process analyses – further the communication within the group. All of these aspects of "We" can then, as part of a TCI-formulated theme (a "We" theme), be discussed and made the subject of the group conversation.

3.2 Disturbances as Expressions of "We" Processes

A further element of TCI-typical methods with regard to the "We" is the way it deals with the Disturbance Postulate.[11] Sometimes, an aspect of the "We" process surfaces in the reaction (experience) of an individual group member. Someone becomes very angry, begins to cry, berates others, complains about the leadership, etc. From the objective per-

8 In group dynamics or in psychoanalytic therapy groups, this process is initially left to chance and then, with the help of the group leader, worked through and interpreted. The course of such group phases depends greatly on the particular style of the leader and on the amount of relationship interaction the leader offers. This course is different in psychoanalytic groups that have a different understanding of leadership.

9 For a broader understanding of the TCI vision, see Walter Lotz (2003).

10 On this, see the controversy that broke out between Kroeger and Rubner (1993) in the journal *Themenzentrierte Interaktion, 7*(1), pp. 57–59).

11 See "Störung als Beitrag zum Gruppengeschehen" (Disturbance as a Contribution to Group Activities) (Rubner, 1992).

spective of the group goal, these interruptions are unfortunate disturbances; from the perspective of the inner workings of the group, these events can be an expression of the "We" dynamics.[12] With the postulate "disturbances take precedence," Ruth Cohn demanded that such "passionate feelings" be openly introduced into the group process. Disturbances belong to every group and further the development of the "We." Some disturbances serve to point out previously overlooked group processes, that, if not properly understood and taken into account, may turn into a crisis for the person in question or for the entire group.[13]

The psychoanalytic model of group development by Rubner and Rubner (1992) can be very helpful especially if we want to understand the unconscious psychodynamics active in group processes. This is particularly true for the psychoanalytic theorems of conflict, transference, and defense mechanisms, as discussed by these authors in connection with the group process. Being aware of the mechanisms behind the development of groups and the successive development phases analogous to individual development can sharpen one's perception of the dynamics that lie below the surface (see in this regard Rubner, 1992, pp. 18–32). This approach also increases our tolerance toward disturbances and reduces the fear of intense emotions; it honors the necessity of confrontations, dissociations, and crises.

3.3 Outlook and Further Development

Against the background of the insights provided by Humanistic Psychology, today we can reasonably say what is necessary for ensuring that a group can truly further the personality development of its members (Rogers, 1974). Thanks to the input provided by Ruth Cohn and her extensive experience with group processes in TCI groups, TCI now has a number of leadership methods at its disposal which contribute to creating a "sufficiently well-developed We" in various groups with different tasks.

The TCI method of group leadership, however, could also be increasingly employed as a model for social learning in school classes, especially those suffering from a difficult composition. The theoretical discussion surrounding social learning has failed to mention this possibility explicitly. In the practical guidelines on improving communication, on the other hand, individual elements of TCI methodology (such as its auxiliary rules or the Disturbance Postulate) do appear, albeit unfortunately without a sufficient understanding of the entire concept.

There have also been some successful implementations of TCI in the area of team development (Burkhardt & Schneider-Landolf, 2009; Greimel, 2003; Stahl, 1998).

---

12 One should note that not all disturbances concern the "We," that is, the interpersonal relationships in a group. In some instances, they may also be solely a concern of an individual "I" and its own personal conflicts.

13 For this reason, the training to become a TCI group leader also comprises "crisis courses."

The "It"

Martina Emme and Jochen Spielmann

1 Definition

In addition to the "I," the "We," and the "Globe," the "It" is one of the four factors in the four-factor model.

A First Approach

In TCI, the factor "It" refers to "things," "contents," "objects," "subject matter" (for learning), etc. The "It" can comprise anything from nature, the environment, society, culture, religion, etc. It is typical of TCI that contents are taken just as seriously and have the same importance as the other factors "I" and "We" (= the equivalence hypothesis). This makes TCI (like organizational development) one of the few comprehensive social concepts to attach such importance to functional matters.

A Second Approach

Matthias Kroeger introduced into TCI the thought that people have a basic need to deal with *something*, with a *thing*, with "It" – both with regard to themselves and in conjunction with others. "TCI says that a human being becomes a human being [. . .] only when confronted with tasks, with things that they can make their own. The dialogic of TCI, that is, the fact of being-in-a-relationship, refers largely not to persons [. . .], but to things, the material world and its humane or inhumane conditions [. . .]. Objects and tasks are, in the sense of TCI, not things that (unfortunately) burden and bother our pure humanity – our 'true' human relationships and feelings (meaning we would be more human and freer without them). Rather, they are requisite to and an unshakable, undeniable element of our humanity, necessary for the depth of our humanity. We become human when we accept such themes, especially those that go beyond our own pure personality. That is the central presumption of TCI" (Kroeger, 1992, pp. 111 f.). This "essential theme orientation" (ibid., p. 96) allows TCI to unfold a potential that allows us to "outgrow" ourselves.

A Third Approach

In an extension of this thought, the concept of TCI assumes that people who work together on some project will develop both as individuals and socially because of this common task. The contents, i.e., the respective objects of the group's concern, binds them together. That is the "third thing" that is able to bring people together and keep them together. Thus, in this sense, the "It" denotes a thing, an object, a task that draws a number of people *together* to work on that task *together*. In fact, people become a group only *because* and *whenever* they come together to deal with something that needs to be done or dealt with. It is Ruth Cohn's special merit that she discovered how the "cohesive" power and the "pull" of a common interest becomes an active, structural factor in group processes; this is what makes TCI group work so unique. Without an "It" there is no group. This aspect of a common concern was so important to Ruth Cohn that she made it one of the corners of her TCI triangle.

In her writings, Ruth Cohn employed a number of paraphrases for "It":

- "the small part or aspect of the world of things and events around which a group gathers" (Matzdorf & Cohn, 1992, p. 72; see also Farau & Cohn, 1984, p. 355).
- "the common task" (Matzdorf & Cohn, 1992, p. 70).
- "the mini-part of the Globe to which a person or persons in a group direct their attention" (personal communication of Ruth Cohn, 1986, to Helmut Reiser, quoted in Reiser, 1987, p. 41).

"It," then, is what brings individuals together and gives them a reason to deal with something. The "It" is what keeps the group together. If and because it is in the interest of all members of such a group to work on the matter at hand, a community-creating connection ensues that forces a qualitative leap into action: "If [...] the task of all 'I's is made one's own personal task, and if this relationship to one another is desired and supported, then that is the optimal work situation" (Farau & Cohn, 1984, p. 354). "It" thus implies the comprehensive theme with which a group is occupied – not a preformulated, formalized theme (from the course, meeting, etc.) – and not the → TCI Theme (Matzdorf & Cohn, 1992, p. 78).

A Fourth Approach

For Ruth Cohn, however, not every "It" was acceptable. Whether a particular thing, object, or content is beneficial to the individual and to the environment must first be subjected to a reality and value check. Without such orientation, even group solidarity and performance can be dangerous. An example: "A military team is discussing a snatch and retaliatory strike. [...] Caring, life-promoting themes are something different indeed – they concern general, humanistic values and the needs of human beings. They cannot be based on creating corpses in some faraway country or some distant future" (Matzdorf & Cohn,

1992, p. 72). Thus, for Ruth Cohn, the "It" is inseparably connected with the → axioms and postulates.

Why Ruth Cohn chose to use the term "It" for things, objects, contents, tasks, etc., is not known. She likely was drawn to the grammatical structure of "I – We – It." There would not appear to be any other hidden meaning in her choice.

The "It" of TCI, however, should be confused with the "Id" of psychoanalysis. The two terms signify something completely different.

2 Origin

According to Kroeger (1992, p. 112), the emphasis TCI places on *being in a relationship with things* is "shared with the basic socialist impulse and with core Marxist teachings. For Marx, real-world things relate to the very core being of humans. For this reason, he called real-world things 'essence materials' in the true sense of the word: Because we are, with all that we are, unalterably in a relationship to these objects and they to us, they determine us in our being, consciously or unconsciously, desired or not. We can free ourselves from them at best only partially. If we do not shape them in a humane way, they will intervene negatively in our being and, because of their essentiality, make us inhumane. They have the capacity to deform us, to alienate us – from ourselves and from others and from the real world of objects." Kroeger claims that Ruth Cohn was influenced by the writings of Marx.

Ruth Cohn herself was a great observer of her own professional and private life in which again and again concrete matters, objects, contents, and tasks occurred – being a working mother, raising children, emigrating from Germany, immigrating to the United States, politics, etc. She observed and reflected on everything, and from her experiences came to the conclusion to provide the "It" with equal factor status in her four-factor model.

Ruth Cohn used the term "It" in the philosophical sense of Martin Buber. In his dialogical principle, Buber differentiated between principles of encounter, his basic relationships: "I-It" and "I-You." The world of "It" is that of objects and objectivized experiences: "I perceive something. I feel something. I think something [...]. All of this and the like together form the realm of It" (Buber, 1979, p. 8). In contrast lies the "I-You" relationship, which according to Buber is what makes humans human: a dialogical principle, a relationship, mutuality, presence. Here, other laws are valid: The keywords are openness, involvement, receptiveness (Emme, 1996, pp. 19 ff.).

Sensu Buber is Ruth Cohn thoroughly dialogical (Emme, 1996, Chap. 4, pp. 151–215). She is always concerned about ensuring the quality of a living and comprehensive communication that includes one's counterpart. However, she brings Buber's transcendental dialogical principle down to Earth: Her approach is and remains pragmatic. Common concerns, formulated as themes (→ Theme), pave the way for true encounters.

3 Explanations

3.1 Reception

For a long time, many uncertainties and misunderstandings were prevalent concerning the "It." In 1997, Kügler (p. 23) made the following appraisal: "A [. . .] look at the working materials distributed in courses [. . .] as well as at the relevant literature reveals that there is presently no consensus concerning the correct way to refer to the 'third corner' of the triangle." Again and again, "It" was wrongly equated with → theme. Unfortunately, Ruth Cohn, through her choice of words in her writings, contributed to the confusion: "The It is the theme of the group, the small part or aspect of the world of things and events on which a group concentrates" (Matzdorf & Cohn, 1992, p. 72). In her own teachings, she always clearly delineated the "It" from the formulated "TCI theme." In his article Kügler says very clearly: "'It' and 'Theme' are two different things [. . .]. I would suggest retaining the term 'It' for the 'It corner' of the triangle" (1997, p. 27). The "Theme" a group is working on, in turn, is influenced by all four factors and not just by the "It." That is what separates TCI from other approaches. In this handbook, we treat "It" and "Theme" as different matters.

In the 1970s, Ruth Cohn's insistence that "It" consists only of life-affirming matters led to the adoption of an unchallenged dogma that, at least initially, tended to hinder work on questions emerging from the business world. Since about the mid-1980s, however, the discussion on values has taken place on a much broader plane and now expressly includes subjects of economic interest.

3.2 Criticism

There has been little criticism concerning the equal weight assigned to the "It" and the other factors; rather, criticism has been expressed toward the long-term practice in many TCI courses of choosing subject matters based on very individual and biographically oriented concerns. In contrast, topics from nature, the environment, society, culture, and religion were more rarely chosen. Only recently have more "hard facts" come to be used and discussed as "It."

3.3 Explanations

Just what can be an "It"? The image of an iceberg is helpful here to illustrate the many-leveled possibilities of "It." What we see above the waterline may be described using synonyms with a more cognitive meaning, such as work object, aspect, thing, question, object, subject matter, project, factual issue, performance demand. What lies below the waterline, on the other hand, in the hidden area, adds dimensions of more emotional relevance to the "It": interests, tasks, concerns, challenges, or problems. In the deeper layers, "It" is thus what might be called unexpressed commonalities, taboos, hopes, etc. Whatever we humans encounter in life and gives us the impulse to grasp, understand, question, or clarify is also contained in the "It."

These very different ways to see "It" may be divided into narrower and broader circumstances:

a) *The "It" is a more or less prescribed, given subject.*
The "It" could be something that a group or a team is confronted with – some topic for instruction in a school class or the agenda of a business meeting. Here, the group does not actually *choose* the "It," but rather *must* deal with an "It" that someone else (or some circumstance) provides for them. This sort of "forced group" generally consists of members who did not come to the group of their own free will.

b) *The "It" is freely chosen.*
A group comes together to do exactly what that group wants to do: A citizens' initiative is concerned with public transportation in their community, a project group is preparing a theater performance, a team is working on a suggestion for a new product, etc. Such groups are formed voluntarily and work together on an "It" that also glues the group together.

c) *The "It" can, within limits, be chosen by the group.*
Today, many organizations use variations of the above-mentioned alternatives. The "It" may exist, but only broadly, and is then specified according to individual and group-specific criteria by a group that does not come together solely of their own free will. Examples would be a school class that determines a number of focal points within a prescribed curriculum or a team that prepares new strategies in a company on the basis of certain guidelines.

d) *The "It" is determined through communication.*
Walter Lotz asked (2003, p. 159): "What about the It in situations and worklife in which no specific theme has been prescribed, no clearly defined object, and no generally designated task?" Lotz is thinking about social situations, such as the encounter between a shopper and a sales person in a store, parents dining with their child in a restaurant, a counselor and a client in a counseling center. In such cases, the "It" is not predetermined from the very beginning, but rather the participants must come to some consensus about a common "It." Lotz continues: "In order to determine the It, I would look at some term, something of major importance in the scenario. In social situations [...] I have to gather this information through my own interpretation – much different than a subject matter that has been prepared for all the I's and the We present. Rather, it emerges from the dynamics of the relationship and is the product of device" (Lotz, 2003, p. 161). Here, the "It" represents the objectification of a psychosocial construct based on a very differentiated perception of the overall situation. Such objectifying detachment allows the TCI concept to be employed in many different types of counseling situations (→ TCI and Counseling; → TCI and Supervision; → TCI and Organizational Development).

The "Globe"

Walter Nelhiebel

1 Definition

Like the "I," the "It," and the "We," the "Globe" belongs to the four elements of the TCI structure model, which describes the four categories of factors active in groups. "The Globe consists of people and events beyond the Here-and-Now-group. This external world – the familial, the professional, the hierarchical, the ecological facets, etc. – is always active within a group, though situated on the outside" (Farau & Cohn, 1984, p. 354).

Ruth Cohn describes various aspects of the "Globe" in "concentric circles" or "shells" that define the "I-It-We" triangle. She emphasizes the interaction of the "I," the "It," and the "We" with the "Globe": "We must pay attention to how the Globe affects us and to how we affect the Globe. Otherwise, we are like the captain at sea who knows his own ship but pays no heed to the conditions of the ocean, the wind, and the geographical circumstances. If you don't know the Globe, the Globe will eat you up" (Farau & Cohn, 1984, p. 355).

Ruth Cohn (1989) differentiated three "shells" of the "Globe":

1. First, "Globe" means, pragmatically, the surroundings of a course or workgroup and its members: the people involved, the events and institutional circumstances. These things influence the group and are influenced by the group. This is true for the place where the group meets, the time, the composition of the group members (social stratum, sex, age, level of education, etc.). But it also means the existing hierarchies that determine the course, the curriculum, operational changes, church services, or political action. On this topic, Ruth Cohn writes: "If we fail to become acquainted with the economic, political, social, and societal map of a school or a business or a country, and if we do not include the extended environment in our planning and decisions, then the actions of the body in question will be irrelevant or even dangerous. An example would be not looking a recession in the eye and searching for alternative solutions, but rather remaining bogged down in irrelevant themes that prevent us from discovering new and creative possibilities" (Farau & Cohn, 1984, p. 356).
2. Second, "Globe" means all the individual members of the group or employees of a company, citizens of a city, of a country, members of a society, etc. For Ruth Cohn, this designation is not neutral, i.e., there is a definite political dimension to it. In her conversation with Schulz von Thun she said the following: "My whole person is a stake-

holder in this world, by the very fact of my living in this world. Whether I like or not, my being a stakeholder means I have the task of living my life politically, that is, for the community" (Cohn & Schulz von Thun, 1994, p. 53).

3. Third, the term "Globe" can also designate more distant people as well as historical, planetary, and astronomic events. This includes things passed on in words and writing, past and present institutions, visible and invisible heavenly bodies, known and unknown material and intellectual forces. "The Globe expands to include the cosmos. Everything is connected to everything else and to everyone else, whenever and wherever it happened, happens, or will happen" (Farau & Cohn, 1984, p. 355).

2 Origin

The word "Globe" originally designated a term loaned from the Latin original "globus" and used from the 15th century on to mean a "ball, sphere, lump," in particular the spherical Earth in the geographical or astronomical sense. The adjective "global" means "pertaining to the whole world" and is also used in the figurative sense to mean "worldwide, comprehensive; broadly, approximately."

Between 1963 and 1965, Ruth Cohn attempted to outline the complexity of her insights about the various factors that influence group processes. She came up with the image of the pyramid with the four factors as four corners. The graphical representation eventually was changed from the symbol of a pyramid to that of a triangle inside a sphere, which is optically easier to grasp (Farau & Cohn, 1984, pp. 343 f.).

3 Explanations

3.1 Reception and Criticism

In his critical contribution entitled "Globe – die unbekannte Größe" (Globe – The Unknown Factor), Schreyögg (1993, pp. 12 f.) notes that, except for psychodrama, TCI was originally the only agogic action model that proposed to include not just individual and relationship factors, but also the context ("Globe"). TCI is both an educational-therapeutic and a social approach (an action model) that can be employed to humanize task-driven social systems.

The role of the "Globe" in TCI should be seen against the background in the changes that took place in the *zeitgeist* since the 1940s. The ideal image of a human being became one of a unique and individual being in continual development over the course of his or her life, a being who goes beyond the limits of institutional involvement.

On the other side there were bureaucratically structured work environments, where the individual, like a machine, is integrated into a preprogrammed, collaborative structure. Some authors (e.g., Argyris, 1975) thought such an environment robbed humans of their distinctive individuality and alienated them.

The goal of enabling direct, human encounters became the gold standard for all relationships. In all confrontations with professional and political systems the primary objective was to locate pressing problems.

Against this background it is not surprising that the themes represented by the "Globe" in TCI turned out to be rather impressionistic: The "Globe" was generally held to be the source of disturbances (Schreyögg, 1993, p. 14) (→ Disturbance Postulate). There was little understanding for the fact that the structures of social system do not precipitate only constraints and destruction, but also carry with them the potential for stabilization. The goal cannot lie in eliminating or surmounting all institutionalizations with their organizational constraints, but in shaping them to be livable and pleasant.

In the 1980s and 1990s, positive methods for structuring work conditions became the main task conceived for projects on humanizing worklife. And up to this very day it remains one of the main premises of organizational development to maintain a balance between the "competitiveness of an organization," on the one hand, and "employee satisfaction," on the other hand (Becker & Langosch, 2002) (→ TCI for Managers).

Statzer's (1995) analysis of the course offerings of WILL (Workshop Institute for Living Learning) over a period of 8 years showed that in TCI "Globe" themes are generally discussed via the "I": How does the Globe affect me? How do I affect the Globe? That has likely not changed recently. Statzer's theory, in short, says the following: Discussing the Globe via "I" leads to a culture of powerlessness; the secret power lies in stabilizing the status quo. This was surely not Ruth Cohn's intention: She preferred to see TCI as socially and politically engaged in effecting social change (→ Historical and Political Fundamentals).

3.2 Relationship to Other Technical Terms

Schreyögg (1993) noted critically that the idea of "Globe" needs to be more precise. In the following I would like to show how this term can be understood in the context of other social-scientific technical terms and the respective theories: What questions can be deduced from these theories and applied to our understanding of TCI's "Globe"?

1. The initial meaning of Ruth Cohn's concept of "Globe" may be best described by the term *context* – what surrounds us. This includes, in the sociological sense, certain characteristics of environments, situations, and milieus. The important term is *situation*, which means a spatially and temporally structured complex of objective determinants of a social relationship embedded within other circumstances. These determinants affect an active subject who is presently behaving in a certain way. The question is: What is the connection to the task at hand? What is presently affecting that person's behavior?[1]

---

1 "Situation" is a central term in sociological action theory. Noteworthy are Kempski (1954), Parsons (1961), and Dreitzel (1968).

2. Every group member and every group represents an element in a number of various *systems* (family, company, city, etc.). The term system is a basic keyword in sociology used when analyzing interactions, i.e., how several individuals, groups, or organizations act toward one another (interdependent behavior). This fits the second meaning of the term "Globe" (every group member is an employee, a citizen, etc.). Every system has its limits and interacts with the surrounding environment. The questions regarding "Globe" analysis are: What system or systems are we talking about here? Which are the relevant system environments and what effect are they presently having on the respective system?
   In contrast to system theory, which takes a neutral position, Ruth Cohn staked a political claim. She saw it as a human obligation to be political, that is, to be active in the community. Further, she considered the emotional dimension to be of great importance: "It's all about feeling sympathy for others" (cf. Cohn, 1989). In a "Globe" analysis, the question is: What *task* or *mission* motivates the group members and what moves them?
   Every system offers a certain amount of integration and coherence in the relationship of its elements to one another, i.e., it has a *structure*. Structure is a relatively stable entity that is subject to certain regularities in the way it creates and maintains the relationships among the system elements. We then study certain specific areas in such a structure, such as way expectations, norms, positions, roles, groups, organizations, institutions, layers, or classes are ordered.[2] "Globe" analysis is thus concerned with the structure, the fabric into which the individual group members or the entire group in their respective system are woven.
   Which *values* determine the action within a system? Under "values" we understand the opinions shared by individuals, groups, or organizations as to what is desirable or worthwhile, which in turn limit and influence the possible procedures, means, and goals available.
   What are the *norms* that determine behavior? What should one do or not do? "Norms" are generally accepted rules of conduct; behavioral demands made of those in certain social roles. They regulate how each individual member of a social entity (a group, an organization, a society) should act in a particular situation or should act toward another member of that social entity.
3. The third meaning of "Globe" may be described as *culture* (→ Interculturality). Under "culture" we understand the totality of all life forms, guiding principles, and living conditions precipitated by human activities among a population within a historically and regionally circumscribed time and space. Culture includes:
   - All material forms of the physical environment that have been inherited from earlier generations and are subject to further development and change (buildings, tools, machines).

2 Durkheim (1895) first used the term "systemic" in his work *Les règles de la méthode sociologique*. Together with the idea of function, this is the central research goal of the Structural-Functional Theory (Parsons, 1960: Structure and Process in Modern Societies). The latter research approach was developed further by Luhmann to become system theory (1984, *Soziale Systeme*; 1997, *Die Gesellschaft der Gesellschaft*).

- The knowledge and use of lawfully based natural processes including human life (science and technology).
- All ideas, values, ideals, and meanings.
- Methods and institutions of human coexistence.

Corporate and *organizational* cultures are relevant to "Globe" analysis (among other things). These terms originated in organizational psychology and the teachings of business organization. The concept of organizational culture transfers the idea of culture from cultural anthropology to organizations. Accordingly, every organization has its own culture that is largely responsible for organized behavior. This culture results from the interaction of values, norms, attitudes, and paradigms the employees have in common. The organizational culture shapes life within the organization and its external appearance. This culture plays a major role in the creation of a corporate identity and a corporate design of the company or organization[3] (→ TCI and Organizational Development).

3.3 Controversies and Divisive Issues

In principle is TCI, with its context-based model of action, the ideal method for → organizational development or – in terms of systems theory – for reconstructing the "Globe."

"If I assume that *my Globe* does not exist independently of me, but that I as an observer 'construct' the Globe; if I assume that there is a reality that is independent of me, while assuming at the same time that I cannot objectively recognize it, but rather can only perceive what it possible to perceive with my own senses, which corresponds to the extent of my observational possibilities. My Globe is not your Globe – so what is the Globe?"[4]

TCI offers a methodological approach for looking at our own individual constructions of the respective organization and, if necessary, to reconstruct them both individually and collectively.

To date, the practice of TCI does not have at its disposal a model for systematically analyzing the construction of the respective "Globe" and for creating a methodological approach to change. Such a model would be helpful in counteracting the frequently experienced powerlessness we feel when confronted with "Globe" conditions. The only thing available is a catalog of questions that can be operatively implemented in advance of course planning as a means of analyzing the initial situation. Langmaack notes such examples for the causal component of the "Globe" of various target audiences (2001, pp. 130f.), and Greving (2003, pp. 69f.) includes them for → dynamic balance.

3 Cf. Wikipedia Organizational Culture. It is important also to point to E. H. Schein (2007).
4 This quote is taken from an unpublished speech held by Helmut Reiser on the thoughts of N. Luhmann about system theory and the construction of the Globe in the further development of TCI, held during the RCI theory workshop in 2008.

In light of the challenges posed by the "Globe," the threats to the ecological system called Earth, and to the living conditions of future generations (and in light of the aspirations of TCI), this matter is all the more pressing. Ruth Cohn was convinced: "Humanity has to become more potent in the 20th century than ever before" (Cohn, 1988, p. 5). And, I would add, this state of affairs has not changed in the 21st century!

To this end, training and continued education in TCI should devote even more valuable space to the "Globe."

3.4 Further Development

A further development in our understanding of "Globe" might occur on two levels: First, on the theoretical level, where we are concerned with understanding "Globe" interconnections, there should be a construction kit from which various system models could be built, in particular ones dealing with social contexts (Schreyögg, 1993). To this end, we could use approaches from system theory and organizational theory. As part of a RCI theory workshop held in 2008, the participants studied this task against the background of the system theory of Niklas Luhmann.[5] It is also necessary to expand this theory with insights stemming from organizational development. Second, on the practical level, instruments should be made available for preparing a well-grounded "Globe" analysis, and with which interventions could be launched via the processes that go beyond the individual group and affect the entire organization. If we are to reach this goal, it will be necessary to strengthen the standing of organizational development within TCI.

The combination of the most important elements of TCI – personality development, authenticity, empowerment, and empathy as well as the mission derived from the axioms – with a (system) theoretically well-founded epistemology and the knowledge of organizational change processes would lay claim to one of the pivotal characteristics and chances contained in TCI.

5 Here there is to date only an unpublished workshop report by Helmut Reiser.

Dynamic Balance

Jochen Spielmann

1 Definition

The term "dynamic balance" contains both a *figure of thought* as well as a concrete *instruction* for leadership. "Dynamic balance is a very general life concept: the necessity of including opposite poles in life [...]. Life is characterized not by static states, but by our being exposed to constant reorientation. The idea of dynamic balance is one way of demonstrating how to favor living learning/teaching and a vibrant life" (Farau & Cohn, 1984, pp. 353 f.).

The *figure of thought* contained in dynamic balance is a thought process that embraces opposites and paradoxes; it has the task of perceiving opposites by constantly changing the perspective. It also introduces them into the leadership role, demanding constant reshifting and rebalancing, if only for a very short time, only to take a new perspective once again. "The idea of 'dynamic balance' means integrating contradictory forces and tendencies as well as combining different individual aspects (examples are intellect and feeling, I – We – It – Globe). Such an idea accommodates the presumption of holism and at the same time resolves the problem of mediating between opposites and differences by assuming that, when we view things dialectically or equivocally, we are put in the position of creating a 'dynamic balance' by synthesizing the opposites or by continually changing our perspective" (Lotz, 1995, pp. 78 f.). Helmut Reiser's position is also plausible: "In contrast to other 'humanistic' concepts of group work, in TCI methodology the contradiction is considered an integral part of the balance achieved, the interruption of the flow that occurs in a group" (1995, p. 25). Reiser continues: "The operative rule in the methodological model of TCI lies in the contradiction inherent in the establishment of connections and the respect for different perspectives. Unity and diversity are the opposites that are synthesized in the figure called 'dynamic balance': The more I perceive of the autonomy of the respective other perspective, the better I can make contact to other perspectives. The more I am aware of the interdependence of perspectives, the more I can do justice to the internal dynamics of the respective perspectives" (1995, p. 25).

The *instruction* involved in dynamic balance refers to the continual effort on the part of the leader to rebalance the four factors "I," "We," "It," and "Globe." It is the task of the leader to ensure that the equality of the four factors does not cause stagnation and sterility. This means that, at least for a while, there will be an imbalance. Ruth Cohn said it like this: "The statement that the I, We, and It of a group must be seen as equal does not mean that these factors will always demand equal attention" (Farau & Cohn, 1984, p. 598). "They should [...], depending on the respective situation, receive a variable amount of intensity and attention" (Matzdorf & Cohn, 1992, p. 74). Ruth Cohn used the image of a "bicycle with three pedals named 'I,' 'We,' and 'It'" (1989, p. 50). "If the group is overly concerned with, say, one particular participant, then I can press on the 'We' pedal or the 'It' pedal to bring back the balance" (ibid., p. 50). "There are nearly unlimited verbal and nonverbal techniques for switching from one 'pedal' to another. This change within I-We-It-Globe brings life to the dynamic interaction and is the driving force behind the liveliness of a TCI group" (ibid., pp. 50 f.).

The idea of continually changing perspectives, however, does not refer only to the four factors. "Other 'polarities' that stand in a holistic relationship to one another, such as nearness and distance, participation and independence, security and the willingness to bear risks, may also adhere to the principle of dynamic change" (Matzdorf & Cohn, 1992, p. 91). "'Dynamic balance' [...] can be used with other life factors, too, for example, the dynamic balance between our need for security and our willingness to run risks, between feeling and thinking, between femininity and masculinity, between giving and taking, between nearness and distance, between listening and speaking, between activity and quietude, etc." (ibid., p. 74).

Over the course of many years, dynamic balance developed from a *synchronic* to a *diachronic* affair. In her 1984 publication entitled *Gelebte Geschichte der Psychotherapie* (The Living History of Psychotherapy), Ruth Cohn spoke of a synchronic dynamic balance: "In the process of group work the emphasis on the individual factors is variable; but the *dynamic balance*, both as a principle and as a compass, remains constant and is always reestablished within a short period of time" (Farau & Cohn, 1984, p. 353). In a contribution she published together with Paul Matzdorf in 1992, "Das Konzept der Themenzentrierten Interaktion" (The Concept of Theme-Centered Interaction), however, her understanding of dynamic balance had undergone a revision. There she writes: "The four factors (I, We, It, Globe) cannot persist longer than perhaps a few minutes in complete balance. Yet they can be treated in a diachronic balance, that is, in a consecutive series of interactions" (Matzdorf & Cohn, 1992, p. 91). Then, the idea of "diachronic balance" is expanded upon: "Dynamic balance is generally speaking the compass for every session of a TCI workgroup. Yet there are often groups in which, in addition to moments of synchronism – the simultaneous effort at achieving balance – instead a sequentiality, a diachronic balance, occurs and is in fact desirable. Intellectual phases follow emotional phases; personal exchanges replace practical work (or vice versa), individual work is followed by group work, physical activity by reflection, short speeches by long discussions" (ibid., p. 75).

2 Origin

In her *Gelebte Geschichte der Psychotherapie* (The Living History of Psychotherapy), Ruth Cohn wrote the following: "I needed a long time, and then only with the help of my friend Toni Horn, to find what I was looking for – the idea of 'dynamic balance'" (Farau & Cohn, 1984, p. 621). This term clearly sums up Ruth Cohn's ideas of working with paradoxes (→ Educational Fundamentals) and combines a number of her philosophical, spiritual, and scientific concepts:

- "'Dynamic balance' is a very general life concept: the necessity of including opposite poles in life, much as in the Chinese concept of Yin and Yang" (Farau & Cohn, 1984, pp. 353 f.).
- "Dynamic balance is one of the core ideas in TCI. It refers to the task of always reestablishing a balance within an existential paradox (we're a biological unit and at the same time a social-cosmic being). This is a balance between the I-We-It factors of the group; a balance between physical, emotional, intellectual, and spiritual needs and desires; a balance between giving and taking, listening and speaking, activity and quietude, etc." (Cohn, 1975, p. 161).
- "In modern physics the universe reveals itself to be a dynamic, indivisible totality that necessarily includes the observer. This is where traditional terms, such as space, time, isolated objects, or cause and effect, become meaningless. This insight is related to the experiences referred to by Eastern mystics" (Farau & Cohn, 1984, p. 621). In her *Gelebte Geschichte der Psychotherapie* (The Living History of Psychotherapy), Ruth Cohn refers to, among others, Fritjof Capra and even quotes from the Introduction to his book from 1984 entitled "The Turning Point": "To achieve such a state of dynamic balance, a radically different social and economic structure will be needed: a cultural revolution in the true sense of the world. The survival of our whole civilization may depend on whether we can bring about such a change" (quoted in Farau & Cohn, 1984, p. 621).

3 Explanations

3.1 Background

The term *dynamic balance* was coined by Ruth Cohn, and the linguistic polarity contained therein is intentional: Whereas "balance" generally describes the idea of something having achieved equilibrium, the "dynamic" part contains the idea of change. The task of continually reestablishing a balance is present more in the term *dynamic balancing* than in the term *dynamic balance*. The opposite, in Ruth Cohn's view, is "vertigo" (or disequilibrium). "Vertigo disorders occur when individuals neglect shifting from work to quietude, from give to take, to spending too much time with children and too little time with adults (or vice versa), too much training or too little practice, etc." (Farau & Cohn, 1984, p. 353).

Ruth Cohn used a number of different terms and descriptions:
- "Dynamic-organic equilibrium" (Cohn, 1975, p. 210),
- "Dynamic balance" (Farau & Cohn, 1984, p. 353),
- "Dynamic balancing" (Matzdorf & Cohn, 1992, p. 75),
- "Dynamic equilibrium" (Matzdorf & Cohn, 1992, p. 75),
- "Dynamic change" (Matzdorf & Cohn, 1992, p. 91).

In addition, Ruth Cohn described the function of this term very differently: *Dynamic balance* is sometimes referred to as a "compass" (Matzdorf & Cohn, 1992, p. 75), other times as a "principle" (ibid., p. 91), then again as an "attention tool" (Farau & Cohn, 1984, p. 354), and again as a "general life concept" (ibid., pp. 353 f.).

To Ruth Cohn, balance is always a dynamic thing. She writes: "Static equilibrium exists in principle only at death, and even there things only appear to be static. Every living creature, every movement, is based on the possibility that one can lose one's balance and recover it once again. Holding on to something, even at the highest moment of equilibrium, quickly becomes a desperate disorder and a fossilization" (Matzdorf & Cohn, 1992, p. 75).

The concept of TCI contains two hypotheses that are closely connected to each other:
1. "The equilibrium hypothesis [...] says that the interactional group does not just work theme-centered, but equally person-centered, group-centered, theme-centered, and globe-centered. [...] The four factors are equal moments within a holistically determined life and group course" (Matzdorf & Cohn, 1992, p. 74).
2. "The idea of dynamic balance goes beyond the triangle within the sphere" (Farau & Cohn, 1984, p. 353).

The first hypothesis is concerned with "what" happens, the second with "how" it happens. The first hypothesis denotes and describes the four concrete factors and their relationship to one another, whereas the second one comprises many more elements that go beyond the four elements in the first hypothesis and designates a concrete goal.

3.2 Reception

Dynamic balance was received and understood in two very different ways. The first direction took up the thought of *balance* – the idea of reaching a certain equilibrium that is to be maintained: the concept of being balanced, of being even keel or along a plumb line. This approach contains the desire to reach this state as quickly as possible and to stay there as long as possible. The everyday use of the terms balance and equilibrium correspond to this approach. *Dynamic balance* and TCI were often (wrongly) accused of projecting a harmonizing worldview (→ Critical Approaches to the Concept). Sarah Hoffmann and Elisabeth Gores-Pieper in their contribution to this handbook formulated it as follows:

"The progressive and educational impetus of Ruth Cohn's early writings tended to deflect from the reflexive orientation of TCI and led to the assumption that Ruth Cohn was following her vision of world harmony when she conceived the idea of dynamic balance. Yet the strength of the TCI model lies in the way it approaches polarities and sees in them productive conflicts and the potential for growth" (→ Rivalry and Competition).

The other direction was oriented more toward these productive conflicts, putting the idea of balancing at the forefront, i.e., the idea of promoting what has previously been ignored. "Balancing yourself means looking at the other side of the coin" (Osswald, 1984, p. 139).

Most of the images and symbols used for this phenomenon tend to correspond more to "keeping one's balance" than to "balancing."

3.3 Critique

Especially the idea of synchronic balance, which is connected to the idea of harmony, garnered much criticism. Helmut Reiser (1995, p. 25) formulated it as follows: "In my opinion, having as a goal the harmonious flow of development in a group rather hinders the development of autonomy and interdependence and encourages harmonizing tendencies. It stops the group from looking at opposites, at the 'dark side' of things, at 'disorders.' In the sense of a humanistic-holistic conviction and terminology, this puts too much emphasis on creating a harmonious entity through dynamic balancing. The way I see it, the desire for bonding is the root of hidden, that is, unconscious (self-)deceptions. The important first step toward become conscious is missed: formulating the opposite side, which is often considered a 'disruption,' a 'disturbance.' In such cases of 'disturbing' interventions, the balance returns as a spontaneous mental effort on the part of the individual and the group at a higher and more satisfying level than is possible if the leader had attempted to force it."

Hartmut Raguse (1992b, pp. 271 f.) was even more severe in his criticism: "The balance principle is an illusion. For me this is true also for the balance between I, We, and It. I am not opposed to a certain measure of balance, but I think it's more meaningful to learn to accept unavoidable frustrations with a certain serenity. To that end, it would seem to me to be necessary to develop an inner, friendly stance that allows me to be kind to myself, to encourage myself, to console myself, and sometimes even to be proud of myself and to enjoy being better at something that others. In this sense, balance is something like an inner counterweight to external stress and disappointment. Perhaps it can give me the freedom to persevere and once in a while also to be forbearing. – If 'balance' is to be saved at all, it needs a measure of 'nonbalance.'"

3.4 Outlook

Apart from the major change from synchronic to diachronic balance, the idea of *dynamic balance* did not experience much development over time. The idea of Diether Craemer

(1988, p. 32) to use the term homeostasis known from the natural sciences in TCI has yet to catch on. Outside of TCI, on the other hand, the idea of *dynamic balancing* did turn up in a number of approaches and concepts, particularly in so-called life-work-balance approaches. It remains an open question whether it would be wise to rename the term to *dynamic balancing*.

Living Learning

Dietrich Stollberg and Mina Schneider-Landolf

1 Definition

Living learning is a method or an attitude Ruth Cohn introduced to TCI. On the one hand, it makes clear that the TCI method is concerned with learning processes, and, on the other hand, that she did not think conventional learning/teaching settings were very lively.

In the sense of progressive education[1] and experiential education[2], Ruth Cohn drew on ideas from → Humanistic Psychology to propagate overcoming a practice of teaching that is oriented solely toward instilling and then testing "sterile information." Such learning and teaching settings can become living ones only if they are not boring, that is, uninteresting to both young and older learners, purely informative, and cognitively oriented. Living learning is more – it is holistic because it pays attention to the intellect, the emotions, the body, the thoughts, the feelings, and the actions of the pupil.

Life means movement. Being statically fixed or sitting still is anathema to living learning.[3] The rhythm of quiet and movement, concentration and relaxation helps to create vitality and furthers the creative skills that are necessary to live and survive.

On the one hand, living learning is a specific method of learning and teaching to be used in school and vocational settings, as part of a greater educational concept (Matzdorf, 1993; Reiser & Lotz, 1995). On the other hand, it characterizes learning processes that take place in TCI-led groups, even if they do not convene for the purpose of learning something (e.g., workgroups, project groups, therapy groups, encounter groups). A process become "living" if everyone present, including the leader, are involved with their whole

1 Around the turn of the 20th century intensive efforts arose to create alternative educational concepts. These new concepts were influenced by and in turn influenced the youth movement and the critical intellectual currents of the day, which came to be found in expressionistic and existentialist art and literature (see on this Schmid, 1973).

2 Among others, Kurt Hahn used sailing trips and other excursions as educational forays. This was an alternative encounter method with youths who were taught to engage the powers of nature (ocean, forest, wilderness) through emotional experiences and independent actions and thus compensate for previous educational deficits.

3 Wilhelm Reich considered sitting to be a life-threatening activity. For him, moving rhythmically in the sense of expansion and contraction were the cornerstones of vitality. See the book "TZI bewegt und bewegende TZI" (TCI Moves and Moving TCI) by Buschmann and Kröner (2000).

personality and are willing to encounter the other participants as well as be concerned with the objective matter at hand.

"Learning something from an encounter with another means retaining something of you in me [...]. Let's take an example: We are both watching a painter paint a picture. At that point in time, there are at least three different ideas about this picture: that of the painter, yours, and mine. If we three then exchange our impressions, our knowledge of that picture grows to beyond us and the picture itself" (Cohn, 1989, p. 16).

This TCI-specific aspect of learning by interaction in a group may be found in the typical encounter groups of the 1970s. The primary goal of such groups was personality building and claimed to further personality development in the participants. Today, the learning implied would be considered emotional learning and social learning, the goal being to develop ego-competence, emotional competence, and social competence.

Korte (1999) describes the simple three-part formula of living – learning – encountering in his article "Alle guten Dinge sind drei" (The Best Things Come in Threes). His emphasis lies on the relationship between the teacher and the pupil, though that is not something completely new to TCI. For Ruth Cohn, understanding encounters also means understanding the encounters that take place among the group members. One of the specific contributions TCI made to living learning was to use the "We" of the group (in the sense of collecting new insights into group interaction) in order to learn about one another from the dialectic of dependence and independence.

2 Origin

Ruth Cohn first used the term "lebendiges Lernen" (living learning) in a German-language publication in 1975. The complete term was "living learning encounter" (Cohn, 1971), to refer to a new approach coined during the foundation phase of the WILL Institute in New York. According to Ruth Cohn, Norman Lieberman, one of the founding members of the Institute who went on to teach TCI in Europe, was the one who thought up this phrase. His version clearly shows that this term refers to a sort of learning that has a connection to life (the experiences of body and soul) and is concerned with the encounter (between the learner and the teacher).

A closer look reveals that the learning style being (rightly) criticized in this phrase is that of "dead learning," a deformed type of learning rejected by enlightened teachers throughout history – from antiquity ("non scholae sed vitae discimus"[4]) to the onset of modern times by reform pedagogues under the influence of humanism, by Comenius, by the teachings of classical pietism, by Pestalozzi (learning with "head, heart, and hand"), by the progressive educationists in the early 20th century, all the way to the antiauthori-

4 The original, more critical version by Seneca reads "Non vitae, sed scholae discimus."

tarian movement of A. S. Neill and finally by the representatives of experiential pedagogics (→ Educational Fundamentals).

Ruth Cohn herself derived her concept of living learning not primarily from the approaches preached by other educational movements, but rather from her own manifold experiences gathered while teaching. Her work as a "student teacher" and later as a psychotherapist in the Bankstreet School[5] in New York revealed to her a type of "progressive education" that she liked. This sort of teaching was shaped by American pragmatism[6] while also reflecting insights from psychoanalysis. There she learned a radical form of respect for the individual child and for self-determined learning.[7] She came to understand how to best preserve and maintain a child's natural enthusiasm and spontaneous will to learn. "In the Bankstreet School children were real and important people, not educational objects [...]. When I look back, I see that Bankstreet was the source of living learning for me" (Cohn, 1994, p. 327).

In her later teaching activities at the Psychoanalytic Institute, she noticed the differences between the vitality of the learning processes in encounter groups and the rigidity found in the conventional lectures at the university (Cohn, 1994, pp. 325–333). Her reflection on the causes of these differences led her to formulate her insights concerning "living learning."

There is a striking similarity between her thoughts and those contained in the less well-known concept of learning and teaching offered by Carl Rogers (1974), who drew conclusions about how best to teach and learn at school and at the university based on his insights gained from research into person-centered psychotherapy at about the same time as Ruth Cohn.[8] Both shared a fundamentally optimistic attitude toward learners – a deep trust in their willingness to learn and in the curiosity of children in general. He too criticized a directive and controlling teaching style that led learners down the path to passivity. There are, however, no indications that Ruth Cohn was aware of his writings on this matter at the time.[9]

5 In order to work as a practicing psychoanalyst, during her initial years in the United States, Ruth Cohn first had to take a "detour" by obtaining a license as a teacher. First, she worked as a "student teacher," then as a psychologist in the Bankstreet School, an institution where progressive educational principles were being applied to instructing teachers as well as pupils in the Institute's own grade schools and research projects.

6 The Bankstreet Schools were primarily oriented toward the educational approaches of G. H. Mead and J. Dewey.

7 In Europe, the antiauthoritarian approach of A. S. Neill became popular. Progressive education in its most radical form, however, was rejected by German educationists. On this see the explanations of D. Tröhler and J. Oehlkers (2005, pp. 7–16) in their book entitled "Pragmatismus und Pädagogik" (Pragmatism and Pedagogics) on the reservations expressed by German educators toward American pragmatism.

8 These parallels are discussed in detail in Kroeger (1973) and in Schneider-Landolf (1987).

9 Rogers' book "The Freedom to Learn" first appeared in German in 1974 under the title "Lernen in Freiheit" (1969 originally published in English). His title "Freedom to Learn for the 80's" (published

3 Explanations

3.1 Reception

This part of the TCI learning concept was best and most decidedly implemented in religious and public → adult education as well as in part at the university level (Kroeger, 1973; Stollberg, 1982; Matzdorf, 1993). Its quality as an intermediary between theory-based and practice-based teaching as well as its usefulness in the development of the "teacher personality" were recognized in the training of teachers and in advanced teacher training (Osswald, 1990). Particularly students of psychology, education, and didactics in Switzerland, Austria, and Germany practiced TCI in their own courses and seminars as well as implementing it as a method for carrying out group lessons and for social learning. Further, TCI came to be appreciated early on as a useful instrument for analysis and reflection in the evaluation of classroom teaching during the second phase of teacher training ("referendariat" = student teaching in the classroom) and in advanced teacher training.[10]

TCI was used quite extensively in the classroom (Cohn, 1992) at the Ecole d'Humanité, a Swiss boarding school that succeeded the earlier boarding schools (under the name of *Landerziehungsheime*). A list of further implementations in schools may be found in Cohn and Terfurth (1993).[11]

At the university level, on the other hand, the educational and didactical discussion of the TCI concept of living learning had little impact, save for the writings of Stollberg (1982, 1995) and Gudjons (1995).[12] This remains an area where this method of cooperative learning and research could be implemented as an efficient method of productive group work as well as a model for social learning. Perhaps newer relevant publications from educational science, like those of Reiser and Lotz (1995) and Ewert (2008), will further this goal.

---

in English in 1982) was published under the title "Freiheit und Engagement: Personenzentriertes Lehrer und Lernen."

10 For many years the advanced teacher training in Bern, Basel, and at the Bavarian Academy for Teacher Training in Dillingen acquainted many of their trainees with the TCI concept of living learning. For information on the reception in German teacher training, see Költze (1993). Concerning TCI-based concepts of teacher training, see Osswald (1995) and Schneider-Landolf (1996).

11 The anthology edited by Cohn and Terfurth "Lebendiges Lehren und Lernen" (Living Teaching and Living Learning) (1993) contains an overview. A scientific study of the experiences gained with TCI in educational practice was done by Ewert (2008).

12 The reason likely lies in the broad emphasis put on experience instead of reflection, paired with a latent opposition by some TCI teachers to theoretical constructs. Their mistrust of "dry theory" goes back to the origins of TCI where this stance was a reaction to the outdated and lifeless methods used in schools and universities, with their one-sided emphasis on cognitive learning processes. The alternative model of learning emphasized learning with all one's senses, using bodily exercises, and interaction games without necessarily resorting to scientific publications or empirical research.

3.2 Discussion

A cursory look at the multitude of educational reform concepts prompts the question: Wherein lies the originality of the TCI method of living learning? The educational concept of TCI, with its → four-factor model and its hypothesis of the equal importance of all four factors offers a clear theoretical framework for allowing the subject matter ("It"), the person doing the learning ("I"), and the group process in the learning group ("We") to be equally involved in planning which methods are to be used. This presumes a careful advance analysis of the initial situation with such key components as task, curriculum, and time perspective ("Globe"). The TCI-specific methodological elements of seeing to it that the subject matter (→ Theme) is adapted to the interests and needs of the learners and preparing work and social forms conducive to learning pave the way for a → dynamic balance between "I," "We," and "It." Formulating the theme directs the group's attention to the subject matter, the social form chosen, and the working method, and it also drives the group process forward. It stimulates self-reflection and process-reflection. The → chairperson postulate and the → disturbance postulate allow pupils to exert their influence from the very beginning and to shape the group work – and thus to take responsibility for how the learning process proceeds.

Thus, TCI offers a complex educational concept that is open to many other teaching methods (including those particular to a specific field).[13] TCI offers a comprehensive framework both for planning and for analyzing learning situations and learning processes. Depending on the situation, emphasis may be placed on the goal of imparting certain factual contents, on educational goals, on personality development, or on social learning. The vision of "living learning" should not omit any of the three factors "I," "We," or "It." In accordance with the hypothesis of equivalence, dynamically balancing the three aspects is what makes living learning possible: The subject matter, the learning person, and the group are all elements of the teaching-learning system and mutually affect each other. Each of the three factors (as well as the "Globe" as fourth factor to be considered) can stimulate and support or hinder and inhibit living learning.

A TCI-trained teacher shapes and supports this process by choosing the proper methodology, by applying specific interventions, and by introducing his or her own personality into the process according to the TCI system. The result is → participative leadership.

Finally, I would like to illustrate the vision of living learning by listing ten of its most prominent characteristics:

1) *Trust in the human willingness to learn:* The teacher trusts that, in their hearts, both children and adults want to learn, and that they are naturally inquisitive. If you let

13 For example, today the many methodological elements and work forms noted by Klippert (2006) may be meaningfully integrated into the overall concept of TCI. The short-term transferral of knowledge in the form of method trainings, however, did not prove to be very effective for creating a sustainable improvement in teaching methods.

people learn what interests them, they learn on their own; you must artificially motivate them only when they have to learn things that do not interest them. The teacher does not ask: How do I motivate them? The teacher asks: How do I discover my pupils' motivation?

2) Living learning has as its goal *self-determined and autonomous learning*. It does this by systematically exploring and considering the learning situation. Even when presenting prescribed subject matter, the teacher strives to determine a connection with the pupils' present life situation. This calls for individualized and differential offers (e.g., in small groups with different foci) that can be chosen on demand.
3) Living learning is *oriented toward experiences*, by making direct experiences in everyday life (e.g., in exercises, experiments, interactive games, role-playing, etc.) and the pupils' present setting the objects of learning – and by moving their own practical and professional experiences to the center of attention.
4) Living learning is *oriented toward behavior*. It is centered around those tasks the pupils have to solve in their daily life or professional life (e.g., in the scope of continuing education) in the learning situation or by offering new learning situations to try out, experiment with, or practice ("learning by doing").
5) Living learning views the *group as a source of learning*, by encouraging personal encounters and interactions among the pupils via the respective social forms (e.g., small groups and plenary sessions). The continual back and forth between autonomy and dependence with the other participants serves to support or question, to solidify or break down, one's own position.
6) Living learning is *emancipatory in nature*, by supporting self-leadership and responsibility for the learning process as well as reducing the dependence on the teacher in favor of concentration on the theme.
7) The teacher has two main tasks: *teaching and leading*. The teacher is at once the instructor and expert on the subject matter at hand, while also the organizer of the teaching situation and companion to the group process. The latter also contains the task of ensuring a dynamic balance between "I," "We," and "It."[14] To this end, the teacher maps out the methodology to be used (theme and social form, work form).
8) *Planning and process:* The vitality in a group occurs because of the unpredictable process that takes place when a theme and a planned method are combined with the actual participating members and their interactions. This process begins as soon as they commence dealing with the theme and with one another.
9) The result of living learning according to TCI is thus *only partially predictable*. It can be encouraged and furthered by the method, but it can never be completely controlled ("goal-directed"). Living learning in the presence of a prescribed subject matter produces a different process in every situation and with every new group. Thus, for the

14 On the problem of leading a TCI group, see Stollberg (1998).

teacher, even if the subject matter remains the same, learning situations are full of surprises and can stimulate one's own learning process.

10) *TCI teachers are always also learners*: That is what make the whole process so interesting! Set curricula and burnout are two things rarely found in TCI-trained teachers. Teaching according to TCI is what keeps the teachers in touch with life.

Part III

The TCI System: Practice

Theme

Mina Schneider-Landolf

1 Definition

Ruth Cohn called her educational-therapeutic model "theme-centered interaction" (Cohn, 1975), and to this day it is still known under the abbreviation TCI.[1] This designation also contains the central meaning of the term "theme" contained within this approach.

The theme sets down the common reason for a group of people to come together. That may be a common task (e.g., a church committee is discussing the renovation of the church house), a project (e.g., the staff of a counseling service is formulating its mission statement), a problem (e.g., conflicts in a management team), an assignment (e.g., to make cuts in a budget), or a curriculum (a prescribed teaching plan).

"In the TCI system, 'theme' means whatever is being addressed. In any group that is the central, the generally verbally formulated focus of attention. In a best-case scenario, the theme corresponds to the actual concern of the participants, which is usually formulated by the group leader or by some commissioning group. If the theme has been dictated by some external party, then it may not correspond to the true concern of the group participants, but rather to some particular curriculum, to some demands from the company hierarchy, or to an unreflected tradition. In such cases, only a good formulation of the theme can pique the interest of the group" (Farau & Cohn, 1984, p. 365).

Thus, a TCI theme is always very deliberately formulated, usually by the group leader or a planning team before the group meeting actually begins. The trick lies in finding a clear and precise description that engages the respective individuals with all their own experiences, knowledge, concerns, feelings, attitudes, phantasies, and questions; one that invites them to participate in the ensuing group conversation. That is how a lively process of exchange ensues among the participants: theme-centered interaction. The formulation of the theme should not lie solely at the factual level, but rather should use all the possibilities language has to express itself through poetics, metaphors, and fantasy. A theme can serve to stimulate, bore, irritate, raise curiosity, please, or annoy. Put succinctly, it

1 In the original German translations of her English writings, Ruth Cohn used the term "thematische interaktionelle Methode, TIM" (literally thematic interactional method).

speaks to the whole human being in his/her entire body-soul composition. If a theme-centered interaction is to succeed in the sense of Ruth Cohn, then it has to produce both a cognitive process and a personal growth process. "Turning 'dead' and dry subjects with no sense of relationship in small, manageable steps into human-oriented themes befitting the classroom situation or workgroups is the true passion of TCI. TCI is deeply committed to the basic assumption of the vital role the theme plays [...]. The way TCI takes on the relationship humans have toward factual matters is the secret passion of TCI" (Kroeger, 1992, p. 114).

This holistic approach to learning and working in groups is supported by the TCI-specific methodology, whereby the theme, together with other structural elements such as → social form, → work form, and timeframe, is just one of the leadership instruments that provide structure and control the process. The theme, with its precise declarations, assumes a leadership function: It centers the participants' attention – like a ball that is being thrown around by the group; it becomes the "unexplored space" (Matzdorf & Cohn, 1992, p. 78) that the individual participants can enter in their own particular way. This assumes that the leader retreats somewhat after introducing the theme, trusting in the effect the theme will have on the group and thus allowing a living process of interaction to occur among the group members. This act of trusting in the process is something only experienced TCI leaders command (→ Structure – Process – Trust).

Yet a theme can (and indeed at times must) be modified based on the contributions of the individual group members. New aspects are added or some particular aspect works its way to the top. In contrast to what is generally done in school, the leader need not intervene here. That is what differentiates a TCI theme from a more purposeful work assignment that demands exact control and intervention on the part of the teacher. In TCI, an intervention by the group leader is necessary only if the group strays completely from the theme at hand.

Themes thus have the role of stimulating and controlling the discussion – and of centering the group's attention. This presumes a certain artful way of formulating the theme on the part of the group leader. The art of formulating a theme can be learned and practiced in methodological seminars of the Ruth Cohn Institute; it is something that cannot be grasped solely through reading matter and the practical guidelines given there.

Further suggestions on formulating themes may be found in Kroeger (1983, pp. 196–200), Cohn (1982, pp. 366–368), Wrage (1985, pp. 69–91), Langmaack and Braune-Krickau (1989, pp. 82–96), and Langmaack (2001, pp. 109–123).

1.1 The Anthropological Meaning of Theme Orientation

The basis of this theme-oriented methodological approach to group leadership or moderation goes back to a basic anthropological statement: In order to properly develop, humans need to encounter other humans and deal with factual circumstances – with themes.

"In TCI, human beings become human beings by addressing themes, tasks, things that they can call their own" (Kroeger, 1992, p. 111) (→ It). In counseling and therapy, it is important that personal problems be formulated and understood as themes (cf. Kroeger, 1983).

It a theme is broad enough to concern everyone, it can become a moment of cohesion in a group; it becomes a common task that glues the group together – as opposed to a simple collection of people who happen to be at the same place at the same time. "The theme represents a link between the individual and the group. If everyone, each in his or her own way, is connected to the same content of a theme at the same time, then group cohesion ensues" (Cohn, 1975, p. 117).

Finding important, common themes furthers the process of developing cooperation in the group (→ We, Phase Models of Group Development).

2 Background

Controlling a group process with the help of a theme was one of the original thrusts of the TCI concept of Ruth Cohn. It was central to TCI, if not the most important difference between TCI and other group-therapy approaches (Kroeger, 1992), such as group-dynamic laboratories, gestalt-therapy group, encounter groups, and psychoanalytical therapy groups. It is not surprising that one of the first publications by Ruth Cohn in German carried the title "Das Thema als Mittelpunkt interaktioneller Gruppen" (The Theme as the Center Point of Interactional Groups) (Cohn, 1975, p. 111).

Ruth Cohn herself derived the meaning of the theme for group work mainly from her own experiences as the leader of seminars for social workers, management teams, and hospital staff, to which she had been invited as both a psychologist and psychotherapist (Cohn, 1984). She mentions how, at the beginning of the seminars, she always asked the participants to first report on their own work situation and their difficulties, instead of beginning with a lecture as was usual at the time. Her own experience as a trained psychoanalytic listener helped her to slowly filter out a preliminary common theme from the personal contributions of the group members – which she then took up, (re)formulated, and used to provoke a lively group discussion – theme-centered interaction. "I spoke with the group members as someone on the lookout to find a generative theme for them" (Farau & Cohn, 1984, p. 334). The term "generative" here denotes themes that are meaningful to the group members, an idea that goes back to Paolo Freire (1971).[2]

A number of authors have also pointed out the close relationship between Ruth Cohn's theme-oriented approach and the trinity of Martin Buber's basic concepts of I – You – It (Schiffer, 1996). This relationship was discussed in detail in the contribution on → It.

---

2 On this, see Matzdorf (1991), who compares the two approaches, and Schneider-Pannewick (1996), who looks in detail at the parallels between the approaches of Ruth Cohn and Paolo Freire.

Another interesting connection for understanding the meaning of themes is that with the language psychologist Karl Bühler (1982), whereby it is not known whether or not Ruth Cohn was acquainted with his writings.[3]

3 Explanations

3.1 Reception

In light of the rapid spread of TCI as a group method in Europe, the central importance of theme as a leadership instrument came up short, whereas the simpler and more accessible → TCI auxiliary rules or the → disturbance postulate were misunderstood as providing the "true" TCI methodology. Even many of those trained in the TCI systematic placed determination of a theme as the subject of group discussion at the beginning of the session (oftentimes complemented by preparing a written version thereof on a flipchart), only to weaken its effect by adding instructions and exercises or by employing leader-centered moderation. Clearly, this betrays a missing trust in the effectivity of the theme-based nature of TCI.

The theme-based method of TCI largely came to be known (up to the present day in fact) through the TCI training seminars. On the one hand, it was taught in personality courses or encounter courses[4] and, on the other hand, in specific TCI methods courses, where the attendees (more and sometimes less deeply) experienced how themes function. It is not surprising that, over the 30-year history of TCI, a number of very different – and sometime rather unclear – interpretations of the term "theme" have been propagated by authorized TCI teachers:

1. In many publications, "theme" was equated in illustrations of the TCI triangle with the "It" (thing, task, subject matter) – sometimes even in the early writings of Ruth Cohn herself (Cohn, 1975, p. 113) – but also in the introductions to TCI by Langmaack (1991, pp. 24 ff.)[5] and in Stollberg (1982, p. 32). In Ruth Cohn's later publications, this equation of theme and "It" as part of the TCI triangle has disappeared: The four-factor model/structure model clearly shows "It" and no longer "theme" (Farau & Cohn, 1984; Matzdorf & Cohn, 1992).
2. Many TCI methods courses (among others, by M. Zollmann and M. Kroeger) as well as many educational publications used in teacher training and adult continuing education early on made a clear distinction between "It" (thing, task, contents, subject mat-

3 It is, however, known that she had contact with Charlotte Bühler.

4 In the 1970s, a number of expressions came to be seen as typical of TCI; the language arose from the wide implementation of TCI in encounter groups and therapy groups directed toward personality development. Today, the expressions used are more specific to the respective professional fields and target groups.

5 The completely revised edition from 2001 with the new title "Einführung in die TCI" (Introduction to TCI) now makes a clear distinction between theme and "It."

ter) and the TIC notion of theme derived from "It" (Kielholz, 1975; Platzer-Wedderwill, 1996; Reiser & Lotz, 1995; Schneider-Landolf, 1996; Zollmann, 1976[6]).

The ambiguity in the relationship between "It" and theme was taken up by Kügler (1997) in his "Plädoyer für eine präzise Begrifflichkeit" (Plea for a Precise Terminology), which spurred a critical discussion among TCI educators and in the TCI house journal as well. This was later examined in detail by Lotz (1999) from an epistemological point of view, who came to the conclusion that a differentiation was (epistemologically speaking) not necessary, albeit pragmatically useful.

3.2 Results: "It" Is Not Yet the Theme

From the above we may make the following differentiations for learning the TCI methodology and for understanding the TCI theory are meaningful and necessary:

1. The colloquial use of the term "theme": When a group is concerned with a common subject matter or a task, one would, in colloquial terms, generally say that is the present "theme" of the group. In the four-factor model of TCI theory it is the → It.
2. A TCI theme is present only when the task or subject matter has been formulated according to methodological criteria to form a short and succinct statement that addresses the individual members personally, (inter)connects the members, and initiates a group conversation.
3. A TCI theme can have as content a subject matter ("It"), a relationship ("Wir"), the subjective and personal level of experience ("I"), or some aspect of the "Globe." Thus, we can speak of It-themes, I-themes, We-themes, and Globe-themes. Often the emphasis of a theme lies somewhere in between (Klein, 1992, p. 196).

3.3 The Theme Is a Leadership Instrument

In connection with and if supported by the proper → structure and → social form, a fitting and well-formulated TCI theme should (and indeed can) achieve the following during a group process:

- It provides food for thought; it challenges the individual members, invites them, and encourages them to deal with it.
- It is relevant to all present and enables them to enjoy their own personal access to it.
- It becomes a way to join in a common group conversation, and it invites the members to exchange ideas among themselves.

---

6 Unpublished worksheets of Marianne Zollmann, who as a TCI trainer together with Ruth Cohn procured a number of seminar teachers and lecturers to provide TCI teacher training in Switzerland.

Figure 1. Leading with a theme. Controlling the Dynamic Balance: Formulating themes with an emphasis on I-We-It-Globe.

- It leads and centers the discussion and thus unburdens the leader.
- Setting a theme controls the → dynamic balance between the task, the individual, and the group. The proper formulation of themes can thus lead the group to explore the objective level (It-themes), the emotional and personal level (I-themes), or encourage the group to deal with the various viewpoints present (We-themes).

In this sense, we interpret the theme as being a central instrument of TCI for leading and controlling groups. For this reason, in the classification system of the overall concept theme is considered part of the methodological principles (leading with theme and structure), whereas in the four-factor model/TCI structure model, the "It" is considered to be on the theoretical level. This assignment is derived from the work of Schreyögg (1993) and von Lotz (1995).[7] However, the considerations of the basic role of themes in human life, as formulated by Matzdorf (1992) and Kroeger (1992, p. 111), were directed more toward the "It" and thus delegated to the philosophical-anthropological principles of TCI.

3.4 Further Development

Leading a group with TCI themes in the above-mentioned sense provides a broad choice of applications (see Section VI: Interactions: TCI and "," which go far beyond the original situation envisioned for encounter groups and personality courses. Using TCI themes means being able to treat a vast array of different subject matters (e.g., from education, business, social issues) in very differently composed groups, such as learning groups, school classes, teams, workgroups, committees, large groups, work sessions, conflict coun-

7 In agreement with Lotz (1995, p. 56), I consider leading with theme and structure to be one of the basic educational principles of TCI and not simply a "technique," as postulated by Reiser (1995, p. 17). In Matzdorf's (1993, p. 339) depiction of TCI as an educational action system, with the image of the TCI house, the theme as a central methodological element is missing altogether. For this reason, I would assume that Matzdorf too failed to clearly differentiate between "It" and "theme."

seling, decision-making consultations, research processes, etc. The leaders of such groups must necessarily have the professional and technical competence in the respective field as well as a solid understanding of TCI.

Structure

Irene Klein

1 Definition

In TCI, structure means how a concrete procedure involving a theme and the group process control takes place. Defining the structure is primarily the task of the group leader.

Structure can be understood in a broad or a strict sense. A *strict interpretation* of structure means being concerned with → types of work activities – for example, brainstorming, walkabout, and role-playing – as well as with → social forms, such as plenary session, individual work, and group work. The group leader is responsible for introducing these elements during a session, a work unit, or class lesson. The leader decides which form and which procedure are to be used during the available time and at the chosen locality in order to best reach all individual members of the group, to connect them to each other, and to have them deal with the theme at hand. A *broad interpretation* of structure denotes everything that is involved in a leader's conscious controlling and shaping of a group. Thus, in this sense structure means:

- *Choice of room and interior design* thereof, for example, size, lighting and air conditions; furnishings (with or without table), seating arrangements (special spot for leader); recording of results (whiteboard, pinboard, flipboard).
- *Strategic objectives*, for example, dedicated beginning and end phases; length of input phase; individual or group work; plenary session.
- *Size of group*, for example, treat theme in small groups or in groups of varying size; assignment of tasks and group tasks.
- *Specific instructions*, for example, "please pay special attention to the present situation [. . .], please relax and remain silent [. . .], please pause to recall earlier experiences and thoughts" (Cohn, 1975, p. 116) as well as formulating explicit tasks and assignments (Raguse, 1984, p. 59).

Very broadly and very generally speaking, structure can also refer to the themes chosen and their introduction into the group: "The best way to provide structure in TCI is by making the theme the central focus of the group" (Matzdorf & Cohn, 1992, p. 82). Structure and theme are indelibly connected to each other. "Structures represent the fulfillment and the facilitation of the central role of the theme in TCI" (Kroeger, 1992, p. 121). Likewise, the communication and → auxiliary rules provide structure by creating a background for the group leader's behavior and by influencing the way in which the process proceeds as well as how the participants react. Structure in the sense of conscious influence may also be seen in the choice of words in a particular group, in the nonverbal expressions and gestures, reactions, etc. All of these factors serve to provide the group and work processes with structure.

Thus, structures represent the totality of the inner construction of a unit. Specifying and applying a structure is a conscious act, an act of control, an intervention on the part of the group leader (as well as on the part of the participants); it provides the conditions – the flooring and the railing – under which a group orders its work and interaction processes. In this sense, it is at once a limitation (since now not everything is wide open and possible) and the wide-open playing field for gathering new information and new experiences according to the axioms of TCI.

1.1 Structure and Process

The structures of a unit can be mapped out with an eye toward the participants (and in light of the past), the goal, the task, and the "Globe." Yet, they may have to be modified during the actual group process. "TCI structure means: doing the proper preplanning with all available facts and probabilities, while being open to what happens in the Here-and-Now-process, in order to make the necessary adjustments. Rigid planning or the complete lack thereof are equally impractical" (Cohn, 1975, p. 206). Which structures are enacted depends on the present development level of the group (→ Group Phases).

Overall *orientation for determining the structures* is provided by the four-factor model, which represents the compass directing the leader to the factors that flow into decisions about structure. Structures are a way to achieve a → dynamic balance between the "I," the "We," the "It," and the "Globe." This includes paying attention to the corner points ("I," "We," "It," "Globe") and the connections between the corner points ("I – We," "I – It," etc.). Here are some examples of such formulations:

- Which structures best engage the "I"s and enable them to adopt self-management (→ I, → Chairperson)?
- Which structure best enables the various "I"s in the existing social situation in the group (school class, course, committee) to connect and cooperate with one another – in their concrete "We" ("I-We" connection; → We Aspect)?
- Which structure best establishes connections between the individual "I"s and the "It" ("I-It" connection; → It Aspect), so that themes/tasks can effectively be worked on?
- Which structure best fits the → Globe, for example, school, university, company, youth work – time and space?[1]

---

1 More detailed thoughts on this, in the sense of a self-supervision, may be found in Kroeger (1983, p. 229).

The four-factor model, however, represents "only" the methodological part of such orientation. The true starting point for any structuring effort lies in the → axioms, the value system behind TCI. TCI lays claim to always working within the scope of its axioms, striking a balance between autonomy and interdependence, while fostering the development and growth of each individual and expanding limitations by recognizing limitations. "The TCI axioms form the basis for understanding the TCI methodology. Without the axioms, TCI is only as 'effective' as a burning match in a haystack" (Farau & Cohn, 1984, p. 357).

The arbitrary use of techniques and the juxtaposition of shifting forms of activation do not correspond to the idea behind TCI. Only when these forms have been consciously chosen and are consistent with the above-mentioned axioms are they true TCI structures.

Applying structures with the proper reference is what make TCI so difficult, and it is also the reason behind the long training TCI novices have to undergo. No two decision-making situations are alike. And even if, for example, a teacher treats the same theme in a parallel class of the same grade, the situation will be a completely new one: The "I"s in the class are different, the "We" situation is different, the entire context is different.

2 Origin

2.1 The Anthropological Meaning of Structure

In her first book, "Von der Psychoanalyse zur Themenzentrierten Interaktion" (From Psychoanalysis to Theme-Centered Interaction) (1975), Ruth Cohn discusses structure in a very basic way that is important because it eventually became one of the most important features of TCI, indeed one of its trademarks: "This method has a definitive structure [...] I believe that only a firm structure enables freedom" (Farau & Cohn, 1984, p. 113). This is one of the fundamental convictions of TCI which influences the entire methodological background: People need a certain minimum amount of safety and freedom from fear if they are to feel free and powerful and open toward both ideas and other people, i.e., if they are to be functioning, viable humans. The need for orientation, for security, for safety, for belongingness all comprise the most elementary and basic necessities of human life (cf. Klein, 2005, p. 20; Overbeck, 1994, p. 12; Rubner, 1992, p. 230). Only if these needs can be properly met does room for growth develop. Group situations, in particular the situation in a new group, can trigger existential fears of being rejected or losing one's identity – and block all powers to grow. For this reason, TCI is particularly concerned that the initial situation be well structured in order to provide the participants a sense of safety toward the other participants, the theme at hand, and indeed the entire situation (Langmaack, 2001, pp. 103, 162). A clear structure enables orientation, it calms fears, and it frees up creative powers.

"In TCI work the structures are the variables that create and round out the developmental possibilities this method offers. They are the payback and the fulfillment of the fundamental considerations behind TCI concerning development and growth. The all-important skill lies in [...] developing structures that provide an atmosphere for the participants to live and breathe in, where they can take the risk of truly learning to deal with themes that contain critical and biographically painful moments" (Kroeger, 1992, p. 121).

2.2 The Historical Background

The role of structures was not originally one of Ruth Cohn's major commitments. The reason lies in her psychoanalytical background: She came to discover the effectiveness of supportive structures only upon using TCI early on in educational and business situations (→ Educational Foundations). This contrasted with other contemporary models, such as that of Carl Rogers's "encounter groups" (1970). "It was my early, intuitive conviction that group processes are characterized not simply by acceptance, but by the fact that they profit from a proper structure. Only much later did I discover quite deductively just how effective such structural planning could be" (Farau & Cohn, 1984, p. 348).

3 Explanations

3.1 Further Development

Walter Lotz (1995) depicted TCI as an educational action method. He saw the idea of structure in TCI on the level of educational concepts and thus put this term front and center. The TCI axioms represent the theoretical starting point of the educational concept; attached to the axioms, on the lower level so to speak, are concrete methods that can be employed in educational settings. "Theme and structure are methodological work principles that must be attended to during the learning process. As such they are not techniques [...]; rather, when mistakenly interpreted as being techniques, they become banal, everyday practices whose deeper meaning as what controls the process – as a methodological force – is lost. Seen as part of the method, on the other hand, they are revealed to be essential tools" (ibid., p. 56).

The link between the four-factor model of TCI and the concept of the "Berlin Model,"[2] well-known from didactics and originally developed for use in schools, came to be broadly accepted in other educational settings as well. In the Berlin Model, the connection is made between the clear teaching and learning situations of "Goals – Contents – Methods – Media" involving decision-making as the relevant structural elements of each and every planned unit with the value-backed dimensions of "I" – "We" – "It" – "Globe" in TCI. The

2 A more detailed depiction of the Berlin Model, which is a structure model for teaching situations and does not necessarily provide orientation for value discussions, as well as the Hamburg Model, which includes key values similar to those found in TCI (competence – autonomy – solidarity), may be found in Peterßen (1982, p. 82) and Gudjons (2001, p. 240).

decision-making and value factors from the Berlin Model and TCI are interwoven in order to better delineate decision-making situations. The value of this step lies in increasing consciousness of the systemic connection between the various decisions (implication connection) and their interdependence (Klein, 2005, p. 154).

3.2 Criticism

Again and again the fear (or criticism) was expressed that the structures found in TCI might lead to adaption or conformity on the part of the participants, thus effectively retarding their dealing with conflicts, confrontations, and aggression. Yet, this danger is present in every group and primarily depends on the personality of the group leader. Of course, setting down a structure can be (mis)used by leaders to cover up their own tendency to dominate or to conform, or to disguise their fears of confrontation or conflict. The overall concept of TCI, however, like the considerations on how to best employ structures, works in the opposite direction. This is something the axioms as well as the many comments regarding the → chairperson postulate and the → disturbance postulate clearly reveal.

Establishing a structure is a dynamic act. By providing structure a leader provides support, which helps further self-confidence and security; the self-leadership skills of the participants can grow in that protected area. Their dealings with the inherent differences in the group makeup become more open and more differentiated, and they can learn to deal productively and not destructively with aggression. The certain orientation toward the leader at the very beginning is then gradually replaced by the development of each participant's own "chairperson" (Overbeck, 1994, p. 9; Raguse, 1994, p. 122).

What is important to see is that TCI is primarily concerned with "I"- and "We"-oriented *theme work*. In this sense, it is true that structures can be implemented in order to improve the group's work capacity (and thus reduce unnecessary disturbances). Confrontations and conflicts are not *per se* ostensible themes for the group and need not be continually provoked. But they become important and serve as themes whenever they become necessary to the group process or when they hinder the group's working on the actual theme. They are part of the learning process and belong to how we understand process-oriented learning.

The fact that these matters receive so much attention may be seen in their fixed role they play in the central learning and theme areas of TCI training.

Work Forms and Social Forms

Irene Klein

1 Definition

The following statements are closely connected to those made in the previous chapter on → structure. Achieving a → dynamic balance between the factors "I," "We," "It," and "Globe" is done in concrete situations through the use of various *work and action forms* as well as *techniques and learning procedures* (all of which are synonymous), in addition to social forms. These terms were lifted from the didactical concepts of teaching employed in both adolescent and adult education. Sometimes the term "method" is also used, though today that term is generally avoided since "method" designates the higher-level unit, for example, "methodological work" or "the TCI method" (→ TCI System). In the following, I use the term "work forms" and "social forms." Of course, other designations may appear in some quotes.

Work forms are methodological elements that provide an approach to and means of dealing with a particular theme; they may also stimulate or enhance communication and cooperation among the participants. Examples are verbal and nonverbal exercises, brainstorming, lightning, walkabout, lecture/theory impulse, structured exchange of experiences, marketplace, silentium, (body) exercise, painting, diary, games, metaphor meditation, role-playing, mindmap, moderation techniques, and certain rituals such as day/hour start.[1]

Social forms, on the other hand, concern the structure of the relationships (Meyer, 1994, p. 136). They describe the way participants work or deal with one another, the way they approach the learning process or the task at hand; examples are individual work, partner work, groups of 3/4/5 . . ., half-plenary, plenary et al. Also part of the social forms is the way in which groups are constituted or composed; examples are freely chosen groups, accidental groups, groups meetings according to certain criteria, groups put together by the leader, etc.

1 There are any number of books available concerning "methods" and interaction games for both adolescents and adults and for school settings. Generally, these have the form of a list that is ordered according to certain areas of learning and experience (e.g., Klaus Vopel, Monika Kalnius, Bernd Weidenmann, Harald Groß). A good example of a discussion on such work forms according to TCI may be found in Cohn and Klein (1993, p. 132) and in Klein (2005, p. 179).

2 Origin

As far as I am aware of, Ruth Cohn herself did not participate in the discussion that took place in didactics and the educational sciences (→ Educational Foundations). Her methodological approach was more intuitive and creative, based on her own discoveries concerning the background of → living learning. The later use in TCI of a broad range of different methodological structures occurred through the work of TCI colleagues from various disciplines such as school, education, church, and business. It was also the result of the introduction of TCI to Germany parallel to the spread of group-pedagogical and group-dynamic literature in the 1960s and 1970s. It was a time when many experiments were being done with different forms of self-activated and independent learning with adolescents and later with adults as well.

3 Explanations

3.1 Work and Social Forms

Some work forms have proved to be so successful in TCI work that they are now seen as TCI-specific techniques, for example, the fishbowl[2], lightning[3], or interrupting input/presentations by sequences of small-group conversations (so-called murmur groups). And yet, there are no officially TCI-specific work forms – the exception being "silentium," which Ruth Cohn from the very beginning considered an important part of TCI work like the method of "passing the anti-interaction egg."[4] All work forms taken from other methodological approaches, whether from school and didactics, organizational development, or therapy, can also be used as long as they correspond to the TCI value system. "TCI can

2 Representatives from the group or individual participants from subgroups form an inner circle to discuss a theme (e.g., the result of some group task), whereas all others only listen. One chair in the inner circle, however, is always left empty, so that others can alternately take part for a short time.

3 This is a "snapshot" of the respective status of each participant on a certain matter or situation. One after another the participants say a sentence or maybe even just a word on the subject in question. For example, "What do I consider particularly important in this work unit?" or "How much does this theme affect me?" or "My feelings right now." There is no immediate interaction, no immediate questions, though some may emerge at the end of the entire session.

4 This exercise has the goal of stimulating all participants in a group to express their thoughts and thus to increase the transparency of the entire group situation. First, a short, summary matter is chosen following a theme sequence or during the group process (e.g., when everybody is no longer involved or when attention is focused on sorting out or holding onto some important personal events or clearing up a group matter). Then, after the question has been described and the participants have had a short time to ponder it, an object (a rock, an egg . . .) is passed around. Whoever has the object in their hands speaks, and the other group members listen. "Anti-interaction egg" was Ruth Cohn's term for this. She used an egg-formed semiprecious stone for this purpose, thus the name. While the object is making its way around the circuit there is no exchange of comments (Cohn & Terfurth, 1993, p. 310).

encompass all group techniques that do not contradict the axioms and that prove helpful to the respective situation of the participants and the work group" (Farau & Cohn, 1984, p. 369).

TCI can be employed in nearly all fields of work – and yet the use of work and social forms is different because the respective situation, the Globe, the goals, the persons, and the groups are different. A university lecture or seminar demands different types of work and social forms than, say, leading a team discussion or a board meeting, instructing a class, or giving a TCI seminar. It suffices to glance at the TCI triangle to see the truth of this statement, that is, at the various different requirements put on the participants and the leader, the specific social situation, and the many different themes and goals.

Structures are there to serve! Work and social forms are chosen because of their ability to produce effective work and because of the basic anthropological assumptions of TCI (→ Axioms). They are employed in order to activate and enable the → "I," to facilitate interaction and cooperation, or to elucidate a particular theme. The immediate goal is to establish a balanced and quiet working situation, which is the first prerequisite to self-determined and self-responsible work. Work and social forms do limit the necessity for continuous self-restructuring on the part of the participants, which in turn leads to greater working capacity and cooperation of both the individuals and the group. On the other hand, in accordance with the axioms, there is a need for forms that – over time – foster self-structuring and self-leadership.

"Working with TCI means developing a culture of work forms that are self-determined (i.e., without the need for continual leadership) and that can work with themes, whereby the → theme (the subject matter, the task) is such that, if necessary, the theme and the structure can proceed without a leader. [...] In the sense of TCI, structures present a free and reasonable space to work in" (Kroeger, 1992, p. 122).

The use of work and social forms serves to further holistic work and learning processes. They address all parts of our being – our heads, our hands, our bodies, our hearts, our senses and feelings. The goal is → living learning and living working. This demands a variety of forms: Some address more intellectual needs, other emotional needs. Switching from individual to group to plenary work engages different aspects of the participants and furthers their ability to self-express as well as, through some other approach, their developmental potentials.

3.2 The Effects of Work and Social Forms

Work and social forms work on several levels and in multiple ways. Many action forms produce experiences, in some cases quite purposefully, though always open-endedly. The leader must be able to evaluate what a particular action form or social form will precipitate, and whether that form will be able to deal with any unexpected effects, for example, with the deeper dimensions in the participants. Here, especially nonverbal exercises and work forms taken from therapeutic settings have proved to be fitting. Properly applying action forms demands great sensitivity and the ability to foresee impending situations and react responsibly.

A group leader's combination of skill and experience provides the best way to approach an existing situation. Besides analyzing the "I" and the "We" situation, the leader must also analyze the effect of the respective form. Here are a few examples of such situations:

Work Form: Passing an Object[5]

- *The effect on the "I":* Everyone in the group must spontaneously react and overcome personal inhibitions; everyone must decide how much to tell and how personal to get about things. Everyone is seen and heard by the entire group. For some people, who have difficulty speaking up in plenary sessions, this is their chance to break their own silence.
- *The effect on the "We":* Reciprocal knowledge ensues, along with the growing interest and sympathy of the others. The senses are sharpened, equality and inequality become evident, respect and attention grow. A positive norm arises that everyone present is important.
- *The effect on the "It":* Various aspects are combined; themes are summarized or exposed. If the matter at hand is a process theme, then "secret agendas" and differences become conspicuous.

Social Form: Plenum

The plenum is the normal form of the group – and for many the most challenging form of all. The larger the group, the more stressful and challenging it can be to the participants. The plenum is one of the most important instruments in TCI and is viewed as a "learning chance" (→ Structure – Process – Trust) for the following reasons:
- *For the "I"s on the personal/social level:* Being in the public eye; standing up for yourself and your own opinions; deciding what and how much to say or show; putting yourself in relationship to others by agreeing or disagreeing; enduring the fact that you cannot judge the effect of your own statements; giving others space or being forceful and combative; being empathetic and understanding.
- *For the "I"s with respect to the "We" and "Theme" levels:* Dealing with the opinions of others; enduring the breadth of opinions and thoughts expressed; being willing to expand one's own horizon; developing respect for other thought processes and lifestyle choices; recognizing differences as productive ways of development.

5 Cf. the footnote above in section 3.1 on the "anti-interaction egg"

These "learning chances" do not just occur on their own. Leading a plenum is a high art indeed and requires skills both on the personal and professional level. This is what is taught during TCI training.

Social Form: Individual Work

This too is an important social form in TCI. Individual work can mean the following: a short moment's pause to contemplate a question so that everyone can collect themselves before answering; 5 + minutes time following a question to prepare oneself and make some notes; personal time after a work unit to jot down important things and consider them further; collecting oneself during a work pause in order to reorient and readjust.

This concerns some of the central matters of TCI: conscious (re)action, the ability to perceive things, the personal and inner participation of each member, accepting responsibility for one's own self, making repeated decisions – or, taken together, developing an inner chairperson (→ Chairperson Postulate).

Social Form: Groups of 2/3/4

The size of a group when doing group work should not be left to chance; every size has its own rules and effects. Ever simple decisions can have many implications:

- *The dyad* can be protective as well as exposing; the "I" is always upfront and called upon; no one can evade attention or withdraw. An intimate space is created ("We") that offers the chance of experiencing a personal encounter. In a difficult constellation this may, however, lead to overload.
- *The triad* is somewhat more pliable and viable; each member is eventually heard; attention is directed toward the other two; thematic contributions are broader in scope. However, sometimes a "triangulation" occurs: two against one, which may be reminiscent of difficult experiences in life of being excluded (father – mother – child; mother – child – child, etc.).
- *The group of four* offers an even greater range and spread of attention as well as more possible thematic and experiential diversity. This means that each has a greater shot at self-management. But it takes a lot of time for everyone to be heard.

The decision which of these social forms (and which work form) is the right one for a particular situation may be made based on the following questions:

- What is the primary goal for what content? What is the final summit to be reached?
- What is the situation of the group and how can its ability to communicate be furthered?
- What do individual members need or bring to the table and how can their participation, their contribution, and their responsibility be strengthened?
- What does the "Globe" allow or forbid?

3.3 Critical Remarks

One of the characteristics of TCI is that the use of structures as well as work and social forms is always connected to the existence of the axioms and the → four-factor model as well as to the goals and issues that are being addressed in any one concrete work situation or work unit. This clearly excludes simply daisy-chaining one action or social form to another, like an endless TV program – regardless of how exciting that may seem. Putting the methodological elements ahead of the goals and the contents inevitably leads to superficiality and empty actionism. These comments are necessary because in some books on methods such work and social forms are provided like cookbook recipes, with no reference taken to the respective concrete situation.[6]

The link between the structures and the value system and the conception of human life found in TCI makes working with work and social forms an art that must be first learned and then continually developed.

6 The article "Mit gemischten Gefühlen" (With Mixed Feelings) by Manfred Krämer perfectly describes the distance that must be maintained to this temptation. He uses the TCI orientation to show his reaction to the books of Heinz Klippert "Übungsbausteine für den Unterricht" (Exercise Blocks for Teachers) in the journal "GEW-Zeitschrift" from the German Teachers' Union, issue 9/2004.

Structure – Process – Trust

Werner Sperber

1 Definition

The *interplay of structure – process – trust* represents, on the one hand, a tool that can be used to help provide a leader with orientation when analyzing, planning, and leading groups. This combination clearly shows how important structure is – just as important as promoting processes and encouraging trust in the group members and the group.

On the other hand, it reflects a genuine humanistic approach. In contrast to other group methods, such as group dynamics (see Schütz, 1983), group leadership in TCI was always concerned with maintaining a friendly and trusting atmosphere in the group. Besides a respectful climate, such an atmosphere of trust needs supportive structures and a process characterized by both consideration and challenge.

The meaning of the triad of structure – process – trust may be seen immediately by taking a look at the "shadow triangle" created by Dietrich Stollberg (1982), which also contains chaos – distrust – stagnation (see Figure 1).

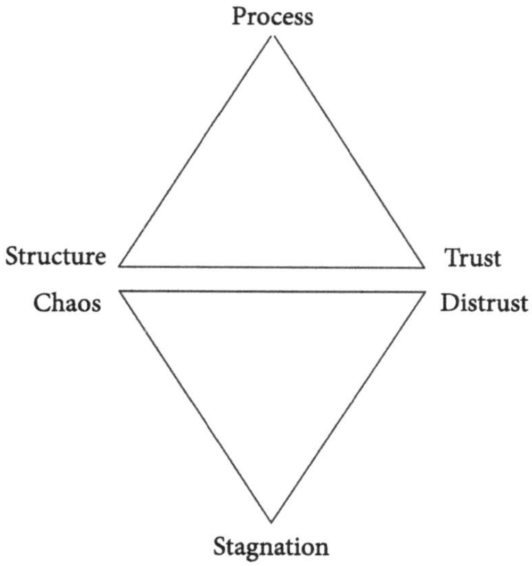

Figure 1. The shadow triangle according to Stollberg.

1.1 Structure

The → theme is a central structural element in TCI. It provides the members of a group with orientation, by giving them a common starting point and an indication of where the journey is going. It unites the thoughts of many individuals and thus represents a connective medium between them.

Part of the methodological structure of working with a theme, however, is also the conscious use of → work forms and → social forms. In addition to the setting of a theme, the way the various social forms control the group process is very important, i.e., working in the plenum (the entire group, see further below) or in small groups of varying sizes, with various work forms such as role-playing, fishbowl, and other exercises, which serve above all methodological and didactic purposes.

1.2 Process

A process (from the Latin *procedere*, to go forward) is the entire qualitative course a group takes, from the beginning to the end, during which things develop and change. In sociology, "social processes" are "the ways in which individuals and groups interact, adjust and readjust and establish relationships and patterns of behavior, which are again modified through social interactions" or more broadly "those activities, actions, and operations that involve interaction between people" (Dictionary of Sociology).

Group processes are affected by the individual participants, who interact with each other and communicate among themselves. They are also influenced by the task at hand and the goal of the group as well as its relationship to the context (Schattenhofer, 2001).

The group process can be further divided into the following parts:

- A *group-dynamic process* that reflects the development of the relationships between the participants and thus the development of their working capacity as a group ("We" process).
- A *psychodynamic process* that represents the unconscious transference processes, projections, and the development of the individual members ("I" process/personality development).
- A *thematic process* that includes the development of the theme, the group work, and any solution to that task ("It" process).

Every group has its own unique and distinct character, and every group develops its own immanent, self-perpetuating, and evolving dynamics (→ We). Thus, a group process cannot be stopped – not as long as the group continues to exists. But it can be influenced by an intervention (e.g., on the part of the group leader) and take a new route; the communication levels can shift over the course of the process. The latter means that the level of action and reaction can (temporarily) be abandoned in order to observe and reflect on the process from the metalevel. Here, from above, as it were, with some emotional distance and a better "view" of everything, the individual members can visualize what group-dynamic events ("We"), what psychodynamic events ("I"), and what thematic events ("It") have taken place in the most recent phase. The question is also how the individual participants and the leader have affected these processes.

1.3 Trust

Trust is a very special qualitative relation that occurs within a relationship. According to the dictionary, trust also means the expectation that a certain thing will in fact happen, that someone will behave in a way that I had hoped or foreseen.

Olaf Germanis calls trust a *social resource*. He says "trust reduces the overall complexity and enables cooperation. Solidarity, neighborly help, and, generally speaking, the reciprocal expectation of mutuality are the result of trust-based interaction" (2002, p. 69).

Sprenger (2002) proposes several different levels of trust: the basic sense of trust, trust as a social convention, trust as competence, trust as a decision, and trust in cooperation.

The basic human sense of trust (Erikson, 1950) plays a major role in this equation. Helga Herrmann says that, in TCI, the goal is to provide "room to develop, room to prosper,"[1] which can arise only through trust. How much trust I as a group leader put in the participants and in the group as an organism with a living process depends greatly on my own level of basic human trust: The more trust or self-trust a human develops over his or her lifetime, the more that person can forgo narrow and inappropriate structures and dispense with control mechanisms. This opens up the chance for the development of a positive learning and working atmosphere – a form of cooperation that does not suppress differences and can constructively deal with conflicts.

Of course, when I trust someone, I can be disappointed or I can deceive myself. That's just part of the deal. Then, a new beginning is called for, especially if I responsible for another person.

2 Origin

In 1974, Ruth Cohn presented this second TCI triangle (structure – process – trust) to a small circle. She said that her experience as a counselor had showed her how important it was that trust lie at the basis of the therapeutic relationship – something that is also true when working with groups. "Not everyone possesses this basic human trust and feels important and valuable." She assumed that "trust develops when someone truly listens,

1 In a personal communication, Matthias Kroeger said this concept originally stems from Helga Herrmann, though there is no source for it. He himself used the idea in some of his writings.

counters, takes things seriously, continues, and does not always have to be right" (Cohn, 1975, p. 213).

Only in 1983 did Ruth Cohn bring her thoughts on "structure – process – trust" to paper (Matzdorf & Cohn, 1983/1993).[2] By then she no longer spoke of a second triangle. In the following, however, I continue to speak of a second triangle, since that image best describes the mutual relationship.

3 Explanations: Structure – Process – Trust in Groups

3.1 The Effect of Structure on Trust and Process

"In order to [. . .] produce a trustful atmosphere, you have to be aware of many structures and the considerations that determine which structure is best in which situation. Like children who cannot learn to trust if they experience no support or experience too much caution, trust arises in a group when its interactions do not receive too much or too little support" (Matzdorf & Cohn, 1993, pp. 81 f.).

A group leader has to ask him- or herself again and again: Which structure do I choose? What am I trying to do? How much support do I provide? How much do I let things run their course? This is where risk-taking begins: Do I react to a risky situation with trust or does my skepticism kick in? Structures that are more open and more demanding produce more process, albeit at the cost of sometimes causing alarm and a loss of confidence if employed at the wrong time.

3.2 The Plenum as a Special Structure

The plenum – the entire group in one place – reflects the true social reality of a group. According to Theodor M. Mills, groups are in fact microcosms of larger society and thus mirror in miniature the situation of broader social scales (1971, p. 12). Participants are more or less "forced" to deal with the situation, to accept the others, and to come to terms with their own personalities and their own behavior. What happens or is said in the plenum is a "public" matter for everyone to see. And because our perceptions are always subjective, there will necessarily be different interpretations, assessments, and opinions, which in turn calls for finding a common understanding if the members of the group are to live or work together.

On the symbolic level, the plenum consists of father, mother, and the children (the family) sitting at the table. This type of "reconstruction" revives, among other things, the respective transferences and projections known from childhood (→ We). Also, in the plenum the participants latently experience a situation fraught with → competition and rivalry.

2 The same text was also printed in 1993 in Löhmer and Standhardt (pp. 81 ff.).

The multitude of relationships that occur in the plenum (depending on the size of the group) may make it difficult or tedious to satisfy all the social needs, as opposed to the situation in a small group or a dyad. Thus, the chance of satisfying needs is reciprocal to the size of the group (i.e., a dyad is quick to provide the satisfaction of social needs). Also, uncertainties and fears surface more quickly in large groups, so that "opening up" can seem to be more momentous to an individual in a plenum than in a smaller group: In the plenum the emotional threshold to be surmounted may be considerably higher. This is the reasoning behind my statement concerning the therapeutic value of the plenum.[3]

3.3 Trust Affects the Process and Enables Different Structures

As already mentioned, whether a process is successful and a group is efficient greatly depends on the trust the participants have toward one another and toward the leader – and on the trust the leader has in the individual, in the group, and toward themselves.

If there is a high level of trust, then the results will be qualitatively better than when the trust level is low. Thus, trust or the lack thereof influences the group process and the group's ability to be productive. If sufficient trust is present, then the leader can initiate looser, more challenging, more demanding structures. If, however, the trust within a group or a certain system is generally low, then insecurity and fear can spread. To ensure productivity, the leader should adopt more supportive and guiding structures in order to prevent insecurity and fear (see above).

3.4 Trust as Approach

The model of the second TCI triangle also contains a specific approach to life and worldview. Trust is an extremely subjective, emotional component, whereas structure and process tend to be more objective, manageable organizational systems. "Structure" and "process" are likely to be accompanied by such terms as "result" and "productivity." And yet, Ruth Cohn added "trust" as a third factor. Her basic assumption is that trust, being a basic quality of relationships between human beings, is an important and necessary category for working together and for achieving results, just like structural components and processual operations.

A very different assumption and worldview may be found in Lenin's famous proclamation (as it is usually quoted): "Trust is good but control is better." This puts control squarely in the forefront, since trust is too precarious. In this model of leadership distrust rules – the result being narrow structures and sophisticated control mechanisms with little

3 In a conversation on this matter, Mina Schneider Landolf noted that these statements may not apply to people who have hysterical inclinations: They love to be on the "stage" of the plenum and in fact feel uncomfortable in the intimacy of a small group.

room for error. Trust is seen as a risk factor. Like Sprenger I do not agree with the statement that trust itself it not the risk, but rather that "the risk lies before trust." The risky situation, which can have several different outcomes, makes us choose whether to evoke trust or not (Sprenger, 2002).

The opposite of "trust is good but control is better"[4] lies in Ruth Cohn's model, which assumes that trust is absolutely necessary[5], and that the three factors (structure – process – trust) possess a meaningful, reciprocal relationship to one another. Put another way: They need each other!

Trust is a resource and is important because a group leader is acting in a risky situation: Most of the parameters are unknown, and the process is continually changing. The value system, the approach, and the method propagated by TCI says that we can in fact extend our trust to the individual members and to the group as a whole. The relevant structures are important for establishing such trust, as can be seen in the following quote by Ruth Cohn: "It is my experience that every work situation in which the structures do not serve the needs of the situation causes trust to diminish – even between people who are quite willing to trust each other. [...] If the structures, however, do correspond to the needs of the situation and of the people in that situation, then trust increases and the quality of the processes as well – more so than when one tries to improve the processes while leaving the structures unchanged" (Matzdorf & Cohn, 1993, p. 83).

4 The quote by Lenin, as reproduced here, is in fact not completely correct. According to Sprenger, who himself quotes the Russian Academy for Language and Poetry, the actual quote reads: "Trust, but also control" (Sprenger, 2002, p. 72). Thus, in this sense, control is not seen as the opposite of trust. If we follow the statements of Germanis (2002, see above), a trustful relationship always contains some measure of control since the expectations we implicitly imply with trust in fact exert some control over the behavior of the person I am extending my trust to.

5 Sprenger says that trust is the theme of the future. He quote the philosopher Sloterdijk: "The society of the future is damned to trust one another" (Sprenger, 2002, p. 62). I would add: This is because control is dwindling in our globalized world, and the cost of control is becoming prohibitively high.

Participative Leadership

Regina Hintner, Theo Middelkoop, and Janny Wolf-Hollander

1 Definition

Participative leadership (PL) is the designation for a leadership concept of TCI that has the goal of allowing individuals, groups, teams, and organizations to reflect on, diagnose, and control learning and work processes. The two concepts contained in this term show the complexity of the leadership task in TCI: leading and participating.

Ruth Cohn said the following: "Group leaders are primarily participants, that is, human beings with their own specific interests, preferences, thoughts, and feelings. Only secondarily are they group leaders with a special function in the group. And this function is mainly concerned with maintaining a dynamic balance between the I, the We, the It and their connections to the Globe" (Cohn, 1984, p. 368). PL comprises the basic dialectical structure of TCI, the function being to strike a synthesis between abstinence and participation (Reiser, 1995, pp. 16–21).

We were unable to find a definition of PL in the secondary literature. For this reason, we formulated a working definition ourselves and would like to back it up by looking at the literature and the developments that have taken place on this matter. In Sections 3.2 and 3.3 we complement these thoughts with our own ideas.

Definition: PL calls on leaders to be cognizant of their own conscious and unconscious actions and reactions by responding to the other participants and the entire process. They do this by selectively and authentically establishing a balance between diagnostic distance and personal involvement.

PL was important principle from the very beginning of the development of TCI. However, it never got a prominent place in the description of the system (Reiser, 1997, p. 26). Ruth Cohn never defined this term, describing it more as a way for leaders to orient themselves than anything else. *Selective authenticity*, on the other hand, did assume a central place in TCI. Matzdorf and Cohn (1992, p. 91) summarized these aspects of TCI as follows:

- "Leadership is understood as a form of 'leading-yourself-and-the-group.'"
- "Leaders are participating members who bear the responsibility for the structures, the dynamic balance of the process, and for heeding the interests and needs of the individuals."
- "Functional, non-status-oriented group leadership."

- "Dismantling of authoritarian and nonauthoritarian positions (selective authenticity, securing adequate communication, distribution of functions, transparency in the democratic workings of the group)."

2 Origin

The term PL was used in the early writings of Ruth Cohn (1975, p. 97) to refer to a further development of the psychoanalytic practice that demands the abstinence of the therapist. The call for selectivity contains a measure of abstinence, whereas the call for active participation toward the client limits that abstinence. Taking her cues from experiential therapy, Ruth Cohn (Matzdorf & Cohn, 1992, p. 43) developed the "principle of partnership of the participative leader" as one of the five principles characterizing experiential therapies. "They have in common that the therapist or teacher is not some 'neutral' or controlling being, but rather someone who participates and inserts himself into the events" (Cohn, 1975, p. 97). When Ruth Cohn herself led workshops on countertransference as part of the training to become a psychoanalyst, she made the unusual decision to act just like the other group members and take part in the group. This step led to her developing the understanding of the role of the leader that later was so decisive for TCI: "A leader is someone who becomes an educationally therapeutic helper and catalyzer by being authentic and congruent in all statements. [...] As leader I am a participant like the others: I am a leader, I am the chairman of myself and the 'chairman of the group.' As the chairman of the group I use myself as an instrument – however I may feel at that moment. It is my responsibility not to extract myself from the leadership function – from myself, from the group, or from the theme. I feel, I think, I am bothered, I am calm, I am apathetic, I am impassioned – however I may feel at that moment. I do not want to remove myself from things, but rather I want to direct my attention to you and support the theme. I am optimally (not maximally!) transparent to you" (Cohn, 1975, pp. 188f.).

3 Explanations

3.1 Reception

Here we must differentiate between two levels: the ideological and the educational justification and implementation.

Ideological Approach

Ruth Cohn (Ockel & Cohn, 1992, p. 198) forwarded an ideological justification. Reducing the hierarchical role of the leader has a social relevance – and it is her full intention that there be a political ramification. The leader of a group has the task of assuming the necessary leader function and the (initial) power that rests with that position, while also participating in the overall group process, something Reiser (1995, p. 26) calls "democratic, functional leadership."

One criterion Reiser (1997, p. 47) thinks is necessary for this to succeed is that any interventions on the part of the leader be oriented toward reducing the power of the leader and thus minimizing the transference to the leader. His second criterion (ibid., p. 27) is that the extent of selectivity and authenticity be appropriate to the respective social setting (school, church, business, political group, etc.) and coordinated with them.

Educational Approach

There are any number of concrete impulses and suggestions as to how PL can be educationally implemented and what skills are necessary for this task. Here are a couple of them: Langmaack (2001, p. 200) defends the educational reasoning that the group leader, being a model participant, has to make statements and take other measures to motivate the group, to increase trust, and to have a positive effect on the learning and group-dynamic processes. On this Ruth Cohn wrote: "Everything I say has to be authentic, but not everything that is authentic has to be said" (1984, p. 371).

Dealing within TCI with the transference phenomenon with regard to PL demands very special skills. Different from classical psychoanalysis, where transference is actually increased in order to better work with it, TCI leaders immediately and clearly point up any transference and work through it in order to ensure realistic relationships. Reiser (1997, p. 27) and Raguse (1994, p. 146) think that this model calls for a special, rather impossible, and in fact paradoxical ability to dive into the process and then withdraw oneself just as quickly. Psychoanalytically speaking, we are dealing here with the ability to exhibit parallel both abstinence and empathetic participation. Thus, Raguse (1992a, p. 97) considers it the most important prerequisite that leaders be fearless in the face of their own actions, any criticism they may receive from the other participants, and any difficult matters that may pop up to prevent them from being suppressed in the group. "Every TCI group leader must find ways to [...] understand his own role in relationship patterns. TCI group leaders are more effective if they can continually expand the horizons of their self- and other-knowledge" (Matzdorf & Cohn, 1992, p. 85).

3.2 Controversial Matters

In summary, there are two basic positions:

1) *Leading and participating is difficult if not impossible:* Lemaire (2001, pp. 118–139) considers this a homemade conflict: The authority and power of leaders are being weakened and blurred by the demand for PL, which robs the other participants of the chance (or need) to deal with these things. Vopels (2000, p. 82) argues that the "TCI leader works in a pseudo-participative way [...] he is both the defender and executor of the

theme he himself set." This, he thinks, does not do justice to the actual power differences that exist in the group. However, Vopels reduces PL solely to participative leadership and leaves out the fact that a TCI leader also has the task of dealing with many very different power relationships.

Thus, to sum up this criticism of the concept of PL: Equality is only being pretended, differences are being glossed over, conflicts over leadership, power, and authority are in fact exacerbated, and the leader effectively weakens the participants' attentiveness by introducing his own personal matters – although the general idea of the whole thing is to help the others to learn, grow, and work together.

2) *Leading without participating is impossible:* This is the opposite position to that given above. Here, too, we find references in the literature: "By actively letting oneself be drawn into the group, the leader allows the group process to become his compass. Out of the empathy and involvement he shows grows the security to proceed to the next steps. The leader can feel what is coming. [...] The insight the leader possesses is expressed in his interventions in the group" (Lang-Körsgen, 2001, p. 11). As proof, let us more precisely define "participation" and operationalize the term. Based on our differentiation between participation in the sense of "taking part in," "showing empathy," "making statements about oneself," and "being involved," leadership without participation is simply not possible, something that is also true of all concepts of leadership. In TCI terms, PL means the *conscious, selectively authentic shaping of the participation based on maintaining a balance between diagnostic distance and personal engagement.* If we accept this differentiation, then we may note that the secondary literature mainly treats individual aspects thereof, without drafting an overall image.

3.3 Further Development and Specification

From our own practical experiences, we would make the following four distinctions. How we prioritize them says a lot about the way in which a leader shapes his or her own participation, whether consciously or unconsciously.

1) *Taking part in:* This we understand to mean: doing the same thing (as the others). A leader can participate in a lightning round – or not. If the participants of a seminar are asked to talk about their political involvement, their biographical background, their stance toward right and wrong, then the leader can take part or not take part. A department head can go with her staff to eat a common meal or choose not to do exactly that.
2) *Showing empathy:* Leaders can show their concern for the life, the present situation, the good and the bad experiences, the problems and joys of the participants, employees, subordinates – or not. The extent to which they do this depends on any number of very different factors.
3) *Making statements about oneself:* Leaders can reveal much or little about themselves. This, too, can be influenced by many different reasons, for example, by the type of task

at hand, by the function and role one has, etc. The basic question is: Is this being done purposefully and with what goal? Is the leader acting upon reflection or spontaneously – and to what end? What are the desired and undesired ramifications of this action? What is the price to be paid for such behavior?

4) *Being involved:* Whereas "taking part in," "showing empathy," and "making statements about oneself" represent more or less conscious decisions, this aspect denotes a situation that is difficult to sum up with a single term since it includes both conscious and unconscious behavior. "Being involved" has various facets such as "being engaged," "being entangled in," "having to do with," "being drawn into something," "being embedded in," or even "passionate involvement." In addition, there are the consciously observed feelings, wishes, desires, interests, intentions, and plans of the leader. On the other hand, we find unconscious (partial) aspects such as involvement in the sense of transference, countertransference, and projection. In the end, PL means recognizing that such phenomena may take place and that it is part of the leader's role to reflect on these actions and reactions – and to use them to better lead the group.

4 In Conclusion

Whenever a leader is oriented toward TCI as a methodological basic principle, in our opinion this does not mean that all four aspects of PL are simultaneously being acted upon, but rather only that these are consciously being considered. However a leader applies the four aspects depends on the leader's personality, on the context, on the particular field in question, on the task, and on the other participants. In order to determine how a leader can do this, consider the following table (example shown):

	In a team	In a meeting	As manager	In the family	...
Taking part in	++	–	–	+++	
Showing empathy	++	+	++	++++	
Making statements about oneself	++	–	+	+++	
Being involved	+++	+	+	++++	

The following table may be used to show the differences between the various approaches (example shown):

	TCI	Psychoanalysis	Group dynamics	Gestalt pedagogics	Systemic work
Taking part in	+/–	–	–	+++	+/–
Showing empathy	++	+++	++	+++	+
Making statements about oneself	++	–	–	+++	+/–
Being involved	++	++	++	++	???

The evaluations presented above, however, should not be interpreted as absolute, and in fact they may turn out to be very different depending on the approach and the background. Yet, differences in the roles and functions, between the profit and nonprofit areas, between the respective roles of men and women can be very well inspected in this manner.

For the future it seems to us to above all be important to look at the respective effect of mixing these four aspects.

Leadership Interventions

Janny Wolf-Hollander and Oswald Wiehe

1 Definition

Interventions are an instrument for controlling processes – regardless of what type. TCI in turn is a leadership concept that is appropriate for deliberating on, diagnosing, and controlling the learning and work processes of all types of groups, teams, and organizations. In this contribution we concentrate on leadership interventions on processes that take place in training and advanced training groups. Interventions in teams, organizations, and other formal bodies are more complicated and demand a more differentiated treatment that is beyond the scope of this article.

Our definition of interventions is as follows:

> Interventions are a control instrument employed consciously, deliberately, as well as spontaneously by a group leader during an ongoing group process. Interventions influence the direction, the intensity, and the speed with which personal, group-dynamic, and content-related matters affect the group setting. The goal is to enable living learning and an effective work climate and thus create positive learning processes.

Two aspects of this definition are discussed below.

1.1 Interventions by the Group Leader

The contributions made by the individual participants clearly have a great influence on the processes that occur in a group. In the following we concentrate on those interventions that originate with the leader.

1.2 Interventions During the Ongoing Process

Over time the understanding of the role of interventions in the TCI secondary literature came to include all control actions effected by the group leadership over the group process. This may be found most clearly in the writings of Barbara Langmaack and Michael Braune-Krickau in their volume "Wie die Gruppe laufen lernt" (How the Group Learned to Walk;

1995, pp. 145 ff.). Elfi Stollberg, in her article "Ich kann nicht nicht intervenieren!" (I Can't Not Not Intervene; 2001, pp. 185 ff.), considers all interactions, not just those concerning themes and structures, to be interventions. Braune-Krickau and Stollberg, on the other hand, restrict the term intervention to refer solely to "spontaneous" reactions.

To date, leading TCI groups has been done via exactly formulated themes and carefully considered structures (using → work and social forms). This has proved to have the greatest influence over the processes. But because that skill is well developed in TCI and plays a major role in TCI training, we prefer not to follow Langmaack, Braune-Krickau, and Stollberg and plead rather – much like Schulz von Thun – for viewing interventions as instruments that are intentionally introduced into ongoing processes as means of control.

This differentiation allows us to study the subjects of theme, structure, and interventions separately and to look more closely at the respective actions at work.

Nevertheless, despite the fact that a spontaneous intervention on the part of the group leader can be a very effective control instrument, there is very little literature available, both generally and specifically in TCI, to back it up.

2 Origin

The term "intervention" comes from the Latin root which means "coming between"; in English it means to mediate, occur or happen between, to interfere, to interpose. The term was originally used in political circles to denote the actions of a country to become involved in military conflicts ("military intervention") or control actions effected during economic crises, such as interventions in the stock market. In medicine, this term describes how physicians react to medical crises and how psychotherapists insert themselves into mental crises.

In the 1970s and 1980s, intervention in group dynamics was extended to mean the actions taken by group leaders to manage therapeutic group and counseling processes; it has been discussed and analyzed extensively in the general secondary literature (Bastine, 1975; Fengler, 1976; Schmidt, 1983; Voigt & Antons, 1987).

The term intervention is quite prevalent in the literature on the systemic approach to counseling, therapy, and supervision, where the emphasis lies on studying intention and effect (von Schlippe, 1998; Selvini Palazzoli, 2003). Some authors plead for a very broad understanding of intervention, whereas others prefer a narrower, more instrumental approach.

3 Explanations

3.1 Reception

Ruth Cohn originally used the term intervention only in the usual psychotherapeutic sense to refer to the conscious control mechanism of intervening while leading a group

(1975). Concerning leadership in nontherapeutic groups she wrote: "I allow everyone to do as they please as long as no one is being destructive toward himself or toward others. Only then would I intervene. That way I encourage an accepting, tolerant atmosphere" (1984, p. 343).

In 2001, Elfi Stollberg made the first attempt to define the term in more detail, putting intervention on the same level as communication. Stollberg apparently was concerned with the entire behavior exhibited by both the leader and the group participants.

3.2 Controversial Matters

Reflection on processes plays a major role in TCI. This is where the four-factor model comes in: It offers a basic platform for planning and deciding which aspects (→ Theme) in which form (work forms) and in which settings (social forms) (→ Work Forms and Social Forms) are to be employed. The goal of dynamic balancing provides the orientation to do this.

The control instruments "formulating and introducing themes" as well as "structuring" are expressly taught and practiced during TCI training. Should a work unit proceed differently than planned, the following questions must be answered by the group leaders: Did we gauge and interpret the process differently? Did we choose an improper theme for the process? Did we formulate it incorrectly? Did we introduce the theme poorly? Were the social forms chosen not fitting or the work form inadequate?

The idea that developments in the group can also be influenced by spontaneous interventions is to date only weakly anchored in the TCI concept and in the role of a group leader. Up to now, it has been assumed when a group accepts a theme and the corresponding structure offered by the group leader that it automatically also assumes the responsibility for working through it. Ruth Cohn intervened, as mentioned above, only if things were getting out of hand. There are many places where she says she is primarily concerned with partnership and with dismantling the hierarchical position of the leader. This also has social and political relevance to her, and this aspect is important in that respect. Reiser too (1997, p. 47) said that interventions on the part of the group leader should be directed toward reducing the power position of the leadership and thus minimizing the transference to the group leader (→ Participative Leadership).

We, however, would suggest expressly allowing *spontaneous interventions* on the part of the leader as a conscious control instrument. This means conceding that the leader does have more power and more responsibility. For this reason, we feel that intervening should be a standard subject in TCI training.

3.3 Further Development

It is our assumption that there are no patent recipes for interventions. The existing general criteria for carrying out "good" interventions are limited to aspects of approach and attitude. So how can we support group leaders who are being trained or receiving extended training to react properly in such situations?

We would like to suggest the following topics, which have emerged from our own theoretical and practical experiences with this matter:

Intervention Styles

Participants of seminars are requested to use a questionnaire to describe their own intervention style. This information is then repeatedly used to compare their self-image with the reactions of the other participants. These two elements in turn form the basis for further developments. Specific exercises are offered for this purpose.

Intervention Levels and Intervention Directions

Based on the → four-factor model, we differentiate between interventions that include
- One or more individuals, their concerns, and their learning process,
- The dynamics of the group, their interaction, their cooperation, their individual roles,
- The overall task and the respective details,
- Or the context.

Development, Courses of Action, Effects of Interventions

In seminars, concrete interventions that can be experienced in the Here and Now of the group or observed by the participants with the help of audio-visual means can be examined using the following steps:

Observance

What did the leader just observe, both externally and internally? What led to the *impulse* to do something? Maybe the group "wavelengths" are somehow disturbed; maybe something doesn't "feel" right; maybe something got "out of whack." An inner emotion, a feeling, state, discomfort, need, breach, rivalry, weariness, boredom, impatience, disquietude, affection, idea, thought, insight, duty, nonverbal signal (hands, feet, face, shoulders, teeth . . .) – whatever – demands our attention. Different leaders will be prompted to become active at different times and for different reasons.

Hypothesis

The drive to do something causes the leader to form a hypothesis that is sometimes conscious and quite often unconscious. Such hypotheses may be more or less professionally motivated, whereas others are fed by fears, by intuition, or by rational considerations. One should examine what values are active here or whether we are in effect dealing with "favorite hypotheses," reproducible templates that strongly influence how one judges what is happening. The hypothesis thus affects the way the intervention proceeds.

Intention

The hypothesis leads to the intention to change the situation. Thinking about what should change sometimes produces complex goals.

Intervention

Actually doing something, that is, actually intervening, represents the concrete choice one makes from a multitude of possibilities in accordance with one's own personal limitations. The path finally chosen – how one decides to intervene, for example, resisting, generalizing, intensifying, objecting, objectifying, decelerating, accelerating, etc. – above all says much about how you imagine what is going to work. Whether one tends more toward asking questions or providing answers, whether one emphasizes the commonalities or the differences, whether one identifies with or distances oneself from others, whether one chooses to smooth over differences or pour oil on the fire: Occupying oneself with the problem at hand and the possible solution forces one to confront reality and deal with future perspectives.

Effects

Understanding how the intervention actually affects the participants requires very exact perception as well as the awareness that not everything is perceptible – that some things happen immediately and other things have long-term effects. Also, the foreseen effect may come to pass, but sometimes things happen unintentionally.

Overall, in our experience this method confronts future group leaders with their own personal motives, capacities, and limitations. Their faculties for introspection and reflection are strengthened, and their ability to intervene grows.

4 Personal Opinion, Summary, Outlook

We would expressly argue the case for seeing spontaneous intervention as an important instrument in TCI, one that in fact has always been practiced, though little has been written about it. We think it has its role in both in the theory of TCI and in the practical training of group leaders.

Further, we consider it indispensable to differentiate between interventions carried out in the various types of applications (continuing education, team development, counseling, etc.).

Auxiliary Rules

David Keel

1 Definition

The so-called *auxiliary rules of TCI* comprise a set of suggestions valid for specific situations and concerning the behavior and the interaction in groups. These are introduced in order to support the work in the group and the aspirations of the individual group members to achieve autonomy and interdependence (Cohn, 1975, p. 114).

Several variations of the individual rules as well as the entire set of rules have been published. Ruth Cohn noted in her own publications a varying number[1] of auxiliary rules, whereby, according to Quitmann, she viewed it as a "simple mistake" that the rule on body sphere was sometimes mentioned and sometimes not (Quitmann, 1996, p. 202). Reiser quotes a personal communication of Ruth Cohn according to which auxiliary rules could be deleted or revised as necessary (Reiser & Dlugosch, 1997, p. 29).

The early English and German literature on TCI does not contains the terms auxiliary rules (in German *Hilfsregeln*); rather, the talk is of "ground rules," in German *Grundregeln*. At the time these included what later became known as postulates (→ Chairperson Postulate, → Disturbance Postulate) as well as a number of the modern auxiliary rules (Cohn, 1971, pp. 262 ff.; Gordon & Liberman, 1972, pp. 108 ff.).

The term "rule" comprises norms prescribed externally (directives), internal conventions within a group (agreements), and personal guidelines (life rules). Ruth Cohn did not see the auxiliary rules as directives (Farau & Cohn, 1987/1991, p. 364), but rather as helpful offers. According to Ruth Cohn, the rules should be mentioned as early as possible in the process, but only as a reaction to the course the process is taking (1971, p. 262).

---

1 In her article "Das Thema als Mittelpunkt interaktioneller Gruppen" (The Theme as the Core of Interactional Groups) from 1969/1970, Ruth Cohn quotes a total of seven auxiliary rules (quoted acc. to Cohn, 1975/1986, pp. 115 f.), whereas in her article "Zur Grundlage des themenzentrierten interaktionellen Systems" (The Foundation of the Theme-Centered Interactional System) from 1974 (Cohn, 1975/1986, pp. 124 ff.) she mentions nine rules, and in her 1984 book (Farau & Cohn, 1984, pp. 361 ff.) there are only five, as in the article "Was ist Themenzentrierte Interaction?" (What Is Theme-Centered Interaction?) (Matzdorf & Cohn, 1992, pp. 76 ff.).

Here, a list of the auxiliary rules (my order):

1.1 Self-Organization and Self-Management

- "Be your own chairperson. Decide what you want to do" (Cohn, 1969, quoted acc. to Gordon & Liberman, 1972, p. 108).
- "Be your own chairperson and determine when you want to speak and when you want to be silent and what you want to say" (Cohn, 1975/1986, p. 115).
- "Be yourself in your own statements. Say 'I' and not 'we' or 'one'" (Cohn, 1975/1986, p. 124).
- "Give to this situation what you want to give and get from it" (Cohn, 1969, quoted acc. to Gordon & Liberman, 1972, p. 108).
- "Be authentic and selective in your communications. Be aware of what you are thinking and feeling and choose carefully what you say and do" (Cohn, 1975/1986, p. 125).
- "Try to give and get from every session what you want to give and get yourself" (Cohn, 1975/1986, p. 115) " from the situation, the group, and the theme" (Cohn, 1971, p. 263).

1.2 Self-Statements

- "When you ask a question, say why you are asking it and what this question means to you. Speak for yourself and avoid interviewing" (Cohn, 1975/1986, p. 124).
- "Make as many statements as possible and ask only important questions" (Cohn, 1975, quoted acc. to Gordon & Liberman, 1972, p. 109).
- "Be careful speaking in generalizations" (Cohn, 1975/1986, p. 126).
- "Refrain from interpreting others as long as possible. Instead, voice your own personal reactions" (Cohn, 1975/1986, p. 125).
- "Whenever you say something about some behavior or characteristic of another participant, also mention what it means to you that he is the way he is (i.e., how you see him)" (Cohn, 1975/1986, p. 126).

1.3 Steering Attention

- "Observe the signals that come from your own bodily sphere and observe these signals in the other participants" (Cohn, 1975/1986, p. 115).

1.4 Conversation Organization

- "Interrupt the conversation if you can no longer really participate" (Cohn, 1975/1986, p. 115).

- "Only one person should speak at any one time" (Cohn, 1975/1986, p. 126).
- "If more than one person wants to speak at the same time, agree shortly about what should be discussed" (Cohn, 1975/1986, p. 127).
- "Side conversations have priority: They disrupt and are generally important. They would not be taking place if they were not important ('Would you like to let us know what you're talking about?')" (Cohn, 1975/1986, p. 126).
- "Disturbances and passionate involvements take precedence over the stated theme in order to be resolved" (Cohn, 1969, quoted acc. to Gordon & Liberman, 1972, p. 109).

2 Origin

Ruth Cohn did not quote any sources concerning the auxiliary rules. Her remark that some rules could be applied most everywhere, whereas others arise from the respective situation (Farau & Cohn, 1984, p. 363), may be seen as an indication that the rules were formulated, tried, and revised in real-life group situations.

3 Explanations

3.1 Reception

Hardly any other element of TCI came to be accepted so quickly as the auxiliary rules. In the early 1970s, Schwäbisch and Siems (1974, pp. 242 ff.) reached a large audience with these concepts, as did Schulz von Thun since the 1980s (1981, pp. 126 f.). Schwäbisch and Siems also made some suggestions concerning feedback rules[2] (1978, pp. 69 f.).

In some secondary literature and on the internet these auxiliary rules have been modified[3] and complemented by feedback rules or other rules; some are declared *pars pro toto* to belong to TCI. Yet, a number thereof fail to differentiate between postulates and auxiliary rules (→ Axioms and Postulates).

Outside of the TCI community the auxiliary rules have been (and still are) widely accepted, sometimes rather shallowly. Reiser and Dlugosch (1997, p. 75) speak of an initial

2 For example, "Give your feedback so that everyone can hear it." – "Feedback should not attempt to analyze others." – "Report your impressions as impressions, your presumptions as presumptions, and your feelings as feelings." – "Feedback should be as extensive and concrete as possible," etc. (Schwäbisch & Siems, 1978, pp. 69 f.)

3 Thus, "Side conversations have priority" (Cohn, 2004, p. 126) becomes "Avoid side conversations and submit your contribution directly to the group so that no one feels excluded" (Höser & Loheit, 2004, worksheet 5.10). In another instance, Ruth Cohn is quoted as having said "Do not demean yourself and the others, your possibilities and your skills as well as those of the others" (retrieved on 25 July 2008 from http://www.ub.uni-konstanz.de/kops/volltexte/2000/401/html/ress18.html).

misunderstanding among some that the auxiliary rules actually represent TCI or that they may serve as recipes for conducting discussion groups.

Today, the auxiliary rules have a relatively low standing within the TCI community. Funke even made the following statement: "The auxiliary rules belong to the periphery of TCI, not to its core, unlike many descriptions" (1984, p. 260). Ruth Cohn took a very sober view of how the auxiliary rules came to be received: "My original enthusiasm for the communication auxiliary rules was dampened by the cold and mechanized ways in which 'Cohn's rules' were nailed to the walls of some institutions and burned into the brains of their inhabitants – without knowing or recognizing hardly a shred of the soul of the axioms and postulates the rules were conceived to support" (Farau & Cohn, 1984, p. 361).

The most popular auxiliary rule in TCI literature is surely "Be aware of bodily signals," a rule that even got its own book-long treatment (Hahn, Schraut, Schütz, & Wagner, 1991). Kroeger (1991, p. 170) notes that this auxiliary rule was often misunderstood as the injunction to introduce body work and practices at all TCI events – and not as the invitation it is to perceive the body by observing its signals.

3.2 Controversies

Schwäbisch and Siems see the auxiliary rules as norms: Because group members often realize only much later how useful these rules are, they should not be introduced in advance and opened to debate (1974, p. 243).

Funke (1984, p. 295) agrees with those teachers of TCI who say one must differentiate between the theoretical background to the two categories *postulate* and *auxiliary rule.* Funke views the postulates as predecessors to the negotiation process in groups; they are, he says, "anticipated idealizations" of communication and must be fulfilled if interaction is to take place. The auxiliary rules, on the other hand, *follow* the negotiation process; their rigid application does not chime with the claim to emancipation. Effectively, Funke is pleading the case for removing the auxiliary rules from the TCI system altogether. The logical consequence is that their use would encourage the "façade of a personality" instead of the "authentic self." Raguse (1987, p. 129) agrees with this sentiment.

Ruth Cohn (1994, pp. 85 ff.) considered the postulates to possess a universal validity, whereas the auxiliary rules were valid only in the respective situation. However, because the auxiliary rules were valid only in a specific situation, Ruth Cohn thought they should be introduced only verbally and not in a written form (Matzdorf & Cohn, 1992, pp. 77 f.). Vopel quoted the example of the side conversation rule to show that auxiliary rules must conform not only to the situation, but also to the respective culture: Speaking consecutively, as demanded by the rule, is characteristic of Western European culture circles, whereas others cultures, such as African and Southern European cultures, are more tolerant toward simultaneous speaking (2000, p. 79).

Raguse thought it strange that self-responsibility and freedom would be imparted through the use of imperatives. He compared the situation with an "*aristocratic* form that has all good intentions to teach democracy. However, what if the intentions turn out not to be all good?" (1987b, p. 129). The use of rules, he thought, always contains the seed of misuse, which in turn could damage TCI (ibid.).

Reiser and Lotz (1995, p. 29) thought the auxiliary rules provided an orientation for "establishing and maintaining a positive interaction style."

3.3 Further Development

Some authors felt called upon to revise the auxiliary rules, to discover new ones, or propose alternatives. Kroeger, for example, coined the modernized rule "Don't think so much about what you want to do, but also about what you must and should do" (1992, p. 49). Ruth Cohn regarded Hoppe's suggestion for a third postulate "Get involved! Take action!" as an auxiliary rule for an active group (1994, p. 87).

Besides the further development of individual auxiliary rules as well as the entire collection of such rules, there is still a need to rethink the entire status of the auxiliary rules and perhaps devise a new understanding thereof, being the "unloved child" of TCI that they are.

In Friedsrichtshafen, along the promenade, the city erected a sign that reads: "Reasonable people do not ride their bicycles here. For everyone else: it's forbidden here." This statement couples insight (an enlightened understanding for the necessity of rules) with the threat of sanctions and the fear of raising the ire of the authorities. In this case, the use of sanctions is based on the educational concept of obeying the rules. And yet the sequence of "follow the rules – get your reward or break the rules – be sanctioned" doesn't correspond to the TCI view of human life. Rather, TCI strives to enable everyone to become their own chairperson and to consciously assume responsibility.

If a group democratically sets down a set of rules, these represent, on the one hand, the fruit of their common insights; on the other hand, enlightenment does not prevent conditioning. Setting rules may lead to having to enforce them.

Raguse replaced the auxiliary rules with model participation. He thought it better "to do away with all rules and postulates and limit oneself to action. As a leader I do not need to say anything about what someone should or should not do. Rather, I act the way I think is right for me and perhaps also for the others" (1987b, p. 130). Raguse the leader thus respected the metanorm of not declaring his own values to be absolutely valid for others.

Stabenau (2000, p. 45) deduced from the joint reflection on the group process a number of rules that were explicitly or implicitly valid in groups. He then leaves it to the group to decide whether these rules are expedient. Thus, for Stabenau rules are first of all descriptive and only later, through a common decision-making process, do they become normative.

In addition to their descriptive and normative function, TCI auxiliary rules also contains suggestions. For example, the rule "Interrupt the conversation if you cannot properly participate" implicitly assigns me the courage to actually interrupt a conversation. What I can learn from this suggestion is that I need not be concerned with whether or not I in fact have the ability and the courage to carry out action, but rather that in the future I should act as if I had these competences and the willingness to carry out the action.

Phase Models of Group Development

Gernot Klemmer

1 Definition

A phase is understood to be a section that is qualitatively different from the situations that preceded and followed that section. Developmental phases, for example, describe the typical segments in the process a group experiences over the course of its existence. There are several different phase models that describe this developmental process, all of which attempt to chart the course of group processes using more or less logical steps.

TCI groups work with various different phase models, and some authors have developed their own developmental models for TCI groups (Belz, 1988; Rubner & Rubner, 1991).

In this regard, reference is often made to a development toward more cooperation. If this cooperation is successful, the extent of the mutual trust increases and with it the group cohesion. This may be seen in the open, serious, and respectful way the participants treat each other, including their use of humor. Then the group passes to a new phase that is qualitatively different from the previous one. Unclear and controversial, however, is the question whether such phases necessarily occur in all groups and under all circumstances.

2 Origin

The term "development phase" (sometimes longer sections are called "steps") has been in use in psychology since the early 1900s to describe the principles of child development. In developmental psychology, Oerter (1969, pp. 48, 53), among others, questioned whether the idea of whether phases truly depict mental development since the majority of the results of psychological research points to a more fluid, continuous development in life.

Most phase models of group development refer back to Bion's (1961) well-known formula:

Forming	Storming	Norming	Performing
Orientation	Contestation	Acknowledgment of rules	Cooperation

Bion developed his model based on his experiences as a group therapist. He preferred the psychoanalytic understanding of the therapeutic relationship as one in which the therapist holds back and moderates the group with "participative restraint" (Battegay, 1969). Later authors broadened this view to postulate the orderly development of groups according to these phases, independent of the respective behavior of the group leader.

3 Explanations

3.1 Helga Belz's Cooperation Model

The concept of how TCI groups develop authored by Helga Belz (1988) was expressly directed toward workgroups, teams, and learning groups, where the emphasis lies on *learning together* or *working together.* An important developmental goal of such groups is the ability to cooperate and work in concert. That lies behind the title of her book *Auf dem Weg zur arbeitsfähigen Gruppe* (The Path to Functioning Groups) (ibid.). The following table shows the scheme she devised to describe the five group phases (ibid., p. 15).

Orientation	**Motivation**	**Own initiative**	**Confrontation**	**Cooperation**
Getting to know one another through facts	Establishing a personal relationship to the main theme	Concrete necessities within the main theme	Personal encounters that enable working together	Joint specification and design of work details
Informational level	Understanding and comprehension level	Desire level	Interactional experience level	Work level

3.2 Group Phase Model of Angelika Rubner and Eike Rubner

Rubner and Rubner (1992, 1993) introduced their model of group development in 1991 in the TCI journal in their article entitled "Entwicklungslinien in einer TCI-Gruppe" (Lines of Development in a TCI Group). Their sources were, among others, Bion, Foulkes, Grindberg, Langer, and Rodrigue as well as later Heigl-Evers. They clearly also lean on Brocher. These many forerunners reveal that their model emerged from psychoanalytical group theory based on findings from analytical therapy groups (→ Psychoanalytical Foundations). They are consistent with the assumptions and research results from these schools of thought.

Their model comprises five phases; below are solely the categories "characteristics" and "behaviors." The original text has five further categories on the various states of and relationships between the group and the group leader.

Table 1. Developmental phases of a group (acc. to Rubner & Rubner, 1992, p. 250).

Orientation and dependence	Fight and flight	Autonomy and interdependence	Trust and intimacy	Dissolution and separation
– Getting to know one another through facts – Providing information and accepting information – Strong relationship to leader – Objective relationship to theme – Fluctuation between intimacy and reticence	– Rise of criticism, troubles, attacks – Competition and rivalry among members – Power struggles between members and leader – Tendency to denigrate the theme – Wish for autonomy – Development of group norms – Danger of dropout	– Solidarity – Clear rules and customs within the group – Mutual support – Open and fruitful communication and cooperation – Creativity and productivity – Large willingness to absorb and learn – Common planning and activities	– Strong interpersonal communication – Openness – Mutual trust and relationships – Theme is treated personally and emotionally – Rivalry and solidarity between persons of the same sex and wooing of opposite sex – Pairing	– Presence of external relationships – External orientation – Transfer – Review and assessment – Sorrow – Flight – Taking leave

A new, unpublished version of this overview is now available which includes an additional phase entitled "Approach and cooperation" (as second column); the 6th and final phase was renamed as "Separation and taking leave." There are also differences in the description of the individual aspects, for example, "Defense mechanism" becomes "Basic anxiety" and "Basic conflicts."

3.3 Further Concepts of Group Development

Very different from the Rubner and Rubner model is the alternative model by Rohner (1992), which puts more emphasis on the development of the capacity of a group to work together – and doubts the necessity of a "fight and flight" phase completely. Instead, the group leader should intervene in the process, something psychoanalysts would call being "directive." After the *initial phase*, there follows the *first work phase*, which is characterized by positive initial successes and then by experiences that may be rather sobering or perhaps even disappointing: The disappointment over heightened expectations may often lead to aggressions, resulting in turn in power struggles. During the subsequent *reflection and regulation phase*, attention is turned to providing feedback and assessment. Only during the *second work phase* does self-determined cooperative attention to the theme become possible. The *final phase* is devoted to a last look at things before dispersing and for preparing the next steps (Rohner, 1992, pp. 53–55, abbreviated).

In the early 1990s, I (Klemmer, 1993) prepared a concept for TCI-based learning groups drawn from teaching methodology. I suggested four phases for the holistic treatment of subject matters: prereflection and planning, holistic preparation of the subject matter (including phases devoted to formulation, processing, application, and transferral), contemplation and final reflection. The "We" development is integrated into the intentional work as part of the joint contents and themes (ibid., pp. 267–274).

3.4 Discussion

As far as the phases of group development are concerned, authors have very differing opinions, with some describing clearly delineated sections that occur in practically every group (Foulkes, Rubner), whereas others consider phase models to be completely superfluous, even in developmental psychology (Oerter, 1976).

A comparison of the above-mentioned phase models for TCI groups shows that Rubner and Rubner take their arguments from the psychotherapeutic basis of earlier approaches from group therapy and group dynamics. Their model is very precise in its descriptions of the individual phases and clearly differentiates them. Of course, that makes it less flexible. That led to considerable criticism (Brake, 1992; Kroeger, 1992; Rohner, 1992), which they aggressively confronted (Rubner & Rubner, 1993). Their publications, on the other hand, unfortunately contain no comments on the older concept forwarded by Helga Belz or the standard article by Konrad Thomas from the year 1987, which appeared in the very first issue of the TCI journal.

Belz, Rohner, and Gernot Klemmer take up the phenomenological arguments of other teachers of TCI on the phases of TCI learning groups. They start from their own experiences with the large bandwidth of possible courses groups can take, projected against the enlightened background of humanistic anthropology, education, and of course psychology.

What they do agree on is that appropriate themes and structures support the development of a cooperative atmosphere in workgroups. This in turn changes the course of group development and with it the various phases it goes through. Rohner emphasizes "group diversity and media diversity." For me, however, the independence and the purposefulness of the group members are just as important as supporting creativity, fantasy, and humor. In all three approaches the psychotherapeutic aspect is balanced out by the educational aspect: Belz emphasizes the didactic aspect more, whereas I accentuate the methodological aspect, meaning that both educational science and educational methodology behind these sources.

Inasmuch as every human being has a unique personality, every group also develops its own unique and individual *gestalt* (→ We). Nevertheless, we can make out some very basic patterns behind group development:

1. *Processes that correspond to* (or are at least similar to) *the model of Rubner and Rubner.* Here, the success of constructive coping with the "storming" phase is decisive for group development.
2. *Processes in which the group development proceeds so fluidly that there are no breaks or fissures.* Eventually, the tension from the onset passes; trust and the ability to cooperate grow continuously; positive statements on the joint task increase; and more and more laughter is heard. Disturbances on the part of individuals, small subgroups, or even larger elements are taken up and dealt with without much ado. The end of the course is regretted by some, not so much by others. The feelings that are shown are generally commensurate with the situation.

3. *Processes in which individual situations occur that may be categorized like the five (or six) phases proposed by Rubner.*

However, their intensity, number, length, and order of these phases can be very different. In one course, for instance, one phase or another may occur only fleetingly, whereas in another the overall process takes place within a single phase (e.g., gets stuck on a conflict). In yet another, the phases occur only at the start and at the very end – or go missing completely. Some groups prove to be cooperative from beginning to end. Because of the multitude of various possibilities, I clearly cannot list all variations here.

In the end, however, the various critical opinions concerning the phases of TCI groups do not differ as much as one might presume based on the articles published in this regard. Rubner and Rubner (1991), in the summary of their statements on the developmental phases of a group, even said the following: "The phenomena described here [...] reflect important aspects of these phases, but they are not dogmatic specifications." The main reason why the group processes proceed so differently, they say, lies in the role of the group leader: "The leader's personality and style of leadership [...] support and/or prevent some phases as well the solving of phase-specific conflicts or their evasion" (ibid, p. 48). In comparison, in a remarkable contribution based on the group theory of Sartre, Kamps (1991) also emphasized the overall well-accepted meaning of the leader's influence.

In summary, based on the discussions in the literature, on discussions held with a number of TCI colleagues, and on my own 30 years of experience in TCI groups, I would offer the following hypotheses:

The phases described by Rubner and Rubner can occur in TCI groups at nearly all times. However, the fact is that they rarely occur exactly according to the model proposed. If the leader or the group itself, however, intensively expects – or fears – that the group process will take a certain course, then the chances increase that the anticipated phases will indeed come about. But if the leader emphasizes the psychotherapeutic aspect of TCI, more classic group dynamics tend to emerge. If the leader stresses the educational aspect and from the very beginning works toward cooperation, the group processes will become more open, more creative, and more diverse. The leader need not necessarily become the object of the group's criticism, from some unconscious level of group dynamics; maybe the leader was simply not well prepared to lead the group, maybe the leader failed to find the right tone in a difficult situation, or maybe there were tensions within the team.

How groups develop that have common goals or strive for common intentions is such a complex, diverse, and varied phenomenon that it is hardly possible to foresee the course they will take or the various phases they will pass through. In order to avoid the formation of unconscious group dynamics, it is important to implement theme orientation, reality control, and disturbance processing from the very beginning – and to use humor, fantasy, and creativity to underscore the process.

Part IV

The Differentiation of TCI

TCI as a Professional Educational Concept

Helmut Reiser

1 Definition

Designating TCI as a professional educational concept or as a professional action concept means seeing it as a management system that can shape educational situations of all types. This makes it more than just a group leadership method with the goal of creating interactions to promote group development. It also means creating a realistic understanding of TCI regarding its aspirations, its scope, and its effects. It means creating a new image of TCI. This allows TCI to be compared to other professional educational concepts, such as psychoanalytical pedagogics, systemic pedagogics, person-centered pedagogics, and such educational concepts as Montessori education, Waldorf education, etc. The fact is that TCI is very well able to fulfill the characteristics and requirements made of a professional, educational concept.

In his volume *Wissenschaftstheorie für Pädagogen* (Theory of Science for Educationists), Kron (1999, pp. 77f.) looked at the terms "model" and "concept" with respect to the interaction between theory and practice. There he describes the meaning of the term "concept" in terms of its role in psychology and in the natural sciences: On the one hand, concepts are tools that help to provide mental and conceptual clarity; on the other hand, they are ways to reveal possible paths of action (ibid., p. 78). "In the practice-oriented literature [...] the idea of concept plays a very special role" and can be interpreted as a "symbolically represented connection" (ibid.). If we think of TCI as an *educational concept*, then the idea of "concept" becomes a long-term, overarching, mental overview; *action orientation* is then made equivalent to "conception." The second element, *professional*, is generally understood to mean "of high quality," as opposed to "amateurish" or "mediocre."

Yet, when we speak of a "professional educational concept" we do not intend this popular meaning. Rather, "professional" here designates the action competence of a *profession* in the sense of the theory of professions. A profession deals with an important social task from a scientific vantage point; it has its own regulated, high-quality training and ethical standards, much like the classical professions of medicine and jurisprudence. The most important element of professional actions is that scientific knowledge is not merely being "applied" or practically "implemented," but rather individual cases are being addressed with their own specific situational interpretation. The capacity of a professional lies in this ability to transfer knowledge and to make decisions befitting the respective situation.

In the case of education as a profession, we may assume that there is a rather large gap between theory and practice that cannot be effectively closed by applying or by ignoring scientific knowledge.

Professional educational concepts take place in that transitional space between theory and practice, where "a special type of reflection rules and where mental thought patterns are created, extended, and modified which are not yet actions and no longer science. Compared to pure scientific analysis, in this space we find a lower level of complexity. Based on normative, in part axiomatic assumptions, justifications are favored that reveal a high level of arbitrariness (compared with pure scientific exploration) and that are oriented toward a realistic practicability, a lower level of action, and an intersubjective plausibility in the vocational context" (Reiser, 2006, p. 44).

2 Origin

Helmut Reiser and Walter Lotz worked parallel and independent of each other in their respective educational areas, all the while in constant communication, to move the discussion surrounding the professionalization of education forward. The result was that TCI came to be seen and implemented as a professional concept of education (Reiser) and as a professional action conception (Lotz). The book they wrote together, entitled *TZI als Pädagogik* (TCI as an Educational Methodology) (Reiser & Lotz, 1995), consists of a written dialog between the two authors on a conceptualization of TCI, on the relationship between theory and practice in TCI, and on methods and approaches in TCI. Lotz went on to develop these thoughts using profession theory to include the social-educational approach (Lotz, 2003) and subtitled his work "The Basis of Social Relationships Using TCI." He saw TCI as being on a "middle level of abstraction," something he called the "conceptual reflection level" (ibid., p. 30). Reiser, on the other hand, based his further research on the profession-theoretical findings of Andrea Dlugosch (2003 & 2005) on special needs education, in particular on the special needs found in educational assistance (Reiser, 2005, 2006).

3 Explanations

TCI sees itself and describes itself as being very open to all sorts of philosophical, social, and humanistic theories, including the many individual techniques of group leadership, counseling, control of interactions, etc. – inasmuch as they do not contradict the basic

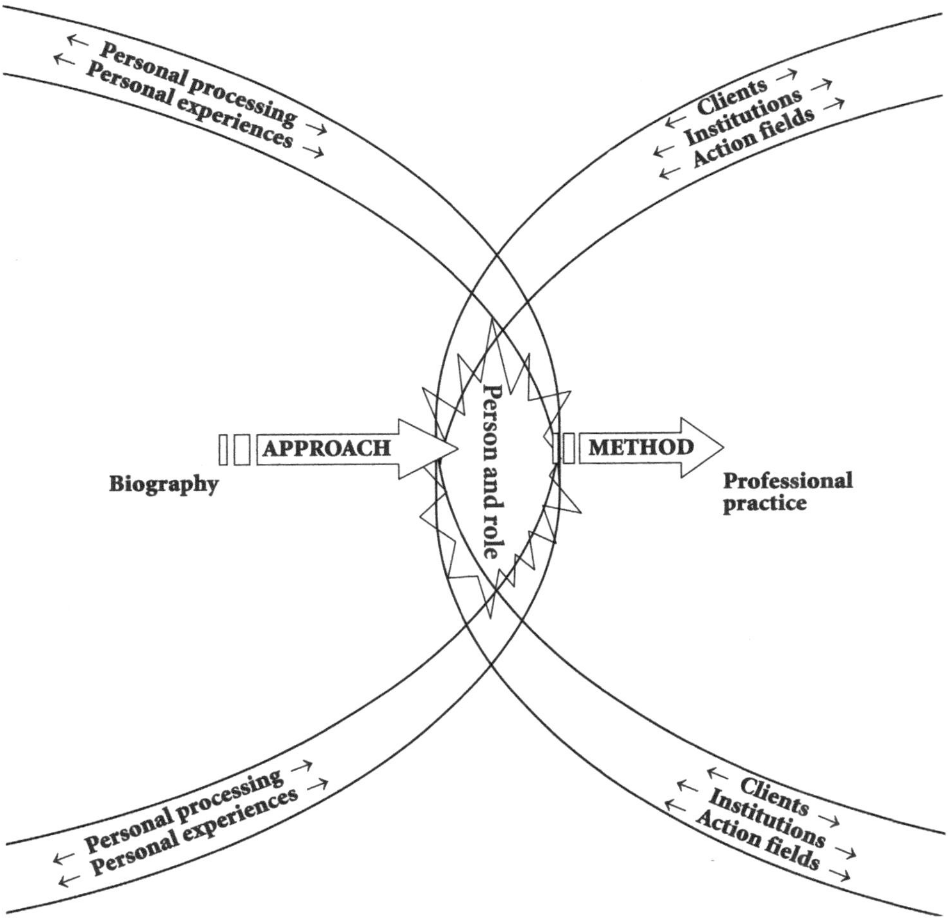

Figure 1. The reciprocal nature of professionalization.

values system of TCI (→ TCI Systematics). This approach is logical when seen from the point of view of the structure of professional educational concepts. "Professional concepts are oriented toward certain reference sciences, even though they may apply them according to their own operative rules that have the role of providing orientation. In order to be able to include all the subjective, contradictory, uncertain, and paradoxical moments of educational tasks and structure (without the need to immediately dissolve these contradictions), they defer to the individual, case-related interpretations by offering rules of interpretation, approaches, categories, examples, and components" (Reiser, 2006, p. 49).

The methodological considerations involved in TCI differ greatly from the patent remedies found in operational sequences and individual techniques; the four-factor model of leadership with its central emphasis on dynamic balance demands a high level of reflection, individual interpretation, and decision making on the part of the group leader.

Individual professional development is a life-long task that includes one's personal and professional identity, which is part of one's approach to a professional educational concept. TCI is characterized by the idea of personality development. "Approach" and "method" are two sides of the same TCI coin.

A further characteristic of TCI is that its operative rules are based on → axioms. "This approach, in my opinion, reveals the design principle of a professional concept. Other professional concepts may lay claim to scientifically sound truths, but here those truths are reduced to subjectively necessary decisions. From this Archimedean juncture onward, the reasoning is turned on its head: Scientific positions, practical procedures, and individual techniques are judged as to whether they agree with these axiomatics" (Reiser, 2006, p. 53).

Thus, TCI offers two types of orientation to educators: "Orientation toward approach and orientation toward content. The approach concentrates on the dialectical unity of opposites as well as a perspective that is attuned to change, i.e., theory is derived from a developmental thought. In conjunction with the first axiom, development may be defined as the reciprocal pervasiveness of increasing autonomy and growing interdependence. The following contents are offered: consciousness raising, the necessity for personal value decisions, and the expansion of both internal and external limits" (Reiser, 2006, p. 55).

Lotz considers the action concept to be the "outline of basic elements that can organize behavior with respect to meaning and with an open attitude toward the situation" (Lotz, 2003, pp. 251 f.). He notes four elements that are necessary for breaking down and working through professional tasks and problems: situation interpretation, vision, approach, and method. Each of these four elements is present in the conception of TCI. He also deals in greater detail with the visionary aspects of TCI and comes to the conclusion that TCI makes these visionary guidelines very concrete through the use of the four-factor model: In the "I-It" connection lies the visionary idea of "education" (ibid., p. 65); in the "I-We" connection lies the visionary guideline of "encounter" (ibid., p. 74); in the "We-It" connection lies the idea of "cooperation" (ibid., p. 86); and in the "Globe" lies the idea of "responsibility" (ibid., p. 63) (→ Differentiation of the Four-Factor Model). He postulates there are "analogies between the elements of a profession and the propositional system of TCI" (ibid., p. 117).

Thus, Lotz (2003) is concerned with the social relationships involved in TCI, whereas Reiser (2006) is concerned more with education and educational support based on TCI. In a further step, Lotz wants to turn the elements and dimensions of the educational action conception of TCI into a model of process analysis according to TCI (Lotz, 2007b).

The question is whether the aspect of professional educational work, which has come more and more to the forefront of TCI in recent years, truly spans all of TCI – or whether other definitions not directed toward professional actions are also necessary in order to describe and conceptualize the workings of TCI, for example, TCI as a "way of life/lifestyle."

Differentiation of the Four-Factor Model

Walter Zitterbarth

One of the best attempts at further differentiating the four-factor model (not, it should be noted, to expand the number of factors) was made by Walter Lotz. In 1997 he presented an "educational conception" of TCI that was not oriented solely toward the corners of the triangle in the sphere, but also denoted the axes and their meaning.

Below I would like to look closer at the meaning of the axes, but first I attempt to clarify what Lotz means by "educational conception." Lotz' thoughts go back to his conviction that the TCI method cannot succeed without recourse to its very basic emphasis on values. This produces the desire to link the normative part of the TCI model (the axioms, the postulates, the value system) with the methodological part, thereby effectively preventing any isolated depiction of the methodological part.

After differentiating the three levels of educational statements, one of these levels, that of "educational conceptions," is linked to the statement system of TCI and then enriched to include a comprehensive orientation for behavior.

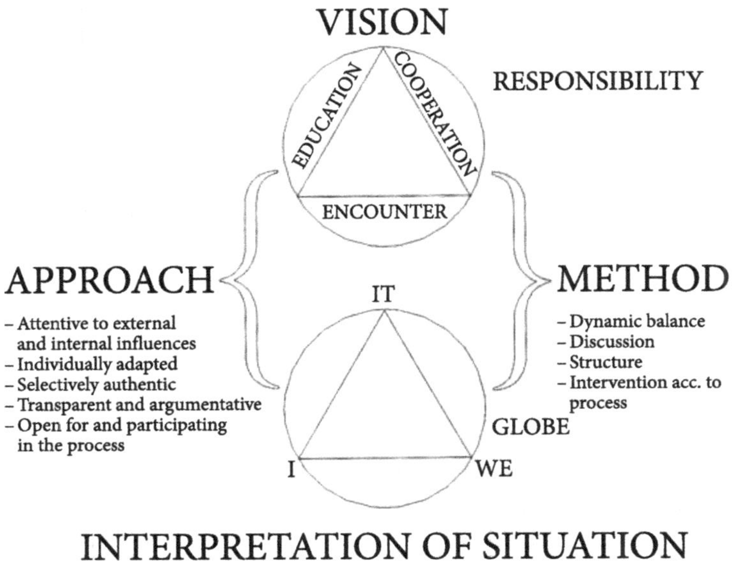

Figure 1. Model of the four conceptional elements.

1 The Levels of Educational Statements

This "level of educational situations" is the attempt to use everyday language to formulate what we perceive about what is happening around us as well as our direct emotional reactions and the subjective assessment we have made in life about what is proper and fitting in any one situation.

The "level of scientific theories" on education, in turn, is the attempt to deduce from the peculiarities of any one situation and to make it understandable using very general terms. The subjectivity of our understanding of a situation is set aside in favor of the verifiability and logical stringency of the statements made.

The "level of educational conceptions" differs from the above-mentioned two terms by formulating the professional competences that result from the problem-solving routines found in everyday worklife. We should recall that this level is connected to the other two levels as well.

2 The Educational Conception of TCI

The TCI statement system as well as the culture of reflection found in practical TCI work fit especially well to the statement level of educational conceptions. The most important aspect when connecting the two statement systems is to differentiate between situation interpretation and vision. Situation interpretation strives to break down a concrete situation according to "I," "We," "It," and "Globe" aspects; it seeks hints and proposals for new steps. If the result is nothing but "the blind leading the blind," a circular march through the four factors, then there is the need to be directed toward a vision founded in values – one that is able to surmount the existing problematic situation and proceed toward more valuable circumstances, one that is able to develop an idea of "the good life" for all involved. If we look at the TCI axiomatics, we can make out an expansion beyond existing limits, a striving toward increasing autonomy and toward interdependence. By employing approach and method we can connect the visionary and the situational.

3 The Visionary Moment of TCI

Because the situational moment, i.e., the triangle within the sphere, has been treated very extensively in TCI literature, we need to look closer at the visionary moment, which too is based on the TCI structure model. In order to better illuminate this visionary dimension in the discussion surrounding the TCI method, it is useful to direct our attention for a while away from the corners of the equilateral triangle and concentrate on the lines that connect these corners. In other words, we want to address the three existential components that, in their totality, represent something like the visionary goal of all "living learning."

1) The "I-We" axis refers to the process of encounter, i.e., a certain quality of human relationships where the other person is not a means, but rather where the space "in-between" becomes the object of attention. The other is not just perceived, but indeed must be personally accepted – even if only as an enemy or a competitor. Because we are open to the other person in a way peculiar to that person, it is only natural that the relationship is unpredictable and unplanable. If we keep the reciprocity of autonomy and interdependence in mind, we discover that any such positive encounter is not the product of an isolated duality, but lies squarely in the context of "We."
2) The "I-It" axis of the triangle refers to a process that concerns the acquisition of objects and the analysis of themes and problems. That is, the dialectical space between the subject and the object propels them into a relationship with one another that does not allow them to be completely independent, but also prevents their complete merger. Objective logic is coupled with the subjective generation of meaning – without completely dissolving in the process. Concrete learning and working conditions are neither totally subjectified nor objectified. The new relationship that emerges between subject and object, between "I" and "It," allows both to retain their independence while also being changed in the process. Wherever this process is successful is what we call "education."
3) Against this background, we see that the unclear differentiation made in large parts of the TCI literature between "It" and "Theme" is disastrous. If "Theme" is inserted where "It" should be (especially at the top of the TCI triangle), we sacrifice the willfulness of the object, which now is relevant only in a subjectively appropriated form; its ability to resist being appropriated is ignored.
4) The "It-We" axis, in its visionary dimension, can be deemed as cooperation. The guiding principle is to find a common approach to themes and tasks which nevertheless leaves the originality of individual approaches intact. The participants should be able to identify with the synthesis we are striving for. The theme principle of TCI also contains the call to retain one's own peculiarities in the search for a common access.
5) Finally, education, encounter, and cooperation are found in the higher-level space of the visionary "Globe." Because of its value system, the autonomous-interdependent self can go beyond its concrete environment and orient itself in an imaginary space full of value-oriented meanings. Initially, Lotz referred to this visionary aspect of "Globe" by noting the trias of "consciousness – responsibility – development" (1997, p. 32); later, he saw it as something more like a transcendental place where the "good life" is situated (2003, pp. 101 f.), a place for which the operational idea of responsibility stands.

4 Outlook

The idea of viewing TCI as a "professional action conception" helped to free up the original thought of differentiating the TCI model from its limitations as a field of activity solely for educational purposes, making it useful in other professional fields.[1]

1 Unfortunately, Lotz mentions only law as a possible application (2007b). However, others are also possible – certainly medicine and pastoral care could be counted as such professions in Lotz' sense of things.

Communicative Theology

Matthias Scharer

1 Definition

Communicative Theology is primarily situated in a specific "culture of practicing theology,"[1] where the Christian understanding of God, mankind, and the world is critically connected to the methods of TCI and where communication is given the role of an intermediary between the two systems. Communication in TCI is thus extended to include the free and unavailable self-communication of God. "Communicative Theology consists of theology derived from living communication processes" (Scharrer & Hilberath, 2003, p. 15). Thus, it goes far beyond just applying the principles of TCI according to Ruth Cohn in a theological setting.

2 Origin

Communicative Theology developed from work being done with TCI in various types of groups using various approaches to the practice and theory of theology. B. J. Hilberath, a systematic theologian, and M. Scharer, a practicing theologian and a teacher of TCI, were invited by K. Ludwig in the 1990s to develop theologically oriented TCI curricula at the Theological-Pastoral Institute in Mainz (TPI). Many TCI teachers subsequently took part in these activities. These efforts to map TCI onto theological subjects were linked to earlier attempts to adapt TCI according to Ruth Cohn for the theological training and education as well as for church pastoral work and religious education.

The first proponents of what eventually (around the year 2000) came to be called "Communicative Theology"[2] were well aware of the gap that exists between academic theology and the concrete needs of practicing pastors and priests as well as their congregations. They were also acquainted with the problem that church structures and church work methods are generally oriented more toward external criteria than pure academic

1 Compare here the subtitle of the American edition of the volume by Scharer and Hilberath: "Introduction to a New Theological Culture" (2008).

2 The term "Communicative Theology" goes back to an idea offered by J. Panhofer, who suggested this terminology while putting together a university curriculum for a theological faculty.

theology.[3] On the other hand, academic theology also suffers from the poor relationship it maintains to practical theological applications. The very broad collection of disciplines present in modern theology point, on the one hand, toward the high scientific standards it has reached; on the other hand, they also effectively limit the meaning and effectiveness academic theology can have in practical matters.

Against this background, it became clear that "Communicative Theology" somehow had to be grounded in what was happening in both theological research and educational settings. Some theology faculties were already working with TCI methods in their seminars, so that the introduction of Communicative Theology fell on fertile ground. Further impetus for the systematic implementation of TCI in theology was provided by the concept of the university course on Communicative Theology offered at the University of Innsbruck, which, beginning in 2001, provided both bachelor and masters students with 5 semesters of instruction in this subject.[4] This program still exists today.

An interdisciplinary and internationally oriented research circle "Communicative Theology" was established in 2003 and meets regularly at symposiums and congresses around the world. Its efforts are supported by many research projects[5] and publications.[6]

3 Explanations

The ideological orientations specific to TCI and Communicative Theology, respectively, do not necessarily contradict each other, inasmuch as God's communication with humans is considered a concrete part of this relationship. Such an approach attributes a very humanistic touch to human communication that is based on the life and fate of a concrete human being, Jesus of Nazareth. The gift of the Holy Spirit in every human soul as the subject of a relationship with other human beings and with God is the expression of the

3 An example may be found in the ongoing analysis of dioceses and other church organizations by management consultants as well as the development plans put forth by the dioceses which (independently) contain a number of implications for theological work and structural and personnel decisions.

4 The connection between the development of a curriculum of Communicative Theology in the Faculty for Theology at the University of Tübingen occurred because of the work of B. J. Hilberath, who together with M. Scharer held an introductory week of seminars directed toward the teaching staff of this university course.

5 See, for example, the project supported by the Foundation for the Support of Scientific Research in Austria (FWF) entitled "Less Violence Due to Increased Encounters? A Critical Look at the Social Relevance of Theme-Centered Interaction According to Ruth C. Cohn (TCI) with Respect to Coping with Conflicts." Furthermore, a number of suggestions were made to include TCI in the doctorate school of the University of Innsbruck as part of the interfaculty research projects entitled "World Order – Religion – Violence."

6 Cf. The two series of publications "Communicative Theology," edited by B. J. Hilberath and M. Scharer, and "Communicative Theology – Interdisciplinary/Communicative Theology – Interdisciplinary Studies," edited by B. J. Hilberath, B. Hinze, and M. Scharer.

communication of God's love for mankind. The spirit of Jesus provides humans with relationships and prohibits any exclusion of individuals or whole groups. This corresponds to the basic intention of TCI as well.

Both approaches to communication, that of TCI and that of Communicative Theology, do not mesh well with the modern social mainstream, which generally sees communication from a more technological and efficiency-oriented vantage point. Thus, in this respect TCI and Communicative Theology share a deeply humanistic approach to life itself (→ Axioms) as well as in the way they strive to prevent violence from occurring in human relationships. From a communicative and theological point of view, this common concern for human connection through relationships may be traced back to the mystery of the Trinity of God, which puts God in a relationship to Himself and has God connecting to others by choice. A further common meeting point between theology and TCI lies in their respective conviction that → living learning is diametrically opposed to "dead learning." The life-oriented approach of TCI may certainly be employed in educational processes to look at the questions of living and dead learning as part of the basic theological inquiry into the meaning of life and the salvation of humankind.

Communicative Theology differentiates between three levels present in the theological process, all of which are seen as producing theological truths and thus continually interlocking. Communicative Theology combines the

- direct level of participation,
- experiential and interpretive level,
- the scientific, reflective level.

True theological insights emerge only when these three levels are linked to one another, which in turn allows all humans to participate in theological processes by introducing their own specific experiences – inasmuch as they have committed to dealing with the basic existential questions involved in theology (whether explicitly or implicitly).

TCI affects Communicative Theology not just in its efforts regarding theology, but also encourages finding, (re)discovering, and (re)defining its own specific places of knowledge (*loci theologici*) in biographical, interactional, traditional, and context-specific ways. This means adapting the four factors of the TCI model (→ Four-Factor Model) – "I," "We," "It," and "Globe" – to the central theological loci, much as R. Siebenrock[7] did with the most important theological premises (cf. Hünermann, 2003, pp. 207–251; Seckler, 1988, pp. 79–104). A combination of the TCI factors with the traditional insights stemming from the loci theologici results in four dimensions decisive to the hermeneutics of Communicative Theology:

- the dimension of personal life and experiences of faith,
- the dimension of social experiences and church attachment,

7 R. Siebenrock is Professor for Systematic Theology in the Theology Faculty of the University of Innsbruck, Austria.

- the dimension of Biblical evidence and their living mediation as well as other religious traditions,
- the dimension of the social context and worldly wisdom.

If we combine the various dimensions and levels of Communicative Theology, we achieve a critical-conflictual dynamic that is theologically relevant. Figure 1 summarizes the patterns of thought and action inherent to Communicative Theology.[8]

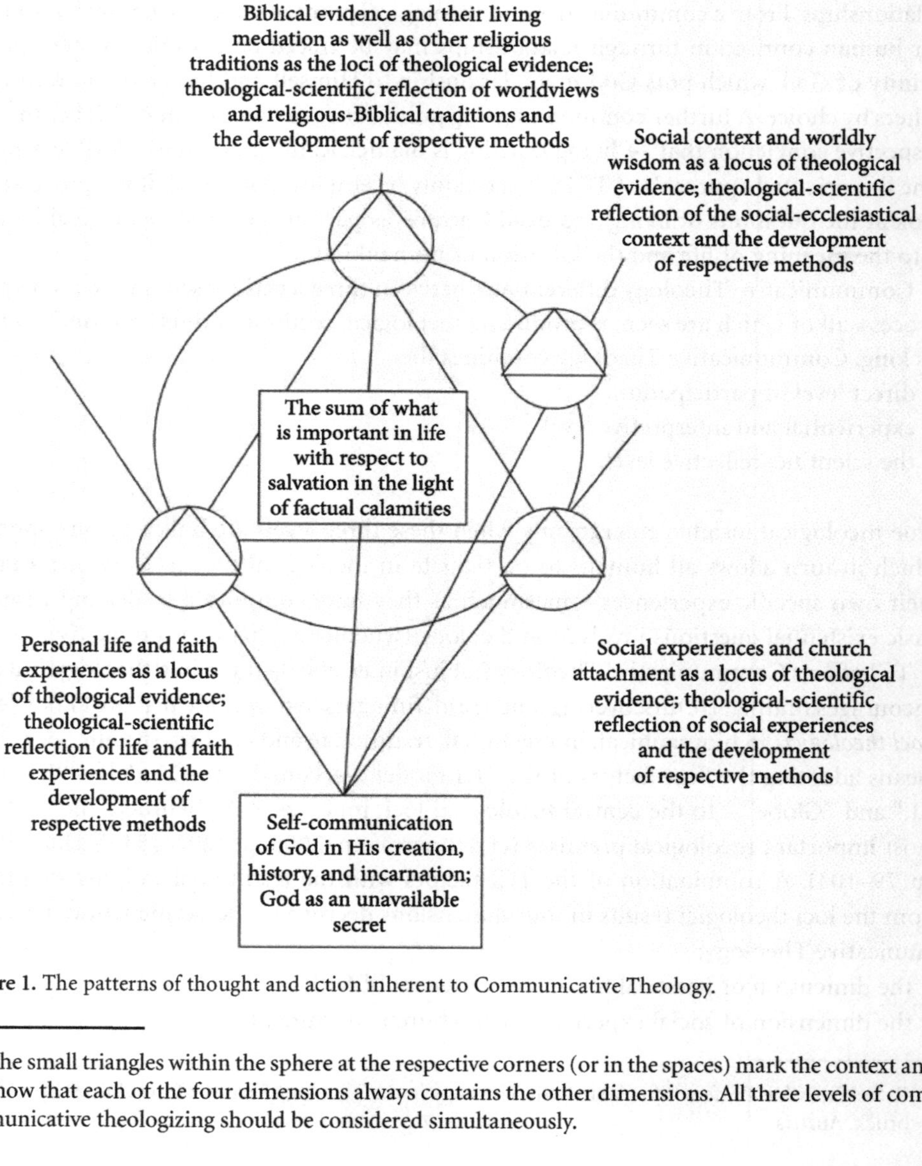

Figure 1. The patterns of thought and action inherent to Communicative Theology.

8 The small triangles within the sphere at the respective corners (or in the spaces) mark the context and show that each of the four dimensions always contains the other dimensions. All three levels of communicative theologizing should be considered simultaneously.

Communicative Theology also reflects the → axioms and postulates of TCI and describes them from the point of view specific to the Jewish-Christian tradition (→ Jewish-Christian Influences). The respective short forms are as follows:

- Axiom 1: Humans in their interactions are both bound and free;
- Axiom 2: Creation and incarnation induce reverence and respect;
- Axiom 3: Limitation and expansion of the limits in light of God's universal will of salvation;
- First Postulate: Chairpersonship as the theological power of judgment;
- Second Postulate: The precedence of disturbances as a theological challenge and interruption.

In accordance with the objective of theology to discern what is important in life with respect to salvation in the light of factual calamities, Communicative Theology adds the following "theological options" to the existing TCI axioms:

- the option of remaining tranquil through grace in the face of feasibility fantasies;
- the option for the poor;
- the option of simply "staying put" when nothing else is possible;
- the option of reverting to contemplation and to the mystical and mystagogical.

TCI as Lifestyle

Jens G. Röhling

TCI originally developed out of psychoanalysis, albeit not as a "means of treating the individual," but as a "way of educating everyone" (Cohn, 1975). Educational theory cannot succeed without some vision of how life itself can be successful. The "philosophy of lifestyle" (or "philosophy of the art of living") is dedicated to the "successful" or "enjoyable" life. Thus, it is completely logical to include TCI in this equation and put a new spin on an old subject. This new accent reflects the changes that took place in the 1960s and 1970s with the creation of a the "new modern" (Schmid, 1998) and the emphasis it placed on the needs of individuals.

1 Definition

The idea of lifestyle (or art of living) reflects the goal of creating something that can be defined by the term "beauty" – the very opposite of a purely ethical outlook on life. Yet what exactly is "beautiful" (or "good") is not defined in the literature concerning lifestyle. What is agreed upon is that it is something that is positively affirmed; that is the formal criterion. The exact determination is left to the individual.

The art of living presumes that humans are in the position to determine such things for themselves, that they are free beings. The correlate is that they have the desire to guide their lives and a method of actually doing so (*áskesis*, Greek for discipline or training). The desire to live a "beautiful" life (synonyms are "worthwhile" and "fulfilling") is one of the basic needs of someone who has arrived at such a state of consciousness (Savater, 2001) and derives from the "concern" one has for oneself (Greek *epimeleia heatou*), which in turn develops from the knowledge of life's limitations. The art of living is thus based on having a favorable attitude toward oneself.

The art of living in question here must, however, be variously delimited. It is more than just a way of living, a method of "designing life" (Schmid, 1998). It is also more than just quality of life, though it does consider ecological aspects. The art of living must also be differentiated from some ideas found in popular self-help literature, such as esoterism, "life-work balance," the "simplify your life" movement, or "positive thinking." It has nothing to do with a look on life that longs only for lightheartedness and pleasure. Those approaches may be included, to be sure; but the "art of living" should be approached from the holistic angle and necessarily includes things that are bothersome and intractable.

2 Origin

In antique philosophy, the major question was: How should I live my life? The educational goal of Plato was *kaloagathia*, that is, the union of what is good and what is beautiful. *Kaloagathia* concerns all of life: the body, the soul, the mind, and the moral side of life. This is where the ethical-moral dimension meets up with the esthetic dimension. Socrates emphasized the idea of "self-care," whereas Aristoteles thought further things of major importance were choice, wisdom, self-empowerment, and asceticism (in the sense of practice). The followers of Epicurus and the Stoics coined the term "self-appropriation." They were also the first to introduce the term "art of living" in both the Greek (*peri bion techne*) and Latin form (*ars vitae, ars vivendi*). Epictetus, who wrote the *Enchairidion* (The Manual of Moral Advice), taught that life is like a material thing that can be artistically formed. Plutarch considered philosophy to be a *techne peri bion*, that is, the art of living. Later, on the threshold of the Modern Era, Montagne wrote about this matter and ushered in the Enlightenment. Kant dedicated his lectures on anthropology (1772/1773) to the subject of the art of living. And in his *Metaphysics of Morals* he developed the thought of striking a balance between our obligations toward others and our obligations toward ourselves as part of the art of living. Kierkegaard, in his work *Either/Or*, discussed various ethical and esthetic approaches to life. Modern existentialism is not possible without the basic thought behind the art of living. According to Schmid (1998), beginning in the late 19th and early 20th centuries, psychoanalysis and psychotherapy came to embrace this theme. In Foucault (and his follower Schmid) philosophy began to take a new look at this matter. In later psychoanalysis, especially Erich Fromm (1992, p. 41) was influential. Schmid says that the rise in interest in the questions of the art of living is closely associated with the increasing freedom and independence humans recently attained from governmental, familial, and religious binds. In this sense, TCI as a form of the art of achieving ethics in education can play a major role.

3 Why Should TCI Be Considered an Art of Living?

Originally, TCI was solely a "professional action concept" (Lotz) for dealing with groups. Matzdorf and Cohn considered the postulates to be "existential" postulates. Especially Langmaack (2001) connected the art of living with the art of group leadership: Only someone who has become his/her own chairperson can lead others in that same task. The idea of TCI as a "action concept" for group leaders is too narrow.

The idea of the "good life" does not exist in the TCI literature (to the best of my knowledge) – even if Ruth Cohn (acc. to Langmaack, 2001, p. 36) did consider esthetics to be of great value. Rather, we find reference to humanization, incarnation, etc. The very use of such terms and goals causes TCI to leave the more "technical" approach to life. TCI as a concept of the art of living assumes that being truly human means living a "good" life – that is where human beings become themselves. In her reasoning for living an ethical life Ruth Cohn quite often referred to esthetics, for example, that an ethical upbringing was clearly dependent on educating one's senses (Matzdorf & Cohn, 1992, p. 60). She links the esthetic lifestyle to the ethical lifestyle. Understanding TCI as an art of living means declaring self-care, the need for a good life, and "wise self-interest" (Schmid, 1998) to be contained within one's social, political, and educational commitment to others. These two directions interact and feed upon one another.

4 TCI as a Lifestyle

In the art of living, what is "beautiful" possesses a "meta-value"; everything else depends on it. In TCI, this meta-value is that which is "humane" (Matzdorf & Cohn, 1992, p. 62). A closer look reveals that the idea of the "humane" is just as vague as that of the "beautiful" – even if Ruth Cohn made it clear that she considered, say, planning a war to be an inhumane act. How to live "humanely" is left unclear. If we understand TCI to be a concept for the art of living, then it *links* the ethical-moral with the esthetical and does not square them off against each other. In the end, this approach prevents formalistic thinking from gaining the upper hand.

4.1 The Axioms as a Vision of the "Good Life"

The TCI axioms describe the way things are, while also addressing how things might (or should) be. In this sense, they project a "vision" (Lotz) of the "good life." It is important to note that this vision is expressed dialectically since that is the only way to describe what it means to live the "good life": by combining things that appear to be incompatible. This points to the ambiguity and incompleteness of a conception of the good life according to TCI. The art of living according to TCI, like dance, is a "performative" art (Sellars, 2007).

The art of living according to TCI means that human beings are "psychobiological units" (Axiom 1), that is, that their mind, body, and soul are equally important. The analogy to art is apparent: Art represents the inextricable union of material-sensual things (the body), of the intuitive-spiritual sphere (the soul), and the intellectual dimension (the mind). That is exactly what the axiom describes: intrapersonal interdependence.

The emphasis placed on interdependence makes it clear that interpersonal interdependence is consciously shaped by the "good life," inasmuch as neither autonomy nor interdependence gain the upper hand. The good life is not some separate entity that can be obtained on its own, but exists only in the interconnection with everyone and everything.

The good life according to TCI understands and applies autonomy and interdependence not as opposites, but as mutually dependent poles.

This part of the axiom may also be interpreted as a meaningful moment if we consider that meaning consists of living within a network of connections to others, and that meaninglessness consists of the absence of such relationships. A meaning in life is not the same as a goal in life or a purpose in life, both of which are products of contemplation; a meaning in life arises from our senses, which connect us to our environment. For this reason, the auxiliary rule "Attend to bodily signals" represents an important methodological adjunct for the art of living.

The second axiom (the "ethical" axiom) says that respect is due all living things. Ruth Cohn expressly included in this statement her own vivacity (e.g., Farau & Cohn, 1984, p. 472), which includes the *epimeleia heautou* mentioned above. Respect is a religious term that belongs more to esthetics than to ethics. Ruth Cohn preferred esthetic arguments and saw them as the basis for ethics. (Compare the explanations of the second axiom in Cohn and Matzdorf, 1984, p. 60.) Again, this is an example of apparent opposites (esthetics and ethics) being regarded as necessary polarities. The good life always begins with self-affirmation.

Further, this axiom points to the necessity of making evaluations in order to express respect toward all living things, that is, living the good life means being aware of the conflicts and contradictions inherent to this responsibility and acknowledging one's own responsibility.

The third axiom (the "pragmatic-political" axiom) is concerned with the polarity of structure and freedom: Freedom without structure is arbitrary, and structure without freedom is anathema to all life. The art of living thus consists of living this polarity, much as art itself is spawned by the tension that exists between form and liveliness. When the internal and external limits are deemed expandable, then a task arises, an exercise in the art of living, namely, to test and expand the limits of freedom.

In the end the concept of "authenticity," which is both the goal and the basis of TCI practice, is a maxim for the art of living. It may be the closest thing to what is considered "good," especially considering that authenticity is an important characteristic of all art.

The term "authenticity" (or "genuineness") does not do it justice. "Authenticity" is based on a static idea of identity which is not fitting in light of the many aspects of TCI considered to be dynamic (e.g., the Chairperson concept). Perhaps it would be better to use Schmid's (1998) term "coherence." In this sense, the art of living generally considers our existence an open matter, capable of growth, whereby this growth can – and indeed must – be actively shaped.

Authenticity emerges less from some core personality than by choice and appropriation. For this reason, it is important (and in one's own best interest) to decide between the various impulses we are confronted with – the woulds, the shoulds, and the coulds – in order to produce the *wants* (Cohn, 1968). At times, authenticity may be nothing more than compliance with what has to be (such as death and decay) or with some prescribed obligation.

"Selective authenticity" is the art of mobilizing those parts of one's personality that are appropriate to the respective situation and to one's counterpart, in order to extend that situation and to hurt others as little as possible.

4.2 The Method of Living the "Good Life" (Postulates, Dynamic Balance, Theme Principle)

The two well-known postulates from TCI are more or less behavioral instructions for living the good life. What connects them is the third thought of self-care, self-appropriation, and self-empowerment. The theme principle has the same goal.

The → chairperson postulate demands and supports autonomy, conscious decision-making, and the balanced consideration of the four factors ("I," "We," "It," "Globe"). TCI ethics comprise the postulate of continual reflection of one's own actions as well as assuming responsibility for oneself and for the entire Earth. It is thus not possible to back up one particular decision or another by quoting TCI, as that would force a moralism not inherent to TCI.

The → disturbance postulate has the goal of creating a holistic, growth-oriented, realistic way of life. In practice, this mean allowing what has been overseen or suppressed to come to the attention of conscious reflection in order to discover new or buried ways of life – and eventually to become the head of one's own household. But this also means that the art of living according to TCI must integrate things that are recalcitrant and bothersome.

The → theme principle, being the "central anthropological assumption" (Kroeger), takes up the idea of the art of living – that life is a malleable thing. The art of living thus consists of the fact that and the way in which one deals with the facts of life, with how this confrontation is considered an opportunity and a way of shaping one's own life. "According to TCI, humans become humans [i.e., a piece of art; the author] by being confronted with themes, with tasks, with things that are made one's own" (Kroeger, 1992, p. 111; similar Schmid, 1998, p. 73).

One of the methodological principles of TCI is → dynamic balance. In this context, it may be seen as a maxim for properly dealing with the polarities of life – the four factors – that determine life and with the "members of one's own inner team" (Schulz von Thun). The classical philosophy of the art of living has the motto: "Nothing in excess" (*meden agan*, Oracle of Delphi), thus ideally a static balance. Dynamic balance, on the other hand, means losing balance in one place and (re)gaining it somewhere else.

The Stoic ideal of *ataraxia* (equanimity, literally: unperturbed), which is achieved by apathy and indifference, meets with Ruth Cohn's thought: "It's all about compassion" (Cohn, 1993), which she derived from the axiom of interdependence. If this is understood as the expression of esthetic categories, then a postulate is born from the moral demand: Compassion serves the beauty of life.

5 The Polarity of Structure and Process

Self-responsibility and the resulting necessity to make decisions are both demanding activities. This effort can, and indeed must, be balanced out by, for example, developing and observing certain rituals and habits. That does not contradict the chairperson postulate, but rather offers the needed relief. These rituals can be freely chosen or perhaps even self-developed. Yet the process can succeed only if it is tempered by the structure, much like life can succeed only if there are fixed structures that life can "hold onto."

6 Conclusion

Today, many different lifestyles are at our disposal. "Individualization" is the catchword that is sometimes (mis)understood to mean "everything goes." The downside is a complete lack of orientation. And for just such a situation, TCI as an art of living offers a concept that enables individuality while demanding and pursuing a clear value orientation to prevent arbitrariness.

Generative Leadership: The Transformative Leadership Concept of TCI

Ivo Callens

1 From Psychoanalysis to TCI, from TCI to Generative Leadership

Both the theory and the practice of TCI are continually being further developed. The evolution of the TCI system into a concept of *generative leadership* ran parallel to a radical and modern redefinition of the entire TCI system: TCI reconsidered. This transformation of the TCI model became necessary if it was to continue to be relevant in a society that itself had undergone a radical transformation over the past 20 years (Callens, 2004, 2005; Callens et al., 2003). "Every new development [...] arises because of both *internal and external dynamics*" (Farau & Cohn, 1984, p. 255). Ruth Cohn used these words to describe a decisive twist in psychotherapy – the rise of group psychotherapy – which later was extended to include experiential therapy and many years of experience with transference workshops to finally flow into the creation of theme-centered interaction (TCI). In her volume *Von der Psychoanalyse zur Themenzentrierten Interaktion* (From Psychoanalysis to Theme-Centered Interaction, 1975) she describes her own transformation from a psychoanalyst and therapist of individuals to an experiential teacher of many (Cohn, 1969). Her intensive interactions during congresses and especially during the many workshops of the newly founded American Academy of Psychotherapists (AAP) with other progressive colleagues led to her experiencing and even shaping the new and changing world of psychotherapy. This fed Ruth Cohn's own inner dynamics. Everything became a living, learning network *avant la lettre*. Knowledge was being created in concert at a point in time at which thankfully theory of knowledge management did not get in the way. Things occurred organically, and there was a great need to pursue things off the trodden path of psychoanalysis and behaviorism and to mutually profit from the experiences of others (Callens, 2005). The new direction taken by those concerned was supposed to be more effective and more humane. This was the wind of change that blew from California to New York, giving Ruth Cohn the feeling of riding a tidal wave and yet swimming of her own accord. What the young people of the day were expressing with the flowers in their (long) hair "stood for rejecting an estrangement from life, for affirming human existence – with sense, with senses, and with sensuality" (Farau & Cohn, 1984, pp. 292f.) (→ Historical and Political Background). Those were the external dynamics.

From a sociological viewpoint, this lived history was an episode embedded in a well-known social phase called the 1960s and the 1970s, a → Globe that was experiencing profound changes. The rise of generative leadership in this context was also deeply rooted in a changed globe – in the social transformation that began in the last 15 years of the last century.

From a sociological perspective, over the past 100 years there were three major transformational periods that spawned social and economic upheavals, whereby each of these periods had its very own specific theme. Here a short overview (taken from the leadership study of Callens et al., 2003; cf. also Lang-Korgen, 2001):

1) The first transformational period may be called *movement and dynamics* and took place from ca. 1895 to 1913. The Industrial Revolution in consequence of the invention of the steam engine set society in motion. The moving picture was invented, *art nouveau* came to life. The leaders of the day were "great men"; organizations were seen as fine-tuned machines. Taylorism with its mechanistic outlook introduced causal-lineal thought patterns, later parodied by Charlie Chaplin in his film *Modern Times*. This time period also includes Freud's development of the extremely innovative psychodynamic view of the human mind (→ Psychoanalytic Fundamentals). However, the fight to loosen the grip of the "linear pattern of cause-effect" was also born in this movement and dynamics period.
2) The second transformational period was that of *growth and change*, lasting from about 1957 through 1974. During this time there was economic growth, the rise and blossoming of rock and pop music, the May uprisings in Paris (1968) as the epicenter of youth revolt, antipedagogics, the antipsychiatry movement, critical psychology and sociology – all of these leveled the discourse between therapist and patient, between teacher and pupil, between manager and employee. Hierarchy was finally being challenged on all levels. Democratic leadership styles and the orientation toward the many capabilities of humans (Maslow) became popular. Humanistic Psychology, in which encounter groups and personal development played a major role, spread throughout the entire Western hemisphere. It was during this time that Ruth Cohn published the original and regenerating idea of TCI and her concepts of → living learning.
3) The third transformational period was one characterized by *turbulence* (1984 to 2002). The introduction of the personal computer, the rise of the internet, the fall of the Berlin Wall – these were the events that led up to the attack on the Twin Towers in New York in 2001 as well as precipitating a number of other unexpected revolutions. The likewise unexpected economic crises caused by the new economic order between East and West, including the weakening economies of the Western world, occurred parallel to these events. The desire for innovation and a new understanding of leadership in a seemingly chaotic world that denied all attempts at predicting the future were clearly articulated. The need arose for a new leadership culture in all areas of society, which in turn was

in the process of becoming an entity consisting of many different self-organizing interaction networks. The various concepts of perceiving and evaluating reality collided with great force, affecting the identity of many institutions and touching the lives of all individuals.

2 New Scientific Findings

In the 20th century, psychoanalysis and experiential psychotherapies were the midwives of TCI. Over the latter period mentioned above, however, new theoretical findings appeared that were quickly combined to support the assumption that the transformation of the TCI system to generative leadership might represent an answer to the developments occurring on our planet.

The systems approach, in all its various facets, eventually developed into one of the most important paradigms in modern history. The most recent developments of systemic thought run parallel to the increasing number of insights emerging from chaos and complexity theory. Biology has also become a breeding ground for new findings on what generates life and on the conditions necessary for living systems to self-organize and transform themselves (cf. Waldrop, 1992).

The systems approach represents an ancient truth about the mystery of life which Ruth Cohn recognized long ago: Individual systems are possible only as parts of even larger systems. Because of their reciprocal relationships, living systems, being parts of larger entities, are permanently growing and changing. "The part is where the whole is made visible" (Senge et al., 2004, p. 7). Perception originating from within the whole reveals in an intimate relationship not only what we see (I-Thou according to Buber), but also what wants to happen (synchronicity; cf. Jaworski, 1996). Generative leadership invites us to take a look from this holistic vantage point (wholeness, cf. Bohm, 1980) and channels our attention toward the transformative process that lies behind what we see (sensing). This results in actions that serve the whole based on our perceptions, feelings, thoughts, and connections with the universe.

The insights presented above converge with another relevant paradigm: organizational learning. This part of organizational theory has grown in importance since the second period to the present day (von Argyris & Schön, 1978, to Senge, 1990). A learning organization is one that is capable not only of adapting to new and changing environment, but one that is also able to generate the future. This points, first, to the purpose of an organization based on its vision and mission – its contribution to the bigger whole such as the communities and, in the end, our entire globe – but also, second, to its ability to survive within this environment (De Geus, 1977). These insights also reveal deeper processes of life and learning as well as the reciprocal implications.

Generative leadership views human organizations (including humans as part of those systems) as living systems that are continually learning from the interdependent, self-regenerating interaction networks in which they are embedded. They are, on the one hand, part of larger networks and thus interact with them. On the other hand, under certain circumstances complex forms arise in the interactions between these networks and within individual networks which can suddenly evoke changes to the interaction patterns and indeed to the character of the entire system. Here, the interaction system *as a whole* is transformed and moreover modifies its entire environment as well as its individual components. This process can be observed and controlled. Systemically we are dealing here with an *ecological* process (Capra, 1996).

Thus, generative leadership based on the principles of living learning – inasmuch as any new insights are grounded in actions (doing) and existence (being) – can provide important impetuses to creating a solid and sustainable society. In this regard a quote from the founder of the Worldwatch Institute and the Earth Policy Institute, Lester Brown: "A sustainable society is one that is able to fulfill its own needs without damaging the means of later generations." That is what Ruth Cohn meant by "generative, life-supportive themes" (Farau & Cohn, 1984, p. 355) (→ It) that the TCI system creates as a sort of *generative core system* (Matzdorf & Cohn, 1992, p. 53).

3 A New Definition of TCI: Generative Leadership

Back when TCI was still called the *theme-centered interactional method*, Ruth Cohn's article "The Existential Leader" (Cohn, 1975a) appeared in which she described the leadership of groups, including her auxiliary rules for interaction. The discovery of interactional group dynamics that went beyond the individual level (which was decidedly influenced by the studies initiated by Lewin) led to the – in those days – new and exciting field of *group dynamics*. Group dynamics, which squarely belonged to the second period mentioned above, has now receded into the background; today, we are well aware of the fact that leadership is manifested in many shifting, sometimes even virtual groups or teams and in complex interactional networks.

This leads us to the most important differential characteristics of generative leadership:

- Generative leadership is the transformational leadership concept of TCI. Through a multitude of centered interactions, it generates transformations and innovative learning and change capabilities in individuals and within interactional systems such as teams, organizations, and social communities.
- Conceptually speaking, generative leadership presumes an inherent system-dynamic connection between the four components ("I," "We," "It," "Globe") on the four levels (physical, emotional, mental, spiritual). When the abstraction "I" is experienced, it becomes the *chairperson*, the "Globe" becomes the *context*, the "We" becomes *concrete interactions*, and the "It" becomes the *living themes* (see Figure 1). Overall, it is a systemic configuration: If any one of the four components or the four levels changes, the

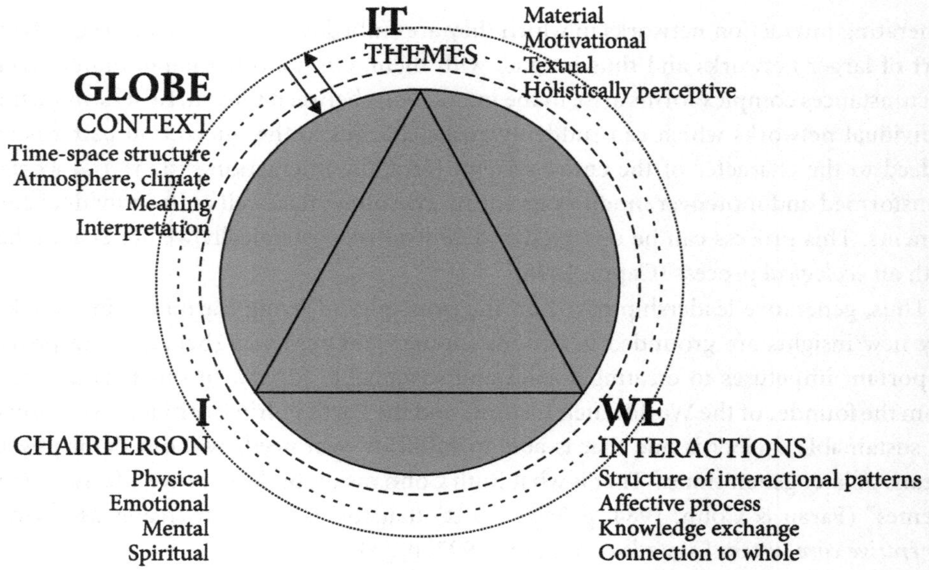

Figure 1. Concept of generative leadership: The systemic-dynamic connection of the four components on the four different levels. © Callens/Centre for Generative Leadership.

whole configuration changes, both in its entirety and in its various parts. This makes this leadership compass a powerful and differentiated concept.

- Operationally speaking, a variety of inspiring interactions are generated concerning the theme. These interactions in turn generate new themes. Every chairperson approaches the themes on as many levels as possible and thus directly introduces him-/herself into the interaction (see Figure 2).
- The systemic-dynamic link between the four components on the four levels produces a ground plan containing 16 leadership components (see Table 1, p. 220). The combination results in 16 fields that are ordered according to their internal or external orientation, resulting in 32 different competences. Moreover, the ecological competence of dynamic balancing ensures the holistic nature of generative leadership.
- The competences present in generative leadership are described more exactly in the "Dynamic Balanced Leadership ScoreCard (DBLS)" (see Figure 3). Depending on the respective personal leadership task (or that of the management team, the directorate, the organization, etc.), one can determine how one's own competence can best be realized (and evaluated) in the areas of self-responsibility (I), environmental consciousness (Globe), result orientation (It), and interpersonal sensitivity (We). This allows assessment of self-image vs. other-image (e.g., by using 360-degree feedback).
- Generative leadership brings existing diversity to life with the help of a variety of interactions. It can bridge differences by focusing on themes – on what is truly at stake: the living themes. Both feminine and masculine qualities are equally important in this concept of leadership (Callens, 2003). *Generative leadership makes a difference.*

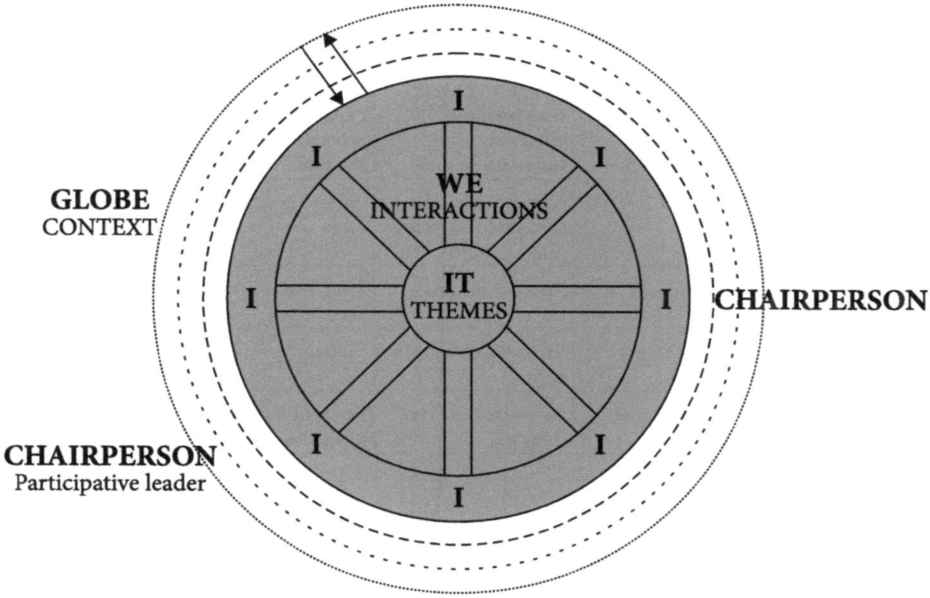

Figure 2. Generative leadership (operational): Every chairperson logs into as many different levels as possible to address the various themes and thus introduces him-/herself into the interaction.

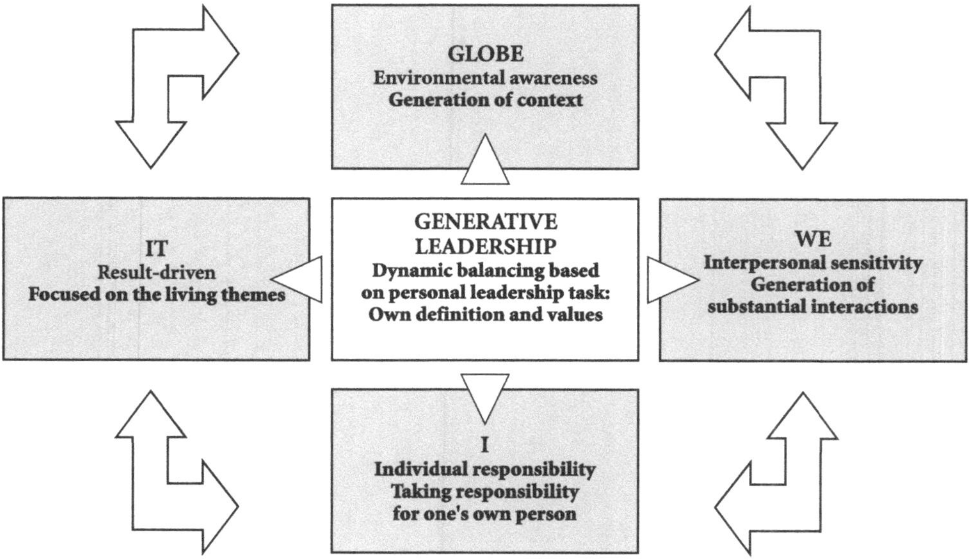

Figure 3. Dynamic Balanced Leadership ScoreCard® (DBLS). The competences as determined by personal values, the definition, and the leadership task at hand. © Callens/Centre for Generative Leadership.

Table 1. Generative leadership: Basic plan for competences.

The 4 components of the TCI system → Levels ↓	I CHAIRPERSON Self-responsibility Internal/external	WE INTERACTIONS Interpersonal sensitivity Internal/external	IT THEMES Experiential orientation Internal/external	GLOBE CONTEXT Ecological awareness Internal/external
Physical	Awareness	Communication structure and interactional pattern	Physical-material form	Physical time-space structure
Emotional	Emotion	Affective process	Motivational influence	Emotional climate and atmosphere
Mental	Cognitive (consciousness)	Exchange of knowledge	Content	Meaning
Spiritual	Soul, inspiration	Connected to everything else	Perception of everything else	Interpretation

Part V

Facets of TCI

Critical Remarks Concerning the Concept

Andrea Dlugosch

1 Scope of the Criticism

This criticism[1] refers to various areas, levels, or parts of TCI[2]. For some, the overall concept of TCI stood at the center of attention; for others, it was the basic assumptions and references (e.g., Geißler & Ebner, 1984/1995), the methodological implications, and/or individual techniques.[3] Further, some differentiated between the level of concept and what occurs when TCI is put into practice in various fields (Lührmann, 2001, p. 101). Finally, there were many critical voices concerning the organizational forms that were used by WILL and RCI to expand the influence of TCI.

2 Phases of Criticism

In the following I would like to differentiate three time periods of criticism. By using these phases I hope to provide pertinent examples within their respective temporal settings. This method also allows me to examine which of the objections raised were valid over a longer timespan and which may be seen as passing phenomena.

2.1 The 1970s and the 1980s

Günther Bittner is one of the most vehement critics of group-dynamic therapies. He considered "postpsychoanalytic therapies" (1976, p. 237), i.e., those conceived by Fritz Perls and Ruth Cohn, to be pure "self-delusions" (ibid.). He felt that TCI, because of its fuzzy and abbreviated self-concept, did not truly contribute to any type of *self-awareness* since

---

1 On the subject of criticism, see Fontius, 2001; Grimm and Grimm, 1873; Holzhey, 1976; Siebenhüner, 2006.

2 During its rise and initial years, TCI itself possessed great social-critical potential and questioned many established values (cf. Raguse, 1995, p. 32).

3 Cf. the criticism leveled by Raguse (1992b, pp. 270f.) at the auxiliary rule to "always speak in the I-form."

it remained stuck in the *experience*. Even after Ruth Cohn's rejoinder (1976), Bittner held to his views, though he did concede to move beyond his earlier, purely destructive criticism (Bittner, 1980, p. 41). He claimed that the problems he had located had blinded TCI to the dark sides of the self (ibid., p. 43). He goes on to describe the "problem of the 'glorified' feelings" (ibid., p. 53), which in turn allowed TCI to "see things through rose-colored glasses, to the point of kitsch" (ibid., pp. 53 f.). With this he means the "didactical approach in its dealings with emotions" (ibid., p. 55). Ermann (1977, p. 273) presumed that a too accepting approach on the part of the group leader might lead to avoiding conflicts and to the suppression of destructive affects. Helga Betz (1979) retorted that destructive tendencies are part of reality and cannot be simply negated. An accepting atmosphere should never exclude working on such matters.

2.2 The 1990s

In his "Critical Survey of TCI," Raguse (1992b, pp. 266 ff.) comments on the criticism expressed by Bittner. Raguse too thinks that TCI is in danger of projecting a too harmonistic view of the world, for example, in its normative assumption of the balance principle. This leads to its missing the opportunity and necessity of "soberly looking evil in the eye" (ibid., p. 271). Raguse even proposed doing away with the idea of disturbance and the associated postulate (cf. Raguse, 1987b, p. 136). Insight into the destructivity of human existence, an important and valuable human heritage in his opinion, should help us to resist all tendencies toward harmonizing and idealizing. Raguse thinks strivings to harmonize lie behind the "condemnation of rivalry" present in TCI (1992b, p. 269).

Raguse formulates a total of eight critical objections to TCI (1992b, pp. 269 ff.) and calls for actions to counteract them, to expand the use of reason, to cultivate reflection, to employ one's intellect, and to "maintain distance and promote understanding" (ibid., p. 272). The rational interpretation of experiences can counteract the "mystification of TCI" even on linguistic level (ibid., p. 275) in light of the inflationary language of TCI in the form of "dead metaphors" (ibid., p. 273). That alone warrants scrutiny of the conceptual terms employed in TCI (e.g., disorder, balance, globe) to ensure "reflection, deconstruction, and renewal" (ibid., p. 273).[4] Moreover, TCI suffers an "ideological overload" (ibid., p. 274). Raguse locates the main danger for TCI "of disappearing within that part of consumer society one might call the 'group scene' through the trivialization of its concepts, the poorly differentiated application thereof, and ideological overload in general. Though it may be well situated there and feel 'safe,' it would lose its liveliness" (ibid., p. 277).

Among the critics of TCI, Raguse discerns two primary tendencies: Most them treat "TCI as it was formulated by Ruth Cohn as a constant, as something to be either rejected

4 Cf. Fontius (2001, p. 454) and Raguse (1995, p. 32) on the use of the term "deconstruction" in Jacques Derrida.

or be subjected to a few desirable modifications" (1992b, p. 268). Yet completely new concepts or far-reaching transformations (which is what Raguse considers his own approach) remain the exception.

Toward the end of the 1990s, like Raguse, Reiser is of the opinion that *trivializations* may be expected "whenever theory is not discussed critically and further developed; when the contents of the theoretical constructs as well as some statements by Ruth Cohn are treated as canonical; when they are interpreted and confirmed as such" (Reiser & Dlugosch, 1998, p. 76). Those parts of TCI devoted to problems, on the other hand, must be retained and not sacrificed to the provision of answers (ibid., pp. 75 f.). You know TCI is being overestimated when TCI comes to see itself is as social criticism or a standalone therapeutic method (ibid., p. 72). The multitude of different fields in which TCI is now employed leads to its being modified, something Reiser greeted, "inasmuch as these modifications do not diverge from the core system of TCI" (ibid., p. 68). The more important thing is that this core system be clearly set forth and described. For this reason, Reiser thought it "necessary to separate individual religious or spiritual connections from the TCI concept in order to maintain the general validity of the overall system" (ibid., p. 73).

With respect to the critical remarks concerning the *incompleteness* of TCI, Reiser quotes the position of Schreyögg (1993a), who like Bittner sees herself as an external critic. She claims that the theory behind TCI is vague, for example, the fuzzy concept of the "Globe." She demands more precise formulations, also and especially in view of its links to social or organizational theories, wherever there is agreement with the anthropological assumptions. She also suggests that TCI could be enriched by adding a "theory kit" (ibid., p. 19).[5]

2.3 The 2000s

At the beginning of the new millennium, Vopel thought he had detected a stagnation of TCI as a group method (2000, p. 69). In his opinion, if TCI is to survive it would need to be updated and improved. Vopel was especially critical of the tendency of TCI to stick by its structures and its failure to scrutinize the original methods (ibid., p. 77). The in principle "static character of the TCI method" (ibid., p. 76) blocked off all further development, something Raguse had pointed out during the 1990s. Vopel too demanded clearer concepts and more exact definitions of the core business of TCI (ibid.). In his opinion, TCI displayed great deficits with respect to its learning-theoretical background, learning goals, evaluations, and methodological tools[6] (ibid., p. 78). Like Schreyögg he also sees the

5 Reiser (Reiser & Dlugosch, 1998) made his own counterproposition to that of Schreyögg (cf. Reiser, 1993) in which he discusses the inner systematics of TCI, thereby rebutting many of the objections. Reiser's rebuttal led Schreyögg to offer an even more pointed version of her criticism (cf. 1993a, p. 71).

6 According to Vopel, it is unfortunate that many resources were invested at the beginning in creating an organization and not in establishing a solid concept and linking it to existing scientific research. This was especially true for the later theoretical discussions.

need for more theoretical underpinning, though he focuses more on existing power and conflict theories (ibid., p. 81). The lack of a solid theoretical foundation leads to some constitutive matters in the social fields being treated only superficially. For example, instead of being adequately exposed, these inadequacies are covered up or concealed by the postulates.[7] Lührmann (2000, pp. 102 ff.) repeats many of the objections quoted above and notes the existing anti-intellectual tendencies, whereby he differentiates between the conceptual level and the practical level, which in his view display a great discrepancy (ibid., p. 101). He also points out the atmosphere in which a "highly dramatically staged value-based discourse" (ibid., p. 102) led to high expectations and claims. He also expresses his distaste for the immanent concepts (ibid., pp. 100 ff.), a charge that goes back at least to Bittner (1976, 1980). Further, Lührmann also attacks the "hypertrophic organizational structure" (2000, p. 101) and the "self-indulgence" of TCI as well as the many deficits in the educational system which eventually led to a crisis (ibid., pp. 99 ff.).

3 Critical Perspectives

In retrospect, we can see that many of these critical objections were repeated over a long period of time. Deficits in the theory of TCI continue to be voiced today, as do the calls for sharper contours of the overall concept and rejection of idealizing tendencies. The rise of harmonizations and idealizations, however, cannot be solely attributed to faults in the overall concept, but may be founded rather in the one-sided way in which it was applied. The "fuzziness" and uncontrolled nature of the concept may also be due to the fact that concepts, unlike terms, generally play a functional role by helping to provide a structure for dealing with problems, and by combining control, effectiveness, and openness (Weisser, 2005, p. 105). "Concepts are developed, whereas terms are set down. [...] Many things can be called a concept, as long as they retain the functional ability to turn unsettled situations and feelings of uneasiness into manageable forms. This is not a matter of deducing and justifying the theories to be applied, but rather one of selecting knowledge and linking that knowledge so that solutions are forthcoming. Concepts always point to conceptual developments, that is, a social process that leads to a sense of direction" (ibid.). Concepts allow social situations to be properly dealt with. This puts the well-known objections to the theoretical vagueness of TCI in a different light. And yet: If TCI is to continue to exist and be taken seriously as a concept, then it will need to continue to orient itself toward scientific theories, in the sense of providing justifications and not deductions.[8] In addi-

7 Cf. the criticism expressed by Vopel (2000, pp. 80 ff.) concerning the Disturbance Postulate, the Chairperson Postulate, Participative Leadership, and the role of Dynamic Balance and the four-factor model.

8 Cf. for example Reiser (2006) and/or the training events for certified TCI instructors and graduates of the RCI for TCI – International.

tion, in all its various manifestations TCI needs to remain true to its commitment to cultivate a critical atmosphere if it is to productively counter the numerous dilemmas, omissions, and gaps that exist. TCI needs to foster a culture of discourse. "Discourse forms the basis and the means of constructive criticism since it creates a distance to convictions held so dearly. [...] Criticism invokes insights that have been gained and in turn questions them, while also questioning the validity of opinions and demanding corroboration of assessments. In this sense, criticism can create alternatives and opens up horizons for both positive and negative options" (Müller-Doohm, 2000, p. 93).

In addition to the self-reflective type of criticism, we can look to TCI to (re)develop new critical potential in light of the ongoing social tendencies – not as a misunderstood political movement, but as a concept that promotes sophistication and differentiates itself from all antirational tendencies so pervasive in society.

Shadows

Eike Rubner

1 Definition

The term "shadow" (cf. Stollberg, 1992) is found in the writings of C. G. Jung (1945), in his concepts "persona" and "shadow," which are interdependent like light and shadow inherently are. "Persona corresponds, first, to our ideal ego and, second, to our idea of how others perceive us" (Kast, 2000, p. 12). Our shadow, on the other hand, is that part of our self we tend to reject, to suppress, or to hide. In other words, whatever fails to correspond to our ideal ego and the demands the superego puts on us – which are then shoved into the darker part of our soul, to the preconscious, or the subconscious: to the *shadow*.

Our shadow "becomes integrated into our ego by our becoming consciously aware of it, by bringing it into the whole" (Jung, 1945, p. 452). The goal of such integration is the union of the positive and the negative factors in our self to become one, whole individual and to release the energy that was previously bound up in the shadow parts of our personality.

2 Light and Shadow in the Theory and Practice of TCI

The view TCI has of the world and of human beings is strictly differentiated according to light (values, humanism) and shadow (un-values, inhumanity). "What is humane is valuable, and what is inhumane threatens our values," Ruth Cohn once wrote (1975, p. 120). Thus, being an innately educational method, TCI has the goal of increasing the humane (light) portion and decreasing the inhumane (shadow) portion in the human soul.

The → axioms emphasize the value basis and the value background of TCI, which also means calling out precisely the shadow thrown by this light:

- In Axiom 1, the *existential-anthropological axiom*, we read: "Human beings are psychological entities, part of the universe, and thus equally autonomous and interdependent. The autonomy of the individual is all the more larger, the more that person is conscious of his or her interdependence with everything and everyone" (Farau & Cohn, 1984,

p. 375). This quote expressly emphasizes both the ideal ego of autonomy and the shadow of dependence, i.e., interdependence.[1]

- Axiom 3, the *pragmatic axiom*, says the following: "Free will occurs within mutually dependent external and internal limits, which can be expanded. Our latitude is larger if we are healthy, intelligent, materially well-off, and spiritually mature than if we are sick, restricted, poor, or otherwise suffer from violence and a lack of maturity" (Cohn, 1975, p. 120). In this sense, freedom is a human ideal juxtaposed to the shadow of limitations. However, one may question whether inner freedom is automatically delimited by an external lack of freedom and by any other limits imposed upon us. Perhaps it is possible for the shadowy sides of life – our having to deal with sickness, poverty, and violence – to lead us to attain more inner freedom and greater personal maturity.
- The *first postulate* says: "Be your own chairperson" (Farau & Cohn, 1984, p. 35), which is clearly directed toward the "bright side" of life: the autonomy of one's self. The "I" can exit from the shadows by consciously saying "I" (Kast, 2000, p. 49).
- The *second postulate* says: "Disturbances and passionate involvements take precedence" (Farau & Cohn, 1984, p. 121). "Disturbances can be all sorts of inner emotional events and external facts that deflect from dealing with the theme or task at hand" (Matzdorf & Cohn, 1992, p. 69). Disturbances and passionate involvements represent the shadowy sides of a group process and in everyday life are often seen as hindrances that must be eliminated on the path toward processing tasks. Yet that would deprive the ego of the possibility of existentially understanding disturbances as emotional, non-ego consternation – of integrating them as the shadows that they are and of becoming whole and learning to be an ego (cf. Raguse, 1987b, pp. 135 f.).

Another, more positive approach and extension of the function of disturbances in the group process may be found in the assumption that every disturbance represents an important contribution, a "shadowy" contribution, to the theme, to the task, to the communication going on in the group (cf. Mahr, 1979, p. 149; Rubner, 1992; Stollberg, 1987, p. 114). If every so-called "disturbance" were seen as the unconscious reaction to a theme, the individuals, the group, the "Globe," or the group leader, then this would lead to a more comprehensive understanding of the situation and a more positive attitude toward the shadow (→ Disturbance Postulate).

- The → four-factor model examines and names the four factors ("I," "We," "It," "Globe") that Ruth Cohn thought cause an accumulation of persons to become a group and that determines how they work together. The management of such a group occurs according to the principle of → dynamic balance. The four-factor model and the concept of dynamic balance give the group leader(s) instruments that can be employed to

1 Axiom 2 is discussed further below since it doesn't exactly fit between Axioms 1 and 3 due to its structure.

highlight the bright sides (e.g., successful processes) and the shadowy sides (e.g., disturbances and conflicts) within the group process – which are relevant to both the individuals and to the group as a whole and must be recognized and controlled by both.
- In TCI practice all → themes, not just the positively formulated ones but those referring to the negative sides as well, fulfill the criteria for accepting and integrating shadows.
- The training offers made by the Ruth Cohn Institute includes special courses that explicitly deal with the integration of shadows: crisis courses on psychopathology, on group crises, and on dealing with aggressions and conflicts.

3 Repressed Shadows in TCI and Their Integration

3.1 Axiom 2

I would like to return to the second axiom, which was not treated above. This is the *philosophical-anthropological axiom* (→ Ethical Axiom): "Respect is due all living things and their development" (Cohn, 1975, p. 120). In contrast to the other two axioms, this axiom is clearly one-sided; it is not dialectical in nature and does not contains opposite poles of any kind. Thus, it postulates that liveliness and growth are ideals to be sought out, whereas stagnation, diminishment, death, and dying are to be suppressed. A more holistic formulation would be: "Respect is due all living things, their growth and their decay."

In this sense, the Conference of TCI Teachers held in 2001 formulated the following statement following a debate on TCI research: "Respect is due to all living things in their growth and decay. This respect qualifies all evaluative decisions."[2]

All human existence consists of reacting to opposites, to antipoles; life takes place in in the tension-filled area that lies between them: light and shadow, good and evil, power and suppression, love and hate. If the shadowy side is suppressed or forced into the unconscious in favor of ideals, the result is ideological, fanatical behavior that runs the risk of becoming destructive.

3.2 Aggression in TCI Groups

The danger that aggression (→ Feelings) might turn into violence and destruction arises when this emotion is suppressed because it is considered to be completely negative in nature. This, in my opinion, was long the case in TCI circles, where aggression was considered to be solely destructive and inhumane, something to be rejected and excluded from all discourse. The discussion surrounding the theme of "aggression in TCI groups" (see Hahn, 1994), which had gone on since 1992, ended with the very Freudian conviction

2 See the minutes of the IGK 2001. This addition to the original wording received a positive response from most of those present at this conference.

that "aggression is a human impulse (like libido) that should be used and properly channeled" (Ruth Cohn at the International Exchange Meeting in 1995 in Vienna).

Aggressive feelings such as anger, irritation, rejection, rivalry, envy, and destruction are the shadowy side of the coin called aggression. On the brighter side lie the positive drives such as delimitation, saying no, self-defense, determination, independence, perseverance, ambition, purposefulness, constructive behavior, commitment, and engagement.

Raguse, like Melanie Klein, thought there were two different types of aggression in groups: *Dyadic aggression* has the goal of "either retaining some state that has been experienced as being positive or freeing oneself from such an early state." *Triadic aggression*, on the other hand, is a more competitive sort (→ Rivalry and Competition), "not geared primarily toward destroying, but to being superior to the enemy" (1994, pp. 134f.).

In TCI groups, we can observe the entire gamut of aggression. At the beginning of a group process (→ Phase Models), for example, where the individual group members are highly dependent on the leadership and on the group in general, primarily dyadic connections are established. The further cooperation that ensues then strengthens the trust of individual group members both in themselves and in the others. At the same time, members become aware of their own characteristics and strengths as well as dependencies. This in turn may lead to dyadic aggression, i.e., the desire to extract oneself from a situation perceived to be restrictive. The confrontation that develops both toward the leadership and toward the other group members culminates in rivalry and competition, the typical triadic aggression. Only when both forms of aggression are allowed to exist and are openly discussed and dealt with can true autonomy and interdependence arise (cf. → Phase Models; Rubner, 1992, pp. 230–251).

4 "Shadiness" in TCI

For reasons of space, the following presents only a few examples of unclear and inexact matters in TCI theory and things that are avoided in practice.

- In the TCI literature, "theme" is often equated to the "It" and thus commingled.[3] The "It" concerns the thing, the contents, the issue at hand – the stuff themes are made of. In the four-factor model, it lies at the head of the triangle within the sphere. A completely worded theme, on the other hand, contains statements about the strategic goal, the task that occurs when treating the "It." In the four-factor model, the theme lies in the middle of the triangle and moves dynamically in that space. The theme is the instrument the leader uses to plan the group sessions to ensure a dynamic balance with the proper theme order (→ Theme).[4] In practice, themes expressed in accordance with

3 Cf. "It (the theme)" in Cohn (1975, p. 115) and in Farau and Cohn (1984, pp. 352ff.). See also Greimel (1992, p. 351).

4 Today, many plead for a clearer differentiation of the terms "It" and "Theme" (cf. Kugler, 1997; Lotz, 1999).

TCI play a rather minor role and are often formulated only as headlines or task descriptions. This neglects one of the most basic concerns and one of the most particular chances inherent to TCI: Formulating a theme is a work of art that can be taught and learned, albeit a form of art to be grasped by the intellect.
- In training courses, the present trend is toward individualization, reflecting perhaps a general tendency in society. The "I," with its own ideas, desires, and expectations ("I want to . . ."), demands ever more space and thereby tends to displace the equally important "We" factor. Interdependence and solidarity are neglected in favor of some presumed autonomy. This may be observed not only in the decreased willingness to adopt "We" themes in the group, but also in the decreased number of "We" themes being offered by group leaders (→ We).
- Recently, in contrast to earlier traditions, training courses tend to address themes concerning gender issues – men/women, eroticism, sexuality – less and less. It is my assumption that here too we are observing a phenomenon stemming from societal trends, the de-eroticization of society that is accompanied, paradoxically, by the complete elimination of all taboos regarding sexuality.

Because TCI claims to be a method that proposes to view and control processes holistically, it must continually recalculate the perception and integration of the shadowy parts of TCI. When Ruth Cohn says "Nothing human is foreign to me," then she is striving for the integration of all light and dark sides of the communication and work processes found in groups. It was Tolstoy who said: "The whole variety, the whole appeal and beauty of life [and the processes that occur in groups; the author] consist of light and shadow."

Spirituality

Hermann Kügler

1 Definition and Background

In the following, "spirituality" is understood as the "basic orientation, and devotion, of humans to what is 'godly' or to 'God and His doings'" (Kügler, 2005, p. 10). This definition has two problematic aspects to it: First, Ruth Cohn never expressly declared what she understood under the term "spirituality," nor do we find any real definition of spirituality in the TCI literature. Second, use of the term has a rather checkered history, being part of the vocabulary employed by the esoteric and New Age movements, in the counseling community as well as by Christian churches and many other religious movements.

Since no single ideology has the prerogative to claim the right interpretation of the meaning of human existence, spirituality is not the privilege of those who believe in a *personal* God. "Devotion to God" is itself not a clear-cut term, much as spirituality is as variable as life itself, like the multitude of ways in which one can address the godly or God.

Nevertheless, despite these complications, there are many good reasons for writing this chapter. First, the conception of human life found in TCI is open to spirituality as defined above. Second, postmodern society has developed its own peculiar search for meaning in life, which is more "spiritual" in nature than tied to any one religion. Third, the history of TCI reveals that the people who attended TCI seminars always profited from being on the lookout for what "lies behind."

2 Origin

Ruth Cohn describes her own spiritual journey in several different places: "I believe that the theories of reason from the 19th and 20th centuries which excluded subjectivity, its transcendence as well as any reference it may have to the universe were in fact *pseudoscientific*. They declared any and all *unproven possibilities to be impossibilities*, for example, *transcendental experiences* – despite the fact that all humans who have ever lived believed in some immanent meaning in life" (1975, p. 231). "What I want to express is the following: Only those forces who serve to unite knowledge and intuition bring a sense to the sensual; only the unifying power of belief gives meaning to sensual and intellectual affairs.

Is our knowledge really as clearcut as scientists would have it? Are our beliefs really so dubious as the 'knowledgeable' would claim? Let us not forget that scientific facts are always related in some manner to the observer, that science without faith is immanently meaningless" (ibid., p. 227). Ruth Cohn also describes how she mediates conflicts using different possible solutions, and how she often discovers that the solution appears "on its own": "Such situations seem to expose the divine in my own self – my inner beyond" (ibid., p. 232).

According to Cohn (1978, pp. 28f.), TCI groups "are concerned with basic human needs and questions, including ethical needs, which comprises, among other often repressed or unconscious matters, religious questions pertaining to the meaning or origin of human life. TCI itself does not make any statements about God or the divine [...] TCI is religiously neutral. Its axiomatics can be grasped religiously, philosophically, or scientifically – or rejected outright. My own personal belief is that religiosity is deeply grounded in the human spirit and, like language, can take on many different timbres and forms. Yet all languages are meaningful; speechlessness would mean great suffering indeed."

These thoughts never failed to captivate Ruth Cohn. "I sought, I questioned, I sobbed and prayed – despite being a nonbeliever – from the desperate hope of somehow finding a redeeming answer to my agonizing insecurity. [...] I speculated: If the divine is in everything, then I will find it not just in myself; rather, the divine must (at least can) be discoverable, even if not directly by our senses" (Farau & Cohn, 1984, p. 520). She summarized the results of her search as follows: "I believe that there is meaning in the world. That there is an inscrutable but nevertheless perceptible Spiritual-Divine being. Of this Being we should make no images. All images of God are mortal. They can and must pass" (Farau & Cohn, 1984, p. 521).

3 Reception and Criticism

The access TCI offers to spirituality developed to date on three different levels.

3.1 Spiritual Elements in TCI Seminars

From the very beginning, TCI teachers and leaders introduced spiritual elements and rituals of all different types from many different cultures, in order to ensure a lively and holistic learning atmosphere. TCI courses have included, among others, Indian and Chinese rituals for beginning a session, for body work, meditation, and evening services (Kügler, 2001). The use of candles and flowers in the middle of a group meeting has long been characteristic of TCI culture, sometimes accompanied by heated discussions for and against such rituals. Generally speaking, however, TCI allows each group member to determine for him-/herself whether they participate in rituals and spiritual acts of this nature. No one should be forced into anything against their will.

3.2 TCI Work on Spiritual Themes

TCI seminars are gatherings of persons with very different religious and ideological convictions. Employing the proper themes can enable spiritual experiences to become experiences of an absolute transcendental reality, which need not be expressed as part of any traditional religious system. Michael Frickel was the first to develop and teach "theme-centered meditation" over the course of years-long group work, which he subsequently wrote about in many publications (1981, 1991, 1992a, 1992b). Frickel presumes the corporeal nature of humans and the resultant experiences, which are available to everyone. It is to Frickel's credit that he illuminated the connection between corporeality, communication, and meditation.

TCI is itself not a specifically religious approach and was never meant to be. Nevertheless, it is oriented toward the values precipitated by the Jewish-Christian cultural tradition. Like the Jewish tradition, Christianity proposes a path crowned by incarnation, not by excarnation. The goal is the redemption of the Earth, not the liberation from the Earth, such as that found in some old Indian religions. "The path of incarnation – in our own body, in our social environment, in our concern for the state of our habitat Earth and the larger community of all mankind – can provide important impulses for TCI. On the other hand, we humans can more consciously shape our search for a spiritual connection to something greater [. . .] if we get to know the implicit intellectual dimensions of TCI and develop them further, both in ourselves and in our TCI activities" (Amann, 1992, p. 174).

In modern continued education offered by churches, there is little or no room for purely theological-systematic debates about God and belief. On the contrary, what people demand are lively encounters centering on discovering the traces of God in one's own biography and on discussing with other matters of belief and disbelief, hope and doubt. Seminars on such true-to-life themes are very popular. TCI in this context is not primarily a highly efficient method of group work, but rather provides the basic axiomatics for shaping such situations (Ludwig, 1997; Scharer, 1997a, 1997b, 2002 ff.).

3.3 How Open Is TCI to Spirituality?

There is presently no general agreement whether or not it is necessary for TCI to address the spiritual dimension of human life. Matthias Kroeger (1992), in his seminal contribution on the anthropological assumptions of TCI, failed to address this matter. In his view, those who use TCI are not members of some church or sect or even a community; rather, TCI provides the background for creating growth processes. Jens Röhling (2005) assumes that TCI does not represent the art of *leadership*, but rather the art of *living*. He, too, does not address the question whether the TCI axiomatics imply some spiritual dimension.

Stollberg and Stollberg (2005, p. 18), on the other hand, think the TCI axiomatics do include religiosity and spirituality. The TCI method has the effect of introducing people to something "very different."

Raguse points out the connection between spirituality and responsible behavior: TCI enables the "rediscovery of one's ego as a believing and theologically driven subject" (quoted in Ludwig, 1997, p. 52). It also provides insights into the possible ways in which the world can change based on such beliefs: the preservation of one's own convictions while simultaneously tolerating the perspectives of others.

Faßhauer is opposed to overemphasizing the spiritual within TCI. The concept of TCI does not, in his opinion, provides any insights into "last things," about the nature of human life or its relationship to the Divine. It cannot and does not provide solutions to existential questions, though it also does not avoid the subject. The professional competence of TCI is not spiritual but intellectual in nature. It is imperative that TCI retain a critical, distanced, and dissociating approach to all spiritual and religious impulses. "TCI enables an emotional approach as well as an objective, theme-based approach to emotionality. That is how it also prevents the continual retreat into pure inner vision and intuition [...] and thus resorting to rather nonpolitical-harmless dealings with one's own subjectivity" (Faßhauer, 2005, p. 26).

An interesting question would be whether the role of spirituality in TCI theory would be treated differently in a different cultural context than that of Central Europe (e.g., India). Research in this direction is, however, only now beginning (Abraham, 2006).

Feelings

Anja von Kanitz

1 Definition

For Ruth Cohn, feelings represented a means of understanding reality which is equal to all thought processes. Typical for her time, she employed common notions of feeling without adhering to any one school or definition. Today, there are any number of different scientific approaches from various disciplines which attempt to differentiate feelings, affects, emotions, moods, etc. Yet no one of them has come up with a generally accepted and binding definition. Ruth Cohn's own fuzziness in dealing with this matter may have been grounded in the inherent difficulty of defining subjectively perceived or experienced phenomena. She viewed feelings as an important source of knowledge that is equally as important as intellectual activity and physical experiences for providing information about both oneself and the world we live in. "Like Farau, I have never subscribed to the positivistic, scientific approach, which assumes that all internal, subjective phenomena are less valuable for scientific argumentation than all the measurable, so-called objective ones. Both those phenomena that are generally quantifiable and those that remain within the domain of a single individual (e.g., some experience or memory) contain reality" (Farau & Cohn, 1984, p. 216).

2 Background

Ruth Cohn attributed the "upgrade" she gave feelings as independent and equal means of gaining insight to the experiences she had had during her own years-long psychoanalysis. There she had learned to permit both feelings and thoughts to direct her on her path. This experience with the unconditional "invasion" of feelings, visions, and fantasies allowed her to look at a particular matter from very different perspectives and let the impressions sink in. It expanded her freedom to make decisions and strengthened the responsibility for her actions (Farau & Cohn, 1984, p. 221). As part of this method of weighing and critically judging the benefits of psychoanalysis, it proved to be a great boon that psychoanalysis embraced subjective experiences as objects of concern while simultaneously using them as tools for scientific inquiry. "Human experiences cannot be tapped into externally, but rather only through the subjective perception and observations of that individual. This demands training in inner awareness – the ability to observe one's own feelings and emotions with great nuance. The goal of such training lies in the search for the authenticity of feelings and for clarity of thought" (ibid., p. 217). These, in Ruth Cohn's opinion, form the basis for responsible decision-making and for taking action.

Ruth Cohn was stimulated by the work done by Elsa Gindler concerning the perception of bodily sensations during healing processes. In her therapeutic work, Ruth Cohn linked matters concerning feelings and thoughts to those concerning bodily sensations. "'Tell me what's happening! What are you feeling? What does your body tell you?' I encouraged patients to listen to what their body was saying to them" (Farau & Cohn, 1984, p. 245). She pursued the idea of linking physical perceptions to perceptions of feelings and thoughts and using the insights gained, and then integrated it into her TCI concept. But this approach effectively cut the ties to standard psychoanalytic teaching and practice, which in her opinion did not lead to a "body-friendly, educational stance" (ibid., p. 248). This decision to treat feelings and thoughts equally and to support decisions based on the knowledge gained from these very different sources was based on her own personal experiences. With it she anticipated later modern concepts of emotional competence or the so-called "emotional intelligence" (especially in the neurosciences).

Because feelings can reflect the truth of a situation, Ruth Cohn thought they also played an important role when working with groups. They could, for example, point to existing disturbances, such as one member's erotic attraction to another member or feelings of irritation toward another member (Cohn, 1992, p. 184). Whether only a single individual lay at the center of attention or the entire group process was being affected, feelings are powerful things that can withdraw much energy from the theme being treated. In Ruth Cohn's opinion, in such cases it is better for the overall work that the feeling not be repressed but addressed. "When feelings are experienced, they change: The boredom, the sadness, the anger become more transparent. One tends to fixate less on them because they are being addressed and because the person having the feelings feels free to be himself" (ibid., 193). The → disturbance postulate in the TCI concept can thus be understood as a system-immanent reminder that strong feelings are important even when they would not seem to befit the task at hand. Ruth Cohn preferred the "emancipation of inner life" (Cohn, 1975, p. 112). This was her vision of all teaching and learning institutes: "Perhaps teachers can concede both to themselves as well as to their students the right to become aware of their feelings and thus replace the secret sabotaging of feelings with a clear right for everyone to experience their own feelings. Both students and teachers have a right to see the reality of their disorders and the truth contained in their creative feelings. I thought it wise to acknowledge this reality and to treat it as a fact instead of repressing it" (ibid.).

In the TCI literature, dealing with feelings is generally linked to the → disturbance postulate as a theme of reflection. Few authors go into more detail about the role feelings play in the overall TCI concept. Kroeger (1989) developed a model of self-supervision that systematically describes how to prepare and carry out thematic work in groups according to TCI principles to ensure living learning. This model combines the basic ideas behind the client-centered therapy of C. R. Rogers with those of TCI. It equally emphasizes training one's means of perception as well as dealing with one's own feelings toward the theme and perceiving the feelings (or presumed feelings) of other group members. Group leaders can pose direct questions and note their observations as part of their dealing with the various factors that go into the four-factor model of TCI. This permits a productive working and learning atmosphere. "The group leader must use fantasies, intuitions, and emotions as well as thoughts as means of perception. That is in fact the only way to understand the decisive levels of the group members and their learning processes" (ibid., p. 243). According to Kroeger, successful TCI group leadership is possible only with the purposeful application of the perception of feelings, both one's own and those of others, both real and future. TCI training à la Kroeger would thus imply the express development of what Rindermann (2006) later came to call "emotional competence."[1]

Rubner and Rubner (1992) provide concrete information for TCI group leaders about how to deal with feelings in the various phases of a group. They refer equally to the feelings of the TCI group leaders and those of the participants. In accordance with their own psychoanalytic background, they think that fear, aggression, and erotic feelings play particularly important roles. In their opinion, the task of TCI leaders is to pay close attention to their own feelings, wishes, and fantasies, so that during the initial phase, for example, "they can properly assess the situation of the group and determine the proper steps and methods necessary to reduce fears and to enhance careful reciprocal approaches" (ibid., p. 236). The group leader's own conscious and unconscious feelings thus, according to Kroeger, help to diagnose and assess the ongoing group processes and to determine which structures and interventions would be most appropriate. When dealing with one's own feelings, the group leader must show selective authenticity, which, depending on the situation, may mean not revealing one's own feelings. Generally speaking, both authors think it important that TCI leaders select their themes and structures such that the participants are encouraged to express their own feelings, including, among others, their negative feelings toward the group leader. The important thing (from Kroeger's point of view) is that the group leader be accepting of all feelings and reactions and avoid all judgments. Group leaders should also be able to introduce their own feelings in a selectively authentic manner. Openly addressing conflicts in the group should enable group members to experience that "aggressions do not kill, but rather represent constructive ways of

1 Rindermann (2006, p. 3) describes emotional competence as a "multidimensional ability to recognize one's own feelings, to recognize the feelings of others, to deal with one's own feelings, and to express feelings." "The model of emotional competence developed here implies that successfully dealing with and expressing feelings depends on first properly perceiving, recognizing, and understanding such feelings. My concept of emotional competence also has the advantage of viewing our understanding, regulation, and expression of feelings as learnable activities. Emotional competence is in short acquirable, susceptible to change, and dependent on one's decisions" (ibid., p. 10).

promoting development" (Kroeger, 1989, p. 242). Registering one's own feelings and those of others, consciously and responsibly dealing with these feelings, as well as being able to select the proper structures, themes, and interventions represent for Rubner and Rubner the central competences of people working with TCI.

The volumes written by Langmaack, on the other hand, which are often considered excellent introductory texts for persons aspiring to learn TCI theory and methods, do not deal explicitly, or only marginally, with feelings (Langmaack, 2001, pp. 200f.), for example, in connection with the iceberg model ("psychosocial level," ibid., p. 59) or with the theme of transference/disturbances (ibid., p. 153). In Langmaack's remarks on planning or analyzing group processes, matters concerning the feelings of the group leader or the group participants play an extremely subordinate role (ibid., pp. 76, 84, 114, 123, 139f., 142, 150, 173, 211 et al.).

Ruth Cohn's criticism of the one-sided approach of the empirical sciences toward rational collection and measurement of facts as well as her conviction of the equality of bodily sensations, feelings, and reason as sources of knowledge was later taken up by Jan Tillmann (2007) on a more theoretical level. This work entitled *Trajektivität* (Trajectivity) proposes a metatheory of all social-work sciences and maps out an extended scientific concept of how the dimensions of feeling and body might look like in the social-work sciences.

3 Controversies

In his critical review of TCI, Raguse (1992b) lamented the one-sided emphasis put on feelings and the expression thereof during TCI seminars – at the expense of abstract analysis and interpretation. He was referring to the statements of group participants who felt that only their feelings and experiences were being respected as expressions of truth ("That's difficult to express – you have to feel it. Stick to your feelings," ibid., p. 265). Raguse's rejoinder to this one-sided emphasis put on the value of feelings was the following statement: "For me it [analytical work with texts and the admission of associations, feelings, ideas; the author] contains an 'intelligence of feelings' only when I understand both how to experience something and to interpret it. [...] I am thankful to Ruth Cohn for calling on us to think about how this process can be instituted also in learning groups with themes that, at least initially, are foreign to us" (ibid., p. 265).

Overall, the tendency remains to attach importance to feelings and the conscious approach to dealing with them as integral parts of the TCI concept, much as Ruth Cohn wanted. Yet clear differences prevail regarding the exact form and intensity with which the emotional competence of the group leader should be made the subject of discussion and encouragement in TCI training and practice. The theoretical basics that support this notion are as inconsistent as the teaching practice itself.

4 Development in the Neurosciences

From the mid-1990s on newly developed methods expanded the horizon of the neurosciences considerably concerning the course of emotional and cognitive processes. This in turn led to a deeper understanding of the role of feelings in learning, thinking, and decision-making processes and furthered overall the holistic concepts of humanistic psychology and education. "Reasonable behavior, the competent interaction with the environment and with other human beings would, according to the newest research results (cf. Damasio, 1995), seem possible only if we integrate emotions and thoughts. [...] Emotions are, in a very subtle way, present everywhere and seem to have penetrated our entire information processing, influencing both the contents thereof as well as the thought processes" (Döring-Seipel, 1999, pp. 39f.). Damasio's neurological research confirms Ruth Cohn's concept that corporeal signals can indeed be used as perceptual tools. Physical processes and the development of emotions are thus inseparably connected, whereby the perception of bodily signals precede the perception of feelings. "In short, the most important role of feelings lies in reflecting a certain bodily condition. The substrate of feelings are neuronal patterns that reflect a certain physical state and that serve to create a mental image of the physical condition. A feeling is above all an idea – of the body or, in some situations, of the inner state of the body. The feeling of an emotion is the idea of a body under the influence of an emotional process" (Damasio, 2003, p. 107). Faßhauer (2004) as well as Reiser and Dlugosch (2007) also studied how modern emotion research scientifically corroborates the presumed truths of the TCI concept and the extent to which the consequences from recent neuroscientific and psychological research is relevant to shaping learning and developmental processes in the educational application of the TCI concept. A more detailed look at this subject, however, has yet to be written. It would be interesting to learn more about the conscious perception of physical feelings and sensations, and how to view them as sources of knowledge and decision-making as well as how the Chairperson and Disturbance Postulates and the methods of subjective approaches to working through factual issues are relevant today.

Rivalry and Competition

Sarah G. Hoffmann and Elisabeth Gores-Pieper

1 Definition

The terms "rivalry" and "competition" are colloquial descriptions of social situations in which it is unclear whether and to what extent those involved can satisfy their needs. The word "rivalry" stems from the Latin *rivalis*, originally meaning a neighbor with whom one shares a waterway of some sort. Today, rivalry refers primarily to a battle for predominance and is used most often to describe a wooing situation, the fight for a sexual partner, or other elementary needs. "Competition," in turn comes from the Latin word *competitio*, meaning a judicial demand, a rivalry, or competition. It refers to a contest or match for some material or immaterial thing. Today, it is found especially in the business world and points to the scarcity of some goods. Competition in sports denotes situations in which a performance order is established. Abstractly speaking, competition is used to indicate ideas or concepts that go up against one another, for example, different laws that regulate the same issue.

One well known and accepted opinion within TCI circles views rivalry as a heightened (and destructive) form of competition.

Rivalry and competition pertain to the dialectic of constructive and destructive forms of cooperation. It is still disputed whether they are helpful as technical terms for better understanding TCI.

2 Rivalry and Competition in TCI Philosophy

Within the context of TCI, rivalry and competition are dealt with on two very different levels. On the one hand, TCI is considered an alternative concept to the principle of rivalry; on the other hand, the role of rivalry and competition within TCI groups is hotly discussed.

2.1 TCI as Alternative to the Rivalry Principle in Inhumane Pedagogics

In an article that appeared in 1973, Ruth Cohn first concerned herself with the subject of rivalry as a principle. In her opinion, the rivalry principle had come to assume a dominant position in both the American and German school systems, which she described as "organizations of undiluted egoism" (Cohn, 1975, p. 154). With the rivalry principle, Cohn thought, the only concern was who won and who lost: "Only you *or* I can succeed. We cannot both succeed" (ibid.). She thought the destructive consequence thereof was a permanent disturbance of the balance of "I-ness" and "We-ness" as well as the absence of any semblance of togetherness. Against the background of a passionate confrontation with rigid educational concepts, Ruth Cohn saw TCI as a cooperative model that offers the principle of dynamic balance instead of rivalry. TCI strives to (re)establish balance: "A balance among the I-We-It factors in the group; a balance between physical, emotional, intellectual, and spiritual needs and desires; a balance between giving and taking, between listening and speaking, between activity and quietude, etc." (ibid., p. 161). In this sense, TCI offers an alternative to the rivalry principle and propagates reducing rivalry through the proper attitude and method and thus encouraging cooperation.

2.2 Rivalry and Competition in TCI Groups

In her later writings, Ruth Cohn did not concern herself much with the themes of rivalry and competition but rather concentrated on answering the question of the methodological steps and attitudes necessary to creating cooperation in groups.

Nevertheless, numerous articles written by leading TCI teachers and researchers (e.g., Belz, 2001; Kroeger, 1985; Lemaire, 2001; Rubner & Rubner, 1992) do deal with this subject. The continuing education courses of the Ruth Cohn Institute often also contain seminars that look at rivalry and competition as an important theme of TCI (in particular those of Rena Krebs, Elisabeth Gores Pieper et al.). How relevant these aspects are in the overall practice of TCI, however, remains controversial.

In his own "critical review of TCI," Raguse (1992b, pp. 269f.) devotes an entire section to the subject of rivalry, saying that this theme is often avoided or shunned in TCI groups. Helga Belz, on the other hand, thinks that feelings of rivalry as well as aggression, envy, and jealousy belong to all group situations (→ Shadows). According to Belz, these "destructive strivings" must be accepted, "as given, albeit not necessarily as something that is viewed positively" (2001, p. 52). Rivalry and competition are thus disturbances that, according to the second postulate, have priority and provide opportunities.

Others have discovered in competition a joyful stimulation, a stimulus, a motivational force. Rubner and Rubner (1992, pp. 230ff.), for example, point out that competition and rivalry as well as power struggles between group members or between members and the group leader are necessary and can act as catalysts for the group process. In their opinion, one important task of the TCI leadership is to look for or create opportunities for "competition and for rivalry on the verbal, physical, and emotional level as well as in the areas of intuition and imagination" (ibid., p. 240).

According to Lemaire (2001), rivalry and competition contain a paradoxical function for TCI: The complex expectations made of the TCI group leader, oscillating between leadership tasks and true participation, often provoke ambiguities in the power structure of the group and can trigger feelings of rivalry and competition (→ Participative Leadership). Depending on the respective relationships present, these feelings are expressed or suppressed. Lemaire thus pleads for intensive reflection on the subjects of power, rivalry, and competition during TCI training.

2.3 Explanations

Ruth Cohn herself noted that her comments on the rivalry principle were not typical for her: "I am doing something here that I've never done in my own training groups: I'm emphasizing the negative aspects before touching on the positive ones" (Cohn, 1975, p. 158). Cohn's thinking usually proceeded gradually and moderately, "oriented pragmatically and dynamically toward life processes" (Kroeger, 1992, p. 98), whereas she used the "reality principle" as her conceptual counterpoint for outlining her own visions and goals.

Regardless of the still very great relevance of Ruth Cohn's descriptions and diagnoses on the subject of rivalry, her comments proved to be confusing for the construction of TCI theory. In the late 1970s, setting the "destructive reality principle" in opposition to the "constructive TCI approach" led to a largely unfruitful debate on rivalry and competition as something to be avoided or even suppressed in TCI practice (cf. Bittner, 1980). The enlightened impetus emerging from Ruth Cohn's early writings concealed the reflexive nature of TCI and led some to assume that Ruth Cohn's idea of → dynamic balance was in fact a vision of world harmony. What was lost was the true strength of the TCI model: the implementation of polarities (→ Jewish-Christian Influences) to develop potential.

3 Discussion

In this section, we summarize what we see as some of the most important aspects of rivalry and competition in TCI.

3.1 Using Theme and Structures in Leadership

Ruth Cohn (1975, p. 158) describes the rivalry principle using a simple experiment: Once, while bird-feeding, she noticed that birds react differently, depending on their eating behavior. When she throws them a large piece of bread, there ensues a great commotion and fight to get a piece thereof, which ends with the victorious bird taking off with the booty away from the others. When she throws them a bunch of little crumbs, on the other hand, the birds pick at them with no or little fuss, even leaving some pieces lying on the ground. These observations led Ruth Cohn to conclude that it depends on the structures whether a shortage of something leads to rivalry or cooperative behavior. She later expanded on this thought in her ideas about the structure of workgroups in space and time and the formulation of a Theme as one of the central tasks in a group (cf. Farau & Cohn, 1984, p. 370). From this perspective, rivalry seems to be less a problematic I- or We-behavior but rather the result of adverse structures and neglect of → globe factors.

3.2 Trust as a Basic Attitude and a Methodological Principle

According to Ruth Cohn (1975, p. 152), the rivalry principle does not conceal some malicious or manipulative intention, but more simply incompetence and insufficient introspection. Vice versa, the humanistic attitude underlying TCI is not based on some diffuse "bleeding heart" approach, but on self-awareness and self-education as well as on the clear orientation toward life-supporting, "generative" themes (ibid., pp. 113 ff.). Ruth Cohn was convinced that intuition, empathy, tactfulness, and courage could be schooled and expanded upon, and that it helps to concern oneself with the positive capabilities humans have rather than with their deficits and faults.

Based on his own personal exchanges with Ruth Cohn, Matthias Kroeger considered TCI to be (psychoanalytically speaking) a largely female-infused orientation, as opposed to the more male-based concepts that emphasize aggression and competition. In this opinion, the TCI approach found in the → chairperson principle and the technique of → setting a theme (cf. Kroeger, 1985, p. 34) stems directly from Ruth Cohn's own personal take that "the primary notion is the love we have for ourselves and for others." In this vision, aggression comes to the forefront at a later point in time and, according to Kroeger, need not be expressed but rather structured. Kroeger (ibid.) questioned whether "this attitude [will remain] the basis for the TCI method" if the following generations applied their own work methods with TCI.

In the meantime, more than 150 teachers of TCI have worked on creating a multifaceted practice of TCI. Precisely because Ruth Cohn was able to transform her personal stance into a methodological principle, people coming from different corners can join together to teach and learn the cooperative principles behind TCI. Belz (2001, p. 52) wrote in this regard: "The quality of a teacher is not revealed in that person's ability to be 'gracious,' but in how well that person is able to project selective authenticity, and how well that person can enable the individual members and the group as a whole to directly experience their thoughts, feelings, and opinions because of that authenticity and tolerance."

3.3 Respect for Interconnectedness

The dominant characteristic of the principle of rivalry according to Ruth Cohn is a one-sided emphasis on the performance and evaluation of individuals. Knowledge and insights are detached from interests and attached and related solely to relevance. The verifiability of knowledge becomes all important.

The cooperative concept behind TCI, on the other hand, views performance as the result of interactional processes, steeped in the idea that humans are psychobiological entities and as part of the universe interconnected with everyone and everything. This implies not just that we humans can learn from one another through cooperation, and that working and learning in a group produces synergetic effects; the theory of interconnectedness, precipitated in the triangle model in the globe, also enables us to reflect holistically on practical and factual problems. The four-factor model (→ Four-Factor Model, → TCI for Managers) may be used as an individual means of reflection on any subject; it helps to understand the social context, to see both the internal and external world, and to gain new perspectives.

3.4 Self-Reflection

Lemaire (2001, p. 123) notes that the lack of differentiation between the TCI employed in workgroups and that employed in training groups has impeded our understanding of the meaning of rivalry and competition. TCI workgroups have the goal of positively applying competition within the group in order to reach the set goals with the greatest efficiency possible. Training groups, on the other hand, are testbeds for experiencing, experimenting with, and reflecting on competitive behaviors.

For this reason, TCI training foresees a large range of different ways to reflect on all the various aspects of rivalry, competition, and cooperation. There participants can discover their own patterns, in particular those present in rivalries with siblings and parents, and practice dealing constructively with feelings of competition. This includes peer groups, written self- and other-evaluations, etc.

A particular challenge may be found in situations in which the ability to lead a TCI group or to teach TCI theory and practices is being tested. In light of the very complex and personal relationships that arise in the course of a training program, one might be tempted to block out the hierarchical and power conditions and thus avoid the themes of rivalry and competition altogether. This fact has influenced the strivings for adequate training structures and forms of evaluation over the course of the history of WILL and RCI (→ Institutionalization of TCI, → Training in Flux).

Interculturality and Diversity

Karl-Ernst Lohmann

Interculturality raises the basic question whether TCI is in fact a universal method of group leadership in the sense of cultural neutrality, or whether it is more strongly culturally shaped than most Central European and North American group leaders would assume. In other words, is TCI basically a Western or even just a German method? Because presently no verifiable data are available on this matter, the following reflects primarily my own personal position.

There is practically no tradition among TCI authors of theoretically addressing intercultural matters. The state of the art of the themes of *culture/interculturality/management of diversity* presented below thus does not stem from TCI authors. The subject of internationality, on the other hand, did play a major role in TCI from the very beginning: It was, and still is, an important practical theme in the organizations that offer TCI training, such as WILL/RCI.

1 Definition

1.1 Interculturality

Cultures are collective manifestations of a material and immaterial nature which serve to find solutions to matters of human cohabitation, in the sense of creating a system of cultural standards for the respective collective. "Culture conveys meaning. [. . .] Culture offers humans ways of being active in both the material and immaterial sense, while also setting limits to individual behavior. [. . .] Culture provides orientation in the midst of a plethora of objects and a continual flow of events" (Schroll-Machl, 2002, pp. 26 f.). Cultures change because of internal and external influences, particularly with respect to globalization, which is a process that uses economic dynamics to connect very different cultures, sometimes resulting in conflicts. The contact between various cultures is referred to as *interculturality*.

1.2 Cultural Models

In modern intercultural training concerned with, for example, a manager's move abroad or the development of a multicultural project team, we generally find cultural models that describe the differences between cultures, in the form of cultural dimensions or standards. Hall (1959) is regarded as the founder of such cultural theories. He proposed a number of criteria for cultural differentiation: time (monochronic vs. polychronic), space (private vs. public), and communication (high-level vs. low-level).

The first empirically valid cultural model was developed based on a famous survey conducted by Hofstede (1991) at the end of the 1960s among employees of IBM. There he worked with the dimensions individualism vs. collectivism, masculinity vs. femininity, low-level vs. high-level power distance, low vs. high insecurity. From this model, Trompenaars (Trompenaars & Hampden-Turner, 1997) developed his own model with the dimensions universalism vs. particularism, individualistic vs. communitarian, specific vs. diffuse, affective vs. neutral. Further dimensions concerned social status (performance vs. attribution), time (sequential vs. synchronous), outside world (internally vs. externally controlled).

All of these models, however, do not in fact *explain* the phenomenon of culture but only describe it. They were created for the purpose of intercultural practice, and they are characterized mainly by their overarching goal of pointing up cultural differences in order to promote cooperation between peoples of very different cultures.

All of these models are subject to the criticism that the act of mere consciousness-raising about cultural differences by pointing out cultural dimensions may in fact promote what one claims to be dismantling, namely, the practice of stereotyping what is foreign. This is a real danger, and the best means of avoiding it is to use these models to reflect on the degree of one's own cultural conditioning.

Further prerequisites for the practical application of the above-mentioned models is the assumption that there is no "best" culture; rather, that all cultures serve to find solutions to the respective problems that arise anywhere and anytime human beings work and live together. The result of a training carried out with a culturally mixed project group is thus a construct: the agreement concerning how this particular group wants to deal with such topics as punctuality, conflicts, information flow, etc.

1.3 Management of Diversity (MoD)

How we deal with diversity has changed considerably since the 1960s (for a historical review, see Thomas & Ely, 1996). Today, MoD is understood to be a management method for organizations that highly value all the differences and varieties present in modern society and attempt to apply them to the advantage of the respective organization and its goals. The persons involved – the employees – should use these differences to grow personally.

The United States was long considered a *melting pot*, a metaphor for the cultural product that emerged from combining the native population and the "immigrants" who entered the country. The result was something uniform, consistent, homogeneous. Today, however, difference and diversity are valued, changing the metaphor to the *salad bowl*: a colorful mélange of various ingredients (cf. the layer model of diversity proposed by Gardenswaartz & Rowe, 1998, Chapter 3).

The conditions for the success in the MoD are as follows:
- Diversity is viewed as a resource that is not only unavoidable but rewarding.
- Behavioral differences among the persons involved are understood to be cultural differences.
- Respect is the professional stance of choice toward cultural differences.
- A constructive attitude toward diversity is not the matter of the individual, but of the organizational culture.
- If an organization wants to be diverse, then it is the responsibility of the management to implement. MoD demands an OE process and must proceed, and be demonstrated, top-down.
- MoD costs money.
- MoD can succeed only if there is a rationally based interest in diversity within the organization.

2 Internationality, Interculturality, and the RCI

From the very beginning, internationality was a innerorganizational them within RCI International[1] (→ Institutionalization of TCI). The smaller, non-German regions were very intent on not allowing the German influence within the RCI to mutate into a German influence elsewhere. Up to 2003 there was even a special committee that dealt with matters of internationality.

Internationality and intercultural understanding were characteristic of the TCI perspectives, not the least because of the political and biographical background of its founder Ruth Cohn. And, indeed, TCI workshops on intercultural understanding were carried out, although it is no accident that this fact is not well known at the RCI (Zieman, 2003).

Today, TCI is not very uniformly widespread, neither on a worldwide basis nor even in the Western hemisphere (for example, the Anglo-Saxon countries are missing) – not even in Europe, where the Romanic, Nordic, and Eastern European countries are weakly represented or missing altogether. German influence in turn remains strong. The number of German regions represented within RCI International and number of persons represented by the organization in those regions lies well beyond 50% of total membership. The TCI house journal is largely written in German, and the staff of RCI International also consists predominantly of German teachers. TCI training contains no obligatory intercultural contents, save for the declaration of intent in the preamble to its charter.

---

1 Previously WILL Europe or WILL International.

All of this suggests that the way in which TCI is being developed, practically applied, and taught (with regard to both its contents and its methods) is clearly influenced by German culture. This viewpoint, however, squarely contradicts the widespread self-image of TCI, which sees itself as a universal method of group leadership based on the themes it treats and the groups it addresses. This leads to the notion that one can use TCI to lead mixed-cultural groups and that one can employ the theme of interculturality while doing so. And, generally speaking, this is indeed the case.

3 Interculturality and TCI

Recently, a number of TCI-oriented authors have addressed the question of how extensively TCI has been conceptually formed by those cultures in which it is best well known (cf. Arend-Herlyn, 2001; Dorison, 2005; Lohmann, 2003). In order to answer that question, in the following I have largely adopted the empirical model proposed by Schroll-Machl (2002), who established seven characteristic standards for the German setting:

1) *Objectivity:* Germans are, relatively speaking, focused on issues and can best connect with strangers via a task to be solved or discussed; other cultures tend to be focused more on relationships.
2) *Appreciation of structures and rules:* In Germany, one finds not only a vast number of rules and regulations, these are also seen by Germans to be necessary and valuable. The German culture is oriented less to situations. This may explain the organizational talents of Germans.
3) *Rule-oriented, internalized control:* If someone is used to adhering to reasonable rules, then that person is reliable and a good neighbor. Germans consider the internalization of rules to be an educational goal. Rules are not adhered to because of the possible punishment in case of violation, but because a citizen see the necessity for their existence.
4) *Separation of personal and professional areas:* Foreigners wonder at the departmentalization of German life, which is separated into professional-private, rational-emotional, role-personality, formal-informal to a much greater extent than in other cultures.
5) *Time planning:* Germans plan their time sequentially and exactly. What task has to be done at what point in time? Time is a precious commodity, so schedules have to be heeded. During contacts with others it is best to concentrate on important matters, on the task at hand. Spontaneous activities are considered disruptive. Punctuality is highly regarded.
6) *Germans prefer communication with a weak context:* Much is explicitly communicated, i.e., not left to interpreting what lies between the lines. What one says is more important than how one says it – content is the most important thing. Orientation to issues dominates communicative styles, and little consideration is given to the sensitivities of one's

counterparts. Regarding communication style, Germans are generally regarded as undiplomatic, even shockingly so, but nevertheless open and honest.

7) *Individualism:* Generally speaking, German society emphasizes the individual more than the collective. Identity means personal identity, which distinguishes one person from others. I am the center of my life – and no one else is allowed to judge that. The boundary lies with other individuals with their respective (and legitimate) interests, a boundary that is guaranteed through any number of existing rules.

This admittedly succinct version of German cultural standards may be found in the TCI theory and likely also in the specific cultural style with which German TCI group leaders understand and practice TCI methodology.

For example, the idea of chairpersonship (→ Chairperson Postulate) may be traced back to the individualism so prevalent in German culture (#7). The preference for hard and fast structures and rules (#2) in TCI, including the time structures (#5), is clearly supported by German cultural values. Indeed, the entire four-factor model (task, individual, group, environment) as well as the demand to balance the factors thematically may be seen against the background of #4 as follows: Experience shows that all four factors influence the group situation. TCI organizes leadership such that the four factors do not get out of control over the course of the group process, but rather remain separate from each other as much as possible and worked through serially. Of course, that plan doesn't always work out – disturbances may arise. According to the prevailing rule (#2), these disturbances take precedence (#7) (→ Disturbance Postulate). The orientation toward objectivity (#1), like the communication style (#6) present in German culture, may be seen in the fact that the group situation tends to deal with very personal themes and sensitivities (including directly addressing conflicts), something that is unthinkable in many other cultures.

If this interpretation that the TCI method is especially compatible with the German culture proves to be tenable, wouldn't it be logical to differentiate between "TCI" and "TCI as practiced today"? Put another way: Is TCI essentially German? Or is it rather something that Germans merely interpret and practice in a very German manner?

TCI is certainly a Western method, if only because its roots lie in an individualistic value system and Western societies have experienced a strong surge of individualism over the past few decades. This causes certain limitations: The TCI personality courses that have been so successful in Central Europe could not be carried out in many countries of Asia (or only without the typically German characteristics), where harmony and avoidance of embarrassment comprise the central social norms. It remains to be seen whether TCI leaders from non-European cultures who have been trained by Europeans are able to adapt TCI to their home countries or cultures.[2]

2 In this regard, an Indian author once wrote: "Let us try to adapt TCI to the Indian situation rather than adopt it" (Abraham, 2006, p. 56). On the cultural challenges faced by TCI in India, which does show great interest in TCI, see the report by Walbrodt et al. (2006).

Gender

Sabine Brombach

In Ruth Cohn's writings, we do not encounter the term "gender." Yet the relationship between the sexes, the sensitivity toward female and male themes as well as the political importance of emancipatory efforts were matters of great importance in the early group-educational activities of TCI. In 1975, Ruth Cohn wrote: "'Theme-centered interaction' helps teachers (and parents), social workers, counselors, psychotherapists, and group-dynamics specialists to lead themselves and their groups. It also serves to enable the leaders and members of all other types of groups, for example, adolescents and organizers of action groups, men's and women's emancipation initiatives, company management, church events, social actions, etc., to free themselves of both consciously and unconsciously entrenched rigidities" (Cohn, 1975, p. 8). On the subject of "theme-centered interaction in the classroom," she notes the following example: "I am a man. I am a woman. I am a boy. I am a girl: What is role and what is reality?" (Cohn, 1990, p. 161).

A person's sex is one of the most important differential characteristics of individuals. Knowing whether a person is male or female helps us to orient ourselves to that person and to establish our position in the interaction with that person as well as determining our own identity. In addition, our sex is an important parameter for the role and status we have in social structures.

1 The History of the Term "Gender"

Women's Studies, which arose from the social sciences and humanities following the events of 1968 and is now established in all disciplines, is credited with making the suppression and repression of the female sex in the past and present a subject of discussion. This gave birth to feministic criticism of patriarchy, which eventually led to two theoretical debates concerning the equality of or differences between the sexes. Today, research in Women's Studies is primarily addressed toward gender themes. Thus, the relationship between the sexes, both internally and with respect to society, now lies at the center of both the scientific and political discussion, for example, in the international demand for gender mainstreaming in order to overcome the discrimination suffered by one sex or the other.

It was Simone de Beauvoir who voiced the now famous sentence: "One is not born, but rather becomes, a woman. No biological, psychological, or economic fate determines the figure that the human female presents in society" (1997, p. 334). This points to the idea that sexual roles are produced by society, and that the category of sex has a social dimension in addition to the biological one. Ann Oakley (1972/2005) introduced to the social sciences the idea of differentiating between *sex* and *gender* propagated by the psychoanalyst Robert Stoller (1969) after his work with hermaphrodites: *Sex* denotes the biological differences between male and female, whereas *gender* the cultural dimension – the social classification of something as being *masculine* or *feminine.*

The use of the differential term *gender* thus assumes that one's sex is determined physically through genetic programming, whereas the manifold social allocations and complex attributions of sexual differences are, historically speaking, products of human invention that are universal throughout all social constructs. Because gender is a socially defined dimension, it is necessarily not a constant; one's "social sex" is not a stable personality characteristic, but rather remains flexible over time. Our gender is constructed through the actions we take in processes of communicative exchange. This creation of sex, sometimes called *doing gender* (West & Zimmermann, 1991), is in part a conscious act, in part an unconscious design of individuals engaged in everyday private and political practice.

A more radical position was assumed by the American philosopher Judith Butler, who began a completely new discussion on physicality (Butler, 1991; Bowald et al., 2002; Villa, 2006). The reception of Judith Butler's theses, which transferred postmodern deconstruction to the category of biological sex, has shaped the scientific debate to this day (Sönser Breen & Blumenfeld, 2005). Butler radically breaks with the idea that one's anatomical sex is biologically determined and thus a given, whereas social constructs alone determine social gender. According to Butler, one cannot escape this discussion; every label depends on language, so that even the designation of a biological sex is merely symbolic: "'Biological sex' is no longer something that is physically construed, something to which the 'social sex' is artificially adjoined. Rather it is a cultural norm that rules the materialization of bodies" (Butler, 1995, p. 22). Both sex and gender are thus politically constructed categories that create the norms of what is masculine and what is feminine as criteria for behavior. This occurs in a social context that has been shaped by hegemonial masculinity (Connell, 1990).

The consequences of deconstruction allow us to "consider gender identity as the multifarious interpretation of sex" (Butler, 1991, p. 22), which, according to Butler, is thinkable up to the very extremes of travesty. If the political consequence of deconstruction is the complete dissolution of sex-based, uniform groups and thus also varying political demands in various dimensions of control, then deconstruction enables a more playful attitude toward gender attributions, roles, and identities at the personal level.

The category of gender is especially challenging at the theoretical and practical level: "Gender is always both a category of analysis and a normative category. On the one hand, sex as category provides a way to see and analyze gender hierarchy; on the other hand, this same gender hierarchy could consolidate and be reinvented again and again as soon as the category of sex is applied. Paradoxically, the feminist idea of gender may create and reinforce something it initially wanted to simply point out and criticize" (Frey & Dingler, 2001, p. 21).

The scientific instrument of analysis should be overcome through political action. This is, on the one hand, an emancipatory venture as well as, on the other hand, the result of *doing-gender processes*, which correspond to processes of social change.

Social scientists from various disciplines support the thesis that the slow erosion of lines of sexual identity directly reflects modern social directions, and that the functional differentiations in our society make all sexual differentiations superfluous. Put another way: Normatively speaking, sex as a category should be dissolved (Thürmer-Rohr, 2001) – at the very least the *ambivalence* of the gender discussion should be kept in mind (Rose, 2007). Does the distinction of two sexes (which for reasons of discrimination is also criticized by the queer movement, cf. among others Hark, 1999) serve any useful purpose? And if it does, to what extent have the methods and attitudes of TCI been influenced by this distinction? Does TCI control a process of doing gender or its deconstructivistic demise?

2 TCI and Gender

TCI is a learning process that proposes to provide a personally important learning experience and thus, in addition to its comprehensive orientation to self-awareness, intersubjective access to specific themes. Within the seminar practice of TCI, the subject of gender has been treated since the 1970s and, in full awareness of its necessity, integrated by group members both thematically and processually. In addition, there have always been (and still are) offers of seminars directed exclusively at men or women or couples.

In institutional settings, emphasis is put on creating a good balance of the sexes. For example, in the guidelines for teacher training at the Ruth Cohn Institute we read: "Both sexes should be represented among the graduates." This demand is also valid for studies leading to certification and diplomas. Positions in the executive boards or management organs of the regional branches of the Ruth Cohn Institute are also balanced for men and women.

This may also be seen in the change that occurred to the category of the "chairman," which Ruth Cohn originally proposed in accordance with the customs of the day, to the present-day "chairperson," which reflects awareness of the necessity of using inclusive language.

During the 1990s, women's issues emerging from the experiences gathered in seminars were taken up in the TCI journal *Themenzentrierte Interaktion* (Theme-Centered Interaction) and other relevant publications (Buschmann & Borgmeier, 1998; Buschmann & Kröner, 2000; Skupnik-Henssler & Wünsche-Pietzka, 1999). Buschmann and Kröner (2000), for example, edited an anthology entitled *TZI bewegt – bewegende TZI* (TCI Moves

– Moving TCI) concerning the new ways group work in continuing education and social work with women was progressing. They conceived of a method of TCI training (cf. also Körner, 1993) that envisioned a holistic form of teaching TCI, providing new impulses for the further development of TCI methodology.

What role can the communicative, holistic, humanistic concept of TCI play in the ongoing gender debate?

3 Explanations

The ethical basis of the TCI system rests on three axioms (Cohn, 1990, p. 120; → Axioms and Postulates), which concern the autonomy, the limitations, and the interdependence of human beings. "Dynamic balancing is one of the basic constructs behind TCI. It refers to the task of continually reestablishing a balance within an existential paradox (our being a biological unit and a social-cosmic being at the same time) – a balance between the I-We-It factors in the group; a balance between physical, emotional, intellectual, and spiritual needs and desires; a balance between giving and taking, listening and speaking, between activity and quietude, etc." (Cohn, 1990, p. 161).

Ruth Cohn's thoughts can serve as a contribution to the debate on gender issues. The goal is to have the biological separation of men and women be as socially acceptable as possible, also by creating a balance of the interaction between the various spheres of human life. Supporting and practicing such a balance can help to overcome the gender problem, inasmuch as it attempts to recognize and pinpoint problems of power and inequality and to surmount them through respectful and humane interactions. This process does not have the goal of leveling the differences between the sexes; rather, the goal is to respect the differences and use them as the starting point for better getting to know oneself and others. As Buschmann and Borgmeier (1998, p. 258) noted: "Recognize yourself – acknowledge others." "The first conclusion [...] says [...]: A confident attitude toward one's own sex role helps to avoid judgmental, polarizing discussions."

And yet, what is *own* and what is *other*? By using this differentiation TCI effectively recognizes the inequality of the sexes. The most important representative of the difference theory, Carol Gilligan, published a critique of Kohlberg's steps of moral development and concluded that there are two forms of morality: a male and a female version, which are of equal value and complement each other (Gilligan, 1984). Everyday experiences provide us with insights into typically male or typically female behavior. So does the concept of Globe introject gender differences into TCI? And how does TCI react?

Based on their experience as supervisors, Buschmann and Borgmeier (1998, p. 269) concluded the following: "The themes introduced into supervision are, depending on the makeup of the group or the team, gender-dependent." They claimed to have observed different approaches to the subject of leadership depending on the sex of the persons involved. And they postulate (ibid.) that men emphasize more the factual/objective level and professional issues, whereas women tend to put more value on relationship matters and exhibit a high level of oral exchange. Whereas women may avoid the subject of competition, men address it head on.

My own research (Brombach, 2006, pp. 20ff.) confirmed the importance of the aspect of gender when leading a seminar, where I asked a group of female students: "Does it matter to you whether the seminar is led by a man or a woman?" The results showed, on the one hand, that it did prove to be important for their personal learning success whether the seminars were being taught by men or women: A mixture of transferences, traditional role models, and gender-specific expectations were bound up in the relationship to the group leader. On the other hand, erotic elements, whether toward the leader or toward other participants, did have an influence on the emotional level in group situations geared toward rational learning. Finally, the sometimes very different assessments of male and female behavior showed that moral demands were seamlessly being deconstructed.

The functional differentiations present in our society (the Globe) have either provoked the assimilation of gender-relevant behavior or more subtly concealed such differences. The continual changes going on in doing gender can be recognized and revealed by using the active process of balancing as practiced in TCI, through the use of intersubjective communication. Ruth Cohn saw leadership as a process of humans negotiating things, thus also between the sexes. Ruth Cohn's statement that "I am not all-powerful, I am not powerless. I am partially powerful" (1990, p. 121) thus reveals the extent of leadership as well as stipulating self-confidence and resistance to hubris to be part of one's personal leadership concept. Buschmann and Borgmeier (1998, p. 274) suggest that "participation be extended to include not just process and theme, but also the effect of gender roles of all involved in the supervision process." To this end, it is necessary to employ language (ibid., pp. 275f.) that includes male and female forms, male and female values, symbols, and metaphors. The goal is to reduce power differentials, to create openness and transparency, and to show an appreciation toward both sexes.

The axioms, the four-factor model, the auxiliary rules – all of these play a part in the gender debate going on with respect to theory and practice. The attitude and the methods of TCI demand a high level of normative prudence when dealing with individual personalities while also taking all sorts of gender-differentiated lifestyles into account. The goal is to recognize the individual and the individual lifestyle as equally valuable in all communicative processes, abolishing in the process everything that divides such as gender attributions.

The Institutionalization of TCI

Hertje Herz

"Institutionalization" means discovering and shaping a specific, organized form of presenting, teaching, and developing TCI. The history of the institutionalization of TCI reveals a dynamic that corresponds to the TCI teachings: the discussion and structuring of a group using process orientation and the interpretation of disturbances as impulses for further development.

1 1966: The Beginnings in the United States: "Now Let's Teach"

TCI first entered an institute in the United States in 1966, when Ruth Cohn and some colleagues established the Workshop Institute for Living Learning (WILL) as a member society. "I've done it – now let's teach!" she exclaimed (Farau & Cohn, 1984, p. 345). This enthusiastic statement by Ruth Cohn marks the beginning of the institutionalization of TCI in the United States. After her famous dream, in which she saw the triangle within a sphere (→ Four-Factor Model), Ruth Cohn developed a model that made teaching TCI practical and above all theoretically learnable. WILL took on the task of making "teaching, researching, and practicing group leadership" possible (ibid.). The term "theme-centered interaction"[1] was chosen by the founders as a way to differentiate this method from other methods that were not devoted to a "theme." The name WILL[2] in turn contained not only the idea of "living learning" in its program, this abbreviation also expressed the willful ego action, the conscious, integrated answer to "I want, I must, I should, I shall" (cf. ibid.) within external and internal limitations. It is the expression of the → chairperson postulate.

The WILL Institute went on to develop a curriculum and a final certificate as well as a WILL faculty in New York for the founding members (Farau & Cohn, 1984, p. 596). Ruth Cohn was its leading benefactor, yet the institute never received her name (cf. those of Fritz Perls, Jacob Moreno et al.). Rather, she chose to have her cause be enshrined in the name.

---

1 Originally coined by Frances Buchanan (Farau & Cohn, 1984, p. 345).
2 Originally coined by Normal Liberman ((Farau & Cohn, 1984, p. 345 & footnote on p. 595).

2 1972–1986: The Founding of WILL Europe – A Democratically Organized and Informal Affair

Especially Austria and Germany had lost out on the scientific developments that took place during the Nazi regime in the fields of psychology, psychotherapy, and education. Now was the time to catch up. Ruth Cohn had become quite well known in psychotherapeutic circles through her many publications; this led to her being invited to speak at congresses and later workshops. In 1971, Ruth Cohn decided to move the main focus of her work to Europe (Farau & Cohn, 1984, pp. 384f.), a decision that was likely decisive in the fact that work with TCI faded in the United States while becoming institutionalized in Europe.

"Once the initial work had been done for setting up 'WILL Europe,' I retreated somewhat at the WILL organization. I didn't want to take on the personal responsibility for the work as I had in New York, since I knew that organizations that did now grow from their own roots usually do not survive their founders and remain vigorous and creative" (Farau & Cohn, 1984, p. 385). On 27 August 1960, Ruth Cohn's 60th birthday, the founding assembly of WILL Europe as a membership society was held according to Swiss law in Küsnacht near Zurich.[3]

The founding and the subsequent work of the WILL Institute was shaped by several impulses that correspond to TCI theory:

- The common connection is based on new experiences and insights gained through TCI, also beyond national borders in a united Europe.
- An official scope of action was formed within the existing social conditions so that it would be possible to provide impulses for change.
- A proper education was offered with very little formal structure and considerable individual freedom and responsibility.
- It emphasized a humanistic attitude, holistic learning surroundings, the meaning of feelings, relationships, and individual approaches to solving issues, whether in the administration, in committees, or in training situations.

The statutes of WILL set down that a yearly general assembly should be carried out to enable the international exchange of information. The statutes also demanded that a high level of consensus reign in all decision-making bodies. It was deemed important that mutual respect as well as personal and professional interactions (the → "We" part of the Four-Factor Model) be institutionalized. The work that went on within the WILL was characterized by great enthusiasm and a pioneer spirit, with all work being done on an honorary basis (teachers, members, students). This succeeded thanks to in part their very

3 Cf. EURO-Info, Supplementum of 27 August 1982: Bojan von Plotho, p. 11, and Farau & Cohn, 1984, p. 602, footnote 5.

generous financial support and a growing number of "family members," including any number of positive and negative entanglements.

3 Crises Lead to Further Development and Restructuring

Any institution that grows rapidly and continuously is bound to experience a number of conflicts. Over time numerous regional groups were founded, some of which were set up as registered associations and were well suited to the needs of their members. Thus, here, too, autonomy and interdependence stood in conflict. Is there really a need for a central organization? Wouldn't a decentralized structure perhaps be the better choice? More and more students and members were becoming interested primarily in developing their own personalities on their own, in using the living methods of TCI, in breaking away from the old patterns – and less so in partaking in administrative work. Hard and fast structures were frowned upon; the "I" gained in reputation. Courses were being offered, and the administration was functioning smoothly without everyone becoming involved in the process. This explains why TCI became ever more prevalent, while at the same time the WILL as an organization remained unknown to many. This situation, I think, marks the beginning of the tendency to separate the educational arm and the administrative arm. The yearly general assemblies and informational exchanges with some 200 participants were characterized by an almost familial structure. Everyone was able to contribute and vote, and few or any of the attendees were prepared in advance to make the necessary decisions, choices, elections, etc. The result was tiresome, emotional disputes, and chance decisions. The demand was made to have more efficiency and professionality in the process, while also retaining the desired exchange and mutual respect.

History eventually caught up with us: The large majority of the members were Germans, and the smaller countries felt outvoted. It became apparent that the past experiences of violent suppression and usurpation at the hand of Nazi Germany had not been worked through enough. Some showed outright resentment and aggressions, others were thankful for belonging to Europe and set their feelings of national identity aside. This process was to continue for many years on end with great diligence.

4 1986–2001: WILL International: The Attempt to Solve Internal Conflicts and Advance an External Profile

In 1986, WILL International was founded to serve as an umbrella associations for the many regional and national WILL organizations, who became the only members of WILL International and received in turn much independence. They participated in preparing the decisions made in the central organization through their appointed delegates and were represented in the international committees that maintained a reasonable and workable size. Internationality was the main thrust – in the name of the central organization, in the mandatory bilingual nature of all international committees, and in the establishment of representation for the national organization. Above all, however, it became a forum for discussion and suggestions on internationality and cultural differences. The board was very consciously called the "Coordination Team," which meant an implicit trust in the competence of the participants, letting the group develop on its own without major attempts at control on the part of the leadership. The organizational work and training were set up in separate structures that existed parallel to one another. In addition to the yearly General Meeting, a Delegate Meeting was also convened with the regional delegates, who enjoyed decision-making authority and appointed an international training commission. In order to participate in the training courses, one had to be a member.

The international exchanges in the form of workshops were divorced from the board meetings. These workshops were directed toward encountering and exchanging ideas about Globe themes and the further development of TCI. The new organizational structure represented the attempt to address the existing internal problems (taking disturbances seriously) (→ Disturbance Postulate) while also helping the organization to raise its game. Yet only few truly understood the structure of this organization: The processes and procedures, the responsibilities and jurisdictions remained in part rather fuzzy or even completely undefined. The familial structure still prevailed. How the organizational work was to be understood above and beyond training efforts was unclear – and is to this very day.

5 WILL 2000 – Transparency and the Simplification of Structures

The General Assembly of 1992 gave the new Coordinating Team the task of looking into the structures of the entire organization with an eye toward greater transparency and simplification. This process came to be called "WILL 2000" and is described in detail by Hildegard Enzinger in the contribution "Wo WILL ist, ist ein Weg! Vom basisdemokratischen Verein zur leistungsfähigen Organisation" (Where There's a WILL, There's a Way! From Grassroots Democracy to an Efficient Organization; Enzinger, 2003, pp. 39–53). The WILL process took place in three basic phases (ibid., pp. 41 f.):

- Up to 1997: examination of the existing structures.
- 1998 to 2001: preparation of new decisions to consolidate the financial situation, to reformulate the goals and objectives of the organization, to combine the organization and its training activities under a single leadership.
- Through 2002: implementation of the new statutes and training guidelines, dissolution of the previous councils, and creation of a new name.

These are the most relevant changes that were made to the structure (Enzinger, 2003, pp. 43ff.):

- A common leadership for all sections.
- The single decision-making organ is the General Assembly (also for all matters concerning training).
- The role of the leadership was redefined to have the Board exercise control powers.
- Members of the organization were no longer only the regional or national branches, but also other associations.
- The training concept was overhauled and a new curriculum put in place.

These were the new tasks (Enzinger, 2003, pp. 45 f.):
- The public face of the organization is the organization as such and not individual members.
- Training is guaranteed and should have a verifiable quality.
- The time necessary to obtain a degree is defined and specific.
- Greater emphasis is put on research and development.
- An important role is explicitly assigned to internationality, cultural exchange, and networking.

6 Since 2002: The Ruth Cohn Institute for TCI – International: A Clear Force in the Training Marketplace

Since May of 2002 the new name of the umbrella organization is The Ruth Cohn Institute for TCI International. This change in name came about for both rational and emotional reasons:
- TCI had become a well-known name, whereas WILL was less well known.
- The term "TCI" could be protected only in conjunction with the name Ruth Cohn.
- Last but not least, it was meant to serve the memory of its founder.

The 1992 task force entitled "WILL 2000" was thus concluded upon adoption of the new statutes.

The circle of member organizations had undergone changes even during the times of WILL International. WILL America and WILL London had withdrawn their membership, leaving only individual members of those organizations. The collapse of the socialist states of Eastern Europe led to new memberships from East Germany, Poland, and Hungary, while at the time presenting great challenges to the cooperation of persons with very different biographies and socialization backgrounds. The full membership of TCI India (2005) was the first encounter with an Asian culture.

In the end, internationalization meant not only establishing a special institute, but also cooperating with other institutions, inasmuch as TCI had been officially adopted there. From the very beginning, there had been many such initiatives, such as the "Westphalia Cooperative Model" in Vlotho (Germany), later the Diaconia Qualification Center in the old German Democratic Republic (TCI could be practiced under Communism only within the walls of a church). There were also cooperation agreements with the Distance University in Hagen (Germany) and the present-day Academy for Teacher Training and Personnel Management in Dillingen (Germany). Today, there are a variety of further cooperation agreements for fixed curricula, including at the University of Tübingen and the Protestant Academy in Meißen. And more are expected.

TCI has clearly established itself as a viable concept. Yet finding the proper institutionalized organizational forms and thus institutionalizing TCI remains an ongoing process.

Training in Flux

Bernhard Lemaire

1 North American Roots

The founding of WILL Europe in August of 1972 brought systematic training in TCI to Europe, even though training courses had unofficially commenced much earlier. The courses, workshops, trainings, etc., introduced by Ruth Cohn in Europe beginning in 1969 had been carried out in various contexts and were effectively educational events in nature. Those courses had concentrated on personality development as well as professional qualification. In North America, in the heyday of WILL New York and Atlanta, there was a complete training program for TCI. In her book *Gelebte Geschichte der Psychotherapie* (The Living History of Psychotherapy) (Farau & Cohn, 1984) she notes that, in 1972, she collaborated with Anita Ockel to establish an "emergency program for the German-speaking countries" based on the training program of WILL New York (ibid., p. 603).

In the protocols of the founders of WILL Europe we read that guidelines for structuring a training program of the then theme-centered interactional model (TIM) had been drawn up as early as 1971.

It is interesting to note that, besides the planned professional qualification of group therapists, teachers, psychologists, and executives (i.e., managers, organizational leaders), the training program in North America included ways of "including individuals in the WILL organization."[1] Thus, the training goal comprised not only qualification of one's work, but also an ideological training intended to bind one to the training institute. It was important to Ruth Cohn that WILL be a *training institute*. Many letters she wrote, in part directed toward the Training Commission (e.g., 18 February 1977), spoke of this desire that WILL be a "Lehrhaus" (the old German/Jewish word for "house of study").

WILL USA attached great importance to group therapists, who could become Associates in Training, whereas others became only Affiliates in Training. In the North American

1 From the Guidelines for Joining WILL, which were translated into German by Anita Ockel (Ausbildungsrichtlinien für WILL USA, New York 1969). The translation itself bears no date, though the accompanying letter, sent to a circle involved in the founding of WILL Europe (Elisabeth v. Godin, Alice Kündig, Franz Heigl, Klaus Vopel, Samuel Kräuchi, and Louis Lambelet), is dated 29 December 1971.

model, later teaching activity was reserved solely for group therapists (the Associates). This rule was discussed at WILL Europe, too, but was not adopted. The reason likely lay in the heterogeneous mixture of persons who participated in the founding of WILL Europe, including therapists, most of whom were medical doctors, as well as theologians, educators, and social workers. The rule that crisis courses should/must be taught only by persons with a therapeutic qualification is presumably a relic from that era.[2]

2 The Beginnings in Europe

A number of in part rival groups from Northern Germany (Hanover), Switzerland, and Southern Germany were involved in drawing up guidelines for the training courses of WILL Europe, all of which were combined by the Training Committee in late 1972 to form a final draft of the guidelines, which assigned great meaning to professional training.[3] There were three sections: the agogen (all sorts of teaching professionals, including those who manage organizations and youth groups), the counselors (which included pastors, couples therapists, nurses, social educationists), and the therapists with their experience in analysis. In addition to the professional qualifications, the various groups had to provide varying prerequisites in order to be admitted to training, for example, proof of having attended basic seminars, crisis-intervention courses, and the like.

Up until 2003, when the guidelines were revised, it was considered a matter of course that Ruth Cohn's suggestion was part of the process: "Because WILL puts a very high value on ideology, individuality, and communication, the program demands that the Training Committee and the students have knowledge of personality, be open, and have the desire to receive the best training possible of individual competences. The training includes both those obligatory demands considered by WILL to be prerequisites as well as the needs of the individual students. This obligatory program should be viewed as a guideline, not as a rigid set of rules. The Training Committee shall cooperate closely with the individual students concerning their respective needs."[4]

Today, the relative importance of these matters has shifted considerably. The Preamble to the 2003 revised version of the Guidelines states: "The Ruth Cohn Institute is an international organization; the promotion of intercultural competence is part of its self-concept. The goal of the training program is to enable students to acquire the competences necessary for working with the theme-centered interaction (TCI) method according to Ruth C. Cohn in agreement with these Guidelines. These competences can, depending on the respective cultural background of the student, be acquired in various ways, inasmuch

2 I have this information only verbally but found no written confirmation. Thus my careful wording. How exactly this rule was applied remains unclear.

3 From the protocol of the meeting of the Training Committee on 17–18 Dec. 1972 in Loccum.

4 Ockel (1972). Appendix to the Draft of the Training Guidelines of 14 August 1972. Unpublished manuscript.

as they serve the overall goals of these Guidelines. The comparability of the different training profiles is guaranteed by RCI International based on these Guidelines."[5]

The promotion of individual variety introduced into the Preamble some 30 years previously (and still found in the seminar directory in the late 1990s[6]) was thus replaced by a culturally oriented, supraindividual variety.

3 Differentiations

One early change may be found in the way the training steps were differentiated. Originally, the only degree awarded was patterned on the North American form of graduation, whereas from 1973 on a sort of precursor was introduced, the so-called FA (for the German term *Fähigkeitsausweis*, a certification or license), whereas the North American model demanded that graduation be followed up by at least 6 months of qualification in "group leadership."

In November 1987, the International Training Commission (IAK) decided to replace the term *Fähigkeitsausweis* by the term "diploma," first to ensure "international applicability"[7] and second to meet the competition going on in the psychosocial sector. Following a 1994 revision of the "International Guidelines for Receiving a Diploma" and the respective commentaries, graduation is no longer mentioned; rather, attaining the qualification to teach was regulated by separate guidelines that were sent out on request.

Once again at the end of the 1990s changes took place in the training landscape of the WILL Institute when the article by R. Hintner and B. Lemaire, who at the time were members of the IAK of WILL International, was published in the section "Mitteilungen von und für WILL-International" (News from and Concerning WILL International) in the journal *Themenzentrierte Interaktion* (Theme-Centered Interaction). In that article, they demanded a further breakdown of the diploma program, based on the argument that the training lasts longer than is necessary for professional life. The result of this process was a change to the training program to make three different degrees possible: certificate, diploma, and graduation (teaching license). An additional further qualification following the diploma was introduced in the early 1990s in the courses leading to qualification as a supervisor.

4 Membership

Yet there was another change that occurred in 2003 that was to influence how the RCI/WILL see themselves. Up to that time, membership and participation in the organization were considered part of the training. The entry colloquium, the gateway to all

5 RCI – The Ruth Cohn Institute International (2003). Training guidelines. Unpublished manuscript.

6 For example, on page 13 of the 1999 seminar directory we find the statement: "This training concept is solely a guideline and not a specific regulation."

7 IAK protocol of 31 January 1988, p. 4.

training courses, was considered a prerequisite to becoming a member of WILL. Even the seminar directory of 2001 still describes this close connection and points out that only membership enables an applicant to receive counseling through the Training Commission, and that personal engagement in the organization is desired.

The seminar directory of 2006, on the other hand, fails to mention the necessity of membership or an entry colloquium in the context of training. The regional organizations are mentioned briefly, and there is no separate membership form for the RCI. The entry colloquium was thus turned into a concept workshop that is part of the diploma curriculum following certification. All of this can be interpreted as part of the professionalization of training and of the separation of the TCI formal organization from professional qualification and further education.

5 Meaning and Goal

The goals of the individual training segments have come to be described in detail only recently. On the one hand, this resulted from a previously rather noncommittal structural culture at WILL; on the other hand, it reflects changes to the social paradigms (e.g., the shift from an input to outcome orientation), which suggest that educational offers should be made with no regard to the standing of the student. The first edition of the annotated training guideline (Ockel & Wrage, 1979) spoke of the "meaning" of education, whereas the 2003 version refers solely to the "goals" that a student has to reach.

What the graduates of the certification track, the diploma track, and the teaching qualification track have to learn was first laid down during the reform (2000–2003). However, it would be wrong to assume that there had previously been no goals. The description[8] of what TCI is and what it can facilitate contains a rather long section on the qualities and competences that lie behind the training guidelines, providing students with an idea of what they *could* learn. The change in emphasis suggests that there has also been a change within therapeutically oriented education toward a more educationally and didactically specific curriculum. Support for this was provided by Schneider-Landolf (2002), who describes the greater meaning attached to self-awareness in early courses than is the case today.

6 WILL 2000

The structure and role of training in the WILL organization[9] underwent a major change during the reorganization process entitled WILL 2000. Up to 2001 only few amendments

---

8 This description was available in a modified form even in the seminar directory of 2006.

9 It would be a significant step to have a separate investigation of the structure that was prevalent at the time concerning the division of labor, the matter of competition, but also the mutual benefit that occurred between the Coordination Team and the Training Commission, and the relationship between the umbrella organization (WILL International) and the regional organizations.

were made to the guidelines (e.g., a second crisis course, peer group). Some of the individual aspects of the training offers, however, were more radically modified, for example, the meaning of what was then called the "long-term courses."[10] This matter had been discussed earlier as well.

Both WILL Switzerland (the so-called *Langzeitobligatorium*, i.e., a long-term mandatory course, from about 1985) and WILL Lage Landen (Netherlands, early 1990s) were involved in heated discussions concerning long-term groups and the respective training curriculum. These forays, however, were strictly rejected both in Switzerland and at WILL International, the stated reason being that such a suggestion would contradict the spirit of TCI, the chairperson principle – and the necessity of getting to know as many different TCI instructors as possible. Nevertheless, WILL Lage Landen did institute a 2 1/2-year training course with a diploma as final degree.

During this time, the Distance University Hagen (Germany) put together a compact offer together with the WILL Coordination Team (i.e., the Board). These initiatives were explained by the need for higher quality and better calculability for both organizers and prospective students.

The present version of the training curriculum does not contain any obligation to complete long-term courses, even if most persons who sign up for the certification courses do in fact prefer such compact tracks.

7 Change

What changes in training curricula can we observe in the seminar directories? Seen from the outside: up to 1999 none at all! The appearance of the directory remained, except for the color chosen for the cover and the headline change from "WILL Europe" to "WILL International," identical for 23 years. Beginning in 2000, however, the design was finally changed, mostly because of the organizational process of WILL 2000. The regional organizations as well, which had offered their own seminars from the early 1980s onward, oriented themselves to the international appearance. In 2004 a completely newly designed directory was published, and since 2006 the courses offered by RCI International have taken a backseat and been extremely pruned.

The themes and the contents of the international courses[11] have also changed, as have the texts on "What is WILL/RCI?" and "What is TCI?" One little noticed modification should be noted since is almost silently opens a completely new door: In the directory

10 The long-term courses refer to the tendering and execution of at least three courses over a period of 5 days by the same leadership with a single group.

11 In addition to the course offers of the RCI International, a number of courses are offered by the regional organizations and other providers, some of which are directed at specific professionals. These offers were not included in the research for this article.

from 1980 we read: “TCI is a *systematic* approach to realizing such enhancements through the practical application of psychodynamic and group-therapeutic process management techniques.”[12] Since 2003, one important word has been changed: “TCI is a *systemic* approach [...].”

This reflects what has been discussed in a number of publications (most recently Reiser, 2006), namely, that Ruth Cohn’s model took up the socioecological perspective and applied both practically and theoretically a systemic approach long before systemic thought[13] entered group work, social work, and supervision via family therapy. It is thus only logical to consider TCI to be a systemic approach.

8 Conclusion

From the very beginning, training in TCI placed very high demands on the students. Although many offers had long had a personality-building, self-therapeutic thrust, there were also courses that were directly concerned with political and organizational themes.

The changes that took place in the structure of the curricula, from extremely individualized training to a more mandatory path, was the necessary answer to the overall growth and structural differentiation that was going on at WILL/RCI as well as in society in general. On the one hand, there was extreme individualization, on the other hand, rapid institutional reform processes (e.g., economization of social affairs and education) (→ Institutionalization of TCI).

12 The text entitled “What is TCI?” presents, among other things, the axioms. The third axiom concerns extending boundaries, which is the subject of this sentence.

13 In this context, the systemic approach means the system-theoretical/constructivistic position that includes the results stemming from psychology, education, and ethics.

Part VI

Interactions: TCI and ...

TCI and Psychotherapy

Christel Wagner

1 Thoughts on the Relationship Between TCI and Psychotherapy

The specific relationships between psychotherapy and TCI as well as the occasional interactions that crop up in the history of TCI result from (1) the fact that TCI developed out of psychotherapy and (2) the fact that its concept has remained geared toward education *and* therapy despite all the changes that took place in the meantime. The → psychoanalytic roots of TCI as well as the experiential-therapeutic (or humanistic-psychological) revisions (→ Psychoanalytic Foundations, → Influence of Humanistic Psychology) are still very much alive in TCI, even though today attention is paid mainly to its educational aspects. TCI may not officially be considered a form of psychotherapy[1], but it remains therapeutic in nature (social-therapeutic, psycho-therapeutic). Psychotherapy research (see here Grawe et al., 1994) refers to the following as characteristics of psychotherapy: the conscious and planned interactional processes that occur between patient and therapist; the verbal and nonverbal communication that serves to shape this relationship; commonly acquired goals that refer not just to the reduction of symptoms, but also to the development of a patient's personality. In the TCI axioms and in its practical application of the axioms in the postulates (→ Axioms and Postulates) lies the model of basic human conflicts as well as a model of mental and social development. Based on this close interaction, there have been repeated attempts to test the compatibility of various therapeutic methods with TCI (examples are Bielander, 1995; Lobos, 1988; Rubner, 1999; Struwe, 1994; Trost, 1998; Wagner, 2007). The authors all come to the conclusion that therapeutic knowledge (psychodynamics, group dynamics) and therapeutic methods and techniques of the various schools of thought did become integrated into TCI (an example being the perception exercises or the treatment of disturbances).

1 The official definition of psychotherapy valid for the German statutory health insurance companies may be found in Section 1 of the German Psychotherapist Act: "[...] any activity that occurs based on scientifically accepted psychotherapeutic methods for the purpose of diagnosing, healing, or alleviating disorders that have been assessed to be diseases." Further, according to this Act, "the appraisal and resolution of social conflicts" do not belong to the realm of psychotherapy.

2 The Historical Development of the Relationship Between TCI and Psychotherapy

I see three main focal points in the history of the relationship between TCI and psychotherapy: (1) the beginnings of TCI, (2) the further development and spread of integrative methods and systemic approaches, (3) the present situation, in which psychotherapists and educationists must react to a changing client base and set special accents based on the results of brain research. The latter represents the rise of a completely new field of action for TCI in psychotherapy and is described below in a separate section.

2.1 The Beginnings of TCI in the United States (1966–)

The beginnings of TCI were shaped above all by psychoanalysts and humanistic-psychological therapists. In Europe, too, the spread of TCI was initially limited to the psychoanalytic community.[2] The early TCI literature describes TCI as a *modification of existing group-psychotherapeutic methods* such as group analysis, gestalt therapy, and experiential therapy (Cohn, 1970, 1975; Liberman & Gordon, 1971).[3] Therein they confirmed the "therapeutic effectiveness" of TCI and its ability to produce "sustainable changes" (even in nontherapeutic groups) (Cohn, 1975, p. 178). Ruth Cohn herself emphasized that TCI should be carried out solely by specially trained psychotherapists under clinical conditions. In this regard, the psychoanalysts Annelise Heigl-Evers and Franz Heigl played a special role: After having learned about TCI, they developed their own Göttingen Model of Psychoanalytic-Interactional Group Methods (Heigl-Evers & Heigl, 1973; Heigl-Evers & Ott, 1994). In this model, therapists did not provide interpretational interventions in groups, but rather reacted to the ongoing events taking place within the respective group. TCI had a major influence on the development of this therapeutic method.[4]

Further, Elisabeth Tomalin (1993), Bojan von Plotho (1985), Anita Ockel (1985), Helga Aschaffenburg (1987), Ruth Ronall (1983), Elisabeth von Godin (1987), Yitzchak Zieman, and Louis Lambelet are examples of psychotherapists who employed TCI in their own

2 The first congresses in Europe attended by Ruth Cohn were the International Congress for Group Psychotherapy in Vienna in 1968, the Congress of the German Society for Group Therapy and Group Dynamics in Bonn in 1969, and the Psychotherapy Weeks in Lindau in 1970–1972 (cf. Cohn, 1984, pp. 376 ff.).

3 Ruth Cohn's article in the journal *Gruppenpsychotherapie und Gruppendynamik* (Group Psychotherapy and Group Dynamics) had as subtitle "A Modification of Group Therapeutic Techniques for the Purpose of Leading Educational and other Communication Groups." The article by Gordon and Liberman describes the process of "TCI therapy."

4 Also, the influence of the publication of the standard volume on group psychotherapy in the United States by Irvin D. Yalom on Heigl-Evers cannot be emphasized enough. Yalom spoke of the meaning of "interpersonal learning" in groups and urged therapists to selectively communicate their own feelings (Yalom, 1996).

clinical practice as well as introducing their own therapeutic potential into TCI and TCI training (and literature).

2.2 The 1980s and 1990s

In the late 1980s and 1990s, the world of psychotherapy changed considerably: Integrative methods and various systemic approaches to therapy were increasingly being introduced. Such integrative models of psychotherapy were interested in connecting various approaches with respect to theory, effectivity, and methods/techniques.

TCI played a role In the psychotherapeutic literature and in the relevant training institutes especially during the 1980s as a social-therapeutic concept as well as a model for group leadership.[5] Astrid Schreyögg (1993), who was, among other things, a psychotherapy trainer at the Fritz Perls Institute, recognized the "edu-therapeutic" background of TCI as the "first 'integrative' model."

The interactions humans have with their environment became the subject of the new systemic forms of therapy.[6] Symptoms were seen as the (paradoxical) attempts to solve problems occurring within rigidified interactional patterns. The special connection between the systemic approach and TCI was cemented during the International Exchange Meeting in Mauloff in 1996[7] where the following was defined concerning the systemic view: "Viewing and understanding individual phenomena within their respective setting, life in its interdependency and ambiguity."[8] Helm Stierlin (1996), the main speaker at that meeting, first described the systemic approach to therapy and counseling. Then Helmut Reiser (1996b) looked at its interrelationships with TCI: The systemic approach may be found in TCI in the first axiom, which concerns the meaning of the → Globe and the principle of → dynamic balance. Yet TCI differs from newer forms of systemic therapies in many central points, for example, the extent of structuring in an interaction, the position of the group leader, how the unconscious is treated, and the respective approach to values. Alexander Trost (1998, 2007) compared TCI and systemic therapy numerous times and emphasized the major differences between the individual schools of systemic thought con-

5 Petzold, inventor of the "integrative therapy" method and founder of the Fritz Perls Institute, wrote in a book he also edited on "resistance" that TCI was one of the many psychotherapeutic methods available. The article by Ockel and Cohn (1981) bore the title "Konzept des Widerstandes in der themenzentrierten Interaktion" (The Concept of Resistance within Theme-Centered Interaction). During my own therapeutic training, I met with many colleagues especially from gestalt-therapeutic institutes who were acquainted with or had been trained in TCI.

6 The most important representatives of this approach were Gregory Bateson, Salvador Minuchin, Maria Selvini Pallazzoli, Paul Watzlawick, Horst-Eberhard Richter, and Helm Stierlin.

7 The official title of this meeting was "Thinking Systemically, Living Politically: Expanding Horizons Within and With TCI."

8 Quoted from the description included in the WILL International Seminar Directory 1996.

cerning the role of values. Nevertheless, he still thinks "the conceptions of human life and ethics of the two approaches are thoroughly compatible" (Trost, 1998).

In addition to the relationships between TCI and the integrative and systemic schools of thought, psychoanalytic thought continues to influence TCI. Rubner and Rubner (1991, 1992, 1993) developed their own detailed concept of the group phases which is still valid today and used in TCI training. Discussions surrounding the disturbance principle and how best to approach aggression in TCI were also influenced by psychoanalytic thought (e.g., Hahn et al., 1994; Raguse, 1995; Rubner, 1992).

2.3 The Present Situation

The modern-day psychotherapeutic scene has been shaped by three aspects: the results of brain research, changes that have occurred in the target clientele and must be taken into consideration, and the overall changes that have occurred in the fields of health, politics, and law concerning psychotherapy. These aspects also play a role in the relationship between TCI and therapy.

Brain research today ("The decade of the brain may be over, but a century of the brain lies before us"; Grawe, 2004) has precipitated a discussion among the various therapeutic schools concerning some very basic matters in the relationship between mental and neuronal processes as well as exactly how psychotherapy works. Reiser (2006) treated a number of important aspects, for example, decision-making ability and free will, that reflect the axioms of TCI. Keywords such as *relationship structure* and *resource activation* became important in both therapeutic change processes as well in those being sought by TCI (cf. Trost, 2007).[9]

The radical sociocultural changes going on in modern society are mirrored in the changes that have occurred in individual mental structures. Psychotherapists, for example, have noted a clear increase in the number of narcissistic and borderline disorders. They are forced to react to many new symptoms that result from negative experiences of self-esteem and disturbed bonding, for example, so-called chatroom socialization. Therapeutic goals today are often directed less toward binding experiences to fulfill needs and more toward emotional, social, and linguistic maturation.

In addition to these vantage points, psychotherapeutic practice must adhere to the increasingly difficult conditions that reign in the modern healthcare system. Treatment based on a number of methods stemming from Humanistic Psychology is no longer covered by statutory health insurance. Despite intense efforts such as effectivity studies, only a choice number of schools of psychotherapy, such as psychoanalysis, psychotherapy

9 In his book entitled *Neuropsychotherapie* (Neuropsychotherapy, 2004, pp. 434 ff.), Grawe suggested, among other things, a number of guidelines for the therapeutic process that would reflect insights emerging from the neurosciences. I think they could be very interesting for TCI as well.

based on depth psychology, and behavioral therapy, are officially recognized as standard procedures.[10] This means that all those psychotherapists who have been trained in other methods, such as humanistic-psychological, systemic, or physical therapies, can no longer be reimbursed by the insurance system. They can effectively practice their learned trade only by integrating them more or less illicitly, inasmuch as they are covered by the directives.

3 TCI in Modern Group Psychotherapy

The importance of group psychotherapy declined considerably over time, though more recently it has once again been revived. Clinics and other institutions largely offer groups for persons with strictly defined disorders: addiction disorders, borderline disorders, depression disorders, eating disorders, sexual misconduct, etc. Many of these people also suffer from deficits in their social behavior, and "the therapy group can serve as a laboratory, a 'mini society,' in order to enable new experiences, new behavior patterns, and new social skills" (Van Hoeck, 2007, p. 37). Different from individual therapy, group interactions (mirroring, testimony, feedback, etc.) can serve as very potent therapeutic factors. Depending on the respective school of thought, each group therapy generally presumes a different theory of personality, in addition to various approaches to groups and group development. Besides the classical methods, many other forms have developed over time that often take an integrative approach, whereby "integrative" here means: The method showing the best results is employed.

Both milieu therapy (today: sociotherapy) and the psychoeducative method are being employed.[11] The main goal is to promote emotional and social competence – to use emotional experiences to achieve maturation. Milieu therapeutic and psychoeducative groups generally work with themes that are determined by the group therapist. Typical examples are information dissemination concerning one's disorder, coping with daily tasks, creating and shaping relationships, stress management, etc. The main thrust always demands assuming responsibility for oneself and for one's own social interactions. In TCI terms, it means developing one's own chairperson. The educative aspect of this work often carries much weight, since especially the psychoeducative side is compatible with TCI with its clear methodological concept and its attention to values. An example is the (healing) TCI work with respect to reality: This means getting to know one's own inner reality – the entire spectrum of one's innate and acquired convictions – and applying this knowledge

10 Conversational psychotherapy has a limited acceptance for chosen clinical syndromes. Gestalt therapy, family therapy, and other methods stemming from Humanistic Psychology, however, are not covered by the (German) statutory health insurance.

11 "Psychoeducation" originally evolved from behavioral therapy and is long established in clinical work done with chronically ill patients, schizophrenics, and addicts.

to external reality. This serves to confirm that we are social beings who are involved in many different contexts (axioms/postulates of TCI), all of which allows us to deal with our own contradictory feelings of omnipotence and impotence.

The TCI vision encompasses "respect for oneself, for others, and for the entire world," which goes back to its original understanding of what therapy is: The Greek work *therapia* does not mean "to heal" but "to serve and show reverence."

In conclusion, I would like to point out that the professional group of psychotherapists in RCI no longer play the major role it once did in the past. Nevertheless, the relationship between TCI and psychotherapy remains a hotly discussed topic. 2004 saw the founding of a *Working Group Therapy and Counseling in RCI.*

TCI and Counseling

Alexander Trost

1 Counseling: The Present Situation, History, and Definition

Counseling today is a method with many facets. Besides the traditional forms of educational counseling and life counseling, it is also home to coaching, organizational development, and supervision (Lotz, 2007a). In the year 2004, there were a total of 30 different associations that offered counseling of some sort or training in counseling, united in the Deutsche Gesellschaft für Beratung (DGfB) (The German Association for Counseling). The Ruth Cohn Institute for TCI International is a member of the DGfB.

But what is counseling exactly? Colloquially speaking it means an expert providing advice to an unknowledgeable client for a fee. Yet as early as 1968, Sprey emphasized the reciprocity of the counseling situation: The counselor too is being influenced and changed by such situations. The advice given can be requested or offered; it can take place before or after some event; it can be expressed directly or indirectly. It can take the form of a simple note or a concrete suggestion, a proposition, a prompt, a request, or an appeal up to a stern warning.

Sprey (1968) describes the following four basic functions of counseling:
1. "Experience-oriented organizational help" for ordering the object of concern in the experiences of the client, for stabilizing behavioral patterns, and for expanding the intellectual horizon.
2. "Reflection-oriented organizational help" for the deliberate and critical analysis of a concern and its context.
3. "Decision assistance" serves to reveal behavioral alternatives and their feasibility – and how to choose the best path among them.
4. "Positive support" for assisting guidance-seekers, encouraging them, and demonstrating trust, tactfulness, and respect (quoted acc. to Textor, 1987, p. 11).

The definition of counseling from the 1960s is still valid today, though modern counseling is no longer seen as an individual problem-solving or decision-making process. Rather, in accordance with the continuing developments in the field, it is now situated within larger systems or as part of quality control.

A more modern definition may be found in Straumann (2001, pp. 61 f.): Professional counseling means providing scientifically qualified assistance for coping with problems, conflicts, or crises which goes beyond providing information, concrete aid, suggestions, and behavioral instructions; it is holistic in nature and always strictly related to the subject in question. It can be integrated in an institution/company or done on a freelance basis; it is a transparent as well as ethically and legally safe relationship based on well-defined qualifications and quality standards. Professional counselors use their theoretical and methodological knowledge to seek – together with the clients – ways of making decisions and solving problems. They strengthen personal competences and skills, set free social potentials, and influence the conditions causing the problems. The goal of counseling is achieved when decisions and alternatives for coping with problems, conflicts, or crises have been found, and when these solutions are known to the client and can be implemented autonomously by the client in his or her own setting.

The counseling contract, the counseling goal, and the resulting counseling relationship may be very diverse, depending on the matter at hand. Anything is possible – from a short suggestion provided by an "expert" to long-term support in the sense of a positive dialog, to an extensive improvement of the behavioral competence of the client. Today, professional counseling often must step in to replace everyday advice in mature social systems.

It is not easy to differentiate between counseling and therapy (Trost, 2007). (Psycho)therapy means treating some sort of disorder; counseling serves to produce a concrete solution to a problem. In practice, however, such differentiations become blurred. In the basic declaration of the DGfB on their understanding of counseling, for example, we find explicitly curative and rehabilitative aspects (www.dachverband-beratung.de, 2007). Further means of differentiating lie in the length of the attention given, the intensity of the professional relationship and methodology as well as the fiscal background (public vs. private vs. insurance coverage). Another important difference between therapy and counseling in my opinion lies in the extent of time devoted by the therapist/counselor to the task. Counseling always presumes a measure of self-guidance in everyday life, whereas therapeutic processes may, if only temporarily, demand that the therapist or the therapeutic group assume the self-guiding interests of the client in order to provide a structural assistance that is not necessary in counseling (Trost, 2007).

2 Reception and Further Development in TCI

The development of TCI and that of counseling in general in the German-speaking countries of Europe run parallel. Both were part of the overall psychologizing of everyday life, the increasing need to reflect on one's own life and one's relationships to others. It seems obvious that TCI as an approach and method would have been integrated into counseling practice early on. Those responsible include Günter Hoppe and Helga Hermann from the Life and Child Guidance Office Düsseldorf of the Protestant Church as well as Annedore

Schultze of the Westphalia Cooperative Model in Vlotho (and many others). On the other hand, relatively few publications deal directly with these two terms, counseling and TCI (examples are Dlugosch & Reiser, 2006; Herrmann, 1995; Langmaack, 2001; Lotz, 2007a; Rubner, 2006; Trost, 2006).

The TCI system makes significant statements t all levels that can contribute to a meta-analysis of the knowledge structure of a counseling setting. These levels include an image of the world, of reality (epistemology), of humanity and human ethics (anthropology), models for reducing complexity, for understanding observed phenomena (explicative theories), an action theory concerning goals, interventions, impact factors, and interaction styles as well as a praxeology: Which approach, method, or technique is meaningful *today*?

Epistemology and anthropology are described in the → axioms of TCI; the explicative theory comprises the → four-factor model and the theory of group phases, the idea of → dynamic balance, etc. At the level of action theory, we find the → postulates "self-management" and "precedence of disturbances," the principle of holistic self-perception and other-perception, the development of "instincts" for dynamic balance, and the aspect of → participative leadership. Practically relevant are the ways in which themes are discovered and formulated, the use of various settings and creative methods, the process-oriented planning, and the employment of → auxiliary rules.

Below I would like to point out some of the special features of counseling with TCI that do not occur in other types of counseling approaches or are not applied systematically.

2.1 The Four-Factor Model of TCI as a Framework for Developing Problem-Solving Concepts

In TCI, the reason prompting counseling always refers to all four dimensions of the TCI model:

- The "Globe" aspect ensures that counseling occurs only within a specific context that corresponds to the output variable and affects the result. In terms of the TCI triangle, the Globe represents the framework in which the need for counseling has arisen; it has the role of being a system factor for the individuals involved and their respective relationships (e.g., a company that needs to lay off employees). Further, the Globe also concerns the context of the actual counseling session(s): When, where, and under what conditions does it take place?
- The "It" aspect refers to the content of the counseling situation (e.g., quitting a job), which, at least initially in the sense of restricting one's actions, affects the "I" of the person being counseled. One's personal assessment of being unable to cope with the problematic affair on one's own generally ensues as the result of both cognitive and affective events. That is the behavioral dilemma: "I must do something, but I don't

know what (or how)!" That means, with respect to the "It," externalizing the matter at hand by describing it or processing it in some other way so that it can become precise, limited, and clear.

- The "I" aspect comprises the experiences, interpretations, and strategies subjects employ with respect to the counseling theme (Lotz, 2007a) (e.g., anger or perhaps relief at ending a stressful situation, with high expectations for the counseling situation). The thought patterns and feelings of the person affected often provide the key for differentiating between what is demanded of one and one's competence. The "I" aspect concerns our own personal history, the early formative experiences that contribute to our present-day dilemma – and sometimes they also contain the key to successful change. Modern research shows that it is imperative to include in TCI especially the early experiences of emotional bonding and support (Trost, 2006).
- The "We" aspect in the counseling relationship reflects the partial identification the counselor develops with the client, the validation of the matter at hand as well as the dissociation from unrealistic expectations, leading to a trustful relationship. This is where transference and countertransference phenomena occur, which in turn enable inferences about the relationship of the clients to their own problem and to other people. The selectively authentic approach represents part of the art of counseling according to TCI. A further, methodologically shaped part of the "We" aspect lies in the solution-oriented perception and designation of both the intrapersonal and interpersonal resources of the client. The client's "We" relationships that lie outside of counseling are just as important, inasmuch as these relationships are affected by the matter at hand and can contribute to limiting or expanding the client's behavioral latitude (e.g., a termination notice may strengthen symbiotic tendencies in a marriage – or reveal existing marital problems).

2.2 Working Through a Theme Using Dynamic Balance

The subject matter of counseling can emerge only from the interactional dynamic that goes on between the "Globe," "It," "I," and "We." This makes the theme part of the overall dynamic process: It brings a relevant part of the matter into focus, allows crucial decisions to be made, and contributes to a goal-oriented structuring of the counseling process. Lotz (2007a) speaks of themes as "nodes in the network of encounter and reference" reflecting the four factors. Different from group leadership, in a counseling relationship the subject is not a common theme; rather, counselors concern themselves with the needs of the clients by helping them to find and work through their own particular theme (Rubner, 2006).

2.3 The Principle of Participative Leadership

The goal of the counseling process is and remains improving the self-leadership capabilities of the client in the sense of the Chairperson Postulate. The goal is to understand and carefully deal with the present dependence of the client. In addition to working on the theme, the client often is searching for the feeling of being understood by someone else, of empathy for his or her position, or, sometimes unconsciously, of being able to let go of the idea of self-control. Participative leadership in the counseling situation thus means communicating affectively as well as effectively applying nonverbal signals and emotional involvement – while at the same time taking a critical look at the problem at hand.

The view of mankind found in TCI and formulated in its axioms reveals a suggestive-hypnotic power – if properly propagated by the counselor. TCI work is meaningful only if I trust the potential of the client (system) and am able to recognize and capitalize on signals of development.

2.4 Paying Attention to Body Signals

This element plays a special role in holistic perception and process structuring. Registering and reflecting on (often involuntary) physical reactions during the counseling process allows both the counselor and the client to obtain long-term insights into the theme and the working relationship. The use of bodily expressions for shaping a situation often confers a greater dynamic in the counseling setting than a simple verbal exchange. Counseling with TCI thus means employing physical techniques and rituals (Wagner, 1991).

2.5 A Side Note: What Are the Consequences of TCI for Counseling?

As mentioned above, the development of TCI and that of counseling in general were closely connected in Germany. Many of the essentials tenets of TCI were integrated into what the DGfB deemed "counseling." Specific methodological contributions made by TCI to effective counseling were mentioned above in sections 2.3 and 2.4, regarding, on the one hand, participative leadership as the proper orientation of the counselor-client relationship while also maintaining a certain professional distance (from an excentric vantage point) (Lotz, 2007a). On the other hand, the conscious inclusion of bodily signals enables an understanding of the analog communication signals of the client, which can be more important for the overall counseling situation than verbalized statements. It would be desirable if these two aspects were to become standards in the training and practice of counselors.

3 Summary

The circular approach to the four factors of the TCI balance model, which works through reflection on the problem, the subjective action dispositions, and the communicative factors all allow the conscious perception and realization of new behavioral options (Lotz,

2007a). This includes the temporal dimensions of "then and there" in the development of the problem (past), the discussion of "here and now" (present), and the search for ways to provide a solution to the problem (future). Against the background of the ethical-anthropological basis of TCI, the reflective debate that goes on between the counseling partners allows them to discover a holistic path toward a solution to the problem at hand. TCI is thus not just a way to lead groups; rather, its thought and behavioral models represents a clear, comprehensive, and manageable way to establish truly successful counseling.

TCI and Supervision

Helmut Reiser

1 Definition: Supervision Based on TCI

- *Definition 1:* Supervision based on TCI is a form of counseling for professional problems, for example, in the areas of self-perception, self-representation, insecurities during interactions with clients, problems in completing work tasks, clarification of institutional cooperation and roles.
- *Definition 2:* The goal behind treating professional problems is the creation/restoration of the ability of the supervisee (or in a team: the supervisees) to bring about a change of perspective, to mobilize their potentials, and to use existing resources to enable both autonomy and solidarity to be implemented in the professional setting.
- *Definition 3:* The professional problem at hand involves the *clarification* of conditional interactions. This is not a matter of determining objective truths, but rather means the development of working hypotheses on the part of the supervisor, the *resolution* of existing fixations and blockages, and the provision of *impulses* for alternative behaviors.[1]

The supervisor initiates this process involving clarifications, resolutions, and impulses, but the process is then continued by the group (in individual supervision, in the dyadic dialog). In the course of things, the supervisee then makes all decisions.

- *Definition 4:* Supervision based on TCI considers the prerequisites and necessities of the overall format[2] of supervision and its various forms. It employs any number of different techniques from psychoanalysis, systemic counseling, and Humanistic Psychology.

---

1 The terms *clarification, resolution*, and *impulses* are introduced here to describe aspects that often occur in sequence during the process, though they can also be interwoven with one another.

2 The term *format* is used here in accordance with a suggestion made by Janny Wolf-Hollanders to denote action forms that can occur in many different work fields and generally adhere to their systematic and operative logic, resulting in specific roles and tasks.

2 Explanations of the Definition

The definition given above describes the goal, the content, and the process of supervision from the vantage point of TCI, even though it could be valid for other methodological approaches as well.

The first definition uses the → four-factor model (model of the group or dyad process) in order to systematize areas of concern in supervision. By focusing on one specific part of the problem (as is always the case with supervision), this guarantees that other areas important to the problem and its solution are not overlooked.

The second definition emphasizes the goal of developing autonomy and interdependence as well as the idea of *chairpersonship* (→ Chairperson Postulate). Increasing the effectivity of professional work is one goal of supervision and is also part of the personal development of the supervisees. The idea of a humanistic development postulates that autonomy and interdependence amplify each other when we make conscious decisions. The important ability to see things from other perspectives goes back to the systematics of the four factors with their respective perspectives. Determining potentials and resources is a positive and optimistic approach that allows disturbances to become the pointers and indications of necessary developmental steps.

The third definition concerns the elements of the supervision process *clarification, resolution*, and *impulses*, which reflects the deconstruction and renewed construction of the viewpoints of the supervisee in direct interaction with the supervisor (in groups with the supervisors). This process proceeds in the sense of Humanistic Psychology as a form of individual self-management of the supervisee, which is neither addressed nor taught by the supervisor, but only supported. Decisions about where the supervisory process is headed must, in the end, be made by the supervisee, even though confrontations concerning existing contradictions and blind spots are necessary; one should not underestimate the momentum of the supervisory process. Concerning the various forms of supervision of groups, in TCI supervision *with the group* is the rule – not individual supervision that takes place in the group, even though in group supervision based on TCI dyadic sessions may prove to be necessary at times. These supervision guidelines addressing the style of supervision makes supervision based on TCI different from other forms of supervision.

The fourth definition is treated below in greater detail. Via mixed methods, something that has largely been established within supervision, and by reminding oneself of the necessities of the format of supervision it is possible to somewhat reduce the differences between the various approaches. Supervision based on TCI, for example, works closely with the psychoanalytical theorem of unconscious internal and interactional processes, in light of phenomena such as transference and countertransference, mirroring, and other matters on various process levels. Yet, generally speaking, it does not work with *interpretations of transference*.[3]

3 Interpretations of transference in psychoanalytic therapy refer to indications concerning repetitions of relationships from early childhood and affects that occur in the relationship toward the therapist.

Humanistic Psychology supplied the many creative techniques for looking at and resolving problems as well as the great importance assigned to affects and bodily signals found in supervision based on TCI. Supervision based on TCI also does not usually work with exercises. The fundamentally constructivistic attitude, the attention paid to the context of all narratives, and the use of circular questions in teamwork all reflect the systemic-constructivistic approach. Because of the way it looks at disturbances and their solutions, supervision based on TCI puts greater emphasis on acknowledging and solving problems and conscious decision-making.

3 The Format of Supervision and Its Effect on Our Understanding of TCI

One thing that is common to all methodological approaches and all forms of supervision are the terms of the format: A supervision session always begins with a narrative in which the supervisee (the protagonist) or other members of a team report on some difficulty that has cropped up at work, for example, a conflict, a relationship problem, or some other uncertainty or problematic situation. Treating this *case* during a session means proceeding according to the protagonist's (or the team's) depiction, without prejudice for the result. Exceptions to this rule are themes that concern the setting itself (see below). The supervisor is responsible for properly working through the problem at hand, yet the supervisor is not responsible for providing instructions or suggestions on eliminating or mitigating the problem. The role of the supervisor is to guide the process empathetically, while also maintaining a professional distance to the affective experiences of the supervisees and a certain level of neutrality concerning any conflicts. The goal agreed upon by the supervisees and the supervisor comprise equally both the professional learning goals of the supervisees as well as an improvement in their job satisfaction and a reduction of psychosocial stress. It is of utmost importance that this agreement concerning the common goal(s) be strictly delineated.

These basic conditions for supervision are also valid for the many variations of supervision[4] that apply to special circumstances. For example, supervision in institutions must reflect complete transparency concerning the triangular relationship between the supervisor, the participants, and the institution. In teams and staffs, personal concerns must be limited to avoid an invasion of privacy that would render the daily work relationships difficult. Maintaining the proper distance-nearness relationship when working within in-

4 Such forms could refer to, for example, individual supervision, leadership supervision, supervision in an openly composed group, the accompaniment of teams and partial teams, staff-based and partially staff-based groups, in institutions, voluntary or prescribed supervision, long-term or short-term supervision, low-frequency or high-frequency supervision. There may also be some overlaps in these various forms. Other, more specialized forms would be case discussions among colleagues and training supervision.

stitutions demands a different approach than, say, in self-selected groups. Individual supervision also requires different techniques than in a group when developing alternative approaches.

These conditions for the format and the alternative forms thereof are also valid for supervision done on the basis of TCI. They can represent quite a challenge to the usual practices of TCI group leadership and, in some cases, even severely test the TCI rules. Compared to a TCI group that consists of adults who have come together of their free will to address certain themes, supervision does not have a preformulated theme, but rather often represents the search for the hidden theme behind some particular case. The successful end to supervision is achieved when the concealed theme of the protagonist has been uncovered. Even if a supervisor who works according to TCI introduces his or her own associations to the case, the overall participation of the leader is less than in, say, a TCI training group. The supervisor exhibits much greater selectivity and distance. Also, there is a greater level of confrontation than is generally found in TCI self-awareness groups; contrary to the guidelines set up by Ruth Cohn, the supervisor may also carry out interviews and provide interpretations. Supervision based on TCI balances out the level of participation and selectivity and the distance-nearness situation of the group leader by applying specific structural methods (e.g., individual work, graduated tasks).

Ruth Cohn developed TCI during the famous countertransference workshops that took place from 1955–1961 as a method of training supervision during psychoanalytic training. Subsequently, supervision became rather commonplace in TCI, first as a training supervision that combined supervisory methods with the art of TCI group leadership, and second as method of group supervision employing a modified version of the TCI group leadership approach. The 1990s was a phase in which "TCI supervision" was conceptualized as a form of group supervision (see Reiser, 1998) that put special emphasis above all on the value orientation of TCI (→ Axioms), its leadership style, the four-factor model, and the principle of structuring.[5] The publication that started this new era in the discussion was entitled *Themenzentrierte Supervision* (Theme-Centered Supervision; Hahn et al., 1998). It soon became clear, however, that it was impossible to establish a special form of TCI supervision (or theme-centered supervision) according to a modified type of TCI training group. The newly founded working group that offered such training in supervision as part of the TCI training according to the standards of the Deutsche Gesellschaft für Supervision (German Association of Supervision) (DGSv)[6] called this "supervision based on TCI." Reichert (2005) spoke of "TCI as the basic concept of supervision."

These expressions clearly point out a change that had occurred in the understanding of TCI because of its work with the format of supervision. TCI came to be seen as a con-

5 Hartmut Raguse's multistage model of case supervision was adopted both within and outside the ranks of TCI as a good example of TCI supervision (Raguse-Stauffer & Raguse, 1980).

6 The pilot project ran from 1990 to 1993. Training management was by Helmut Reichert, Helmut Reiser, Peter Wendt, Janny Wolf-Hollander, and Ulla Wolter.

cept for developing interactions that would further one's own growth and that is then adapted to the respective formats: TCI ceased to be solely a group leadership model. A group of adults who have come together of their own free will in order to receive further social training was historically the standard TCI training group, albeit only one format among many. All formats have in common that TCI basics such participative leadership, selective authenticity, theme orientation, participation of the group in the group leadership, and dynamic balance must be developed according to the respective format. The TCI system demands that these basics principles be observed and adhered to, even though no hard and fast behavioral rules are valid for all forms of interactional work. Supervision suggested that the supervisees think of the → Globe in a system-theoretical way as the sum of all constructions of relevant environmental areas. One task of the supervisor is thus to discuss these constructions and to correlate them to one another.

4 TCI and Its Effects on Supervision

TCI became well known in supervision circles especially as a concept for group supervision. The structured, step-wise supervision according to Raguse came to be used in various models of mutual case supervision, even if the source of this method was not always properly mentioned. One particular contribution of TCI lay in the way in which it designed the sessions of a supervision group or dyad, which were concerned less with a specific case and more with working through the main theme of the setting, that is, establishing the group, reflecting on group work, holding final sessions as well as treating overarching themes stemming from multiple case-related sessions. Such matters were then treated more generally. Sessions with thematic standards were amenable to the rules of the standard TCI format.

Above and beyond these contributions TCI made to supervision, the Society for Further Education in Supervision should be mentioned as an independent approach to supervision. This society was based on TCI and especially the Supervision Expert Group, which was founded in 1992 at the Ruth Cohn Institute. It was adept at combining psychoanalytic, systemic, and humanistic approaches and thus corresponded to the overall development of supervision (cf. Buchinger, 2004). Because the majority of those holding prominent positions at the DGSv[7] also taught TCI, TCI became very well known as a supervisory concept (see Reichert, 2005).

7 Helmut Reichert held various positions at DGSv, and Bernhard Lemaire was also president of the DGSv.

TCI and Organizational Development

Ulrike B. Meyer

1 What Is Organizational Development?

Organizational development (OD) is a consulting method used in organizations which provides developmental and value-oriented answers to the institutional questions that have resulted from the social, political, and economic changes occurring over the past decades.[1]

The core of OD (as opposed to organizational consultation) is described by F. Glasl as follows: "Organizational development makes the attempt to connect the development of human thought patterns, attitudes, and behaviors in organizations with the work on the organizational aspects" (1983, p. 23). Human beings always form the starting point of this approach: "From the concepts of strategies to modify human mental processes grew the later conceptions of organizational development" (ibid.). The main goal is to enable humans and their organizations to achieve self-development.

In OD, the affected humans control and determine their own change processes (Baumgartner et al., 1995, p. 20). The main prerequisite is that management be completely supportive of the envisioned change processes (Jegge & Lehmann, 1983, p. 176).

OD combines the shaping of change with the human search for meaning, in particular against the background of the social and economic demands for autonomy expressed in all areas of modern business (Heintel, 1999, pp. 20 ff.).

2 The History of the Interactions Between TCI and OD

As early as the 1980s we find tendencies emerging from both methodological directions:

- OD began searching for methods that correspond to its own demands for human orientation and value orientation.
- TCI began searching for methods and knowledge that would satisfy its own demand that the Globe also be included in all work settings.

---

1 The goal of OD to shape organizations as special instances of social reality to be more efficient and humane over the long term must be seen against the background of the research that was being conducted in the social sciences, in particular in the so-called critical sciences, during the 1970s.

All processes of OD depend on working with groups, whether large groups (whole systems) or very small groups (control groups). The potential for success lies not only in the person doing the consultation, but also in that person's ability to work with various groups such that changes are effected both within the organizations and in the people who work there. TCI offers an excellent holistic concept, providing methods for leading groups and an approach to (self-)management that correspond to the demand that those affected also are participants. In addition, the disturbance postulate assumed a major role since it made it possible to quickly view conflictual developments.

Put succinctly, TCI is seen solely as a model for group leadership. The TCI concept of dynamic balance would seem to be useful for OD processes as an instrument for both planning and analysis purposes.

There are a number of good reasons to connect the theories behind OD and TCI to form a unified concept. In the past both directions were also open to such interactions. The working group "TCI in Business" had the goal of introducing the TCI concept and its basic foundations to various fields of business. Numerous articles and reports emerged from this "TCI Business Network" (Arbeitskreis TZI und Wirtschaft, 1985) as well as an "Inventory of Scientific Papers and Research Projects on Theme-Centered Interaction (TCI) in Business" (Hannen, 2001).

An example is Marianne Schaper: "This led to our strategy for corporate development, which combines the principles and methods of organizational development with the value orientation, the didactic system, and the respective methods of TCI" (Bauer-Sternberg & Schaper, 1994).

Consulting contracts in the nonprofit field, in particular supervision, had previously been carried out based on good TCI training since they were largely concerned with human beings, their conflicts, etc. However, expanding the consultation to matters of entire organizations opened up a new dimension that demanded much more organizational knowledge (cf. Meyer, 1999).

Elmar Osswald propagated a concept for school development based on TCI and combined it with the results from various management theories. The limits to the applicability of insights emerging from TCI within complex organizations led him to expand the TCI model (→ Four-Factor Model of TCI) (Elmar Osswald, Das Dreieck in der Kugel bekommt die Füße "Leitung" und "Strukturen" [The Triangle in the Sphere Gets Two Feet "Leadership" and "Structures"], n.d.).

3 What Are the Connections Between OD and TCI?

Both OD and TCI assume that humans are social beings and as such have the ability (and the will) to assume responsibility for themselves, their own lives, and their environment.

This *conception of mankind* includes as well the conviction that humans can indeed change over the course of their lifetimes, that they can learn, and that they want to learn.[2]

This common belief led the two approaches to use selected methods and structures to develop the necessary competences in the humans involved.

In TCI terms, this means strengthening the → chairpersonship, the healthy application of autonomy and interdependence, and leading with mutual respect and esteem. Managers should "do everything in their power to enable the unique [...] talents of an individual to reach their complete development" (Flöther, 2001, p. 122).

Methodologically speaking, OD and TCI strive to achieve a high level of transparency of their processes and the participation of all persons involved. Disturbances are seen as invitations to reflect on the process together with those affected. The process-oriented procedures behind both OD and TCI reveal their respective trust in the ability of both humans and organizations to develop. Put another way: Growth is possible.

In conclusion, because of their similar aspirations for change among humans and organizations, OD and TCI are marching in the same direction and reflect nearly the same basic view of mankind and philosophy.

3.1 How One Methodological Approach Can Profit from the Other: Where Do the Limits Lie?

The secondary literature provides only few examples of the connections between OD and TCI. It is particularly noticeable that TCI is nearly completely absent in the secondary literature from the economic sector (where OD is very present) (Hannen, 2001). In TCI literature, in turn, there are a few depictions of the advantages of using TCI in OD, such as in team development (Gores-Pieper, www.structura.de; Greimel, 1992, 2003). TCI seems to be considered especially useful because of its methods of conversational leadership and the structure of groups (cf. Hannen, 2001, p. 31). Glasl (1983, p. 23) mentions an interesting connection that invites us to see the development of chairpersonship at the center of OD: "The more the desired organizational and management models appeal to the independence and inventiveness of the employees, the less such changes can be brought about through purely rational strategies or through compulsion and power."

3.2 TCI Supports OD Consulting Activity

Competences

Training in TCI (→ Training in Flux) focuses primarily on the development of professional competence in leadership of groups – not of organizations (Dörfler, 1998). Practi-

2 Cf. the TCI axioms in Cohn, 1975, Chapter 9.

cally speaking, these management and leadership concepts based on TCI have proved to be very efficient.[3] TCI methods are able to effect value-oriented changes in attitudes and has proved helpful for achieving successful change processes within organizations. This is where the definition of the role of consultation is derived. It would thus seem appropriate to use the TCI-specific competences in OD consultation (Bauer-Steinberg & Schaper, 1994), seeing that the ability to professionally lead groups in the sense of Glasl's (1983, p. 23) "mentality changes" is solidly entrenched among experts in organizational development. My own surveys produced an astonishing result: Many OD colleagues from non-TCI fields in fact employ TCI as the ideal method for working with groups.

A further contribution to the professionalization of OD consultants may be seen in the way TCI approaches *self-competence and social competence* by relying on therapy-oriented training. In their research, Worley and Feyerherm (2005, p. 86) point out the importance of such competences: Efficient OD consultants can trace their success back to their broad background knowledge in methodology, their social competence, and their personality development. Well-established self-competence and social competence are thus important resources for becoming both successful leaders and successful consultants.

Methods

The development of *methods expertise* is one of the major strengths of TCI training, alongside those of processes reflection and self-reflection in light of humanistic values (→ Humanism). The results of action research show that the key to effective and sustainable change lies in self-reflection and system-reflection, which is valid for both behavior and values. The TCI structure model provides an effective orientation through its complex reflection and planning processes.

Concepts such as dynamic balance and participative leadership provide hints as to how the TCI philosophy and concept of mankind can be used methodologically in OD, and how the principle of participation found in OD can be systematically and methodologically applied.

3.3 OD Knowledge Supports Work with TCI

In the four-factor model of TCI, the "Globe" is seen largely as a factor influencing the other three main factors – and less as a factor with its own structural elements and regulations. In the context of organizations, this may pose the risk that TCI knowledge about groups and their dynamics is extended to the entire organization, thus treating the organization as a group and not as the organization it in fact is (cf. Dörfler, 1998). An example would be how conflicts are handled.

---

3 This is also what lies behind the results of a survey of managers from 300 companies (cf. Hannen, 2001, p. 32).

OD theory used the scientific insights about changes in mentality to develop further scientific insights into organizational behavior, individual psychology, group dynamics, management and organizational theory, survey/interview methods, comparative cultural perspectives, and functional knowledge about business affairs (Worles & Feyerherm, 2005, pp. 82f.).[4]

This knowledge about organizations and their dynamics can be of great profit for working with TCI in groups, inasmuch as the task is to understand the Globe context and to include it in the work to be done. This is true for team development and individual counseling as well as for in-house seminars, etc.

Process-oriented work with TCI becomes all the more efficient if it is able to profit from the goal and result orientation of OD and include knowledge about project methodologies. Finally, OD offers good descriptions of the developmental processes that go on in organizations, which in turn may be used to streamline the processes with great transparency.

OD consultants need a high level of *methods expertise* if they are to meet the needs of the broad range of demands: management of the consulting process, analysis and diagnosis, design and selection of appropriate interventions, moderation techniques and forms of process consultation, development of the client's own skills, and evaluation of organizational change (Worles & Feyerherm, 2005, pp. 82f.). Instruments and methods should produce reliable results in short timespans, while also simultaneously providing those affected with great transparency about the ongoing process and allowing management to participate in the entire process.

4 Conclusion

The central tasks and competences of OD lie in the factor "Globe"; those of TCI in the triangle of factors. The central competences are dispersed accordingly. OD can offer TCI its organizational knowledge, whereas TCI can offer OD its axioms for defining the conception of mankind, its dynamic balance for understanding process dynamics, and the concept of participative leadership as a model for the role of the consultant or leader in participative processes.

4 On reengineering, see Oetiker (1998); on total quality management, see Schütt (2003).

TCI and Social Work

Bernhard Lamaire and Walter Lotz

The connection between TCI and social work as well as the way in which professional behavior is seen may be seen from two vantage points: The first (Social Work and TCI) is based on the theoretical concepts on social work proposed by Michael Winkler, Hans Thiersch, and Silvia Staub-Bernasconi, which associate TCI with the theories of social work and its various fields of practice. They do this by offering comparable and thus compatible or sometimes merely worthwhile perspectives. The second (TCI and Social Work) describes how aspects of social work are approached within TCI and what effects TCI has had on the professional behavior of social work.

1 Social Work and TCI

The theoretical foundations of social work and social education do not include TCI. Parts of TCI theory are sometimes included as behavioral guidelines, but little effort is made to put them into perspective. Yet there are a number of overlaps between the theory of social work and that of TCI. In the following we address these based on the concepts and theories of Michael Winkler, Hans Thiersch, and Silvia Staub-Bernasconi.

In his *Theorie der Sozialpädagogik* (Theory of Social Education, 1988), Michael Winkler starts from the two central concepts of *subject* and *place* as the basic principles of social-educational actions. Central to this concept is the self-controlled subject, who, even under great hardship or when afflicted by great shortcomings, must never be seen as a passive victim, but always as an active agent. Herein lies a clear parallel to the TCI concept of chairpersonship (→ Chairperson Postulate). A second parallel may be discovered between Ruth Cohn's idea of "Globe" (→ Globe) and Winkler's category of "place," which on the one hand influences the subject and on the other hand is influenced and shaped by the subject. Differences may be found in the way the unconscious is viewed: Winkler rejects the role of the unconscious as the attempt to exculpate and determine the subject.

In Hans Thiersch's theory of social work, too, the local environment and the relationships that evolve at that place form the starting point. His concept of "lifeworld orientation" (1992) puts the local environment squarely in the middle of all social-educational actions. Thiersch looks at both the structural and the individual aspects of successful and unsuccessful life-plans. Like Ruth Cohn he believes in the ability of humans to grow: Existing situations always contain some measure of potential for development. This approach may be seen as complementing Ruth Cohn's statement concerning human creative possibilities (→ Axiom 3). The alternatives are thus not power or powerlessness; somewhere in the middle lies the chance for partial power. The goal of work carried out in one's normal environment (and not in some therapeutic setting) is to achieve a better everyday life.

Thiersch also looks at the participation of professionals in the work process, especially with how closely their professional life relates to the everyday life of others. This act of being involved is similar to the construct of participative leadership in TCI, something Thiersch describes as the danger that occurs when professionals provide "social-educational assistance at the kitchen table." And yet, despite all the asymmetrical situations, the obstinacy of the recipients remains an important reference point. Without questioning the professionality of the social worker, Thiersch implicitly assumes the equal status of the two parties.

Thiersch's concept is interesting inasmuch as it corresponds with TCI regarding the role of values. Like Ruth Cohn's axiomatics, his concept does not provide a normative approach, but rather proposes a framework for weighing value orientations. More concretely, those involved have to define them in each individual case by means of negotiation or by facing up to the value dialectics described in Ruth Cohn's axiomatics.

The basic position formulated in Silvia Staub-Bernasconi's system-theoretical, process-oriented theory (2007) is very close to that of the first axiom. Similar to Ruth Cohn, she too sees the subject as being able to (self-)reflect and as possessing the skills of self-control in the context of interdependence. The two are also similar in their social-therapeutic perspective: Both authors deem a fair and just society to be of utmost importance.

Yet the reception of TCI in the theories of social work remains inadequate and to date has failed to properly reflect the meaning of TCI. The writings of Lotz (2003) and Reiser (2006) closed that gap.

2 TCI and Social Work

How the field of social work is presented within TCI is revealed in a study of the activities listed in the contributions to the journal *Themenzentrierte Interaktion* as well as an analysis of the vantage points taken there on how TCI functions:[1]

- In the fields of child and adolescent social work, TCI is applied because of its humane and fair approach, which appeals to those working in this area. In some articles, TCI is also presented as an educational approach.
- When the contribution concerns ways of working with elderly groups, then this method is clearly different from offers based purely on entertainment. By taking the TCI pos-

1 The article in question (cf. Lemaire & Lotz, 2002) contains references to the individual texts and literature.

tulates (→ Axioms and Postulates) and the central idea of → dynamic balance seriously, it creates a social cohesion in the group that supports and integrates the individual members.
- Corporate social services use TCI to shape qualification programs when it is important to include the perspective of the employee in the acquisition of skills. This supports a communication culture of flat hierarchies and humanistic principles; it sets the tone in organizations that have their primary thrust in having economic success.
- Education is a field in which TCI has become widely and well established. The reason lies in the fact that the essential properties of theme-centered learning and working fit well with the motivational, process-oriented, and goal-oriented ideas of education.
- In the penal system and rehabilitation, the structured and methodical procedures and the transparent, easily understandable positions taken by TCI leaders proves to be an excellent means of including people in self-reflective learning processes who have experienced dissocial developments. To this end, however, effort must be invested in creating a "therapeutic milieu" that can serve as the framework for such interactional methods.
- As a method of living learning, TCI can combine the aspect of self-awareness with that of continually becoming engaged with new problem areas in counseling and crisis intervention. The theme-centered work principles provide a clear orientation for how to proceed with counseling.
- In the field of clinical therapy, TCI can be used in conjunction with therapeutic insights and competences. Especially group therapy will profit from the processual modification and intense pursuit of themes that emerge from the four factors; this prevents reducing the therapeutic approach to mere individualism.
- TCI-oriented work with teams, organizations, and institutions serve to improve the work organization while simultaneously attending to professional and personal competences and the collaboration of those involved. This is done, for example, through its orientation to the four-factor model.

This overview clearly shows that the connection between TCI and social work is present in many different areas – and that the respective approach to TCI turns can be very different. The effects of TCI described in the individual contributions range from an implicit connection to complete integration of the TCI concepts. In some of the articles the role of TCI in the professional activities of social work goes unmentioned, the plausibility of the connection being related more to the overall atmosphere than to a direct and explicit tie-in.

A second group of texts sees an indirect effect of TCI, largely by its creating a sensitivity for insights or the personality development of an individual, which in turn affects the work being done.

A third, rather large number of contributions prefers an eclectic approach to TCI: Individual elements of the TCI system are included in one's own work, for example, aspects of the approach, the axiomatic principles, or the four-factor model, while at the same time leaving all other TCI matters unmentioned. This selective reference to TCI elements is often accompanied by the note that a complete adoption of TCI was not possible because of certain characteristics specific to the field.

Matzdorf takes up a position that goes beyond that. He wants us to implement the TCI concept by looking at its didactic qualities, which could form the basis for using it in action contexts that clearly differ from "standard procedures." Lotz in turn proposes an approach to TCI as a general orientation framework for action fields of social work, in the sense of a "generative core system that contains a [...] wealth of [...] statements that are in the position to influence and expand the entire system, both in its breadth and in its concrete applications" (1989, p. 58). With this, Lotz lays the foundation for TCI to become a professional action concept for very different forms of activities in social work (2003). Reiser developed a similar conceptual perspective of TCI as a psychoanalytic-systemic educational theory (2006) (→ TCI as a Professional Educational Concept). Thus, the role of TCI in the field of social work remains (internally) unclear, while externally it is still a problem of recognition to be resolved in future developments.

TCI for Managers: Holistic Leadership in a Complex Reality

Ineke van de Braak

This contribution is concerned with the difficulties that managers encounter in the modern economy when they try to meet the demands made on them, and how TCI can help them to achieve that goal.

1 Modern Corporate Management: Demands Made on Managers

Modern corporate managers experience tremendous pressure. The world in which they act is one of ever-increasing complexity and turbulence. Organizations are becoming open systems affected by a multitude of external influences: social developments bringing great insecurity, government regulations at ever smaller intervals, and demands on the part of the unions and other interest groups. Competition is cutthroat, customers are demanding. The expectations of achieving short-term results run high, and the personnel and financial means available often do not suffice to reach the envisioned quality goals. Managers today are confronted by employees with high expectations for their jobs, who are no longer happy with just earning a living. In addition to good primary and secondary working conditions, many of them want to experience a workplace where they can grow personally. Even the differences among the employees – their diversity – are growing. This puts great pressure on the flexibility of the working conditions as well as influencing the culture of cooperation within the company. Managers must deal with conflicting demands, for example, those made by corporate management, which wants to see short-term success, and their own duties to attend to the needs of those employees who are unable to withstand the great performance pressure; their own personal values and the way in which the organizations effects changes; the demands the workplace puts on them and their own personal desire to relax and care for their immediate family.

Many other examples could be noted where managers experience such distress. The pressure from such expectations may cause them to lose contact with their own inner selves, their own needs, their own motives and inspirations, leading to alienation and stress-based illnesses ("burnout") (cf. Assink, 2006; Blekkingh, 2005; Quinn, 2006).

Managers also risk being carried away by their desire for power, status, and wealth as well as the need to secure their own position in difficult times. They may in fact fail in their duties because they are unable to arbitrate between their own possibilities and needs and the external demands being made of them.

Generally speaking, trust in managers today has declined. Increasingly, negative images of their credibility are being spread. How to best survive such a complex situation?

2 A Holistic Approach to Meeting this Challenge

Managers need a frame of reference if they are to understand the changing reality they are faced with. It is important that they grasp the broader context and not become entangled in the many urgent appeals directed at them by the divergent interests that surround them.

Modern management literature emphasizes the importance of establishing an integrated, holistic approach to one's work – a consciousness that everything is connected and that problems cannot be solved on just one level (cf. Beck & Cowen, 1996; Merry, 2006; Ofman, 2006; ten Kate, 2005; Wheatly, 1999). The trick is to understand the complexity of the task in order to best determine what to attend to first. To this end, it is necessary to keep an open mind, take in one's environment, and ascertain those factors that will be responsible for the success of an organization.

TCI offers just such a holistic perspective. The → four-factor model means that managers can keep the tasks to be solved and the envisioned results (the "It") in mind as well as reflecting on employees as individuals (the individual "I"s), their cooperation ("We"), and the organizational culture and the context in which everyone is working (the "Globe"). With TCI, managers learn to differentiate between these perspectives and to directly address the task at hand.

This multidimensional approach is a very important one. Even if one's focus alternates from one to perhaps two perspectives, it is imperative that all four factors be seen as the total system. Every I-We-It-Globe constellation is unique and presents management with a new challenge.

3 Authentic and Transformational Leadership

Besides maintaining a multidimensional vision of reality, the integrated approach also considers the professional effectivity of a manger to never be independent of his or her own personal development. Managers need to possess and display great personal strength if they want to remain genuine: They must be in touch with their inner self and with the people they work with. This demands a fundamentally authentic attitude and the courage to make honest and value-derived decisions. That is what is meant by *authentic leadership* (cf. Assink, 2006; Bateson, 1999; Blekkingh, 2005; Quinn, 2006).

Arie de Geus (1997) listed the four major characteristics of organizations that can survive turbulent times:

- They have a strong sense of identification with their clear mission and a strong commitment on the part of the employees.
- They have mastered the art of putting out their feelers for what is going on around them.
- They possess a high level of flexibility with respect to organizational structure and the space they provide for differences and experiments.
- They maintain solid financial policies and sufficient reserves, which enable them to make quick reactions to ongoing developments.

Organizations that are allowed to develop experience a permanent interaction between their own mission and what happens in their environment. There are both external and internal means of experiencing living processes. To this end, however, such organizations need managers who have the courage to enact change, who dare to take on risks, who leave the trodden path and enable learning processes both on the individual level and on the organizational level: Leaders who view everything that happens within and outside the company with an open mind and provide space for new things (cf. Argyris & Schön, 1978; Senge, 1990; Swieringa & Wierdsma, 1990). Only people who are themselves open to change can inspire others to follow them. Only they are in the position to establish a value orientation within the company and propagate a common focus. That is what is referred to as *transformational leadership* (cf. Avolio, 1999; Bass, 1998; Quinn, 2006; Yukl, 2002).

The axioms of the TCI system provide a good basis for this type of leadership. Being a holistic approach, TCI encourages managers to make value-driven, sustainable decisions that leave enough room for developmental processes and yet are courageous enough to initiate profound changes in oneself and in the organization.

The → chairperson postulate proposes remaining honest and upright in one's perception both when dealing with oneself and when making decisions that affect one's surroundings. It also means opening as many windows as possible to what lies without and within, and not denying any part of reality. This form of perception allows decisions to be made and responsibility to be assumed; it enables a manager to deal with his or her own insecurities, fears, sources of inspiration, desires, and needs. It also permits a manager to address external demands.

The → disturbance postulate prepares managers and employees for tackling anything that seems relevant. Being "honest and open" then becomes the norm of the company's communication culture. It creates an atmosphere in which disturbances take precedence, and it demands authenticity. It initiates learning processes in the sense of organizational learning.

4 Activating Self-Leadership in Employees

One of the greatest challenges facing managers is how to instill self-leadership and creativity in their employees. How can they best ensure that the company's vision is supported and that the employees assume the necessary responsibility for implementing that vision? If managers are able to view the situation from several vantage points and have the courage to grow themselves, then they will be in the position to create the proper conditions for success. They can attend to the skills of the individuals in the company and, together with them, seek ways to expand those skills. This path even allows for a certain tolerance toward diversity. At the same time, such managers remain able to engage in confrontations if the attitude or behavior of the employees fail to live up to the organization's values.

A manager who is able to embrace his or her own learning processes can become a model and an inspiration for others to assume responsibility; they do not experience themselves as victims. Integrity and reliability are important here: A company's vision will receive the support of its employees only if the central values of that vision are being realized in daily practice.

The ITC principle of → participative leadership can play an important role in this process as it encourages the corporate leadership to *assume responsibility and to share responsibility*. Participative corporate leadership is transparent: clear in its values, in its vision, in its goals. It provides clear information about its decisions. It is open to processes that it sees going on around it, and it provides concrete feedback. It proves to be a learning being with its own personal needs, reasoning, fears, and insecurities. Participative leadership represents the *integration of leadership and participation*. This demands of the managers that they become active themselves, be engaged, and be empathetic toward the process – and that they are able to distance themselves enough from it in order to analyze what is happening.

5 Leading with Themes

Leading meetings and conferences with a TCI theme (→ Theme) supports an open dialog. Many authors have pointed out the importance of maintaining a communication culture within organizations which provides the proper space for entertaining the perspectives of all involved; it avoids discussions in which everyone pleads only for their own point of view (cf. Blekkingh, 2005; Senge, 1990). An open dialog permits the integration of many interests. And the TCI theme offers a very concrete method for doing just that.

TCI and School

Erika Arndt

The subject of TCI and school concerns above all school development since TCI is always about how people, tasks, and systems develop in accordance with the values they propose.

In section 1, I look at school reforms and TCI, discuss the common to TCI and the main ideas of early progressive education, especially those of personality development. The educational reforms enacted during the 1970s approached school reform from the viewpoint of psychoanalysis, sociology, and group dynamics. The TCI model provided a good orientation for this task since it systematically linked these aspects under the heading of "dynamic balance."

In section 2, I look at TCI and school development and show how TCI became an integral part of modern school development: The dynamic balance between "I," "We," and "Task" in light of the "Globe" was employed as a model for the three classical areas of school development – curriculum development, personnel development, and organizational development.

1 School Reforms and TCI

The progressive school reform movements at the end of the 19th century and in the early 20th century in Europe and North America proposed educational and classroom goals that were later integrated into the educational concept of TCI (→ Educational Foundations). Out of the mass the cultural and educational criticism expressed at the time, however, very similar values emerged despite differing accentuations: overcoming the gap between formal education and living experience, educating pupils to become active citizens and not just intellectual knowledge-bearers, individualization instead of forced subordination, simultaneous assumption of responsibility for the "community" (→ Chairperson Postulate), support for activities and interests, i.e., the linking of cognitive, manual, and social learning (→ Living Learning). The educational reformers questioned traditional school and classroom structures where pupils were objects of indoctrination processes and thus had little connection to the subjects being taught (Potthoff, 2003). The transformation of the role of the pupil also changed the role of the teacher, who now encouraged the children to cooperate and offered individualized learning processes (→ Participative Leadership).

One part of these reforms resulted in the establishment of the Landerziehungsheime (private boarding schools), founded by persons such as Hermann Lietz and Paul Geheeb. In 1910, Geheeb started the Odenwaldschule and was its director until he was forced to flee the country in 1934. The successor school founded by Geheeb and his wife in Switzerland was the Ecole d'Humanité, which has been located in Goldern near Bern since 1946. Ruth Cohn moved to Goldern in 1974 and assumed a position as a Consultant Psychologist at the Ecole d'Humanité after discovering the same values and goals of TCI at that institution (Cohn, 1984, p. 386) (→ Ruth Cohn). "TCI was introduced into the classroom, into community life, and into the organizational structure [of that facility]. Ruth's introduction of TCI at the Ecole would today be called 'school development,' which it still is, being an important compass and catalyst for the development of the school" (Bernsau & Walter, www.ecole.ch).

The educational reform movement that commenced in the 1970s created new school frameworks (comprehensive schools, secondary school reform) in order to avert an impending educational catastrophe. School structure was now being questioned from new and different angles, namely, from psychoanalytical and sociological points of view (Fürstenau, 1984; Wellendorf, 1973). Publications on interactional education were concerned with the extent to which social behavior could be taught and learned (Fend, 1975; Fritz, 1975; Geißler, 1979; Grundke, 1975; Krappmann, 1975; Schwäbisch & Siems, 1974). Training in group teaching in school represented these new methodological attempts (Fritz, 1975). Tausch and Tausch (1965) took up the discussion going on in North America concerning leadership styles and initiated discussions about the therapeutically oriented handling of conflicts and disturbances. Emotional aspects present in education in general and specifically in the classroom were considered important, inasmuch as self-development, esteem, and performance were thought to be variables that mutually affected each other (Oerter & Weber, 1975).

Ruth Cohn introduced to her model of TCI the experiences and insights she had gained with psychoanalysis, group therapy, and experiential education as well as pointing out new ways of applying active and creative learning (1975, p. 7). This was her answer to the productive uncertainty and sensitivity found among educators of the day: TCI offered them orientation with its systemic concept that made the complexity of school and daily teaching practice comprehensible in the → four-factor model and the idea of a → dynamic balance. This system was open for the new methodological approaches, it provided instructions for constructive communication, and it offered suggestions on how to deal with disturbances – all of which was anchored in a humanistic value system. Ruth Cohn had recognized not only that emotional and cognitive learning are of equal value, she also described the necessary methods and leadership competences as learnable.

2 TCI and School Development

The first ideas that cropped up about necessary changes to the school landscape as Ruth Cohn first envisioned them in 1973 during a workshop for teachers were directed toward the "principles of 'objectification' and competition that completely permeate our schools." These were to be replaced "by humanistic and cooperative approaches. To this end, 'theme-centered interaction' offers a realistic possibility" (Cohn, 1975, p. 175).

School development today consists of three different fields of action:

1. Curriculum development,
2. Personnel development,
3. Organizational development.

The secondary literature on school development uses TCI as a model for connecting these fields and integrating them using varying accents.

2.1 Curriculum Development

The volume *Lebendiges Lehren und Lernen – TZI macht Schule* (Living Teaching and Learning – TCI Goes to School; Cohn & Terfurth, 1993) contains numerous examples of how TCI-oriented teaching and methods can be implemented in the school system, at the university level, and in teacher training. In his *Didaktik zum Anfassen* (Didactics Up Close), Gudjons (2003, p. 77) considers TCI to be the "counterpoint to traditional teaching," in which pupils were "objects of indoctrination [...] instead of subjects of their own learning processes." He sees TCI as a "major hope and chance for humanizing and democratizing the school system and the classroom" (ibid.). Because TCI consistently propagates the equality of learning as an individual, in groups, and using objective facts, it makes a clear statement about values: Every single person ("I") is as important as the group and the group dynamics ("We") and the common matter at hand ("It"). It must be considered to what extent the learning environment ("Globe") enables or prevents such learning processes. That can be done by applying a theme (→ Theme), enabling inner participation and cooperation, and supporting self-responsibility (→ Work and Social Forms). One must keep in mind the existing knowledge that pupils already possess as well as their individual skills and structure classroom events accordingly. Respect should be the basic form of behavior, which is expressed not just in the choice of words, but also in the "allowing everyone to join in and participate, by carefully shaping the interaction and work forms, by ensuring transparency in the objective targets and the assessment standards, and by properly appreciating individual performance" (Reiser, 2006, p. 130). In order to reflect on the classroom situation, Reiser developed a model for the "conditional analysis of teaching according to TCI" (Reiser & Lotz, 1995, p. 125), which describes a system that is ordered according to TCI elements and also employs the insights of general didactics. The importance of the four-factor model and the TCI interaction guidelines for teaching and teacher training were emphasized by Grell (1991, p. 291).

In order to reduce the anxiety and increase the interest, the balance between → structure, process, and trust must be in order (Cohn, 1975, p. 213). *Trust* is based on having had the experience of being taken seriously and being included; it determines our motivation and our courage to act responsibly. Our interaction with others, which includes emotionality, demands the support emerging from clear *structures*, which provide both security and impulses – and enhance the learning process. School education according to TCI always means strengthening the individual (finding a position and defending it), enabling cooperation (influencing as well as perceiving and supporting others), and creating more knowledge and greater skills. The evaluation of a *process* in which the group is working and learning is the standard for whether to continue or modify a curriculum. To this end, TCI offers a number of guidelines for evaluating the process and that can serve as the starting point for further planning (Arndt, 1996, p. 110)

2.2 Personnel Development

A school interaction culture oriented toward TCI serves as the "basis for the success of the work environment and for contentment among the teaching staff" (Fleischer, 1990, p. 101), which is often the direct opposite of an existing organizational structure in the school that is antagonistic to cooperation. When beginning school projects, Philipp (1995, p. 30) suggests establishing among the staff an entry sequence to the standardization agreement according to TCI. Schratz (1996, p. 109) sticks to the four factors of TCI to ensure successful teamwork by presuming the derived competences: "Personal competence = thinking about oneself and one's own behavior; social competence = thinking about one's relationships to other people; professional competence = thinking about goals, contents, and methods; political competence = thinking about the sociocultural conditions and the political context as well as the chosen strategies."

Schratz think TCI is a supervision model suitable for expanding such competences. Miller (1997), on the other hand, calls TCI a "prototypical model" for learning about interactions in the school setting. He continues: "The high demand among teachers for TCI groups reflects the quality and effectivity of this model" (ibid., p. 172). But how best to train the teacher personality during teacher training is also discussed: It must have a stable level of self-competence in order to provide self-confident control of learning processes (Gudjons, 2003). The particularity of group and team supervision according to TCI is also taken up by Reiser (Reiser & Lotz, 1995, p. 147). The anthology entitled *Themenzentrierte Supervision* (Theme-Centered Supervision) contains articles on how to understand TCI supervision and how to implement it in schools (Hahn et al., 1998). Kullmann, in his book on self-supervision in the school, looks to TCI since "it convincingly embodies the process character of working with groups and groupwork" (2000, p. 52). In his research on *Themenzentrierte Interaktion (TZI) und pädagogische Professionalität von Lehrerinnen und Lehrern* (2008, Theme-Centered Interaction (TCI) and the Educational Professionalism of Teachers), Friedrich Ewert used biographically oriented interviews to show how TCI-oriented knowledge and behavior can have a long-term influence on the design of classroom teaching and the teacher's own role in developing a holistic learning atmosphere (ibid., p. 62).

2.3 Organizational Development

TCI today is firmly established as a professional part of school development processes. Klein (1997, p. 165), in his volume on school counseling, writes the following: "A look through the 'filter' of TCI can decisively sharpen one's understanding of the innovation processes. The concept of TCI thus makes a major contribution to controlling and shaping those process elements that are characteristic of and crucial to innovation." Today, it is agreed that acceptance, reliability, and a high level of responsibility and participation should be achieve in the further development of the school system. To that end, the four-factor model may serve as a compass. Our knowledge concerning the importance of resistance in change processes and the constructive approach to disturbances is indispensable. TCI provides orientation for dealing with disturbances (→ Disturbance Postulate) by determining the various sources of disturbances using the four factors: personal distractions ("I"), crises of the group process ("We"), disagreement about goals and values ("It"), and structural restrictions ("Globe") (Langmaack, 2004, p. 147). Disturbances at all levels can lead to considerable problems in everyday school life and in school development work, whereas a constructive approach, like the idea of partial empowerment during change processes, serves to relieve tension.

One example for a political implementation may be found in the school development program launched in Basel, Switzerland: TCI was used as a compass for the reform of the Basel school system as well as for the seminars offered to teachers in preparation for and following the reform. "The role of TCI as a procedural support instrument and organizational development (OD) as a leadership instrument makes them important design principles in a living school environment" (Cohn & Terfurth, 1993, p. 214; Osswald, 2001, p. 265). The new branch entitled "orientation school" was conceived in the 1980s for the city of Basel and was subsequently approved in a referendum in 1989. The previous three-pronged method in secondary schools was replaced by the 3-year orientation phase. Osswald called the concept he developed for this process "OD-TCI," adding to the existing four factors of TCI three further factors for school development: school direction, school structures, and the main visions/goals. To this end, he applied aspects known from school quality research (Osswald, 2001, p. 128).

Following the publication of the results of the PISA study on the international comparison of basic skills in pupils (PISA, 2000), questions surrounding the organization of schools and curricula took on a new importance. TCI has a number of suggestions and answers to both old and new questions:

- How much does the school structure (choice of subjects, curriculum, time structure, . . .) influence the success of learning processes?
- What is the connection between school atmosphere and learning success?
- What is the role of school direction (leadership) in a reformed school?
- Which particular teaching skills are able to encourage self-responsible, sustainable learning?
- Which forms/methods of cooperation support sustainable learning?
- How can we improve the role of process orientation in school development?
- How can we best anchor a competent approach to dealing with resistance and disturbances?
- Which forms and contents are required during teacher training and continued training in order to guarantee cooperation and a willingness to confront conflict as well as methodological and reflective skills?

The political and educational debate triggered by the PISA results quickly grew into one concerned more with the question of how to ensure better results on such comparative tests. No longer were values and attitudes in demand that would provide a better curriculum and school organization in the countries that took part, even though these aspects played a role in the PISA research (PISA-Konsortium, 2001, pp. 22, 490). The principles Ruth Cohn criticized as "objectification" and "competition" once again took up their old positions (→ Rivalry and Competition).

Ulrike B. Meyer and Karl Platzer-Wederwille (in *Themenzentrierte Interaktion*, Issue 2/2004) wrote about the theme of "TCI in the Learning Environment School," saying that, even now after the PISA results, TCI has an important role to play in school development.

3 Conclusions

School development is full of paradoxes and contradictions, especially between traditional patterns and new ideas. School development is a process of building consciousness in heterogeneous groups that have euphoric, disconcerting, and constructive phases. This means reexamining theories and behaviors again and again. School development is always based on value decisions – laid down in guiding principles and school programs that, upon implementation, often quickly meet with the limitations of staff size and inherent resistance. TCI, with its understanding of dynamic balance and the disturbance postulate, may be appropriate as an instrument of diagnosis in such phases of the school-development processes; it can prevent premature solutions from being implemented and use existing ambivalences as a motor for change. The Globe question, namely, how traditional plans, class sizes, classes composed solely of one grade, the divisions between subjects, tight schedules, regulations concerning grade-scoring systems, rigid system structures, and federal rivalry set artificial limitations in the school, remains as topical as ever (Arndt, 2002, p. 50).

TCI and Adult Education

Claudia Nounla

1 The Relationship Between TCI and Adult Education

Adult education represents an important application of TCI. TCI was fundamental in helping it to develop further and also influenced the so-called "Education for All" movement. Not the least, training in TCI in the Ruth Cohn Institute and other educational institutions is considered as belonging to adult education.

Yet the term "adult education" is a multifaceted one that can refer to many things – a field of work, a system structure, or a branch of science. "Adult education is [...] closely linked with politics, culture, economics, everyday life, and history, and as such it does not have its own development, but is rather integrated into the historical development dynamics and determined by them. But it is also, to varying degrees, involved in these dynamics and in this sense also influences them" (Friedenthal-Haase, 2001, p. 15).

The juncture of TCI and adult education is a process characterized by many factors. Historically, it occurred at a time in which there were many major political and social upheavals, particularly during the time of the Nazi terror from 1933 through 1945, which strongly shaped Ruth Cohn's work (→ Historical-Political Foundations). "For the West, the time around 1970 proved to be a turning point that marked the final steps in the renewal of democratic adult education. Simultaneously, such events as the student uprising of 1968 provided new impulses" (Pöggeler, 2001, p. 44).

2 Important Discussions in Adult Education

2.1 Group and Individual as Factors in the Learning Process

During the 1960s, adult education became integrated in the educational system as the fourth branch of education. At the same time, it became a further branch of science, parallel to education generally becoming more professionalized (Pöggeler, 1980, pp. 60f.). The emphasis lay on the structure system of adult education and less on the methods and didactics employed or the learning individual. Toward the end of the 1960s, the influence of group dynamics grew as greater efforts were now being made to find one's own identity and to establish self-determination (Leuninger, 1985, p. 22).

In the early 1970s, continuing education took off in Germany, and the number of persons teaching adult education rose; systematic and continuous cooperation between various facilities for continuing education and scientific institutions was initiated (Pöggeler, 1980, pp. 64f.).

After many years of a shortage of trained specialists, where mostly young adults were the target group for their efforts, adult education turned to lifelong learning (Pöggeler, 2001, p. 51). Insight was gained into the connection between the human learner and the curriculum and the influence that personal characteristics and experiences have on the learning process (Boventer, 1980, p. 149; Pöffeler, 1980, p. 66).

Many new methods and approaches were developed during this period, which was when TCI also first came to be used and discussed as a separate method ("theme-centered interactional method") (Genser et al., 1972). Knoll (1977, p. 87) noted that TCI bore "expressly educational characteristics" in its attempt to connect the factors of "I," "We," and "It," and that TCI is "presently the most advanced attempt to measure and correlate all components of the learning and working processes in groups" (ibid., p. 92). Much attention was also paid to the disturbance postulate.

2.2 Participant Orientation

At the end of the 1960s and the beginning of the 1970s, various socioeducational and interaction-theoretical concepts came at the forefront of adult education. In the 1980s, however, a certain disillusionment set in. "If we look today, after many years of consolidation, at the state of the methodological discussions, we may conclude the following: The integration of social-scientific concepts as a separate scientific branch and methodology for the education of adults has proved to be a difficult and protracted task" (Gerl, 1985, p. 45). Schäffter (1991, p. 85) sees the reason for this in the contradiction that exists between group dynamics-oriented procedures and a sort of "technocratic planning and leadership philosophy." The result is that "group-dynamic conceptions are included in situation- and action-oriented didactical models only with great reservation and then rarely explicitly" (ibid.). The contradiction between what is considered, on the one hand, to be vital planning procedures of learning processes in adult education and, on the other hand, the development of learning themes during the process cannot be resolved. "The meaning of group-dynamic competence for the employees' understanding of tasks in adult education [...] touches a neuralgic point of the entire institutional fabric, namely, the friction that exists between the principle of participant orientation and the necessity of careful and elaborate planning and preparation" (Schäffter, 1991, p. 70).

The all-important catchphrase of adult education in the 1980s was "participant orientation." Here, TCI was seen as being "extremely participant oriented" (Tietgens, 1981, p. 179). Participant orientation was "founded on anthropological and ethical principles" and became the "didactical-methodological ruling principle" (Tietgens, 2001, p. 305).

Some approaches known from TCI were employed, adapted, and integrated into adult education, making their origin rather fuzzy at times (an example is the disturbance postulate) (→ Living Learning).

2.3 Self-Direction, Self-Organization, Constructivism

In the 1990s a new, vehemently waged debate arose in adult education concerning lifelong learning, fanned by political concerns. Terms such as self-direction and self-organization were now being used in adult-educational contexts, replacing the idea of participant orientation (though some said it was merely old wine in new bottles). Here, it becomes clear that important matters surrounding adult education, such as the integration of so-called educationally disadvantaged persons, remain unsolved. Adult education "does not have a broadly based and widely accepted concept of 'teaching'" (Faulstich & Zeuner, 1999, p. 48). Didactic approaches are differentiated to which TCI has no clear relationship, seeing that TCI itself is seen as an educational concept (e.g., Reiser, 1995, p. 12).

Constructivism is an epistemological theory that is at home in any number of different scientific disciplines and has been discussed as the basis for a didactic of adult education. This includes demands for

- "including individual experiences and knowledge background,"
- "enabling interaction concerning the viability of rationales, interpretations of reality, and action strategies,"
- allowing initiative, self-direction, and self-control (Arnold, 2001, p. 177),
- accepting the meaning of emotions, sensory perceptions, and biographical events in learning settings (Siebert, 1998, pp. 21 ff.).

3 IS TCI a Viable Concept for Adult Education?

As early as the 1970s difficulties had cropped up concerning the application of TCI in the institutional context. These in turn led to a disillusionment in the overall debate. Especially the predictability of learning processes proved to be problematic in light of the processual nature of learning with TCI. Adult educators presumed that learning processes could (and indeed should) be completely mapped out in advance, something that becomes clear in the following quote: "Then an outline is made for each individual course unit so that the participants can get an overview of what is to come and can test themselves whether the envisioned goals, contents, and methods as well as their own learning experiences properly fit the course in question" (Knoll, 1977, p. 94). The orientation toward both persons and subjects is employed for the planning stage, but not the process-oriented development of themes in the learning process.

Today, newer developments, in particular constructivism and the biographical orientation in adult education, have triggered a rethinking of the factors related to TCI. This produces many connections through the mutual integration of theoretical lines of thought (e.g., Watzlawick's communication theory):

- "Our sensual impressions, our thinking, our feelings, and our memories all reflect not some external world, but rather create their own reality" (Siebert, 2000, p. 17). Langmaack and Braune-Krickau (2000, p. 161) note that "every human being constructs his or her own view of reality."
- "The construction of reality is [...] not just a cognitive and emotional, but also a physical activity" (Siebert, 2005, p. 55). "The individual human being is a psycho-biological unit" (Cohn, 1986, p. 120).
- "Our consciousness allows us [...] to be responsible for our both our thoughts and our actions" (Siebert, 1998, pp. 16f.; cf. p. 23). "Be your own chairperson" (Cohn, 1986, p. 120).
- Learning processes cannot be planned or controlled (cf. Siebert, 1998, p. 17). "In education [...] implementation does not occur with the help of exactly planned work processes, but is rather the result of human actions in their respective relationship processes" (Reiser, 1995, p. 13).

The truth in these statements questions the extent to which the publications on TCI are being noticed in the adult-education arena. For example, Siebert (2003, p. 229) notes that the question of how learning themes are developed by the group – a cornerstone of work with TCI – has been "neglected to date." The reason may lie in the fact that TCI is oriented toward experiences and less toward building an empirically based scientific background. This has prevented the integration of TCI in the scientific curricula of adult education. If constructivism is seen as a "neuroscientific basis" (Siebert, 1998, p. 18) of existing but non-evidence-based knowledge, this it could also be basis for reviving the relationship between adult learning and TCI.

TCI and Vocational Training

Franz Schapfel-Kaiser

TCI was first introduced to vocational training in the 1980s at a time when discussions were going on about learning methods at vocational schools. It was revived once again when group work and decentralized control of industrial production entered vocational training in the 1990s. This enabled TCI to become part of shaping how training processes were carried out within companies. In the following, I point out some of the influences TCI had on vocational training. First, however, it is necessary to differentiate the role of vocational training from that of university education, continuing education, counseling, and other such fields.

1 The Object of Vocational Training

Narrowly speaking, vocational training is concerned with training young people who are transitioning from school to working life, primarily at the mid-level qualification level, something that goes back to the Medieval training craftsmen and merchants received, and terminating in a qualification as a skilled worker (baker, gardener, typesetter, real-estate dealer, animal husbandry, elderly care, etc.). These professions also have a large number of specialized or more comprehensive advance training occupations that prepare for management positions (master level, administrators). In Germany, this training is done primarily as part of the "dual system," where time divided between the company premises and the vocational school, generally lasting a total of 3 years. To this widespread system a transitional system was recently added, consisting of job orientation, preparation for training, basic professional training (1 year), etc., all of which has the goal of supporting disadvantaged adolescents to reach their vocational goal.

Even this short description clearly shows: First, vocational training in Germany has a broad basis, even if we neglect university education, which effectively also includes professional training. Second, it reveals many parallels to other areas in which TCI plays a major role (school system, social work, management).

In order to avoid repeating what has been mentioned elsewhere in this volume, in the following we concentrate on the area of company-based vocational training, how TCI is implemented there, and the theoretical research being done in this area. That said, it remains difficult to exactly delineate this area from continuing education and counseling.

2 Vocational Training and TCI – A Review

The basis of all vocational training is the vocation in question; the demands made on persons working in a particularly vocation in the respective private or public fields determine the curriculum used in their training. Focusing on the specific demands made by the respective vocation, determined in part by evolving technological innovations, and on the dominance of the traditional craftsmen vocations in vocational training means dealing with the learning methods that are best suited to imparting knowledge from technology and the natural sciences. The training of social and generic qualifications is done elsewhere.

The last 25 years have seen a shift from purely cognitive or job-specific demands to more generic demands, the so-called key qualifications. This in turn means dealing with disadvantaged target groups as well as with the role of constructivism in vocational training, leading to a greater emphasis on subject-oriented approaches. "One consequence of the new Vocational Training Act is that the goal of vocational training now clearly lies in developing the four levels of competence (attitudes, knowledge, competences, skills) and no longer in enabling pure knowledge and skills. [...] The modern working environment is demanding ever more the continuous further development of the key competences, for example, 'communication skills' and 'collaborative skills'" (Aschwanden, 2004, p. 5). Thus, the ability to autonomously apply new information and communication technologies in business environments has become part of the curricula of training programs, as has the training of social skills, in all fields of vocational training.

These shifts have also influenced the discussions surrounding the theory of vocational training and the methods employed. During the 1980s, TCI played a role only in connection with the qualification of teachers in vocational-training facilities (Baum, 1980; Kersten, 1983). Later, the debate turned to the more generic qualifications needed and the newer forms of work organization, emphasizing the subject orientation of the "new" vocational training and leading both to new theoretical approaches to this theme (Auer, 1996; Nohl, 1997; Schapfel-Kaiser, 1996, 1997) as well as to new considerations of the practical qualification measures needed (Senghaas-Knobloch, 1996; Schapfel-Kaiser, 2000).

The use of TCI in vocational training was quickened by the social changes going on, which in short can be described by the terms "risk society," "knowledge society," and the new concept of "manpower entrepreneur" (Voß & Pongratz, 1998), all of which presented new challenges to the self-development of lifeplans. The research on these phenomena, such as that done by Faßhauer (2001), Lehmkuhl (2002), and Immel (2004), used TCI as a concept for increasing "self-competence."

Despite the apparent broad debate that went on, TCI never got a strong footing in the discussion surrounding vocational training. Numerous individual seminars at the university level in institutes for vocational and business education (e.g., in Hamburg, Cologne, Darmstadt, Erfurt) included TCI, as did some handbooks and introductions to vocational

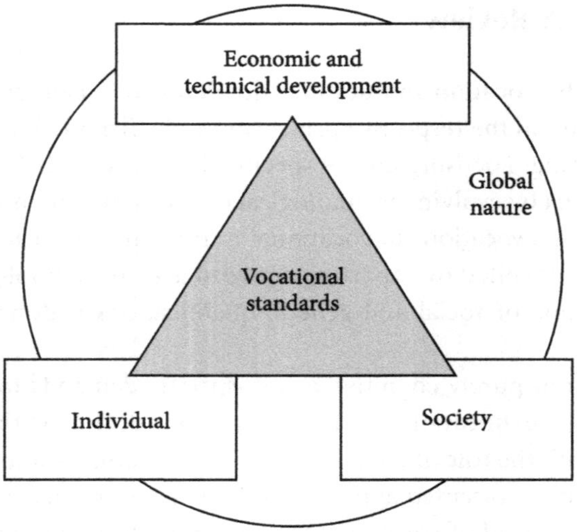

Figure 1. The four-factor model of TCI as a reference point for developing vocational content.

education (such as Pahl & Uhe, 1998). Yet there was no systematic analysis of the relationship between vocational training and TCI, nor did TCI officially gain systematic entry into qualification measures – the exception being an approach taken in Switzerland to qualify vocational teachers (Aschwanden, 2004; WILL Schweiz, 2004).

3 Examples of In-Depth Debates

TCI comes into the focus of attention whenever the methodological and didactical organization of training curricula is being discussed, or when the theoretical discussions concentrate on more subject-oriented matters. The works of Auer (1996) and Nohl (1997), for example, compare TCI to the project method and the textual method and draw their own conclusions for the practical organization, as well as pointing out the contradictions that exist with regard to value orientation. "In the guidelines on management culture, the norm of 'completely identifying with the company' takes the highest priority, regardless of all possible 'unethical' implications" (Nohl, 1997, p. 85). This tension between the new demands being made on the subject in the work arena – characterized by team spirit, planning competence, creativity, and autonomy – must be seen in light of the constitutive elements of subject orientation in the discussion surrounding vocational education (Schapfel, 1996); it highlights the role that TCI plays in subject-oriented vocational training. "An understanding of the interconnections and the dependencies the subject enters into and participates in allows conscious intervention in social and global processes. [...] Wherever there are temporal and spatial connections between action and reflection lie the conditions necessary for the persons involved to make subjective and collective decisions. If they are supported by the common exchange, they can take a position toward the existing demands made in the working environment" (Schapfel, 1996, pp. 78, 84). Here, TCI becomes a very helpful model of orientation for organizing vocational education.

TCI was also applied in a number of pilot projects as well as being integrated into work materials. "The concept of TCI appeared to us to be appropriate for analyzing personnel, social, and other relevant aspects of this process" (Kimmig & Meister, 1995, p. 15). No other attempts are known besides our own work (Schapfel-Kaiser, 1997), in which we attempted to develop the triangle and sphere as a basic guideline for turning learning processes in TCI groups into a general instrument of analysis in vocational educational processes. We applied TCI as an instrument of analysis in learning and work cells by applying Stollberg's shadow triangle, which makes TCI an organizational tool for designing complex vocational curricula, for example, in the expert opinions created for a project of the Worldbank in Turkey (Rützel & Schapfel, 1996).

This model clearly shows that vocational curricula must orient themselves not only to changes going on in technology and work organization ("Theme"), but also to the needs and perspectives of those being trained ("I") which result from the respective economic and political state of affairs of society ("We") and finally also from the global connections between justice and ecological processes ("Globe") – which tend to be ignored. This model played a major role in the debate that took place beginning in 2002 concerning sustainability in vocational education.

4 Outlook

Switzerland has been successful in offering the qualification of training personnel based on TCI together with the Swiss Association for Continuing Education (WILL-Schweiz, 2004). This seems to be one of the best approaches to implementing the goals and methods of TCI in corporate training practices. All other approaches mentioned above are less likely to achieve long-term success and are thus oriented more toward individuals.

Nevertheless, it should be mentioned that vocational training is always the product of negotiations between the national government and the relevant social partners. The value orientation and the methodological concept of TCI can be employed to properly channel these negotiations as well as being integrated into the contents of the vocational educational processes, providing concrete indications for shaping learning situations. Yet TCI should not be overestimated: It cannot replace the systematic analysis of social and economic work processes and the inherent contradictions they have which again and again put limits to the empowerment of the individual, in particular the functional positioning of one's work life, which stretches over one's entire lifetime (Schapfel-Kaiser, 2008).

References

When several years are listed in parentheses, this means authors have quoted from multiple editions.

Abeln, R. (Ed.) (1994). Aggression in Gruppen. Mainz: Grünewald.

Abraham, T. (2006). TCI in India: An Indian's response to its relevance – an analysis of the concept and its application. Themenzentrierte Interaktion, 20 (1), 55–64.

Adler, A. (1911). Theorie und Praxis der Individualpsychologie. Wien.

Amann, I. (1992). Das Dreieck in der Kugel. Spirituelle Aspekte der TZI. In C. Löhmer, R. Standhardt (Eds.), TZI. Pädagogisch-therapeutische Gruppenarbeit nach Ruth C. Cohn (pp. 144–174). Stuttgart: Klett-Cotta

Arbeitskreis "TZI und Wirtschaft" (Ed.) (1985). TZI und Wirtschaft. Reflexionen – Impulse – Praxisberichte. Unveröffentlichtes Manuskript.

Arend-Herlyn, M. (2001). Interkulturelle Kompetenz und TZI. Themenzentrierte Interaktion, 15 (1), 42–50.

Argyle, M. (1969). Social interaction. London: Methuen and Co. (deutsch: Soziale Interaktion. Köln: Kiepenheuer & Witsch, 1972)

Argyris, C., Schön, D. A. (1978). Organizational learning. A Theory of action perspective. Boston: Addison-Wesley.

Arndt, E. (1992). Wie viele Chancen haben Kinder, die eigene Chairperson zu entdecken? Themenzentrierte Interaktion, 6 (2), 93–98.

Arndt, E. (1996). Themenzentrierte Interaktion. In R. Miller (Ed.), Schule selbst gestalten (pp. 98–110). Weinheim/Basel: Beltz.

Arndt, E. (2002). Ruth Cohn und ihre Idee von lebendigen Lernprozessen in der Schule. Themenzentrierte Interaktion, 16 (1), 50–58.

Arnold, R. (2001). Konstruktivismus. In Arnold, R., Nolda, S., Nuissl, E. (Eds.), Wörterbuch Erwachsenenpädagogik (pp. 176–177). Bad Heilbrunn: Klinkhardt.

Aschaffenburg, H. (1987). Selbsterfahrung als Begegnung: TZI-Encounter. In K. Hahn, M. Schraut, K. Schütz, C. Wagner (Eds.), Gruppenarbeit: themenzentriert: Entwicklungsgeschichte, Kritik und Methodenreflexion (pp. 91–100). Mainz: Grünewald.

Aschwanden, K. (2004). Pädagogisches Konzept zur Ausbildung zum/r Fachangestellten Gesundheit. Berufsschule für Pflege Männedorf in der Schweiz. http://www.aschwandenk. ch/download/texte/paedagogisches_konzept_maennedorf.pdf

Assink, P. (2006). Uit het harnas! Vier wegen naar authentiek en verantwoord leiderschap. Amsterdam: Uitgeverij Business Contact.

Auer, K. (1996). Themenzentrierte Interaktion in der Berufsausbildung. Unveröffentlichte Staatsexamensarbeit am Institut für Berufspädagogik, TU-Darmstadt.

Avolio, B. J. (1999). Full leadership development: Building the vital forces in organizations. Thousand Oaks, CA: Sage.

Baier, L. (1993). Hard Multiculturalism. In L. Baier, Die verleugnete Utopie (pp. 126–146). Berlin: Aufbau.

Bales, R. F. (1950). Interaction Process Analysis. Reading, Mass.: Addison Wesley.

Bass, B. M. (1998). Transformational leadership: Industry, military, and educational impact. Mahwah, NJ: Erlbaum.

Bastine, R. (1975). Auf dem Wege zu einer integrierten Psychotherapie. Psychologie heute, 2 (7), 53–59.

Bateson, G. (1999). Steps to an ecology of mind. Chicago: University of Chicago Press.

Battegay, R. (1969). Der Mensch in der Gruppe, Vol. 3: Gruppendynamik und Gruppenpsychotherapie. Bern: Huber.

Battke, A. (1995). Zeit wahrnehmen – Zeit gestalten. Acht Variationen über ein Stiefkind der TZI. Themenzentrierte Interaktion, 9 (2), 66–71.

Bauer, J. (2002). Das Gedächtnis des Körpers. Frankfurt a. M.: Eichborn.

Bauer, J. (2006). Prinzip Menschlichkeit. Warum wir von Natur aus kooperieren. Hamburg: Hoffmann und Campe.

Bauer-Sternberg, D., Schaper, M. (1994). Organisationsentwicklung mit der Themenzentrierten Interaktion. Eine ganzheitliche Strategie zur Unternehmensentwicklung. Gruppendynamik, 25 (4), 421 ff.

Baum, R. (1980). Themenzentrierte Interaktion und Persönlichkeitsentwicklung in der Berufsausbildung (Dissertation). Basel.

Baumgartner, I. et al. (Eds.) (1995, 1996). OE-Prozesse. Die Prinzipien Systemischer Organisationsentwicklung. Stuttgart/Bern: Huber.

Bauriedl, Th. (1994). Auch ohne Couch: Psychoanalyse als Beziehungstheorie und ihre Anwendungen. Stuttgart: Verlag Internationale Psychoanalyse.

Beck, D., Cowan, C. (1996). Spiral dynamics. Oxford: Blackwell.

Beck, U. (1986). Risikogesellschaft. Auf dem Weg in eine andere Moderne. Frankfurt a. M.: Suhrkamp.

Becker, H., Langosch, I. (2002/1987). Produktivität und Menschlichkeit: Organisationsentwicklung und ihre Anwendung in der Praxis. Stuttgart: Lucius & Lucius.

Belz, H. (1979). Über den Umgang mit destruktiven Strebungen in TZI-Gruppen aus der Sicht der Leiterfunktion. Gruppenpsychotherapie und Gruppendynamik, 14 (3/4), 363–373.

Belz, H. (1988). Kooperative Arbeitshaltung in Gruppen durch individuelles Selbstbewusstsein und Reflexion auf der Grundlage der Themenzentrierten Interaktion. In H. Belz et al., Auf dem Weg zur arbeitsfähigen Gruppe. Mainz: Grünewald.

Belz, H. (2001). Über den Umgang mit destruktiven Strebungen in TZI-Gruppen aus der Sicht der Leitungsfunktion. In K. Hahn, M. Schraut, K.-V. Schütz, C. Wagner (Eds.), Kompetente LeiterInnen. Beiträge zum Leitungsverständnis nach TZI (pp. 49–62). Mainz: Grünewald.

Belz, H., Dehm U., Eichberger, M., Roch E. (1988, 1992). Auf dem Weg zur arbeitsfähigen Gruppe. Kooperationskonzept von Helga Belz – Prozeßberichte aus TZI-Gruppen. Mainz: Grünewald.

Ben-Chorin, S. (1971). Der dreidimensionale Mensch in Bibel und Moderne. Trier: Paulinus.

Bernfeld, S. (1973). Sisyphus oder die Grenzen der Erziehung. Frankfurt a. M.: Suhrkamp.

Bernsau, M., Walter, V. (n.d.). Die Themenzentrierte Interaktion – ein "Leitstern" der Ecole d'Humanité. In www.ecole.ch/Fachbeiträge

Bielander, R. (1995). TZI und Gruppenanalyse. Themenzentrierte Interaktion 9 (1), 66–85.
Bieri, P. (2001). Das Handwerk der Freiheit: über die Entdeckung des eigenen Willens. München/Wien: Hanser.
Bion, W. R. (1961a/1971). Erfahrungen in Gruppen und andere Schriften. Stuttgart: Klett-Cotta.
Bion, W. R. (1961b). Experiences in Groups. London: Tavistock.
Birmelin, R. (1985). Struktur – Prozess – Vertrauen. Skizzen einer Organisationsentwicklung. In R. Birmelin et al. (Eds.), Erfahrungen lebendigen Lernens. Grundlagen und Arbeitsfelder der TZI (pp. 118–128). Mainz: Grünewald.
Birmelin, R., Hahn, K., Schraut-Birmelin, M., Schütz, K., Wagner, C. (Eds.) (1985). Erfahrungen lebendigen Lernens: Grundlagen und Arbeitsfelder der TZI. Mainz: Grünewald.
Bittner, G. (1976). Diskussion: Wider die Prächtigkeitsapostel. Gruppendynamik, 7 (1), 237–239.
Bittner, G. (1980). Gruppendynamik – ein ziemlich sicherer Weg sich selbst zu verfehlen. Psychosozial, 3 (1), 41–65.
Blekkingh, B. W. (2005). Authentiek leiderschap. Ontdek en leef je missie. Den Haag: Sdu Uitgevers bv.
Bloch, E. (1974). Das Prinzip Hoffnung. 3 Bde. Frankfurt a. M.: Suhrkamp.
Bohm, D. (1980). Wholeness and the implicate order. New York: Braziller.
Böhme, H., Böhme, G. (1983). Das Andere der Vernunft. Zur Entwicklung von Rationalitätsstrukturen am Beispiel Kants. Frankfurt a. M.: Suhrkamp.
Bönsch, M.; Zach, K. (2006). Seminarkrisen meistern. Erste Hilfe für Trainer, Lehrer, Vortragende. Reinbek: Rowohlt.
Boventer, H. (1980). Meine und deine Freiheit. In F. Henrich, H. Kaiser (Eds.), Erwachsenenbildung. 25 Jahre Entwicklung im Spiegel einer Zeitschrift (pp. 145–150). Düsseldorf: Patmos.
Bowald, B. et al. (2002). KörperSinnE. Körper im Spannungsfeld von Diskurs und Erfahrung. Wettingen: eFeF.
Bradford, L. P., Gibb, J. R., Benne, K. D. (Eds.) (1964). T-group Theory and laboratory method. New York. (deutsch: Gruppen-Training. Stuttgart: Klett, 1972)
Brake, R. (1992). Leserbrief. Themenzentrierte Interaktion 6 (2), 87–89.
Brezinka, W. (1978). Metatheorie der Erziehung. München/Basel: Reinhardt.
Brocher, T. (1967). Gruppendynamik und Erwachsenenbildung: Zum Problem der Entwicklung von Konformismus oder Autonomie in Arbeitsgruppen. Braunschweig: Westermann.
Brombach, S. (2006). TZI im Spannungsfeld von Erotik, Gesellschaft und geschlechtlicher Identität. Themenzentrierte Interaktion, 20 (2), 13–22.
Brown, E. C. (1989). How the Academy began. Voices: The Art and Science of Psychotherapy, Vol. 25, No. 1/2, 70–78.
Buber, M. (1923, 1983, 1984). Ich und Du. In M. Buber, Das dialogische Prinzip. Heidelberg: Lambert Schneider.
Buber, M. (1925, 1960). Reden über Erziehung. Heidelberg: Lambert Schneider.
Buber, M. (1949). Die Erzählungen der Chassidim. Zürich: Manesse.
Buber, M. (1962). Werke. Vol. 1: Zur Philosophie. München-Heidelberg: Kösel.
Buber, M. (1971). Das Problem des Menschen. Heidelberg: Lambert Schneider.
Buber, M. (1973, 1979, 1984). Das dialogische Prinzip. Heidelberg: Lambert Schneider.
Buchinger, H. (2004). Psychoanalyse oder Systemtheorie – eine unangemessene Frage. Supervision, 22 (1), 40–48.
Bühler, C. (1973). Einführung in die humanistische Psychologie. Stuttgart: Klett.

Bühler, K. (1982). Sprachtheorie. Die Darstellungsfunktion der Sprache. Stuttgart: Gustav Fischer.

Bünte-Ludwig, C. (1984). Gestalttherapie – Integrative Therapie. Leben heißt wachsen. In H. Petzold (Ed.), Wege zum Menschen, Volume 1 (pp. 217–308). Paderborn: Junfermann.

Burkhardt, J., Schneider-Landolf, M. (2009). TZI-Phasenmodell und ihr Nutzen für die Teamentwicklung. Themenzentrierte Interaktion, 23 (1), 73–86.

Buschmann, M., Biermann, R., Massing, R. (1997). Themenzentrierte Interaktion (TZI) – ein Modell, das nach Bewegung verlangt. In U. Henkel, G. Pfister (Eds.), Für eine andere Bewegungskultur. Festschrift anlässlich der Emeritierung von Sabine Kröner (pp. 307–336). Pfaffenweiler: Centaurus.

Buschmann, M., Borgmeier, C. M. (1998). FRAU-Sein – MANN-Sein: der Einfluss auf die Supervision. In K. Hahn, M. Schraut, K. V. Schütz, C. Wagner (Eds.), Themenzentrierte Supervision (pp. 256–277). Mainz: Grünewald.

Buschmann, M., Kröner, S. (Eds.) (2000). TZI bewegt – bewegende TZI. Neue Wegebewegungszentrierter Gruppenarbeit in Weiterbildung und Sozialarbeit mit Frauen. Mainz: Grünewald.

Butler, J. (1991). Das Unbehagen der Geschlechter. Frankfurt a. M.: Suhrkamp.

Butler, J. (1995). Körper von Gewicht. Die diskursiven Grenzen des Geschlechts. Berlin: Berlin Verlag.

Callens, I. (1983). Het concept levend leren, proefschrift. Amsterdam: Uitgeverij VU Boekhandel.

Callens, I. (2004). Generative Leadership. Moving towards living learning organisations: the transformational leadership concept of the Theme Centered Interaction (TCI) – vertaling van: Generatief Leiderschap. Op weg naar levende lerende organisaties. Health Management Forum, 1.

Callens, I. (2005). Generatief leiderschap: het innovatieve leiderschapsmodel van de themagecentreerde interactie. In Handboek Werken, leren en leven met groepen. A6500.

Callens, I. (2007). Generative Leadership. Über Leben und Lernen in einer turbulenten Umwelt – vertaling van: Generatief Leiderschap. Het innovatieve leiderschapsmodel van de themagecentreerde interactie (TGI) (2004, 2005). Utrecht: Centre for Generative Leadership.

Callens, I., Bogaard, J. v. d., Doelman, S. (2003). Hoe generatief leiderschap diversiteit bevordert. Utrecht: Centre for Generative Leadership/Amstelveen: Opportunity in Bedrijf.

Capra, F. (1996). The Web of Life, a synthesis of mind and matters. London: HarperCollins Publishers.

Capra, F. (2002). De eenheid van leven. Utrecht: Kosmos-Z&K Uitgevers B. V.

Caruso, I. (1972). Soziale Aspekte der Psychoanalyse. Reinbek: Rowohlt.

Cohn, R. C. (1949). Inmitten aller Sterne. Ed. v. F. Paulsen. New York: Peter Thomas Fisher.

Cohn, R. C. (1968). Ich muß tun, was ich will – für 10 Minuten. In R. C. Cohn (1975), Von der Psychoanalyse zur themenzentrierten Interaktion. Von der Behandlung einzelner zu einer Pädagogik für alle (pp. 145–151). Stuttgart: Klett-Cotta.

Cohn, R. C. (1969). From Couch to Circle to Community. Beginnings of the Theme-Centered Interactional Method. In H. M. Ruitenbeek (Ed.), Group Therapy Today. New York: Atherton Press. Zit. nach Kuebel, M. A. (Ed.) (2002), Living Learning. A Reader in Theme-Centered Interaction (pp. 101–116). Delhi: Media House.

Cohn, R. C. (1970). Das Thema als Mittelpunkt interaktioneller Gruppen. Gruppenpsychotherapie und Gruppendynamik, 3 (2), 251–259.

Cohn, R. C. (1971). Living-Learning Encounters: The Theme-Centered Interactional Method. In L. Blank, G. B. Gottsegen, M. G. Gottsegen (Eds.), Confrontations. Encounters in self and interpersonal awareness (pp. 245–271). New York: Macmillan und London, Collier-Macmillan Limited.

Cohn, R. C. (1975, 1981, 1983, 1986, 1990, 1992, 2000). Von der Psychoanalyse zur Themenzentrierten Interaktion. Stuttgart: Klett-Cotta.

Cohn, R. C. (1975a). The existential leader. In B. Lift (Ed.), The leader in the group. New York: Aronson.

Cohn, R. C. (1976). Kommentar zu Günther Bittner: "Wider die Prächtigkeitsapostel." Gruppendynamik, 7 (1), 239–240.

Cohn, R. C. (1978). Interview mit Prof. Dr. Pöhlmann, Karlsruhe, Deutsche evangelische Arbeitsgemeinschaft für Erwachsenenbildung, unveröffentlichtes Manuskript. In gekürzter Bearbeitung durch Elfi Stollberg (2005) erschienen in Themenzentrierte Interaktion, 19 (2), 19–22.

Cohn, R. C. (1979). Themenzentrierte Interaktion. Ein Ansatz zum Sich-selbst und Gruppenleiten. In A. Heigl-Evers (Ed.), Die Psychologie des 20. Jahrhunderts, Vol. VIII: Lewin und die Folgen. Sozialpsychologie – Gruppendynamik – Gruppentherapie (pp. 873– 883). Zürich: Kindler.

Cohn, R. C. (1985). Über die Bedeutung des Politischen und Kosmischen für mein Denken. Ein Gespräch mit Hilarion Petzold. Integrative Therapie, 11, 264–272.

Cohn, R. C. (1985). Aus einem Gespräch mit Ruth C. Cohn. In R. Birmelin et al. (Eds.). Erfahrungen lebendigen Lernens. Grundlagen und Arbeitsfelder der TZI (pp. 9–22). Mainz: Grünewald.

Cohn, R. C. (1988). Wir sind Teil des Universums und wir nehmen Anteil: Der Globe. Themenzentrierte Interaktion, 2 (1), 3–6.

Cohn, R. C. (1989). Es geht ums Anteilnehmen. Perspektiven der Persönlichkeitsentfaltung in der Gesellschaft der Jahrtausendwende. Freiburg i. Br.: Herder.

Cohn, R. C. (1994). Gucklöcher. Zur Lebensgeschichte von TZI und Ruth C. Cohn. Gruppendynamik, 25 (4), 345–370.

Cohn, R. C. (1994). Verantworte dein Tun und dein Lassen, persönlich und gesellschaftlich. Offener Brief an Günter Hoppe. Themenzentrierte Interaktion, 8 (2), 85–87.

Cohn, R. C. (1997). Van psychoanalyse naar themagecentreerde interactie – Basisteksten. Baarn: Nelissen.

Cohn, R. C., Klein, I. (1993). Großgruppen gestalten mit Themenzentrierter Interaktion. Ein Weg zur lebendigen Balance zwischen Einzelnen, Aufgaben und Gruppe. Mainz: Grünewald.

Cohn, R. C., Ockel, A. (1992). Das Konzept des Widerstands in der Themenzentrierten Interaktion. Vom psychoanalytischen Konzept des Widerstands über das TZI-Konzept der Störung zum Ansatz einer Gesellschaftstherapie. In C. Löhmer, R. Standhardt (Eds.), TZI. Pädagogisch-therapeutische Gruppenarbeit nach Ruth C. Cohn (pp. 177– 206). Stuttgart: Klett-Cotta (originally in H. Petzold [Ed.], Widerstand. Ein strittiges Konzept in der Psychotherapie, pp. 255–282, Paderborn: Junfermann, 1981).

Cohn, R. C., Schulz von Thun, F. (1994). Wir sind Politiker und Politikerinnen – wir alle! Ein Gespräch über mögliche Hilfen von TZI und Kommunikationslehre. In R. Standhardt, C. Löhmer (Eds.) (1994), Zur Tat befreien. Gesellschaftspolitische Perspektiven der TZI-Gruppenarbeit (pp. 30–62). Mainz: Grünewald.

Cohn, R. C., Terfurth, C. (Eds.) (1993, 1995). Lebendiges Lehren und Lernen. TZI macht Schule. Stuttgart: Klett-Cotta.

Cohn, R. C., Krämer, M. (2002). Ruth Cohn im Gespräch mit Manfred Krämer am 12./13. Januar 2002. Themenzentrierte Interaktion, 16 (1), 16–29.

Connell, R. W. (1999). Der gemachte Mann. Konstruktion und Krise von Männlichkeiten. Opladen: Leske + Budrich.

Craemer, D. (1988). Die dynamische Balance: Zwei-Klang, Drei-Pol, Vier-Takt. Themenzentrierte Interaktion, 2 (1), 26–32.

Craemer, D. (1998). Das TZI-Fünfeck: ein Hinweis für Leitungs-Interventionen. Themenzentrierte Interaktion, 12 (1), 88–104.

Damasio, A. (1995). Descartes' Irrtum. Fühlen, Denken und das menschliche Gehirn. München: List.

Damasio, A. (1999). Ich fühle, also bin ich. Die Entschlüsselung des Bewusstseins. München: List.

Damasio, A. (2003). Der Spinoza-Effekt – Wie Gefühle unser Leben bestimmen. München: List.

Dewey, J. (1939). Theory of Valuation. In J. Dewey (1992). Later Works, Vol. 13. Carbondale and Edwardsville, Illinois: Southern Illinois University Press.

Dlugosch, A. (2003). Professionelle Entwicklung und Biographie. Impulse für universitäre Bildungsprozesse im Kontext schulischer Erziehungshilfe. Bad Heilbrunn: Klinkhardt.

Dlugosch, A. (2005). Professionelle Entwicklung in sonderpädagogischen Kontexten. In D. Horster et al. (Eds.), Sonderpädagogische Professionalität. Beiträge zur Entwicklung der Sonderpädagogik als Disziplin und Profession (pp. 27–49). Wiesbaden: VS Verlag für Sozialwissenschaften.

Dlugosch, A., Reiser, H. (2006). Themenzentrierte Interaktion in Bildung und Beratung In U. Sauer-Schiffer, M. Ziemons (Eds.), In der Balance liegt die Chance: themenzentrierte Interaktion in Bildung und Beratung (pp. 23–36). Münster: Waxmann.

Dlugosch, A., Reiser, H. (2007). Themenzentrierte Interaktion in Bildung und Beratung – Fragen und Denkanstöße zur Thematik. Themenzentrierte Interaktion, 21 (1), 7–17.

Doppler, K., Lauterburg, C. (1994), Change Management. Den Unternehmenswandel gestalten. Frankfurt a. M./New York: Campus.

Dörfler, A. (1998). Organisationen sind keine Gruppen. TZI in Organisationen und Gruppen. Themenzentrierte Interaktion, 12 (1), 22–32.

Döring-Seipel, E., Sanne, C. (1999). Emotionale Intelligenz. Gruppendynamik, 30 (1), 37–50.

Dorison, F. (2005). TZI in Frankreich: kein großes Interesse? Themenzentrierte Interaktion, 19 (1), 40–45.

Dreitzel, H. P. (1968). Die gesellschaftlichen Leiden und das Leiden an der Gesellschaft. Stuttgart: Ferdinand Enke.

Duden (1963, 1997). Bd 7: Etymologie: Herkunftswörterbuch der deutschen Sprache (2nd ed.). Bearbeitet von Günter Drosdowski. Mannheim: Dudenverlag.

Durkheim, E. (1895). Les règles de la méthode sociologique. Paris: Félix Alcan.

Ehlich, H., Majewski, I. (1995). Die humanistisch-philosophische Basis der TZI. Utrecht-Hannover: Eigenverlag.

Eicke, D. (Ed.) (1977). Psychologie des 20. Jahrhunderts. Volume 3. Zürich: Kindler.

Emme, M. (1996). "Der Versuch, den Feind zu verstehen": ein pädagogischer Beitrag zur moralisch-politischen Dimension von Empathie und Dialog. Frankfurt a. M.: IKO – Verl. für Interkulturelle Kommunikation.

Engelen, E.-M. (2007). Gefühle. Stuttgart: Reclam.

Enzinger, H. (2003). Wo WILL ist, ist ein Weg! Vom basisdemokratischen Verein zur leistungsfähigen Organisation. Themenzentrierte Interaktion, 17 (2), 39–53.

Erikson, E. H. (1950). Childhood and society. New York. (deutsch: Kindheit und Gesellschaft. Stuttgart: Ernst Klett, 1969)

Ermann, M. (1977). Die themenzentrierte Interaktion (TZI) in Gruppenarbeit und Gruppenpsychotherapie. Gruppenpsychotherapie und Gruppendynamik, 12 (3), 266–277.

Erwachsenenbildung. In E. Schmitz, H. Tietgens (Eds.), Enzyklopädie Erziehungswissenschaften, Vol. 11: Erwachsenenbildung (pp. 160–170). Stuttgart: Klett-Cotta.

Ewen, J. (2003). Ethik für Führungskräfte. Überlegungen aus der Praxis. Themenzentrierte Interaktion (TZI), 17 (2), 91–103.

Ewert, F. (2008). Themenzentrierte Interaktion (TZI) und pädagogische Professionalität von Lehrerinnen und Lehrern. Wiesbaden: VS Verlag.

Farau, A., Cohn, R. C. (1984). Gelebte Geschichte der Psychotherapie. Zwei Perspektiven. Stuttgart: Klett-Cotta.

Faßhauer, U. (2001). Emotionale Leistungsfähigkeit im Kontext beruflicher Bildung (Dissertation, Darmstadt). Bielefeld: Bertelsmann.

Faßhauer, U. (2004). Die "Logik der Sachen" mit der "Logik der Emotionen" vermitteln. Ein Beitrag der TZI zur Didaktik und Professionalisierung in der beruflichen Bildung. Themenzentrierte Interaktion, 18 (2), 32–42.

Faßhauer, U. (2005). Anmerkungen gegen eine Überbetonung des Spirituellen in der TZI. Themenzentrierte Interaktion, 19 (2), 23–28.

Faßhauer, U., Schapfel-Kaiser, F. (2008). TZI als Gestaltungs- und Analyseansatz für berufliche Bildungsprozesse. Eintrag im Kommunikations- und Informationssystem berufliche Bildung, http://www.kibb.de.

Faulstich, P., Zeuner, C. (1999). Erwachsenenbildung: eine handlungsorientierte Einführung. Weinheim/München: Juventa.

Feder, G. (1999). Joseph Haydn. Die Schöpfung. Kassel: Bärenreiter.

Fend, H. (1975). Perspektiven der Forschung zum sozialen Lernen im Kontext der Schule. In H. Roth, D. Friedrich (Eds.), Bildungsforschung: Probleme – Perspektiven – Prioritäten (Part 1). Deutscher Bildungsrat: Gutachten und Studien der Bildungskommission, Vol. 50, pp. 155–213. Stuttgart: Klett-Cotta.

Fengler, J. (1981). Grenzen der Gruppendynamik. In C. H. Bachmann (Ed.), Kritik der Gruppendynamik (pp. 118–156). Frankfurt a. M.: Fischer.

Fengler, J. (1976). Strukturelle Interventionen. Arbeitspapier. Gruppendynamik im Bildungsbereich, 2 (3), 60–61.

Fleischer, T. (1990). Zur Verbesserung der Sozialkompetenz von Lehrern und Schulleitern. Kommunikationskompetenz und Interaktionskultur als Systemanforderung in der Schule. Hohengeren: Schneider.

Flöther, E. (2001). Es könnte so einfach sein. brand eins, H 3, 118 ff.

Fontius, M. (2001). Kritisch/Kritik. In K. Barck, M. Fontius, D. Schlenstedt, B. Steinwachs, F. Wolfzettel (Eds.), Ästhetische Grundbegriffe. Historisches Wörterbuch in sieben Bänden, Vol. 3 (pp. 450–489). Stuttgart: J. B. Metzler.

Foulkes, S. H. (1964). Therapeutic group analysis. London: Allen and Unwin.

Foulkes, S. H. (1974). Gruppenanalytische Psychotherapie (Geist und Psyche). München: Pfeiffer.

Freire, P. (1971). Pädagogik der Unterdrückten. Stuttgart: Kreuz.

Freire, P. (1974). Erziehung als Praxis der Freiheit. Stuttgart: Kreuz.

Freud, S. (1900). Die Traumdeutung. GW Vol. II–III.

Freud, S. (1910). Über Psychoanalyse. GW Vol. VIII.

Freud, S. (1912b). Zur Dynamik der Übertragung. GW Vol. VIII.

Frey, R., Dingler, J. (2001). Wie Theorien Geschlechter konstruieren. Ein Debattenüberblick. In Alles gender? Oder was? Theoretische Ansätze zur Konstruktion von Geschlecht(ern) und ihre Relevanz für die Praxis in Bildung, Beratung und Politik. Dokumentation einer Fachtagung der Heinrich-Böll-Stiftung und des "Forum Männer" in Theorie und Praxis der Geschlechterverhältnisse am 9./10. März 2001 in Berlin.

Frickel, M. (1981). Themenzentrierte Meditation oder: lebendiger Umgang mit Lernstoffen. In A. Biesinger (Ed.), Meditation im Religionsunterricht (pp. 123–143). Düsseldorf: Patmos.

Frickel, M. (1991). Die Grundstrukturen des Daseins in Beziehung zur Leibgestalt und zu den Grundelementen der TZI. In K. Hahn et al. (Eds.), "Beachte die Körpersignale": Körpererfahrung in der Gruppenarbeit (pp. 94–116). Mainz: Grünewald.

Frickel, M. (1992a). Von der TZI zur Themenzentrierten Meditation. Grund und Ziel einer Änderung. In C. Löhmer, R. Standhardt (Eds.), TZI. Pädagogisch-therapeutische Gruppenarbeit nach Ruth C. Cohn (pp. 218–229). Stuttgart: Klett-Cotta.

Frickel, M. (1992b). Symphonie des Daseins, Meditationen themenzentriert. Mainz: Grünewald.

Friedenthal-Haase, M. (2001). Deutsche Erwachsenenbildung in ihrer Zeit – Entwicklungen und Kategorien im 20. Jahrhundert. In M. Friedenthal-Haase (Ed.), Erwachsenenbildung im 20. Jahrhundert – Was war wesentlich? (pp. 13–32). München: Rainer Hampp.

Fritz, J. (1975a). Gruppendynamisches Training in der Schule. Heidelberg: Quelle & Meyer.

Fritz, J. (1975b). Interaktionspädagogik. Methoden und Modelle. München: Juventa.

Fromm, E. (1992). Psychoanalyse und Ethik: Bausteine zu einer humanistischen Charakterologie. München: dtv.

Fürstenau, P. (1964). Zur Psychoanalyse der Schule als Institution. Das Argument, 29, 65–78.

Funke, D. (1984). Verkündigung zwischen Tradition und Interaktion. Praktisch-theologische Studien zur Themenzentrierten Interaktion nach Ruth C. Cohn. Frankfurt a. M.: Peter Lang.

Gagliardi, P. (1995). Organisationsentwicklung (OE), organisatorischer Wandel, und Cultural Change. Organisationsberatung Supervision Clinical Management, 1(1), 7–14.

Galuske, M. (2005). Die Methoden der Sozialen Arbeit. Weinheim/München: Juventa.

Gamm, H.-J. (1979). Das Judentum. Eine Einführung. Frankfurt a. M./New York: Campus.

Gardenswaartz, L., Rowe, A. (1998). Managing Diversity. A Complete Desk Reference and Planning Guide. Rev. ed. New York: McGraw-Hill.

Geißler, K. A. (Ed.) (1979). Gruppendynamik für Lehrer: was Lehrer verändern können. Reinbek: Rowohlt.

Geißler, K. A., Ebner, H. G. (1984, 1995). Interaktionsstrukturen in der Erwachsenenbildung. In E. Schmitz, H. Tietgens (Eds.), Enzyklopädie der Erziehungswissenschaften, Vol. 11: Erwachsenenbildung (pp. 160–170). Stuttgart: Klett-Cotta.

Geißler, K. A., Hege, M. (2001). Konzepte sozialpädagogischen Handelns: ein Leitfaden für soziale Berufe (10th rev. ed.). Weinheim/München: Beltz.

Genser, B. et al. (1972). Lernen in der Gruppe: Theorie und Praxis der themenzentrierten interaktionellen Methode (Ruth C. Cohn). In Blickpunkt Hochschuldidaktik 25, Hamburg.

Gerhardt, V. (1999). Selbstbestimmung. Das Prinzip der Individualität. Stuttgart: Reclam.

Gerl, H. (1985). Methoden der Erwachsenenbildung. In H.-D Raapke et al. (Eds.), Handbuch der Erwachsenenbildung; Vol. 7: Didaktik der Erwachsenenbildung (pp. 43–52). Stuttgart: Kohlhammer.

Germanis, O. (2002). Vertrauen – Die Entdeckung einer sozialen Ressource. Stuttgart: Hirzel.

Geus, A. de (1997). De levende onderneming; over leven en leren in een turbulente omgeving. Uitgeverij Scriptum Management.

Geus, A. de (1997). The Living Company. Habits for Surviving in a Turbulent Business Environment. Boston: HBS Press.

Gilligan, C. (1984). Die andere Stimme – Lebenskonflikte und Moral der Frau. München: dtv.

Glasl, F. (Ed.) (1983). Verwaltungsreform durch Organisationsentwicklung. Stuttgart/Bern: Haupt.

Glasl, F. (1994). Das Unternehmen der Zukunft. Moralische Intuition in der Gestaltung von Organisationen. In Praxis Anthroposophie. Stuttgart: Freies Geistesleben.

Goffman, E. (1975). Stigma. Über Techniken der Bewältigung beschädigter Identität. Frankfurt a. M.: Suhrkamp.

Gordon, M. in cooperation with Liberman, N. (1972). Theme-Centered Interaction. An original focus on counseling and education. Baltimore: National Education Press.

Gordon, M., Liberman, N. (2001/1971). Group Psychotherapy: Being and Becoming. Themenzentrierte Interaktion, 15 (1), 84–92.

Gordon, M., Libermann, N. J. (1972). Theme-Centered Interaction: An Original Focus on Counseling and Education. Baltimore: National Edu. Press.

Gores-Pieper, E. (n.d.). Das Konzept der Themenzentrierten Interaktion (TZI) und seine Bedeutung in der Teamentwicklung: http:/www.structura.de

Gotthardt-Lorenz, A. (1990). Einbeziehung von Leitern in den organisationsbezogenen Beratungsprozess – eine conditio sine qua non? Supervision, 17, 10–19.

Grawe, K. (2004). Neuropsychotherapie. Göttingen: Hogrefe.

Grawe, K., Donati, R., Bernauer, F. (1994). Psychotherapie im Wandel. Von der Konfession zur Profession. Göttingen: Hogrefe.

Greimel, A. (1992). TZI in der Wirtschaft. In C. Löhmer, R. Standhardt (Eds.), TZI. Pädagogisch-therapeutische Gruppenarbeit nach Ruth C. Cohn (pp. 342 ff.). Stuttgart: Klett.

Greimel, A. (2003). Themenzentrierte Teamentwicklung. Themenzentrierte Interaktion, 17 (2), 54–66.

Grell, J., Grell, M. (1991). Unterrichtsrezepte. Weinheim/Basel: Beltz.

Greving, H. (2003). TZI – ein Rädchen im Getriebe eines mächtigen Globe? Oder eine Alternative Lebendigen Lernens? Themenzentrierte Interaktion, 3 (2), 67–80.

Grill, I. (Ed.) (1992). Das Judentum. Zugänge, Herausforderungen, Gespräche. Göttingen: Vandenhoeck & Ruprecht.

Grimm, J., Grimm, W. (1873). Kritik. In J. Grimm, W. Grimm (Eds.), Deutsches Wörterbuch, Vol. 5 (pp. 2333–2340). Leipzig: S. Hirzel.

Grinberg, L., Langer, M., Rodrigué, E. (1974). Psychoanalytische Gruppentherapie: Praxis und theoretische Grundlagen. München: Kindler.

Groß, H., Boden, B., Boden, N. (2000). Munterrichtsmethoden. 22 aktivierende Lehrmethoden für die Seminarpraxis. Berlin: Schilling.

Grubrich-Simitis, I. (1999). Sprache: Königsweg zum Unbewussten. Psyche – Zeitschrift für Psychoanalyse und ihre Anwendungen, 53 (1), 1–7.

Grundke, P. (1975). Interaktionserziehung in der Schule. Modell eines therapeutischen Unterrichts. München: Juventa.

Gudjons, H. (1995). Die Themenzentrierte Interaktion. Pädagogik (11), 95.

Gudjons, H. (2001). Pädagogisches Grundwissen. Bad Heilbrunn: Klinkhardt.

Gudjons, H. (2003). Didaktik zum Anfassen. Lehrer/in-Persönlichkeit und lebendiger Unterricht. Bad Heilbrunn: Klinkhardt.

Hahn, K., Schraut, M., Schütz K.-V., Wagner, C. (Eds.), Aspekte Themenzentrierter Interaktion. Mainz: Grünewald.

Hahn, K., Schraut, M., Schütz K.-V., Wagner, C. (Eds.) (1991). Beachte die Körpersignale. Körpererfahrung in der Gruppenarbeit. Mainz: Grünewald.

Hahn, K., Schraut, M., Schütz, K.-V., Wagner, C. (Eds.) (1994). Aggression in Gruppen. Mainz: Grünewald.

Hahn, K., Schraut, M., Schütz, K.-V., Wagner, C. (Eds.) (1998). Themenzentrierte Supervision. Mainz: Grünewald.

Hahn, K., Schraut, M., Schütz, K.-V., Wagner, C. (Eds.) (2001). Kompetente LeiterInnen. Beiträge zum Leitungsverständnis nach TZI. Mainz: Grünewald.

Hall, E. (1959). The silent language. New York: Anchor.

Hannen, H. (2001). Bestandsaufnahme von wissenschaftlichen Arbeiten und Forschungsprojekten über die Themenzentrierte Interaktion (TZI) in der Wirtschaft. Themenzentrierte Interaktion, 14 (2), 69 ff.

Hanusa, B. (2006). Die religiöse Dimension der Reformpädagogik Paul Geheebs. Die Frage nach der Religion in der Reformpädagogik. Leipzig: Evangelische Verlagsanstalt.

Hark, S. (1999). Deviante Subjekte. Die paradoxe Politik der Identität (2nd ed.). Opladen: Leske + Budrich.

Hartmann, H. (1973). Psychoanalyse und moralische Werte, Stuttgart: Klett-Cotta.

Heidbrink, H. (1992). Interview mit Ruth C. Cohn, Teil 1. Gruppendynamik, 23 (3), 315–325.

Heigl-Evers, A., Heigl. F. (1973). Die Themenzentrierte Interaktionelle Gruppenmethode (R. C. Cohn). Erfahrungen, Überlegungen, Modifikationen. Gruppenpsychotherapie und Gruppendynamik, 7 (3), 237–255.

Heigl-Evers, A., Heigl, F. (1984). Die themenzentrierte interaktionelle Gruppenmethode: Erfahrungen, Überlegungen, Modifikationen. Will-Europa Info Sondernummer 1984. Lebendig lernen. Grundfragen der themenzentrierten Interaktion. Arlesheim: Will Europa.

Heigl-Evers, A., Ott. J. (Eds.) (1994). Die psychoanalytisch-interaktionelle Methode: Theorie und Praxis. Göttingen: Vandenhoeck & Ruprecht.

Heinichen, F. A. (n. d.). Der Taschen-Heinichen Lateinisch-Deutsch (10th ed.). Stuttgart: Klett.

Heintel, P. (1999). Supervision als selbstreflexive Steuerungshilfe von Organisationen. In H. Pühl (Ed.), Supervision und Organisationsentwicklung. Opladen: Leske + Budrich.

Henrich, F., Kaiser, H. (Eds.) (1980). Erwachsenenbildung. 25 Jahre Entwicklung im Spiegel einer Zeitschrift. Düsseldorf: Patmos.

Hermann, H. (1995). Der Einsatz der TZI in therapeutischer Beratung und in Selbsterfahrungsworkshops. Themenzentrierte Interaktion, 9 (2) 86–103.

Hermann, U. (Ed.) (2006). Neurodidaktik: Grundlagen und Vorschläge für gehirngerechtes Lehren und Lernen. Weinheim/Basel: Beltz.

Herrmann, H. (1992). Ruth C. Cohn – ein Porträt. In C. Löhmer, R. Standhardt (Ed.), TZI. Pädagogisch-therapeutische Gruppenarbeit nach Ruth C. Cohn (pp. 19–36). Stuttgart: Klett-Cotta.

Herzer, M. et al. (1997). Management im Dilemma – Zur Rolle von Führung im lernenden Unternehmen. Organisationsentwicklung, H 1, 8 ff.

Herzog, W. (1982). Die wissenschaftstheoretische Problematik der Integration psychotherapeutischer Methoden. In H. Petzold (Ed.), Methodenintegration in der Psychotherapie. Paderborn: Junfermann.

Hilberath, B. J., Hinze, B., Scharer, M. (Eds.), Publikationsreihe "Kommunikative Theologie – interdisziplinär/Communicative Theology – Interdisciplinary Studies" (Vol. 1–11). Münster: Lit-Verlag.

Hilberath, B. J., Scharer, Publikationsreihe "Kommunikative Theologie" (Vol. 1–13). Mainz: Matthias-Grünewald-Verlag. (from Vol. 8) Ostfildern-Ruit: Der Schwabenverlag.

Hillmann, K.-H. (2007). Wörterbuch der Soziologie. Stuttgart: Kröner.

Hintner, R., Lemaire, B. (1998). Gedanken über die Zukunft der Ausbildung in themenzentrierter Interaktion. Mitteilung von und für WILL-International, Supplement to Issue 1/1998 Themenzentrierte Interaktion, 13 (2).

Höser, C., Loheit, U. (2004). Einladende Gemeinde – mitgestalten – mitverantworten, Handbuch für die Kirchenältesten in der Evangelisch-Lutherischen Landeskirche Mecklenburgs. http://www.kirche-mv.de/fileadmin/ELLM-Down loadtexte/Kirchenaelteste. pdf

Hoffmann, S. G. (2005). Irritation als Lernanlass – eine pädagogische Begründung und Interpretation des Störungspostulats. Themenzentrierte Interaktion, 19 (1), 82–93.

Hoffmann, S. G. (2008). TZI im Diskurs. Ein Werkstattbericht. Themenzentrierte Interaktion, 22 (2), 80–85.

Hofstätter, P. R. (1970, 1973). Sozialpsychologie. Berlin: de Gruyter.

Hofstede, G. (1991). Cultures and Organizations. Software of the mind. Intercultural cooperation and its importance for survival. New York: McGraw-Hill.

Holzhey, H. (1976). Kritik. In J. Ritter, K. Gründer, G. Gabriel (Eds.), Historisches Wörterbuch der Philosophie, Vol. 4, I-K (pp. 1250–1282). Basel u. Stuttgart: Schwabe.

Honneth, A. (1994). Kampf um Anerkennung. Zur moralischen Grammatik sozialer Konflikte. Frankfurt a. M.: Suhrkamp.

Hoppe, G. (1993). "Misch Dich ein! Greif ein!" Ein drittes Postulat für die TZI? Themenzentrierte Interaktion, 7 (2), 31–40.

Hoppe, G. (1994). "Misch Dich ein! Greif ein!" Ein drittes Postulat für die TZI? In C. Löhmer, R. Standhardt (Eds.), Zur Tat befreien. Gesellschaftspolitische Perspektiven der TZI-Gruppenarbeit (pp. 17–29). Mainz: Grünewald.

Horx, M. (1996). Trendbuch 2. Megatrends für die späten neunziger Jahre. Düsseldorf: Econ.

Hühn, H. (2004). Wir. In J. Ritter, K. Gründer, G. Gabriel (Eds.), Historisches Wörterbuch der Philosophie. Volume 12. Basel: Schwabe.

Hünermann, P. (2003). Dogmatische Prinzipienlehre. Glaube – Überlieferung – Theologien als Sprach- und Wahrheitsgeschehen. Münster: Aschendorff.

Immel, S. (2004). Gestaltpädagogische Elemente in der Berufspädagogik. Potentielle Erträge gestaltpädagogischer Ansätze für die berufliche Bildung. Dissertation, Universität Kassel.

Jäger, W. (1996). Zukunftsorientierte Aus- und Weiterbildung. Neue Konzepte für eine moderne Arbeitsorganisation. Diplomarbeit, Augsburg.

James, W. (1897). Der Wille zum Glauben. In W. James (1948), Essays über Glaube und Ethik (pp. 40–67). Gütersloh: Bertelsmann.

Jaworski, J. (1996). Synchronicity. The inner path of leadership. San Francisco: Berret-Koehler Publishers.

Jegge, D., Lehmann, H. (1983). Ansätze zur Organisationsentwicklung in der Schweizerischen Bundesverwaltung. In F. Glasl (Ed.), Verwaltungsreform durch Organisationsentwicklung (pp. 175 ff.). Bern: Haupt.

Johach, H. (1994). Auf dem Marsch durch die Institutionen oder: Wieweit kann TZI die Gesellschaft verändern? In C. Löhmer, R. Standhardt (Eds.), Zur Tat befreien. Gesellschaftspolitische Perspektiven der TZI-Gruppenarbeit (pp. 77–98). Mainz: Grünewald.

Johach, H. (1999). Das Erbe der jüdischen Emigranten in der Humanistischen Psychologie. Themenzentrierte Interaktion, 13 (1), 7–28.

Jung, C. G. (1945). Psychologie der Übertragung. GW 16. Olten: Walter.

Jung, C. G. (1958). Praxis der Psychotherapie. GW 16. Olten: Walter.

Jung, C. G. (1973). Symbole der Wandlung. GW 5. Olten: Walter (Originally published in 1912 in the Jahrbuch psychoanalytische psychopathologische Forschung, IV, under the title "Wandlungen und Symbole der Libido. Beiträge zu einer Entwicklungsgeschichte des Denkens")

Kähler, R. (2005). Konfliktfähigkeit und jüdisch-christliche Spiritualität. Themenzentrierte Interaktion, 19 (2), 29–41.

Kalnins, M., Röschmann, D. (2000). Icebreaker. Wege bahnen für Lernprozesse. Ein Logbuch für Trainer. Hamburg: Windmühle.

Kamps, W. (1991). Handlungsorientierter Unterricht und TZI. Themenzentrierte Interaktion, 5 (2), 49–62.

Karmann, G. (1987). Humanistische Psychologie und Pädagogik. Bad-Heilbrunn: Klinkhardt.

Kast, V. (2000). Der Schatten in uns: die subversive Lebenskraft. Düsseldorf/Zurich: Walter.

Keese, J. A. (1996). Humane Arbeitswelt in profitorientierten Unternehmen. Organisations- und Personalentwicklung mit Themenzentrierter Interaktion. Mainz: Grünewald.

Kempski, J. v. (1954). Handlung, Maxime und Situation. Studium Generale, 7, 60–68.

Kersten, J. T. (1983). Themenzentrierte Interaktion in der Berufsschullehrerausbildung. Dissertation. Unpublished manuscript.

Kielholz, J. (1975). Themenzentrierte Interaktion und Lehrerfortbildung. Schweizer Schule, 62 (9), 294–302.

Kielholz, J. (1976). TZI – ein pädagogisches Modell für lebendiges Lernen. Gymnasium helveticum, (2), 70–84.

Kimmig, M., Meister, H. (1995). Ganzheitliches Lehren und Lernen in der Kaufmännischen Berufsschule. Konzepte und Erfahrungen der wissenschaftlichen Begleitung eines Modellversuchs. Arbeitsbericht aus der Fachrichtung Erziehungswissenschaft der Universität des Saarlandes, Saarbrücken.

Klafki, W. (1997). Neue Studien zur Bildungstheorie und Didaktik (2nd exp. ed.). Weinheim/Basel: Beltz.

Klebert, K., Schrader, E., Straub, W. (1987). Kurzmoderation. Anwendung der Moderationsmethode in Betrieb, Schule und Hochschule, Kirche und Politik, Sozialbereich und Familie, bei Besprechungen und Präsentationen (2nd ed.). Hamburg: Windmühle.

Klein, G. (1997). Schulen brauchen Beratung. Kollegiumsorientierte Innovationsberatung als Beitrag zur Schulentwicklung. Marquartstein: PimS.

Klein, I. (1992, 2002, 2005). Gruppenleiten ohne Angst. München: Pfeiffer/Donauwörth: Auer.

Klemmer, G. (1993). Die Wüste lebt. Lebendige Stoffvermittlung mit TZI. In R. C. Cohn, C. Terfurth (Eds.), Lebendiges Lehren und Lernen. TZI macht Schule (pp. 265–287). Stuttgart: Klett-Cotta.

Klemmer, G. (1993). Themenzentrierte Interaktion als therapeutisch-pädagogisches und politisches Handeln in Schule und Hochschule. In R. C. Cohn, C. Terfurth (Eds.), Lebendiges Lehren und Lernen. TZI macht Schule (pp. 105–114). Stuttgart: Klett-Cotta.

Klippert, H. (2006). Methodentraining: Übungsbausteine für den Unterricht. Weinheim/Basel: Beltz.

Kluge, F. (1989). Etymologisches Wörterbuch der deutschen Sprache. (22nd ed.). Berlin: de Gruyter.

Knoll, J. (1977). Gruppentherapie und pädagogische Praxis. Ansätze, Arbeitsformen und Konsequenzen für die Arbeit mit Gruppen in Schule und Erwachsenenbildung. Bad Heilbrunn: Julius Klinkhardt.

Kohlberg, L. (1974). Zur kognitiven Entwicklung des Kindes. Frankfurt a. M.: Suhrkamp.

Költze, H. (1993). Lehrerbildung im Wandel. In R. C. Cohn, C. Terfurth (Eds.), Lebendiges Lehren und Lernen. TZI macht Schule (pp. 192–212). Stuttgart: Klett-Cotta.

König, O. (2002). Macht in Gruppen. Gruppendynamische Prozesse und Interventionen (2nd ed.). Stuttgart: Klett-Cotta.

König, R. (1975). Studien zur Soziologie. Frankfurt a. M.: Fischer-Bücherei.

Korte, N. (1999). Aller guten Dinge sind drei. Themenzentrierte Interaktion, 13 (2), 21–26.

Krämer, M. (2001). TZI und Politik. Themenzentrierte Interaktion, 14 (2), 23–34.

Krämer, M., Zitterbarth, W. (2006). Ist TZI politisch? Ein Kontroversgespräch zwischen Manfred Krämer (am 23.4.2005 verstorben) und Walter Zitterbarth während einer Redaktionssitzung in Berlin am 6.11.2004. Themenzentrierte Interaktion, 20 (1), 8–15.

Krappmann, L. (1975). Kommunikation und Interaktion im Spiel. Deutscher Bildungsrat, Gutachten und Studien der Bildungskommission 48/1. Die Eingangsstufe des Primarbereichs Vol. 2/1 Spielen und Gestalten. Stuttgart: Klett-Cotta.

Kroeger, M. (1973, 1976, 1983, 1989). Themenzentrierte Seelsorge. Über die Kombination Klientzentrierter und Themenzentrierter Arbeit nach Carl R. Rogers u. Ruth C. Cohn in der Theologie. Stuttgart: Kohlhammer.

Kroeger, M. (1985). Profile der Themenzentrierten Interaktion. In R. Birmelin, K. Hahn et al. (Eds.), Erfahrungen lebendigen Lernens. Grundlagen und Arbeitsfelder der TZI (pp. 23–47). Mainz: Grünewald.

Kroeger, M. (1991). Körpersprache und Körperarbeit in der TZI – eine verbreitete Verwechslung. In K. Hahn, M. Schraut, K.-V. Schütz, C. Wagner (Eds.), Beachte die Körpersignale. Körpererfahrung in der Gruppenarbeit (pp. 169–177). Mainz: Grünewald.

Kroeger, M. (1992, 1993). Anthropologische Grundannahmen der Themenzentrierten Interaktion. In C. Löhmer, R. Standhardt (Eds.), TZI. Pädagogisch-therapeutische Gruppenarbeit nach Ruth C. Cohn (pp. 93–124). Stuttgart: Klett-Cotta.

Kroeger, M. (1992). Ruth C. Cohn 80 – WILL 25 – WILL Europa 20. Festrede beim Jubiläumsakt in Gwatt am 24.4.1992. Themenzentrierte Interaktion, 6 (2), 37–53.

Kron, F. W. (1999). Wissenschaftstheorie für Pädagogen. München/Basel: Reinhardt.

Kröner, S. (Ed.) (1993). Annäherungen an eine andere Bewegungskultur. Pfaffenweiler: Centaurus.

Kuebel, M. A. (2002). Living Learning. A Reader in Theme-Centered Interaction, Delhi: Media House.

Kügler, H. (1997). Es oder Thema? Plädoyer für eine präzise Begrifflichkeit. Themenzentrierte Interaktion, 11 (1), 23–28.

Kügler, H. (2001). "Priester-Monat" – ein Projekt, welches Grenzen verschiebt. In B. Langmaack (Ed.), Einführung in die Themenzentrierte Interaktion (pp. 229–242). Weinheim/Basel: Beltz.

Kügler, H. (2005). Überlegungen zur spirituellen Dimension der TZI-Konzeption. Themenzentrierte Interaktion, 19 (2), 7–15.

Kügler, H. (2008). Was ist Zeit? Annäherung an ein unbearbeitetes Thema. Themenzentrierte Interaktion, 22 (1), 9–17.

Kullmann, V. J. E. (2000). Selbst-Supervision in der Schule. Neuwied: Luchterhand.

Kursbuch (1985). Die Therapiegesellschaft. Berlin: Kursbuch.

Lang-Körsgen, R. (2001). Veränderungen im TZI Leitungsverständnis durch gesellschaftspolitische Veränderungen. In K. Hahn, M. Schraut, K. V. Schütz, C. Wagner (Eds.), Kompetente LeiterInnen. Beiträge zum Leitungsverständnis nach TZI (pp. 9–28). Mainz: Grünewald.

Langmaack, B. (1991, 1992). Themenzentrierte Interaktion. Einführende Texte rund ums Dreieck. München: Psychologie Verlags Union.

Langmaack, B. (1996, 2000). Themenzentrierte Interaktion. Einführende Texte rund ums Dreieck (3rd ed.). Weinheim/Basel: Beltz.

Langmaack, B. (2000, 2001, 2004). Einführung in die Themenzentrierte Interaktion TZI. Leben rund ums Dreieck. Weinheim/Basel: Beltz.

Langmaack, B., Braune-Krickau, M. (1985, 1989). Wie die Gruppe laufen lernt. München: Psychologie Verlags Union.

Langmaack, B., Braune-Krickau, M. (1995, 2000). Wie die Gruppe laufen lernt. Weinheim/Basel: Beltz.

Laplanche, J., Pontalis, J.-B. (1973). Das Vokabular der Psychoanalyse. Zweiter Band. Frankfurt a. M.: Suhrkamp.

Ledoux, J. (2001). Das Netz der Gefühle. Wie Emotionen entstehen. München: dtv.

Lehmkuhl, K. (2002). Unbewusstes bewusst machen. Selbstreflexive Kompetenz und neue Arbeitsorganisation. Hamburg: VSA.

Lemaire, B. (2001). Partizipierend Leiten – wem oder was nützt der vorprogrammierte Rollenkonflikt. In K. Hahn, M. Schraut, K. V. Schütz, C. Wagner (Eds.), Kompetente LeiterInnen. Beiträge zum Leitungsverständnis nach TZI (pp. 118–139). Mainz: Grünewald.

Lemaire, B. (2007). Beratung von Ehrenamtlichen. In W. Lotz, C. Wagner (Eds.), Themenzentrierte Interaktion in der Beratung und Therapie. Ostfildern: Grünewald.

Lemaire, B., Lotz, W. (2002). TZI und Soziale Arbeit – Soziale Arbeit und TZI. Themenzentrierte Interaktion, 16 (1 und 2), 95–108 und 26–39.

Leuninger, E. (1985). Bildungsarbeit und Arbeiterbildung. Ein Vergleich der Erwachsenenbildungskonzeptionen von katholischer Kirche und Gewerkschaften. München: Hueber.

Liberman, N., Gordon, M. (1971). Group Psychotherapy: Being and Becoming (wiederabgedruckt 2001). Themenzentrierte Interaktion, 15 (1), 84–92.

Lindzey, G., Aronson, E. (1968) (Eds.). The Handbook of Social Psychology. Vol. 4: Group Psychology and Phenomena of Interaction. Reading, MA: Addison-Wesley.

Lobos, R. (1988). Die TZI in der Gestaltung des Therapeutischen Milieus. Themenzentrierte Interaktion, 2 (1), 7–16.

Lohmann, K.-E. (2003). Interkulturelle Gruppen leiten. Themenzentrierte Interaktion, 17 (1), 7–16 & 17 (2), 81–90.

Löhmer, C. (1994). Am Anfang war der Globe. Die themenzentrierte Interaktion unter besonderer Berücksichtigung ihrer politischen Dimension. In C. Löhmer, R. Standhardt (Eds.), Zur Tat befreien. Gesellschaftspolitische Perspektiven der TZI-Gruppenarbeit (pp. 30–62). Mainz: Grünewald.

Löhmer, C., Standhardt, R. (Eds.) (1992, 1993). TZI. Pädagogisch-therapeutische Gruppenarbeit nach Ruth Cohn. Stuttgart: Klett-Cotta.

Löhmer, C., Standhardt, R. (Eds.) (1994). Zur Tat befreien. Gesellschaftspolitische Perspektiven der TZI-Gruppenarbeit. Mainz: Grünewald.

Löhmer, C., Standhardt, R. (1995). Tabellarische Lebensübersicht von Ruth C. Cohn. In C. Löhmer, R. Standhardt (Eds.), TZI. Pädagogisch-therapeutische Gruppenarbeit nach Ruth C. Cohn (pp. 447–450). Stuttgart. Klett-Cotta.

Löhmer, C., Standhardt, R. (1995). TZI. Pädagogisch-therapeutische Gruppenarbeit nach Ruth C. Cohn (3rd exp. ed.). Stuttgart: Klett-Cotta.

Löhmer, C., Standardt, R. (2006). TZI – Die Kunst, sich selbst und eine Gruppe zu leiten. Stuttgart: Klett-Cotta.

Lotz, W. (1997). Zur pädagogischen Konzeption der Themenzentrierten Interaktion. Themenzentrierte Interaktion, 11 (2), 23–34.

Lotz, W. (1999). Das ES als Gegenstand und Vergegenständlichung. Themenzentrierte Interaktion, 13 (2), 82–96.

Lotz, W. (2001). Partizipierende Leitung und szenisches Verstehen. In K. Hahn, M. Schraut, K. V. Schütz, C. Wagner (Eds.), Kompetente LeiterInnen. Beiträge zum Leitungsverständnis nach TZI (pp. 93–117). Mainz: Grünewald.

Lotz, W. (2003). Sozialpädagogisches Handeln. Eine Grundlegung sozialer Beziehungsarbeit mit themenzentrierter Interaktion. Mainz: Grünewald.

Lotz, W. (2007a). Beratung auf der Grundlage der TZI. In W. Lotz, C. Wagner (Eds.), TZI in Beratung und Therapie. Stuttgart: Grünewald/Schwabenverlag.

Lotz, W. (2007b). Themenzentrierte Prozessanalyse – ein Instrument zur Sicherung der Qualität professionellen kommunikativen Handelns. Themenzentrierte Interaktion, 21 (1), 58–71.

Lotz, W., Reiser, H. (1995). Themenzentrierte Interaktion als Pädagogik. Mainz: Grünewald.

Ludwig, K.-J. (Ed.) (1997). Im Ursprung ist Beziehung. Theologisches Lernen als themenzentrierte Interaktion. Mainz: Grünewald.

Luhmann, N. (1984). Soziale Systeme: Grundriss einer allgemeinen Theorie. Frankfurt a. M.: Suhrkamp.

Luhmann, N. (1997). Die Gesellschaft der Gesellschaft. Frankfurt a. M.: Suhrkamp.

Lührmann, W. (2000). Ach Teezettieh. Anmerkungen zur persönlichen Bedeutung und zur institutionellen Krise der Themenzentrierten Interaktion. Themenzentrierte Interaktion, 14 (1), 99–110.

Luther, H. (1992). Religion und Alltag. Bausteine zu einer praktischen Theologie des Subjekts. Stuttgart: Radius.

Lüthi, A., Lüthi-Peterson, N., Richard, A., Richard-Hudspith, S. (1995). TZI an der Ecole d'Humanité – vier Zugänge. In C. Löhmer, R. Standhardt (Eds.), TZI: Pädagogisch-therapeutische Gruppenarbeit nach Ruth C. Cohn (pp. 281–301). Stuttgart: Klett-Cotta.

Mahlmann, M. (1999). Rationalismus in der praktischen Theorie. Baden-Baden: Nomos.

Mahr, A. (1979). Die Störungsprioritätsregel in TZI-Gruppen. Psychoanalytische und empirische Studien. Göttingen: Vandenhoeck & Ruprecht.

Maslow, A. (1968). Toward a Psychology of Being. New Jersey: van Nostrand.

Matzdorf, P. (1985). Die humanistischen Axiome der TZI. Grundlagen und Perspektiven für pädagogisches, therapeutisches und politisches Handeln. In R. Birmelin et al. (Eds.), Erfahrungen lebendigen Lernens (pp. 48–58). Mainz: Grünewald.

Matzdorf, P. (1989). Arbeitspapier zu "Jugendarbeit: Methoden- und handlungsbezogene Vorbereitung" und "Praxisberatung." Themenzentrierte Interaktion, 3 (1), 36–53.

Matzdorf, P. (1991). Die problemformulierende Methode Paolo Freires und Ruth Cohns Themenzentrierte Interaktion. Themenzentrierte Interaktion, 5 (2), 64–77 und 6 (1), 56–79.

Matzdorf, P. (1993). Das TZI-Haus. Zur praxisnahen Grundlegung eines pädagogischen Handlungssystems. In R. C. Cohn, C. Terfurth (Eds.), Lebendiges Lehren und Lernen. TZI macht Schule (pp. 332–387). Stuttgart: Klett-Cotta.

Matzdorf, P., Cohn, R. C. (1983). Das Konzept der Themenzentrierte Interaktion. In R. Corsini (Ed.), Handbuch der Psychotherapie, Volume 2 (pp. 1272 ff.). Weinheim/Basel: Beltz.

Matzdorf, P., Cohn, R. C. (1992, 1993). Das Konzept der Themenzentrierten Interaktion. In C. Löhmer, R. Standhardt (Eds.), TZI. Pädagogisch-therapeutische Gruppenarbeit nach Ruth C. Cohn (pp. 39–92). Stuttgart: Klett-Cotta.

Maurer, A. (1996). Supervision in Organisationen als politischer Anspruch. Supervision, 29, 74–80.

May, R. (1958). Existence. New York: Basic Books.

Mead, G. H. (1934). Mind, self and society. Chicago.

Mead, G. H. (1968). Geist, Identität und Gesellschaft. Frankfurt a. M.: Suhrkamp.

Meditationsgruppe Düsseldorf (2002). Im Vorraum des Unergründlichen. Ein Gespräch mit Ruth Cohn über TZI. Themenzentrierte Interaktion, 16 (1), 8–94.

Merry, P. (2006). Evolutionair leiderschap. Integraal leiderschap voor een steeds complexere wereld. Haarlem: Altamira-Becht.

Meyer, H. (1994). Unterrichtsmethoden. I. Theorieband. Frankfurt a. M.: Cornelsen Scriptor.

Meyer, U. B. (1999). Supervision in Verwaltungsorganisationen im Spannungsfeld zur OE. In H. Pühl (Ed.), Supervision und Organisationsentwicklung (pp. 418–428). Opladen: Leske + Budrich.

Meyer, U. B. (2004). TZI als Haltung und Methode – ein Beitrag zur Bildungsentwicklung. Themenzentrierte Interaktion, 18 (2), 16–31.

Miller, R. (1997). Beziehungsdidaktik. Weinheim/Basel: Beltz.

Mills, Th. M. (1971). Soziologie der Gruppe. München: Juventa.

Mollenhauer, K. (1982). Theorien zum Erziehungsprozeß: zur Einführung in erziehungswissenschaftliche Fragestellungen. München: Juventa.

Müller, E. F., Thomas, A. (1974). Einführung in die Sozialpsychologie. Göttingen: Hogrefe.

Müller-Doohm, S. (2000). Kritik in kritischen Theorien oder: Wie kritisches Denken selbst zu rechtfertigen sei. In S. Müller-Doohm (Ed.), Das Interesse der Vernunft: Rückblicke auf das Werk von Jürgen Habermas seit "Erkenntnis und Interesse" (pp. 71–106). Frankfurt a. M.: Suhrkamp.

Nagl, L. (1998). Pragmatismus. Frankfurt a. M.: Campus.

Neill, A. S. (1969). Theorie und Praxis der antiautoritären Erziehung. Reinbek: Rowohlt.

Nohl, M. (1997). Zur didaktischen Basis der Themenzentrierten Interaktion. Jüdische Wurzeln und berufspädagogische Perspektiven. Staatsexamensarbeit an der TU Darmstadt.

Oakley, A. (1972/2005). The Ann Oakley Reader: Gender, women and social science. Bristol: Policy Press.

Ockel, A. (1985). Ich bin mein eigen' chairman. In R. Birmelin et al. (Eds.), Erfahrungen lebendigen Lernens. Grundlagen und Arbeitsfelder der TZI (pp. 59–67). Mainz: Grünewald.

Ockel, A., Cohn, R. C. (1981). Das Konzept des Widerstandes in der themenzentrierten Interaktion. In H. Petzold (Ed.), Widerstand. Ein strittiges Konzept in der Psychotherapie. Paderborn: Jungfermann.

Ockel, A., Cohn, R. C. (1992). Das Konzept des Widerstands in der Themenzentrierten Interaktion. In C. Löhmer, R. Standhardt (Eds.), TZI. Pädagogisch-therapeutische Gruppenarbeit nach Ruth C. Cohn (pp. 177–206). Stuttgart: Klett-Cotta.

Ockel, A., Wrage, K.-H. (1979). Wegweiser. Unveröffentlichtes Manuskript.

Oerter, R. (1969). Moderne Entwicklungspsychologie. Donauwörth: Auer.

Oerter, R., Weber, E. (Eds.) (1975). Der Aspekt des Emotionalen in Unterricht und Erziehung. Donauwörth: Auer.

Oetiker, K. L. (1998). Der Mensch als ein Teil des Process Reengineering. Themenzentrierte Interaktion, 11 (1), 65 ff.

Ofman, D., Verpaalen, G. (2006). Hét is niet te geloven. Van reactief naar creatief leiderschap. Utrecht/Antwerpen: Servire/Kosmos-Z&K Uitgevers.

Olbrich, J. (2001). Geschichte der Erwachsenenbildung in Deutschland. Bonn: Bundeszentrale für Politische Bildung.

Olszowi, E. (1976). Zu den Grundlagen der Themenzentrierten Interaktion. Menschenbild und Struktur der TZI. Gruppenpsychotherapie und Gruppendynamik, 10 (1), 78–116.

Olszowi, E. (1987). Überlegungen zu den anthropologischen Grundlagen der TZI. In Hahn, K. et al. (Eds.), Gruppenarbeit themenzentriert. Entwicklungsgeschichte, Kritik und Methodenreflexion (pp. 24–37). Mainz: Grünewald.

Osswald, E. (1984). Sachzentrierter Unterricht nach TZI in der Staatsschule. In Lebendig Lernen. Grundfragen der TZI (pp. 135–146). Ed. von WILL-Europa.

Osswald, E. (1990). Gemeinsam statt einsam. Arbeitsplatzbezogene LehrerInnenfortbildung. Kriens: Brunner.

Osswald, E. (1993). Gestalten statt verwalten. Die lebendige Schule und ihre Schulleitung. In R. C. Cohn, C. Terfurth (Eds.), Lebendiges Lehren und Lernen. TZI macht Schule (pp. 214–247). Stuttgart: Klett-Cotta.

Osswald, E. (1995). Stilwandel. Weg zur Schule der Zukunft. Kriens: Brunner.

Osswald, E. (2001). In der Balance liegt die Chance. Schulen auf dem Weg ins 21. Jahrhundert: Problemlösungen lehren und Probleme lösen lernen, Effizienz/Effektivität und Demokratie, Professionalität und Menschlichkeit. Kriens: Brunner.

Ott, B. (2007). Grundlagen des beruflichen Lernens und Lehrens. Ganzheitliches Lernen in der beruflichen Bildung. Berlin: Cornelsen.

Overbeck, A. (1994). Aggression und Gewalt – erregend, ängstigend, beruhigend. Zur existentiellen Situation des Individuums zwischen Selbstbestimmung und sozialem Bezogensein. In. K. Hahn et al. (Eds.), Aggression in Gruppen (pp. 9–43). Mainz: Grünewald.

Pahl, J.-P., Uhe, E. (Eds.) (1998). Betrifft: Berufsbildung: Begriffe von A–Z für Praxis und Theorie in Betrieb und Schule. Seelze-Velber: Kallmeyer.

Parsons, T. (1960). Structure and Process in Modern Societies, Glencoe: Free Press.

Parsons, T. (1967, 1937). The structure of social action. Glencoe: Free Press.

Perls, F., Hefferline, R., Goodman, P (1977). Gestalt Therapy. New York: Bantam.

Peterßen, W. H. (1982, 2000). Handbuch Unterrichtsplanung. Grundfragen, Modelle, Stufen, Dimensionen. München: Oldenbourg.

Petuchowski, J. J. (1980). Neue rabbinische Geschichten. Freiburg i.Br.: Herder.

Philipp, E. (1995). Gute Schule verwirklichen. Weinheim/Basel: Beltz.

PISA-Konsortium (Ed.) (2001). PISA 2000. Opladen: Leske + Budrich.

Platzer-Wedderwille, K. (1996). Humanisierung des Berufsfeldes Schule. Welche konkreten Aufgaben kann die TZI übernehmen? Didaktische Überlegungen und praktische Einsichten. Themenzentrierte Interaktion, 10 (1), 96–107.

Platzer-Wedderwille, K. (2004). Pisa als Chance für TZI und Schule. Themenzentrierte Interaktion, 18 (2), 43–52.

Plotho, B. von (1985). Lebendiges Lernen in, durch und mit Krisen. In R. Birmelin, K. Hahn, M. Schraut, K. Schütz, C. Wagner (Eds.), Erfahrungen lebendigen Lernens: Grundlagen und Arbeitsfelder der TZI (pp. 92–117). Mainz: Grünewald.

Pöggeler, F. (1980). Vom Pragmatismus zur wissenschaftlichen Fundierung. In F. Henrich, H. Kaiser (Eds.), Erwachsenenbildung. 25 Jahre Entwicklung im Spiegel einer Zeitschrift (pp. 57–73). Düsseldorf: Patmos.

Pöggeler, F. (2001). Demokratisierung durch Bildung: Ideen, Entwicklungen und Erträge der deutschen Erwachsenenbildung im 20. Jahrhundert. In M. Friedenthal-Haase (Ed.), Erwachsenenbildung im 20. Jahrhundert – Was war wesentlich? (pp. 33–56). München: Rainer Hampp.

Pöhlmann, H. G., Cohn, R. C. (2005). Interview zu TZI, Religion und Politik. Themenzentrierte Interaktion, 19 (2), 19–22.

Pohnke, H., Rosin, U., Alberti, L. (1987). Leiterinterventionen in Balint-Gruppen. Gruppenpsychotherapie und Gruppendynamik, 23 (1), 62–71.

Potthoff, W. (2003). Einführung in die Reformpädagogik. Von der klassischen zur aktuellen Reformpädagogik (4th ed.). Freiburg: Reformpädagogischer Verlag.

Prior, M. (2004). MiniMax-Interventionen. 15 minimale Interventionen mit maximaler Wirkung. Heidelberg: Carl-Auer-Systeme Verlag.

Quinn, R. E. (2006). Diepgaande verandering. Ontdek de leider in jezelf. Den Haag: Sdu Uitgevers. Original title: Deep Change. San Francisco: Jossey-Bass, 1996.

Quitmann, H. (1985/1996). Humanistische Psychologie. Zentrale Konzepte und philosophischer Hintergrund. Göttingen: Hogrefe.

Raguse, H. (1984). Was ist Themenzentrierte Interaktion? In WILL-Europa (Ed.), Lebendig lernen. Grundfragen der Themenzentrierten Interaktion. Euro-Info Sondernummer 1984, 55–78.

Raguse, H. (1987a). Einige Gedanken über Krisen in TZI-Gruppen. Themenzentrierte Interaktion, 1 (1), 25–36.

Raguse, H. (1987b). Was ist themenzentrierte Interaktion? In R. Birmelin, K. Hahn, M. Schraut-Birmelin, K. Schütz, C. Wagner (Eds.), Gruppenarbeit: themenzentriert. Entwicklungsgeschichte, Kritik und Methodenreflexion (pp. 117–143). Mainz: Grünewald.

Raguse, H. (1989, 1992a). Vermiedene Themen in Gruppen am Beispiel der TZI. Praxis Spiel + Gruppe, 2 (3), 92–96; und Themenzentrierte Interaktion, 6 (1), 92–98.

Raguse, H. (1992b, 1995). Kritische Bestandsaufnahme der TZI. In C. Löhmer, R. Standhardt (Eds.), TZI. Pädagogisch-therapeutische Gruppenarbeit nach Ruth C. Cohn (pp. 264– 277). Stuttgart: Klett-Cotta.

Raguse, H. (1994). Aggression und Destruktion in der Arbeit mit TZI-Gruppen. In R. Abeln (Ed.), Aggression in Gruppen (pp. 122–150). Mainz: Grünewald.

Raguse, H. (1995). Von der Psychoanalyse zur Themenzentrierten Interaktion und weiter ... oder vielleicht auch wieder zurück? Themenzentrierte Interaktion, 9 (2), 31–43.

Raguse, H. (1997). Theologische Implikationen der TZI. In K.-H. Ludwig (Ed.), Im Ursprung ist Beziehung (pp. 29–53). Mainz: Grünewald.

Raguse-Stauffer, B., Raguse, H. (1980). Ein TZI-Modell der Supervision. Gruppenpsychotherapie und Gruppendynamik, 15 (1), 79–90.

Rappe-Giesecke, K. (1996). Von der Teamsupervision zur Organisationsberatung. Supervision, 29, 6ff.

Reichert, H. (2005). Die TZI als Basiskonzept für Supervision. Supervision, 23 (4), 12–15.

Reiser, H. (1983). Die Themenzentrierte Interaktion als pädagogisches System im Vergleich zur Gestaltpädagogik. In A. Prengel (Ed.), Gestaltpädagogik: Therapie, Politik und Selbsterkenntnis in der Schule (pp. 253–277). Weinheim/Basel: Beltz

Reiser, H. (1987). Ruth Cohn und Martin Buber. Anmerkungen zu den axiomatischen Grundlagen der TZI. In K. Hahn et al. (Eds.), Gruppenarbeit: themenzentriert (pp. 38–46). Mainz: Grünewald.

Reiser, H. (1993). Die TZI als pädagogisches System. Themenzentrierte Interaktion, 7 (2), 52–70.

Reiser, H. (1995). TZI als pädagogisches System. In H. Reiser, W. Lotz (Eds.), Themenzentrierte Interaktion als Pädagogik (pp. 11–53). Mainz: Grünewald.

Reiser, H. (1996a). "Politisch leben" mit TZI. Themenzentrierte Interaktion, 9 (2), 26–39.

Reiser, H. (1996b). Statement: TZI und systemisches Denken in Therapie und Pädagogik. Themenzentrierte Interaktion, 10 (2), 22–25.

Reiser, H. (1998). Die Themenzentrierte Interaktion als Rahmenkonzept für Supervision. In K. Hahn, M. Schraut, K.-V. Schütz, C. Wagner (Eds.), Themenzentrierte Supervision (pp. 9–36). Mainz: Grünewald.

Reiser, H. (2004). Gruppe und Gruppenleitung aus der Sicht der themenzentrierten Interaktion und des systemisch-konstruktivistischen Ansatzes. Themenzentrierte Interaktion, 18 (1), 44–63.

Reiser, H. (2005). Professionelle Konzepte und das Handlungsfeld Sonderpädagogik. In D. Horster et al. (Eds.), Sonderpädagogische Professionalität. Beiträge zur Entwicklung der Sonderpädagogik als Disziplin und Profession (pp. 133–150). Wiesbaden: VS Verlag für Sozialwissenschaften.

Reiser, H. (2006). Psychoanalytisch-systemische Pädagogik. Erziehung auf der Grundlage der Themenzentrierten Interaktion. Stuttgart: Kohlhammer.

Reiser, H., Dlugosch, A. (1997, 1998). Einführung in die Themenzentrierte Interaktion. Skript Fern-Universität in Hagen, Kurt-Lewin-Institut für Psychologie.

Reiser, H., Lotz, W. (1995). Themenzentrierte Interaktion als Pädagogik. Mainz: Grünewald.

Revenstorf, D. (1983). Psychotherapeutische Verfahren, Volume III, Humanistische Therapien. Stuttgart: Kohlhammer.

Revenstorf, D. (1985). Psychotherapeutische Verfahren, Volume IV, Gruppen-, Paar-, Familientherapie. Stuttgart: Kohlhammer.

Rindermann, H. (2006). Emotionale-Kompetenz-Fragebogen. Ein Verfahren zur Einschätzung emotionaler Kompetenzen und emotionaler Intelligenz aus Selbst- und Fremdsicht.

Rogers, C. (1942/1972). Client-Centered Therapy. Boston: Houghton Mifflin.

Rogers, C. (1961). On Becoming a Person. Boston: Houghton Mifflin.

Rogers, C. (1969). On Encounter Groups. New York: Harper and Row.

Rogers, C. (1972). Die nicht-direktive Beratung: Counseling and psychotherapy. München: Kindler.

Rogers, C. (1974). Encounter Gruppen. Das Erlebnis der menschlichen Begegnung. München: Kindler.

Rogers, C. (1974). Lernen in Freiheit: zur Bildungsreform in Schule und Universität. München: Kösel.

Rogers, C. (1979, 1982). Entwicklung der Persönlichkeit: Psychotherapie aus der Sicht eines Therapeuten. Stuttgart: Klett-Cotta.

Rogers, C. (1984). Freiheit und Engagement: Personzentriertes Lehren und Lernen. München: Kösel.

Röhling, J. G. (2000). Gesichtspunkte aus der TZI zum Gewaltproblem. Themenzentrierte Interaktion, 14 (2), 44–67.

Röhling, J. G. (2005). TZI und "Philosophie der Lebenskunst." Themenzentrierte Interaktion, 19 (1), 24–39.

Rohner, P. (1992). Phasentheorie und Gruppenvielfalt. Gedanken zu einem neuen Modell. Themenzentrierte Interaktion, 6 (1), 50–55.

Ronall, R., Feder, B. (1983). Gestaltgruppen. Stuttgart: Klett-Cotta.

Rose, L. (2007). Gender und Soziale Arbeit. Annäherungen jenseits des Mainstreams der Genderdebatte. Baltmannsweiler: Schneider.

Roth, G. (2004). Fühlen, Denken, Handeln. Wie das Gehirn unser Verhalten steuert. Frankfurt a. M.: Suhrkamp.

Rubner, A. (1992). Über die Wechselwirkung zwischen der Rolle des einzelnen, der Gegenübertragung des Leiters und dem Prozess der Gruppe. Themenzentrierte Interaktion, 6 (2), 54–66.

Rubner, A. (1999). Psychoanalyse und Themenzentrierte Interaktion: ein Vergleich. Themenzentrierte Interaktion, 13 (2), 61–81.

Rubner, A. (2006). Zur Erarbeitung des Themas eines Beratungsgesprächs. In U. Sauer-Schiffer, M. Ziemons (Eds.), In der Balance liegt die Chance: themenzentrierte Interaktion in Bildung und Beratung (pp. 91–108). Münster: Waxmann.

Rubner, A., Rubner, E. (1991). Entwicklungsphasen einer Gruppe. Themenzentrierte Interaktion, 5 (2), 34–48.

Rubner, A., Rubner, E. (1992). Die Entwicklungsphasen einer Gruppe – Grundkonflikt, Einstellungen dem Leiter gegenüber und Leiterinterventionen. In C. Löhmer, R. Standthard (Eds.), TZI. Pädagogisch-therapeutische Gruppenarbeit nach Ruth C. Cohn (pp. 230–251). Stuttgart: Klett-Cotta.

Rubner, A., Rubner, E. (1993). Ein Modell der Entwicklungsphasen von Gruppen? Themenzentrierte Interaktion, 7 (1), 50–64.

Rubner, E. (Ed.) (1992). Störung als Beitrag zum Gruppengeschehen. Zum Verständnis des Störungspostulats der TZI in Gruppen. Mainz: Grünewald.

Rubner, P. (2008). Das System der TZI – Das 3 × Vier-Faktoren-Modell. Themenzentrierte Interaktion, 22 (2), 86–95.

Rützel, J., Schapfel, F. (1996). Die Rolle und Funktion beruflicher Standards in der Bundesrepublik Deutschland bezogen auf Berufsbildung und Arbeitsmarkt. Gutachten. Bundesinstitut für Berufsbildung, Bonn. http://www.bibb.de/dokumente/pdf/wd_24_rolle_funktion_beruflicher_standards_brd.pdf

Sartre, J.-P. (1961). Ist der Existentialismus ein Humanismus? Drei Essays. Berlin: Ullstein.

Sartre, J.-P. (1943, 1980). Das Sein und das Nichts. Versuch einer phänomenologischen Ontologie. Reinbek: Rowohlt.

Sartre, J.-P. (2005). Der Existentialismus ist ein Humanismus und andere philosophische Essays 1943–1948 (3rd ed.). Reinbek: Rowohlt.

Sauer-Schiffer, U. (2006). Beratungskompetenz als neue Herausforderung. In U. Sauer-Schiffer, M. Ziemons (Eds.), In der Balance liegt die Chance: themenzentrierte Interaktion in Bildung und Beratung (pp. 13–22). Münster: Waxmann.

Sauer-Schiffer, U., Ziemons. M. (Eds.) (2006). In der Balance liegt die Chance: themenzentrierte Interaktion in Bildung und Beratung. Münster: Waxmann.

Savater, F. (2001). Tu, was du willst. Ethik für die Erwachsenen von morgen. Frankfurt a. M.: Campus.

Schäffter, O. (1991). Gruppendynamik und die Reflexionsfunktion der Erwachsenenbildung. In Pädagogische Arbeitsstelle des Deutschen Volkshochschulverbandes (Ed.), Kommunikation in Lehr-Lern-Prozessen mit Erwachsenen (pp. 70–93). Frankfurt a. M.

Schapfel, F. (1996). Zum Spannungsverhältnis von neuen beruflichen Anforderungen und Subjektwerdung. Betriebliche Berufsausbildung, Subjektorientierung und Themenzentrierte Interaktion. Themenzentrierte Interaktion, 10 (1), 56–66.

Schapfel-Kaiser, F. (1997). Die Themenzentrierte Interaktion als Gestaltungsinstrument und Forschungshilfe für berufliche Bildungsprozesse in aktuellen Wandlungsprozessen. Chancen und Grenzen eines pädagogisch-therapeutischen Zugangs im Zusammenhang mit einem betrieblichen Modellversuch. Zeitschrift für Berufs- und Wirtschaftspädagogik, 93 (10).

Schapfel-Kaiser, F. (2000). Praxisbezogene Qualitätsanalyse mit TZI am Beispiel einer Qualitätsschulung. In J. Rützel (Ed.), Entwicklung und Umsetzung von Qualitätsstandards in der Berufsbildung. Bielefeld: Bertelsmann.

Schapfel-Kaiser, F. (2008). Beruf und Zeit. (Reihe Berichte zur beruflichen Bildung). Bielefeld: Bertelsmann.

Scharer, M. (1988). Leben – Glauben – Lernen: lebendig und persönlich bedeutsam: Handbuch zu "Miteinander glauben lernen." Salzburg: O. Müller.

Scharer, M. (1997a). TZI – Theologie – Glaubenserschließung. In K. J. Ludwig (Ed.), Im Ursprung ist Beziehung. Theologisches Lernen als themenzentrierte Interaktion (pp. 90– 105). Mainz: Grünewald.

Scharer, M. (1997b). Theologie, Glaubenskommunikation und Themenzentrierte Interaktion. In K. J. Ludwig (Ed.), Im Ursprung ist Beziehung. Theologisches Lernen als themenzentrierte Interaktion (pp. 121–127). Mainz: Grünewald.

Scharer, M. (2002). "Der Geist weht, wo er will." Zur spannungsreichen Beziehung zwischen Kirche(n) und TZI. Themenzentrierte Interaktion, 16 (1), 70–80.

Scharer, M., Hilberath, B. J. (2003). Kommunikative Theologie. Eine Grundlegung. Mainz: Grünewald.

Scharer, M., Hilberath B. J. (2008). The Practice of Communicative Theology. Introduction to a New Theological Culture. New York: Crossroad Publishing Company.

Schattenhofer, K. (2001). In K. Antons et al. (Eds.), Gruppenprozesse verstehen: gruppendynamische Forschung und Praxis (pp. 281–294). Opladen: Leske + Budrich.

Schein, E. H. (1985/2007). Organizational Culture and Leadership. San Francisco: Jossey-Bass.

Schiffer, W. (1996). Das "Wir" ist keine Gruppe: Vergleich der Grundworte innerhalb der TZI und der Dialogik Martin Bubers. Themenzentrierte Interaktion, 10 (2), 49–57.

Schleißheimer, B. (2003). Ethik heute. Eine Antwort auf die Frage nach dem guten Leben. Würzburg: Königshausen & Neumann.

Schley, W. (1995). Organisationsentwicklung und Schulkultur. Organisationsberatung Supervision Clinical Management, 157 ff.

Schlippe, A. von, Schweitzer, J. (1998). Lehrbuch der systemischen Therapie und Beratung. Göttingen: Vandenhoeck & Ruprecht.

Schmid, J. R. (1973). Freiheitspädagogik. Schulreform und Schulrevolution in Deutschland. Reinbek: Rowohlt.

Schmid, W. (1998). Philosophie der Lebenskunst. Eine Grundlegung. Frankfurt a. M.: Suhrkamp.

Schmid, W. (2004). Mit sich selbst befreundet sein. Frankfurt a. M.: Suhrkamp.

Schmid, W. (1998). Philosophie der Lebenskunst. Frankfurt a. M.: Suhrkamp.

Schmidt, J. (1983). Design und Intervention in berufsbezogenen gruppendynamischen Trainings. Gruppenpsychotherapie und Gruppendynamik, 18 (1), 127–143 & 18 (2), 305–321.

Schneider-Landolf, M. (1987). Was hat der Therapeut Carl Rogers dem Lehrer zu sagen? Brennpunkt: Schweizerische Gesellschaft für Gesprächspsychotherapie. Sondernummer zum Tode von Carl Rogers, 9 (31), 85–90.

Schneider-Landolf, M. (1996). Themenzentrierte Interaktion: Ein Beitrag zu einer neuen Lernkultur in der Lehrerfortbildung. In J. Bohne, U. Hallwirt, C. Scheilke (Eds.), Lehrer bilden sich: Fortbildung in den ersten Dienstjahren – ein Modell der Evangelischen Schulstiftung in Bayern (pp. 96–113). Münster: Comenius-Institut.

Schneider-Landolf, M. (2002). 30 Jahre TZI – was hat sich verändert? Themenzentrierte Interaktion, 16 (1), 141–151.

Schneider-Pannewick, W. (1996). Mitten im Grauen der Welt – die Kultur des Schweigens beenden! Die gesellschaftliche Relevanz der TZI aus der Sicht der Pädagogik Paulo Freires. Diplomarbeit FH Nürnberg.

Schratz, M. (1996). Gemeinsam Schule lebendig gestalten: zu Schulentwicklung und didaktischer Erneuerung. Weinheim/Basel: Beltz.

Schreyögg, A. (1993). "Globe" – die unbekannte Größe. Themenzentrierte Interaktion, 7 (1), 12–28.

Schreyögg, A. (1993a). Erwiderung von Astrid Schreyögg. Themenzentrierte Interaktion, 7 (2), 70–72.

Schroll-Machl, S. (2002). Die Deutschen – Wir Deutsche. Fremdwahrnehmung und Selbstsicht im Berufsleben. Göttingen: Vandenhoeck & Ruprecht.

Schulz von Thun, F. (1980). Laudatio auf Ruth Cohn. Zeitschrift für Humanistische Psychologie, 4, 7–12

Schulz von Thun, F. (1980). Laudatio auf Ruth Cohn. Festschrift für Ruth Cohn. Der Zeitschrift humanistischer Psychologie, 3 (4), 15–20.

Schulz von Thun, F. (1981). Miteinander reden. Teil 1: Störungen und Klärungen: Psychologie der zwischenmenschlichen Kommunikation. Reinbek: Rowohlt.

Schwäbisch, L., Siems, M. (1978). Anleitung zum sozialen Lernen für Paare, Gruppen und Erzieher. Reinbek: Rowohlt.

Schulz von Thun, F. (1998). Miteinander reden, 3. Teil: Das "innere Team" und situationsgerechte Kommunikation. Reinbek: Rowohlt.

Schulz, W. (1980). Unterrichtsplanung. München: Urban und Schwarzenberg.

Schulze, A. (1995). TZI als lebendiges Lernen in Gruppen – Versuch einer Darstellung mit Hilfe eines Baumes. TZI-Info Will-Franken, 1, 1995.

Schütt, M. (2003). Die TZI als Element des TQMs – Eine "Brücke" zum humanen Management sowie einem werteorientierten Unternehmen. Themenzentrierte Interaktion, 16 (2), 25 ff.

Schütz, K.-V. (1987, 1993). TZI zwischen Gruppendynamik, Gruppenpädagogik und Gruppenpsychotherapie. In K. Hahn et al. (Eds.), Gruppenarbeit: Themenzentriert (pp. 11–23). Mainz: Grünewald.

Schütz, K.-V. (1992). Glossar zur TZI. In C. Löhmer, R. Standhart (Eds.), TZI. Pädagogisch-therapeutische Gruppenarbeit nach Ruth C. Cohn (pp. 385–437). Stuttgart: Klett-Cotta.

Schwäbisch, L., Siems, M. R. (1974). Anleitung zum sozialen Lernen für Paare, Gruppen und Erzieher. Kommunikations- und Verhaltenstraining. Reinbek: Rowohlt.

Schweitzer, A. (1984). Die Ehrfurcht vor dem Leben. Grundtexte aus fünf Jahrzehnten (4th ed.). München: Beck.

Seckler, M. (1988). Die schiefen Wände des Lehrhauses. Katholizität als Herausforderung. Freiburg i. Br: Herder.

Seiwert, L., J., Tracy, B. (2002). Lifetime-Management: mehr Lebensqualität durch Worklife-Balance. Offenbach: Gabal.

Sellars, J. (2007). Téchnê perì tòn bíon. Zur stoischen Konzeption von Kunst und Leben. In W. Kersting, C. Langbehn (Eds.), Kritik der Lebenskunst (pp. 91–117). Frankfurt a. M: Suhrkamp.

Selvini Palazzoli, M., Boscolo, L., Cecchin, G., Prata, G. (2003). Paradoxon und Gegenparadoxon: ein neues Therapiemodell für die Familie mit schizophrener Störung (10th ed.). Stuttgart: Klett-Cotta.

Senge, P. (1990). De vijfde discipline. Schiedam: scriptum.

Senge, P. M. (1990, 2006). The Fifth Discipline. The Art and Practice of the Learning Organization. New York: Doubleday.

Senge, P. M. (2008). Die fünfte Disziplin: Kunst und Praxis der lernenden Organisation (10th ed.). Stuttgart: Schäffer-Poeschel.

Senge, P. M., Scharmer, C. O., Jaworski, J., Flowers, B. S. (2004). Presence. Exploring Profound Change in People, Organizations and Society. London: Nicolas Brealey.

Senghaas-Knobloch, E., Nagler, B., Dohms, A. (1996). Zukunft der industriellen Arbeitskultur. Persönliche Sinnansprüche und Gruppenarbeit. Münster: Lit-Verlag.

Siebenhüner, B. (2006). Wirtschaftsethik als kritische Sozialwissenschaft. http://www.sozial-oekologische-forschung.org/intern/upload/literatur/siebenhuener_wissen schaftsethik_ge.pdf

Siebert, H. (1998). Konstruktivismus. Konsequenzen für Bildungsmanagement und Seminargestaltung. Frankfurt a. M.: DIE.

Siebert, H. (2000). Didaktisches Handeln in der Erwachsenenbildung. Didaktik aus konstruktivistischer Sicht. Neuwied: Kriftel.

Siebert, H. (2003). Didaktisches Handeln in der Erwachsenenbildung. Didaktik aus konstruktivistischer Sicht (4th ed.). München: Luchterhand.

Siebert, H. (2005). Pädagogischer Konstruktivismus. Lernzentrierte Pädagogik in Schule und Erwachsenenbildung (3rd ed.). Weinheim/Basel: Beltz.

Skupnik-Henssler, A., Wünsche-Pietzka, H. (1999). Ein anderes "Magdeburger Modell" – politische Frauenbildung im Dialog. Themenzentrierte Interaktion, 13, 1, 78–90.

Sönser Breen, M., Blumenfeld W. (Eds.) (2005). Butler Matters. Judith Butler's Impact on Feminist an Queer Studies. London: Ashgate.

SPIEGEL (2006). Mit Anstand auf die Welt. Issue 51, pp. 136f.

SPIEGEL (2007). Die Grammatik des Guten. Issue 31, pp. 108–116.

Sprenger, R. K. (2002). Vertrauen führt: worauf es im Unternehmen wirklich ankommt. Frankfurt a. M.: Campus.

Sprey, T. (1968). Beraten und Ratgeben in der Erziehung. Zur Differenzierung einer pädagogischen Handlungsform. Weinheim/Basel: Beltz.

Stabenau, H.-J. (2000). Wie viele Spielregeln braucht eine Gruppe, um arbeitsfähig zu sein? Chancen und Risiken von Regeln, insbesondere der "technischen Hilfsregeln" von TZI – im Umfeld von (betrieblicher) Erwachsenenbildung. Themenzentrierte Interaktion, 14 (1), 30–49.

Stahl, E. (2002). Dynamik in Gruppen. Handbuch der Gruppenleitung. Weinheim/Basel: Beltz.
Stahl, C. (1998). Teamentwicklung mit TZI. Themenzentrierte Interaktion, 12 (2), 126–131.
Stämmler, F. (1999). Gestalttherapeutische Methoden und Techniken. In R. Fuhr (Ed.), Handbuch der Gestalttherapie (pp. 439–460). Göttingen: Hogrefe.
Standhardt, R., Löhmer, C. (Eds.) (1995). Lebendiges Lernen in toten Räumen. Zur Verbesserung der Lehre an der Hochschule. Gießen: Focus.
Standhardt, R., Löhmer, C. (Eds.) (1994). Zur Tat Befreien. Gesellschaftspolitische Perspektiven der TZI-Gruppenarbeit. Mainz: Grünewald.
Statzer, M. (1995). "Wer den 'Globe' nicht kennt, den frisst er." Themenzentrierte Interaktion, 9 (1), 91–97
Staub-Bernasconi, S. (2007). Soziale Arbeit als Handlungswissenschaft. Bern et al.: Haupt.
Steffensky, F. (2002). Das Haus, das die Träume verwaltet (7th ed.). Würzburg: Echter.
Stierlin, H. (1996). Der systemische Ansatz in Therapie und Beratung – illustriert am Beispiel der Alkoholabhängigkeit. Themenzentrierte Interaktion, 10 (2), 6–21.
Stollberg, D. (1982/1990). Lernen, weil es Freude macht. Eine Einführung in die Themenzentrierte Interaktion. München: Kösel.
Stollberg, D. (1987). Vermeidungen in der Themenzentrierten Interaktion. In K. Hahn et al. (Eds.), Aggression in Gruppe (pp. 101–116). Mainz: Grünewald.
Stollberg, D. (1991a). TZI zwischen humanistischen Idealen und psychosozialer Wirklichkeit. Themenzentrierte Interaktion, 5 (2), 23–31.
Stollberg, D. (1991b). Zum Problem der Schuld – aus pastoralpsychologischer Perspektive. Una Sancta, 46 (3), 200–207.
Stollberg, D. (1992). Wo viel Licht ist, ist viel Schatten. Zum Begriffs des Schattens in der TZI. In C. Löhmer, R. Standhardt (Eds.), TZI – Pädagogisch-therapeutische Gruppenarbeit nach Ruth C. Cohn (pp. 207–217). Stuttgart: Klett-Cotta.
Stollberg, D. (1995). Lebendiges Lernen will gelernt sein. Zur didaktischen Situation der Dozentinnen und Dozenten an deutschen Hochschulen. In R. Standhardt, C. Löhmer (Eds.), Lebendiges Lernen in toten Räumen. Zur Verbesserung der Lehre an der Hochschule (pp. 128–132). Gießen: Focus.
Stollberg, D. (1998). Ich leite, du leitest – wer leitet? Leiten in TZI-Gruppen. Themenzentrierte Interaktion, 12 (1), 88–97.
Stollberg, D. (2006). "Wer den Globe nicht kennt, den frisst er." Zur Bedeutung des Umfeldes in der themenzentriert-interaktionellen Arbeit. Themenzentrierte Interaktion, 20 (1), 28–39.
Stollberg, D., Stollberg, E. (2005). TZI und Spiritualität. Themenzentrierte Interaktion, 19 (2), 16–22.
Stollberg, E. (2001). "Ich kann nicht nicht intervenieren!" Zur Intervention von Leiterinnen und Leitern in der TZI. In K. Hahn, M. Schraut, K. V. Schütz, C. Wagner (Eds.), Kompetente LeiterInnen. Beiträge zum Leitungsverständnis nach TZI (pp. 178–200). Mainz: Grünewald.
Stollberg, E. (2002). Was ist "TZI" an der TZI? Themenzentrierte Interaktion, 16 (2), 42–48.
Stoller, R. J. (1969). Sex and Gender: On the Development of Masculinity and Femininity, Vol. 1. International Psycho-Analysis Library: Chatto and Windus.
Straumann, U. (2001). Professionelle Beratung – Bausteine zur Qualitätsentwicklung und Qualitätssicherung. Heidelberg: Asanger.
Streeck, U., Bell, K. (Eds.) (1994). Die Psychoanalyse schwerer psychischer Erkrankungen. München: Pfeiffer.
Struwe, G. (1994). Blick über den Zaun: TZI und NLP. Themenzentrierte Interaktion, 8 (1), 107–117.

Sullivan, H. S. (1947). Conception of modern psychiatry, Washington D. C.: Second Printing.
Swieringa, J., Wierdsma, A. (1990). Op weg naar een lerende organisatie. Groningen: Wolters Noordhoff Management.
Der Taschenheinichen (n.d.). Lateinisch-Deutsches Taschenwörterbuch (10th ed.). Bearbeitet von H. Bauer, R. Rau, H. Zimmermann. Stuttgart: Klett.
Tausch, R., Tausch, A. (1965). Erziehungspsychologie. Göttingen: Hogrefe.
Ten Kate, G. (2005). Stabiel leiderschap. Pearson Education Benelux.
Textor, M. (1987). Beratung, Erziehung, Psychotherapie. Eine Begriffsbestimmung. Psychologie in Erziehung und Unterricht, 34 (1), 1–13.
Thiersch, H. (1992). Lebensweltorientierte Soziale Arbeit. Weinheim/Basel: Beltz.
Thomann, C., Schulz von Thun, F. (1988/1997). Klärungshilfe. Handbuch für Therapeuten, Gesprächshelfer und Moderatoren in schwierigen Gesprächen. Reinbek: Rowohlt.
Thomas, D. A., Ely, J. J. (1996). Making Differences Matter: A New Paradigm for Managing Diversity. Harvard Business Review, 74, 79–91.
Thomas, K. (1987). Gruppenprozesse: mimetisch oder authentisch? Themenzentrierte Interaktion, 1 (1), 14–24.
Thomas, K. (1991). Dürfen wir vielleicht doch aggressiv sein? Themenzentrierte Interaktion, 5 (1), 57–63.
Thürmer-Rohr, C. (2001). Vagabundinnen. Feministische Essays. Berlin: Orlanda.
Tietgens, H. (1981). Die Erwachsenenbildung. München: Juventa.
Tietgens, H. (2001). Teilnehmerorientierung. In R. Arnold, S. Nolda, E. Nuissl (Eds.), Wörterbuch Erwachsenenpädagogik (pp. 304–305). Bad Heilbrunn: Klinkhardt.
Tillmann, J. (2007). Trajektivität. Anstöße für eine Metatheorie der Sozialarbeitswissenschaft. Schriftenreihe der Fakultät V – Diakonie, Gesundheit und Soziales der Fachhochschule Hannover, Vol. 14. Hannover: Blumhardt.
Tomalin, E., Schauwecker, P. (1989). Interaktionelle Kunst- und Gestaltungstherapie in der Gruppe. Köln: Claus Richter.
Tröhler, D., Oelkers, J. (Eds.) (2005). Pragmatismus und Pädagogik. Zürich: Pestalozzianum.
Trompenaars, F., Hampden-Turner, C. (1998). Riding the Waves of Culture (2nd ed.). London: Nicholas Brealey.
Trost, A. (1998). TZI und systemische Therapie: spielend kreative Lösungen (erfinden). Themenzentrierte Interaktion, 12 (2), 61–87.
Trost, A. (2006). Bindung anbieten, Halt geben, Lösungen finden: Ein etwas anderes Balancemodell für die Beratung mit TZI. In U. Sauer-Schiffer, M. Ziemons (Eds.), In der Balance liegt die Chance: themenzentrierte Interaktion in Bildung und Beratung (pp. 65–90). Münster: Waxmann.
Trost, A. (2007). Therapeutische Dimensionen der Themenzentrierten Interaktion – TZI in therapeutischen Prozessen. In W. Lotz, C. Wagner (Eds.), Themenzentrierte Interaktion in der Beratung und in therapeutischen Prozessen. Ostfildern: Grünewald.
Tugendhat, E. (2003). Egozentrizität und Mystik. Eine anthropologische Studie. München: Beck.
van de Braak, I. (2003). TZI – Themenzentrierte Interaktion – eine integrative und wertebezogene Herangehensweise an Leitung. Themenzentrierte Interaktion, 16 (2), 9ff.
Van Hoeck, K. (2007). TZI in der ambulanten Gruppentherapie mit Sexualstraftätern. Themenzentrierte Interaktion, 21 (1), 32–45.
Villa, P.-I. (2002). Sexy bodies. Eine soziologische Reise durch den Geschlechtskörper (3rd rev. ed.). Wiesbaden: VS Verlag für Sozialwissenschaften.

Vogt, H., Cohn, R. C. (1975). Diskussion: Kann das themenzentriert interaktionelle System eine Methode emanzipatorischer Erwachsenenbildung sein? Kommentar zu Vogts Überlegungen. Gruppendynamik 6 (5), 380–384.

Voigt, B., Antons, K. (1997). Systematische Anmerkungen zur Intervention in Gruppen. In O. König (Ed.), Gruppendynamik. Geschichte, Theorien, Methoden, Anwendungen, Ausbildung (2nd ed.) (pp. 224–246). München: Profil.

Von Godin, E. (1987). TZI und Gestalttherapie. In K. Hahn, M. Schraut, K. Schütz, C. Wagner (Eds.), Gruppenarbeit: themenzentriert: Entwicklungsgeschichte, Kritik und Methodenreflexion. Mainz: Grünewald.

Vopel, K. W. (2000). Ein Update für die TZI. Themenzentrierte Interaktion, 14 (2), 69–83.

Voß, G. G., Pongratz, H. J. (1998). Der Arbeitskraftunternehmer. Eine neue Grundform der Ware Arbeitskraft? KZfSS – Kölner Zeitschrift für Soziologie und Sozialpsychologie, 50 (1), 131–158.

Votsmeier, A. (1996). Kurt Goldstein and Holism. Lecture held at the GTILA-Summer-Residential-Program Barcelone.

Wagner, A. (2003). Partizipierende Leitung als Aspekt der themenzentrierten Interaktion. Hagen, Schriftliche Hausarbeit, angefertigt im Hauptfach Soziale Verhaltenswissenschaften, Fernuniversität in Hagen.

Wagner, C. (1991). Körper signalisieren – wie und was sind unsere Fragen. Gespräch mit Ruth Cohn. In K. Hahn (Ed.), "Beachte die Körpersignale ..." Körpererfahrung in der Gruppenarbeit. Mainz: Grünewald.

Wagner, C. (2007). Psychotherapie in der Gruppe nach Albert Pesso und TZI. In W. Lotz, C. Wagner (Eds.), Themenzentrierte Interaktion in der Beratung und in therapeutischen Prozessen. Ostfildern: Grünewald.

Walbrod, H., Eppler, H., Krock, B., Debrunner, A., Pöpel, K. (2006). TZI Grundausbildung in Indien. Ein Pilotprojekt. Themenzentrierte Interaktion, 20 (1), 65–96.

Waldrop, M. (1992). Complexity: the Emerging Science at the Edge of Order and Chaos. New York: Simon & Schuster.

Watzlawick, P., Beavin, J. H. Jackson, D. D. (1969). Menschliche Kommunikation: Formen, Störungen, Parodoxien. Bern: Huber.

Weatley, M. (1999). Leadership and the New Science. San Francisco: Berret-Koehler.

Weidenmann, B. (2006). Handbuch active Training. Die besten Methoden für lebendige Seminare. Weinheim/Basel: Beltz.

Weisser, J. (2005). Sonderpädagogische Probleme formulieren: Konzepte und die Logik sonderpädagogischen Wissens. In D. Horster, U. Hoyningen-Süess, C. Liesen (Eds.), Sonderpädagogische Professionalität. Beiträge zur Entwicklung der Sonderpädagogik als Disziplin und Profession (pp. 97–115). Wiesbaden: Verlag für Sozialwissenschaften.

Wellendorf, F. (1973). Schulische Sozialisation und Identität. Weinheim/Basel: Beltz.

Werner, G. (2005). Macht Glaube glücklich? Freiheit und Bezogenheit als Erfahrung persönlicher Heilszusage. Regensburg: Pustet.

West, C., Zimmermann, D.-H. (1991). Doing Gender. In J. Lorber, S. A. Farrell (Eds.), The Social Construction of Gender (pp. 13–37). Newbury Park: Sage.

Wheeler, G. (1993). Kontakt und Widerstand. Köln: Edition Humanistische Psychologie.

WILL-Europa (Ed.) (1982). EURO-INFO. Sondernummer zum 27. August 1982. 10 Jahre WILL-Europa und seine Regionen.

WILL Schweiz (Ed.) (2004). Lehrgang Ausbilder/in auf der Grundlage der Themenzentrierten Interaktion. St. Gallen: Werkstatt Institut für lebendiges Lernen. http://www. kibb.de/cps/rde/xbcr/SID-3C5594CA-21B69BD4/kibb/ada_broschuere.pdf

Winkler, M. (1988). Eine Theorie der Sozialpädagogik. Stuttgart: Klett-Cotta.

Worley, C., Feyerherm, A. (2005). Überlegungen zur Zukunft der Organisationsentwicklung. Organisationsentwicklung, 1, 80 ff.

Wrage, K. H. (1985), Themen finden – Themen einführen. In R. Birmelin et al. (Eds.). Erfahrungen lebendigen Lernens. Grundlagen und Arbeitsfelder der TZI (pp. 68–91). Mainz: Grünewald.

www.dachverband-beratung.de/pa_060711jmt/Dokumente_06. htm (01.04.2007) und: Vorstand der Deutschen Gesellschaft für Beratung (Ed.) (2006). Die Deutsche Gesellschaft für Beratung e. V. (DGfB) – ein Forum für Qualität und Zukunft von Beratung. Köln.

Yalom, I. D. (1996). Theorie und Praxis der Gruppenpsychotherapie. München: Pfeiffer.

Yalom, I. D. (2005). Theorie und Praxis der Gruppenpsychotherapie (8th ed.). Stuttgart: Klett-Cotta.

Yukl, G. (2002). Leadership in organization. Englewood Cliffs, NJ: Prentice Hall.

Zieman, Y. (2002). Völkerverständigung durch TZI. Themenzentrierte Interaktion, 16 (1), 161–168.

Zitterbarth, W. (2001). TZI und Ethik. Themenzentrierte Interaktion, 15 (2), 102–104.

Zundel, E. (1991). Ruth Cohn: Themenzentrierte Interaktion. In E. Zundel, R. Zundel (Eds.), Leitfiguren der neueren Psychotherapie. Leben und Werk (pp. 66–82). München: dtv.